Sassoon

Sassoon

THE WORLDS OF PHILIP AND SYBIL

Peter Stansky

Yale University Press
New Haven and London

For information about this and other Yale University Press publications, please contact:
U.S. Office: sales.press@yale.edu   yalebooks.com
Europe Office: sales@yaleup.co.uk   www.yaleup.co.uk

Set in Minion by Fakenham Photosetting
Printed in China through Worldprint

Library of Congress Cataloging-in-Publication Data

Stansky, Peter, 1932–
Sassoon: the worlds of Philip and Sybil/Peter Stansky.
p. cm.
Includes bibliographical references and index.
ISBN 0–300–09547–3 (hbk.)
1. Sassoon, Philip, Sir, 1888–1939. 2. Great Britain—Social life and customs—20th century. 3. Politicians—Great Britain—Biography. 4. Art patrons—Great Britain—Biography. 5. Nobility—Great Britain—Biography. 6. Jewish families—Great Britain. 7. Sassoon, Sybil, 1894–1989. 8. Sassoon family. I. Title.
DA566.9.S68 S37 2003   328.41'092—dc21   2002014918

A catalogue record for this book is available from the British Library.

10 9 8 7 6 5 4 3

Frontispiece: John Singer Sargent, Sir Philip Sassoon, 1923. Copyright Tate Gallery, photo: John Webb.

Sassoon

THE WORLDS OF PHILIP AND SYBIL

Peter Stansky

Yale University Press
New Haven and London

For information about this and other Yale University Press publications, please contact:
U.S. Office: sales.press@yale.edu   yalebooks.com
Europe Office: sales@yaleup.co.uk   www.yaleup.co.uk

Set in Minion by Fakenham Photosetting
Printed in China through Worldprint

Library of Congress Cataloging-in-Publication Data

Stansky, Peter, 1932–
Sassoon: the worlds of Philip and Sybil/Peter Stansky.
p. cm.
Includes bibliographical references and index.
ISBN 0–300–09547–3 (hbk.)
1. Sassoon, Philip, Sir, 1888–1939. 2. Great Britain—Social life and customs—20th century. 3. Politicians—Great Britain—Biography. 4. Art patrons—Great Britain—Biography. 5. Nobility—Great Britain—Biography. 6. Jewish families—Great Britain. 7. Sassoon, Sybil, 1894–1989. 8. Sassoon family. I. Title.
DA566.9.S68 S37 2003   328.41'092—dc21   2002014918

A catalogue record for this book is available from the British Library.

10 9 8 7 6 5 4 3

Frontispiece: John Singer Sargent, *Sir Philip Sassoon*, 1923. Copyright Tate Gallery, photo: John Webb.

To Marina and her grandchildren, Emily, Lucy and Kate

Contents

List of Illustrations   *viii*

Preface   *x*

The Walpole, Cholmondeley, Sassoon and Rothschild Families   *xiv*

1   *India: Establishing a Dynasty*   1

2   *England: Becoming English*   11

3   *Philip and Sybil Serve Their Country*   51

4   *Becoming a Politician in the 1920s*   91

5   *Setting the Stage in London and in the Country*   138

6   *The Role of Art: Making an Aesthetic*   185

7   *The Bomber Always Gets Through: Politics in the 1930s*   213

8   *Sybil*   247

Notes   269

Index   283

Illustrations

1. *David Sassoon*, unknown artist, no date. Private Collection.   *page* 4
2. Thomas Woolner, *David Sassoon*, 1869, Bombay. Courtesy of the Witt Library, Courtauld Institute, London.   8
3. Spy (Sir Leslie Ward), *Sir Albert Sassoon, Vanity Fair*, 16 August 1879. Private Collection. Photo: Visual Art Services, Stanford University.   13
4. Aline Sassoon, 1888.   14
5. Sybil with three cousins at her grandparents' château in France, *c.* 1897.   14
6. 25 Park Lane, *The Builder*, 10 October 1896. Copyright: Bodleian Library, University of Oxford.   17
7. John Singer Sargent, *Lady Sassoon*, 1907. Photo: The Bridgeman Art Library.   20
8. Hannah Gubbay at Trent Park, early 1930s.   21
9. Spy (Sir Leslie Ward), *Sir Edward Sassoon, Vanity Fair*, 1 February 1900. Private Collection. Photo: Visual Art Services, Stanford University.   22
10. Philip Sassoon as a boy. Photo: Elliot and Fry.   23
11. Max Beerbohm, *Philip Sassoon in Strange Company*, original drawing, 1913. Max Beerbohm Collection, General Collection, Beinecke Rare Book and Manuscript Library, Yale University. Copyright the Estate of Max Beerbohm, reprinted by permission of London Management.   33
12. Bassano, *Lord Rocksavage*, 1908. By courtesy of the National Portrait Gallery, London.   34
13. John Singer Sargent, *Sybil Sassoon*, 1910.   36
14. John Singer Sargent, *Sybil Sassoon*, 1912.   36
15. John Singer Sargent, *Sybil Sassoon*, 1913. Photo: The Bridgeman Art Library.   37
16. Sir William Orpen, *Countess of Rocksavage*, 1913. Private Collection.   38
17. Bassano, *Sir Philip Sassoon*, 1913. By courtesy of the National Portrait Gallery, London.   41
18. Glyn Philpot, *Sir Philip Sassoon*, 1913. Photo: Simon Warburton.   42
19. Sir William Orpen, *The Drawing Room at 25 Park Lane*, 1912. Private Collection.   43
20. Port Lympne. Country Life Picture Library.   45
21. Mural by José Maria Sert, Port Lympne. Country Life Picture Library.   47
22. Philip de Laszlo, *Sir Philip Sassoon*, 1915. Courtesy of the estate of Philip de Laszlo. Photo: The Bridgeman Art Library.   54
23. Douglas Haig and Philip Sassoon during the First World War.   57
24. John Singer Sargent, *Ruined Cathedral of Arras*, 1918. Photo: The Bridgeman Art Library.   78
25. Philip and the Prince of Wales at Trent Park, 1920.   96
26. John Singer Sargent, *The Prince of Wales*, 1921. The Royal Collection © 2002 Her Majesty Queen Elizabeth II.   100
27. Rex Whistler, *Vignette of Octagon Library, Port Lympne*, 1930. Private Collection. © 2002 Artists Rights Society (ARS), New York/DACS, London.   102
28. Lloyd George and Sybil at Port Lympne, April 1921.   103
29. The Second Hythe Conference, 19–20 June 1920 at Port Lympne.   103
30. The Schneider Trophy, 1913. NMPFT/Science & Society Picture Library.   125

31. Rex Whistler, endpaper for *The Third Route*, 1929. Photo: Visual Art Services, Stanford University. © 2002 Artists Rights Society (ARS), New York/DACS, London. 129

32. Philip setting off on his trip, 29 September 1928. 130

33. Marthe Bibesco at Port Lympne, May 1921. 135

34. Sir Louis Mallet, 1920. 139

35. E. Shepherd, *The Drawing Room at Park Lane*, 1923. Private Collection. 141

36. John Singer Sargent, *The Countess of Rocksavage, later the Marchioness of Cholmondeley*, 1922. Photo: The Bridgeman Art Library. 142

37. Charles Sims, *The Countess of Rocksavage and her son, Lord Malpas*, 1922. Photo: Simon Warburton. 143

38. John Singer Sargent, *Philip, Rock and Sybil at Port Lympne*, August 1920. 145

39. John Singer Sargent, *The Marchioness of Cholmondeley and Paul Manship*, 1923. 146

40. Charles Sims, *The Marchioness of Cholmondeley in the Ballroom at 25 Park Lane, c. 1923*. Private Collection. 147

41. The dining room at Port Lympne. Country Life Picture Library. 149

42. Georges Carpentier, Rock and Philip at Port Lympne, September 1921. 150

43. Lord Louis Mountbatten in the Moorish Courtyard at Port Lympne, August 1923. 150

44. A corridor at Port Lympne. Country Life Picture Library. 150

45. The garden at Port Lympne. 151

46. Rex Whistler, *The Tent Room*, 1932. Port Lympne. © 2002 Artists Rights Society (ARS), New York/DACS, London. Courtesy Howletts and Port Lympne Wild Animal Park. 155

47. Philip and Sybil at Port Lympne, 1921. Private Collection. 157

48. Hannah, Charlie Chaplin, Sybil and Philip, September 1921. 158

49. Lytton Strachey, Philip and Baba Curzon at Port Lympne, September 1922. 161

50. Trent Park in 1893. Country Life Picture Library. 164

51. Rex Whistler, *Trent Park with Philip and Sybil*, 1934. Private Collection. © 2002 Artists Rights Society (ARS), New York/DACS, London. Photo: The Bridgeman Art Library. 165

52. The drawing room at Trent Park. Country Life Picture Library. 167

53. Christmas card of penguins at Trent Park. 169

54. Howard Coster, Philip in the library at Port Lympne, 1929. Photograph courtesy of the National Portrait Gallery. 171

55. Queen Mary, Sybil, Hannah and Lady Cynthia Colville at Trent Park, 1938. Photo: A.C.G Windbrush 172

56. Trent Park Visitors' Book, 1925. 173

57. 12 Kensington Palace Gardens. Country Life Picture Library. 180

58. Sybil with Hugh, Aline and John on a houseboat during a holiday at Key West, Florida, 1928. 182

59. Sybil and her son Hugh and two Bugattis at Houghton before the outbreak of the Second World War. 183

60. Thomas Gainsborough, *Mr and Mrs Browne of Tunstall and their daughter Anna Maria*. 195

61. A Louis XIV ebony and brass and pewter-inlaid brown tortoiseshell *coffres de toilette (mariage)* by André-Charles Boulle, acquired by Philip Sassoon before 1923. © Christie's Images Ltd 2003. 200

62. A pair of Louis XVI gilt-bronze and Chinese powder-blue glazed porcelain pot-pourri vases and covers, acquired by Philip Sassoon before 1927. © Christie's Images Ltd 2003. 201

63. Sybil *c.* 1926–30. Cecil Beaton photography courtesy of Sotheby's London. 205

64. Sybil and Rock. 206

65. Wyndham Lewis, *Sybil Cholmondeley* from *Thirty Personalities*, 1932. Private Collection. Estate of Mrs G.A. Wyndham Lewis. By permission. Photo: Visual Art Services, Stanford University. 209

66. Philip, Winston Churchill, Sybil, Clementine Churchill and Hannah, soon after the First World War. 220

67. Rex Whistler, letters to Philip Sassoon. © 2002 Artists Rights Society (ARS) New York/DACS, London. 233

68. Lee Miller, *The Marchioness of Cholmondeley*, 1945. Photo: Courtesy Lee Miller Archives, Chiddingly, England. 248

69. Sybil and Rock at 12 Kensington Palace Gardens. 260

70. Sybil at Houghton, 1980s. 264

71. Janet Stone, Sybil at Houghton with her portrait by Sargent, 1980s. By permission of Phyllida Gili. Photograph courtesy of the National Portrait Gallery. 267

Preface

In January 1999 my sister, Marina Vaizey, and I went to India. She had gone there several times before but I had never been. I was on leave from my position in the History Department at Stanford University and had a fellowship from the National Endowment for the Humanities and a grant from the Memorial Foundation for Jewish Culture in order to work on a study of the Sassoon family. (I should also like to thank for his assistance Tad Taube through the Taube Center for Jewish Studies at Stanford University.) And needless to say I am profoundly grateful to these organizations for their help. I had decided that I would limit my study to two Sassoons whose lives fascinated me – Sir Philip Sassoon and his sister Sybil, the Marchioness of Cholmondeley, great-grandchildren of the founder of the family fortunes, David Sassoon. It would be the first major project I would embark upon without the advice, except in the preliminary stages, of my companion and collaborator, William Abrahams, who had died the previous June. The year largely away from Stanford also had a therapeutic purpose: to help me recover from his death and the terrible illness of the last five months of his life as he became weaker. We had been together since 1961, had written four books – one also a double study, of John Cornford and Julian Bell – and he had been my constant critic and inspirer.

But I knew that he was unlikely to have enjoyed a trip to India, not because he would not have been interested in the sights and the country, but the challenges and discomforts that go along with travel there would probably have been uncongenial and caused him displeasure. He was right in some senses; travel in India is not easy even if done under the best circumstances. The trip was fascinating: not only visits to the more traditional sights of temples and other buildings but as a way to witness where the saga of the Sassoons began to take its modern shape.

The world that the Sassoons came to occupy in England had intrigued me from the very beginning of my training to be a historian. At one point I thought I might write my dissertation on the Anglo-Jewish peerage. I have always found a compelling question how and to what degree new groups are accepted in English society: the nuances of acceptance and rejection. The Sassoons were always mentioned as part of the Jewish 'Cousinhood', a group of the most prominent and richest English Jews, although the Sassoons were somewhat less involved in Jewish life than were such families as the Rothschilds, the Montefiores, the Samuels and the Montagus. But when I began to think about a similar topic years later, I first considered some sort of study of several such families, and then perhaps just the Sassoons. But as so frequently happens with me, I came to the conclusion that what I would enjoy most, and what might result in the better book, was a study of one or two individuals, and I found myself increasingly fascinated by Philip Sassoon and his sister Sybil. My interest in them was increased by their connections, so intensified by the fact that they were children of Aline de Rothschild, with the world of art as collectors and patrons.

I particularly remembered seeing the great 1922 portrait of Sybil by John Singer Sargent on display in the Country House Exhibition at the National Gallery in Washington in 1985. And the origins of my interest went back even further to the one time I had met Sybil. In 1970 when Houghton, the great Walpole/Cholmondeley house was not yet open to the public, I visited it myself. William Abrahams and I were taken there by the poet Dunstan Thompson (a fellow poet and Harvard contemporary of Billy's) and Philip Trower, a contemporary of her son, Hugh Cholmondeley, at Eton. I had assumed that they already knew Lady Cholmondeley but I discovered years later that they didn't, although as Norfolk residents they had mutual friends. They had simply asked if they could bring some visitors and with great graciousness she consented and gave us a tour of Houghton herself.

I feel very fortunate that I was able to meet her that once. She had an extraordinary quality. She was modestly grand or to put it another way she combined authority and charm. Now I have had the privilege of visiting Houghton several times in the course of my research. I first must profusely thank her grandson David, the present Marquess of Cholmondeley. This is in no sense an authorized study, but it would not have been possible without his graciousness in making available the family archive, his hospitality, his willingness to answer my innumerable questions, the help in so many ways that he gave and the pleasure of his company. All quotations from his grandmother and great-uncle are printed here by his permission and he retains their copyright. The family also has been extremely generous in providing many of the illustrations. And here I wish to express my great gratitude to Todd Bruno who did so much to help me secure these images.

Other members of the Cholmondeley family have been immensely helpful. They kindly read the manuscript, corrected errors, added some material, but did not censor. One of the enriching experiences of the historical enterprise is those one meets along the way and one's gratitude to them for giving so generously of their time. Sybil's daughter, Lady Aline Cholmondeley, did so as did Sybil's daughter-in-law, Lady John Cholmondeley, and her son, Charles Cholmondeley. Sybil Cholmondeley's longtime secretary, Hélène Stopien, assisted me the first time I visited Houghton and entertained me at her home in Cookham. Many others have also helped, and a mere listing can hardly give them the credit and gratitude they deserve. I must record my profound thanks to the Royal Archives at Windsor, the guidance and help there by Lady de Bellaigue and the advice of my fellow historian William Kuhn, wise in the ways of royalty. My quotations from the Royal Archives and from members of the royal family found in other sources are printed with the gracious permission of Her

Majesty Queen Elizabeth II. Quotations from the Earl Haig Papers are courtesy of the present Earl Haig (to whom I am also very grateful for the time he spent in talking to me) and to the Trustees of the National Library of Scotland. The quotation from T.S. Eliot's 'The Love Song of J. Alfred Prufock' is used with permission of Faber and Faber and Harcourt Brace and Company. Quotations from William Plomer are given with the permission of Durham University Library; from Mrs Belloc Lowndes from the Harry Ransom Humanities Research Center, The University of Texas, Austin. The quotation from Siegfried Sassoon's letter to his cousin Philip, copyright Siegfried Sassoon, is reproduced by the kind permission of George Sassoon. The quotation from Siegfried Sassoon's 'Monody on the Demolition of Devonshire House', from *Collected Poems of Siegfried Sassoon* by Siegfried Sassoon is copyright 1918, 1920 by E.P. Dutton and copyright 1936, 1946, 1947 and 1948 by Siegfried Sassoon. Used by permission of George Sassoon and of Viking Penguin, a division of Penguin Putnam Inc. For quotations from Geoffrey Dawson I am grateful to his copyright holders, Mr and Mrs William Bell. Mrs Dudeney's diary is quoted by kind permission of the Library of the Sussex Archaeological Society, Lewes. The quotations from the letters of T.E. Lawrence are used by permission of the Trustees of the Seven Pillars of Wisdom Trust. The quotations from Winston Churchill are reproduced with permission of Curtis Brown Ltd, London, on behalf of the Estate of Sir Winston Churchill. Copyright Winston S. Churchill. Thornton Wilder is quoted by permission of A. Tappan Wilder. All rights reserved. Excerpts from Rex Whistler's letters are quoted by permission of the executors of Sir Laurence Whistler. I am grateful for access to the Archives in London of the National Gallery, the Tate Gallery, the Royal Institute of British Architects, and the Wallace Collection. As with all the work I've done since the beginning of my career, it wouldn't have been possible without access to the British Library: its printed material as well as manuscripts; for this study, the Northcliffe Papers, and a few scattered items in other collections. The staff at my own Library, at Stanford University, have, as always, been helpful far beyond their obligations. I am deeply grateful for their support as well for that of the staff of the University's History Department and the Stanford Humanities Center. I am also grateful to the Library and Archives of the Metropolitan Museum, New York; the Hertfordshire Record Office for the papers of Lady Desborough; the London Metropolitan Archives for the papers of the Northern Hospital; the National Maritime Museum, the Liverpool Record Office for the papers of the Earl Derby and to the present Lord Derby for his kind permission to quote from them. At Churchill College, Cambridge, I consulted the Esher, Churchill, and Swinton Papers. I am grateful to the present Lord Esher for permission to use quotations from his grandfather. At the Cambridge University Library, I consulted the Baldwin and Templewood Papers. I also worked and received great assistance at the Public Record Office, the Imperial War Museum and the Record Office of the Royal Air Force Museum in Hendon. I am grateful to the House of Lords Record Office for the Lloyd George and Bonar Law Papers as well as material in connection with the office of the Lord Great Chamberlain, the Chichester Institute of Higher Education for the Ted Walker Papers, and the Society of Authors for material about the Cholmondeley Prize. Michael Meredith, the Librarian of Eton College, graciously made available material at the College. I am also grateful for the assistance of Moyra Ashford, Pamela Bell, Susan Cleaver, Anya Emerson, Susan England, Erhan Erdem, Max Erdstein, Marc Fecker, Clive Gee, Caryl Hubbard, Elaine Kilmurray, Harvey Sachs, Edwina Sassoon, Leonard Smith, Lynn Zastoupil and Kristin Zimmerman. In the publishing world I would like to thank Fred Hill, Mary Clemmey, Norris Pope, Robert Baldock and his colleagues Kevin Brown, Diana Yeh and Hazel Hutchison of Yale University Press, London and my copy-editor, Beth Humphries. Conversations with the late Percy Baldwin, John Cornforth, Lord Deedes and the late Sir John Plumb were very helpful. The manuscript has profited – and I only regret that I was not able to put their insights and suggestions to better use – from meticulous readings by Susan Bell, Trent Duffy, Sir Michael Howard, James Sheehan, Philippe Tapon, Marina Vaizey, Bernard Wasserstein, and the anonymous readers of the Yale University Press.

I began work on this study in 1996 while teaching at Stanford in Oxford and completed it while there again in 2002. The congeniality of its staff and students made me even more aware of the Anglo-American context in which I have been privileged to spend my life.

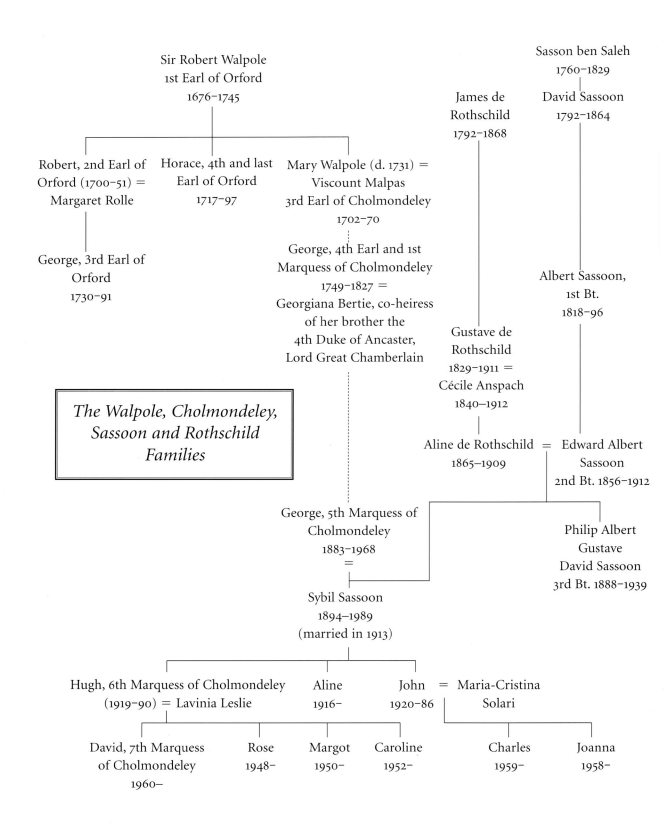

Sir Robert Walpole
1st Earl of Orford
1676–1745

Robert, 2nd Earl of
Orford (1700–51) =
Margaret Rolle

Horace, 4th and last
Earl of Orford
1717–97

Mary Walpole (d. 1731) =
Viscount Malpas
3rd Earl of Cholmondeley
1702–70

George, 3rd Earl of
Orford
1730–91

George, 4th Earl and 1st
Marquess of Cholmondeley
1749–1827 =
Georgiana Bertie, co-heiress
of her brother the
4th Duke of Ancaster,
Lord Great Chamberlain

Sasson ben Saleh
1760–1829

David Sassoon
1792–1864

James de
Rothschild
1792–1868

Albert Sassoon,
1st Bt.
1818–96

Gustave de
Rothschild
1829–1911 =
Cécile Anspach
1840–1912

**The Walpole, Cholmondeley,
Sassoon and Rothschild
Families**

Aline de Rothschild
1865–1909

=

Edward Albert
Sassoon
2nd Bt. 1856–1912

George, 5th Marquess of
Cholmondeley
1883–1968
=

Philip Albert
Gustave
David Sassoon
3rd Bt. 1888–1939

Sybil Sassoon
1894–1989
(married in 1913)

Hugh, 6th Marquess of Cholmondeley
(1919–90) = Lavinia Leslie

Aline
1916–

John   = Maria-Cristina
1920–86   Solari

David, 7th Marquess
of Cholmondeley
1960–

Rose
1948–

Margot
1950–

Caroline
1952–

Charles
1959–

Joanna
1958–

1   *India: Establishing a Dynasty*

Sir Philip Sassoon, Bart. (1888–1939) was one of the best-known and most glamorous figures in Britain in the first forty years of the twentieth century. He was descended from wealthy Baghdadi Jews; the family had made a fortune in India from the opium trade and other enterprises; his grandfather and three of his great-uncles immigrated to England and became close friends of the Prince of Wales, later Edward VII. Philip was the youngest Member of Parliament; he was elected in 1912. Serving as military secretary to Douglas Haig during the First World War, and as parliamentary private secretary to Lloyd George after the war, he was at the centre of the British establishment. He lived in a great town house in London and owned two country houses, one of which he built; the other he extensively altered. He had a wide circle of friends, from the Royal Family down. He was a Minister of the Crown, but not in the Cabinet. He was very active in the world of art as a patron of John Singer Sargent and other painters, as a trustee of major museums, and the stager of ten influential exhibitions.

In his day, he would have been the best-known member of the Sassoon family as his name was frequently mentioned in the press in political, social and artistic contexts. Unless one rises to the very top, as he did not, such fame is fleeting. Sir John Colville, a prominent figure of the time and the secretary of Winston Churchill during the Second World War, compared Philip to a fragrance and as such he is particularly hard to recapture. He was not close to two of his cousins, his contemporaries, who also have some lasting reputation. The family's other baronet, also by inheritance, Sir Victor, was famous in business and racing circles. Best known now is undoubtedly another cousin, the poet Siegfried Sassoon.

Philip never reached the pinnacle of success that he might have wished. Was it because he was Jewish? Anti-Semitism was prevalent in English society, but was neither life threatening nor formalized as it was elsewhere. English attitudes towards Jews can be very complicated. Ever since their readmission to England in the seventeenth century, they had been virtually in the same position as all others who were not Anglicans. During the nineteenth century all restrictions were removed, as they were for others. They were equal citizens of the state and there was little explicit discrimination. Edward VII had bestowed upon his rich Jewish friends a high degree of social acceptance. He enjoyed their company and was grateful to some of them for lending him money. Yet English Jews ran the risk of being despised as vulgar plutocrats or as dangerous radicals. In 1905 Parliament passed the Alien Act, largely designed to exclude poor East European Jews. In the fiction of the time they might figure as decadent aesthetes and dangerous manipulators, such as George du Maurier's Svengali. The figures of Shylock and Fagin have a lasting hold on the English imagination.

Philip Sassoon was the most eligible bachelor of his age, the greatest host of his time, but now, once so famous, he is largely forgotten. His life is, I believe, an intriguing story in itself but it may also provide a picture of the nature of English life, particularly in its highest reaches, in the twentieth century.

In many ways his sister Sybil provides a counterpoint to his life. Six years younger than Philip, Sybil lived much longer, dying in 1989 at the age of 95. The siblings were extremely close but where his life was largely lived on the public stage hers was much more private. The exception was the two world wars, when Sybil served in the high command of the Women's Royal Naval Service. She married into the grandest level of the English aristocracy: her husband Rock, the Marquess of Cholmondeley, was the Lord Great Chamberlain. Sybil played the major part in bringing Houghton, Sir Robert Walpole's magnificent Palladian house in Norfolk that the Cholmondeleys had acquired in the late eighteenth century, back to its earlier greatness.

The Sassoon brother and sister led fascinating lives, significant in their ways and now largely forgotten. To attempt to bring them back is the purpose of the pages that follow.

Philip Sassoon travelled to India when he was Under-Secretary of State for Air in the Tory government of 1924 to 1929. Although he remained in touch over the years with the family firm there, I have run across only one example of his visiting an office in India. He was a senior figure, but quite inactive, in the London office of David Sassoon & Co. He recognized his close connection with the firm in his will, leaving one year's salary to all employees who had been there a year or more (as he did for his domestic servants).

Some thought he was Indian – more specifically, some thought he was a Parsee. It was said that he encouraged that belief. If he did so, it had an ironic coda. In one English country house guidebook, a discussion of his house, Port Lympne in Kent, states that he was a Parsee who converted to Judaism. But because of his famous name, most realized that he was Jewish – or, to put it another way, an Englishman of the Jewish persuasion (no matter how comparatively unpersuaded he might be). Parsees, far rarer in English society, tended to have less trouble in being accepted.

How did Sir Philip's being Jewish influence his life, both his own ideas about himself and how the rest of the world saw him? Hard as this question may be to answer, I will attempt to keep it in mind in the course of this study. I am also interested in another connected one. To what degree was he regarded as an 'outsider' by others, and to what degree did he feel himself to be an 'outsider'? How did these questions play out in the world in which Philip lived – one where high society, high politics and high culture, met? Jews had acquired the right to sit in Parliament in 1858. This was referred to as 'emancipation', the same term as was used when Roman Catholics had become eligible to participate in politics in 1829. But there was an implied contract: in return for the rights of participation, Jewish MPs in effect pledged themselves, with rare exception, not to pursue what might be seen as Jewish interests. Might a certain loss of identity have been the price of acceptance? Was his being Jewish something that Philip chose largely to ignore, but that he couldn't prevent being frequently imposed upon him by others? Was his career hampered by this or did he in his brief life rise as high as his talents deserved? Were the frequent references to Philip as 'oriental', a term of disdain, a sign of admiration for the exoticism of his character, or both?

His ancestors had had less ambivalence about themselves: they were devout Jews. After the arrival of six of the eight Sassoon brothers in England, starting in 1858, they belonged to Bevis Marks, the oldest synagogue in England. (It was founded in 1657, a year after the re-admission of Jews to the country after their exclusion in 1290; its new building opened in the City of London in 1701 and is still used for worship.) Philip's father, Sir Edward Sassoon, was an active member, becoming President of the Elders of the Congregation and a Warden. On his death in 1912, Philip joined and paid his subscription fees regularly. But there is no record of his being involved to any degree in the life of the congregation.[1]

Before the Sassoons came to London, Bombay had been the centre for the making of the family fortune. David Sassoon rose to prominence as a merchant in this city of a quarter million on the west coast of India. But the family soon dispersed; David Sassoon sent his sons about the world, in the manner of the Rothschilds (the Sassoons, although a mercantile rather than a banking family, were known as the Rothschilds of the East), most notably to London. Although only one son, Sassoon David Sassoon, moved to England before David Sassoon's death, Philip's grandfather, Sir Albert, settled there in the 1870s.

Sybil Sassoon had spent six months in India in 1913 on her honeymoon. She had married the Earl of Rocksavage, the heir to the Marquess of Cholmondeley. Earlier he had spent some time in India as an aide-de-camp to the Viceroy. Despite the limited time Philip and Sybil spent in India, it was always there, I should think, in the background. The India I encountered on two trips in 1999, with a population of a billion people, may well have very little resemblance to the India of the Sassoons. Yet I thought it might be significant, and certainly interesting, to see what remained of their India. It would be the setting of the stage. After all, India and the financial empire that grew out of the family business in Bombay allowed Philip and Sybil to lead the lives that they did.

David Sassoon began his business in Bombay in 1833. He came there from Bushire in Persia where he and his father had gone after leaving Baghdad. It is said, and who would deny it, that the Sassoons had been resident in Mesopotamia ever since 586 BC, the year of the fall of Jerusalem, when their ancestors had been carried off from Jerusalem by Nebuchadnezzar. They had declined to return when the Babylonian Captivity ended with the restoration of Jerusalem in 538 BC. The family became 'court Jews' under the Islamic caliphs from the seventh century of the common era on. Rather confusingly, at least according to Stanley Jackson in his study of the Sassoons, and giving support to the idea of their

1. *David Sassoon*, unknown artist, no date.

being called, as they frequently are, Sephardi, they may be descended as well from Sephardic Jews. Jackson stated that the family was connected with the Shoshans of Toledo, and to the seventeenth-century scholar and mystic of Venice, Abraham Sason, who claimed descent from Shephatiah, the fifth son of King David.[2] Presumably the Sephardic Sassoons and the Baghdadi ones may have had common ancestors. At times it was said that the Sassoons were directly descended from the Jews of Toledo. The historian of the English Jews and of the

Sassoons in particular, Cecil Roth, rejects the Sephardi connection in favour of direct descent from the Captivity.[3] In any case, Sephardic is now used as a term to describe Middle Eastern Jews in general, particularly in terms of their religious practices.

Baghdadi Jews – and the term was increasingly used for all Arabic-speaking Jews – began moving to India in the mid-eighteenth century, first to Surat, then the largest Western trading port. At the end of the eighteenth century they went in greater numbers to Calcutta, Poona and Bombay. (There had been a few Arabic-speaking Jews in Bombay as early as 1730. There was also in Bombay an indigenous small Jewish community, the Bene Israel, as well as a long-standing group of Jews elsewhere in India in Cochin.) David Sassoon's father, Sasson ben Saleh, born in 1750, was for thirty-eight years the Nasi, or Prince of the Captivity, the head of the Jewish community in Baghdad. The position frequently carried with it the role of principal finance minister and banker, the Saraf Bashi, for the Governor of Baghdad, then under Turkish rule. This position may well have been held by members of the family in a semi-hereditary fashion. But the city itself was much depleted and had become some-thing of a backwater in the Turkish empire. Sasson ben Saleh took up his position in 1778 but he experienced persecution and incurred fines after retiring in 1817. The last of the Mameluke governors, Daud Pasha, who ruled from 1817 to 1831, was especially hard on the Jews. At the time the Jewish community was about 6,000 and they were mostly traders. They tended to live in their own section of the city but it was not a ghetto. Sasson ben Saleh's son, David, born in 1792, followed him into the family bank. It's possible that even while still in Baghdad, the Sassoons traded with the British, through the agency of the British East India Company. Such opportunities became much greater both in Baghdad and India after 1813, when the monopoly of the East India Company ended.

Because of the persecution by Daud Pasha, David Sassoon was imprisoned; he was released after a heavy bribe and fled to Basra and then immediately on to Bushire in Persia, where his father and family followed him. David already had two sons and was to have six more by a second wife, and five daughters, two by his first wife and three by his second. His father died in 1829 and four years later David moved on to India. Baghdad became an even less attractive place to be in 1831 when it was devastated by plague. Partially as a consequence, the Turks reasserted more direct control of the area, and life for the Jews in Iraq improved. But by that time David Sassoon and his growing family were gone.

David Sassoon started his life in Bombay, the most important commercial city of the area, as a banker, but shortly thereafter he and his sons became extremely successful mer-chants, particularly in the import-export business in the Persian Gulf. They also acquired a considerable amount of real estate in Bombay. The family initially lived modestly, occu-pying quarters over their place of business in the centre of the city. They began as traders in cloth and hides, and moved on to raw cotton. Trade in cotton grew at an extraordinary rate thanks to the cessation of the supply from America at the time of its Civil War. The Sassoons entered the manufacturing of textiles after that war, at a time when many of the textile firms in India were in great financial difficulties. The family next moved into the opium trade.

Opium became an important crop in India during the Raj because of Anglo-Chinese trade policies. The British bought tea and silk from China but had little to sell in return. They found it increasingly uneconomic to pay for goods in silver, as the Chinese required, so they turned to the opium poppy, which was grown in Bengal under a government monopoly as well as in the Malwa region. However, the Chinese did not want Indian-raised opium to be sold in China, so the British smuggled it into the country. In 1839 the Chinese destroyed 20,000 chests of opium, precipitating the first Opium War from 1839 to 1842. When the British were victorious, they were reimbursed for their lost goods and received improved trading rights, including the acquisition of Hong Kong. In 1860, after the second Opium War, the trade was in effect legalized, and the cultivation of opium in India continued until 1917. During the nineteenth century, opium accounted for one-seventh of British income in India – and the Sassoons eventually controlled 70 per cent of the trade. It was said that 'silver and gold, silks, gums and spices, opium and cotton, wool and wheat – whatever moves over sea or land feels the hand or bears the mark of Sassoon and Company'.

While he was establishing the family in India and China, David Sassoon maintained his Arab style of dress, as did his sons until later in their lives. Although multilingual, he never learned English. In 1853 he was naturalized as an Indian subject and from then on members of the family attempted, generally with limited success in the early years, to have themselves considered European rather than Indian.[4] The Sassoons identified completely with the British; for instance at the time of the 1857 uprising, David Sassoon pledged the services of the Bombay Jewish community to the government.[5]

Two firms evolved: upon David's death in 1864, his eldest son, Abdullah, ran David Sassoon & Co.; another, E.D. Sassoon & Co, was founded by David's second son, Elias David, three years later. Abdullah Sassoon, who increasingly became known as Albert (an English approximation of his name), was knighted as a member of the Star of India in 1872, in large part for his considerable philanthropic activities in Bombay. The next year, he received an honorary Freedom of the City of London, the first Jew to acquire that honour, although there had been Jews who had acquired the freedom of the city in the ordinary way. From then on he spent most of his time in England, as did his younger brothers Reuben and Arthur. Quite rapidly they became part of the circle of the Prince of Wales. The Rothschilds, with whom the Sassoons intermarried, probably introduced them and they may have served, with others such as Sir Ernest Cassel, as the Prince's bankers. They also shared his interest in horse racing. Albert, Philip's grandfather, became an English baronet, as Sir Albert of Kensington Gore and Eastern Terrace, Brighton, in 1880. (In good part, he was being rewarded for his heroic entertainment of a difficult guest: the Shah of Persia.) Even earlier the family had established an English connection when, in 1858, Sassoon David Sassoon, David Sassoon's eldest son by his second wife, went to London and his father bought for him the estate of Ashley Park in Surrey.

Most of the employees of the family firms were Baghdadi Jews who spoke a Jewish-Arab dialect, Amrani, and conducted business correspondence in Judaeo-Arabic, or Rashi, written in cursive Hebrew script, which served as a semi-cipher for their dealings. The branches in China handled not only opium and textiles but other goods as well such as tea, indigo, silk and spices, as did the firm in India. Offices were established in Canton, Shanghai, Rangoon, Singapore, Hong Kong and Japan. Albert expanded the operations of the firm extensively into textile manufacturing, as did E.D. Sassoon & Co., as well as into large-scale agriculture and insurance.

The family left concrete legacies in the cities of Bombay and Poona, in some senses similar to those that Philip Sassoon and his sister Sybil would later leave in England. Within a decade of his arrival in India, David Sassoon was the leading member of the Jewish community and had established a reputation for absolute probity. In an article in the *Illustrated London News* a year before his death, it was estimated that he had spent £100,000 on various good works, both buildings and funds to maintain them. The family built two synagogues in Bombay (which still function, although with quite small congregations). As the family became more successful, it moved into the suburb of Byculla. There in 1861 David Sassoon built the Magen David (the Shield of David) synagogue with an imposing clock tower and a classical pillared porch. A plaque in the synagogue points out that the building was done at the 'sole' expense of David Sassoon, Esq. Next to it he built a ritual bath and a school, a Talmud Torah for the younger children as well as a primary school, the David Sassoon Benevolent Institution, which taught English, Hebrew and Arabic as well as book-keeping, and 'God Save the Queen' in Hebrew. An upper school is still at the same location, functioning as the Sir Jacob Sassoon High School. As a plaque at the school states, it was 'for the free education of Jewish boys and girls in Hebrew and English', and was built with the 150,000 rupees given by David's grandson Jacob. In 1910 Sir Jacob Sassoon, having been knighted the previous year, enlarged the synagogue. The Sassoons also built the Kereseth Eiyahoo synagogue in 1884 in the centre of the city, the Fort district.

In Byculla the Sassoons named their mansion Sans Souci after Frederick the Great's house in Potsdam. Now the Masena Hospital, it has a plain yet impressive classical front with a large central courtyard. Two large Sassoon coats of arms, with inscriptions in Latin and Hebrew, are still on the grand staircase. Also in Byculla is an imposing clock tower in the Victoria Gardens given by David Sassoon and erected a year after his death. The Victoria & Albert Museum, founded in 1857 by Sir George Birdwood, is in the Gardens. In the central atrium stands a large statue of Prince Albert, eight feet high, on a pedestal of ten feet. It has both English and Hebrew inscriptions on it, including the following: ' "Dear to Science, Dear to Art, Dear to Thy Land and Ours, A Prince Indeed." Dedicated by David Sassoon 1864.' In central Bombay, a dashing statue by J.E. Boehm of Edward as Prince of Wales stands in front of the Prince of Wales Museum; it was given by Albert Sassoon to mark the visit of the Prince in 1875.

David Sassoon not only honoured the British and his God but he accomplished an extraordinary number of good works in Bombay and Poona. The greatest sense of his presence can be gained at the David Sassoon Library and Reading Room in the Fort district in Bombay. In the entrance hall is an impressive statue of David Sassoon in Arab dress with his hands outstretched. His long thin face is rather similar to that of his namesake, the present head of the senior branch of the family, David, the Marquess of Cholmondeley. (Indeed the

2. Thomas Woolner,
David Sassoon, 1869,
Bombay.

Cholmondeley family has recently given funds for the restoration of the Library.) The statue was dedicated at a memorial meeting in David Sassoon's honour in Bombay, chaired by Sir Bartle Frere, the Governor of Bombay. The subscription was international, including the great Jewish families in England as well as a five-guinea cheque from Mr Gladstone. The sculptor was Thomas Woolner and the work was displayed for six months at the South Kensington Museum (now the Victoria & Albert) in London before being sent to Bombay.

The Library is a characteristic Victorian institution. Begun as a mechanics' institute in 1847, it now occupies an 1863 Venetian Gothic building designed by Colonel F.A. Fuller and funded by Sassoon's gift of 60,000 rupees. In gratitude, the name of the institution was changed from the Bombay Mechanics Institute to the Sassoon Mechanics Institute. The younger Sassoons gave in their father's name the David Sassoon Building at the Elphinstone High School and the David Sassoon Industrial and Reformatory Institution, both in Bombay. Albert Sassoon's contributions to the Reformatory were in two parts: £10,000 to mark the visit to Bombay of the Duke of Edinburgh, Queen Victoria's son, and £5,000 as a thank offering for the recovery from illness of the Prince of Wales.

The benefactions of the Sassoon family to Poona were on a similar scale. The most striking, perhaps, is the Ohél David (The Tent of David) synagogue, known as the Red Temple, finished in 1867. David Sassoon laid its cornerstone on 5 November 1863, shortly before his death.[6] The synagogue, in a plain Gothic style, has a tall clock tower; it almost resembles a church. The large room inside is in the simple style of a typical synagogue. A considerable mausoleum with a Gothic tower, containing the catafalque of David Sassoon, stands next to the synagogue. Within, on the tomb, is his coat of arms with its mottoes in Hebrew, *Emeth ve Emunah* (Truth and Faith) and Latin, *Candide et Constanter*. The coats of arms later adopted by the two baronets in the family were very similar, but omitted the harp and star of David. They kept the Lion of Judah with a sceptre, alluding to the claimed descent from David, the palm tree under which the righteous man flourished, the pomegranate as a Rabbinic symbol of good deeds as well as, with its seeds, a symbol of fertility and wealth, the laurel of concord, and above a dove carrying an olive branch.[7] There are inscriptions in English and Hebrew on the tomb, the latter celebrating David's benefactions not only in India but in Baghdad, Jerusalem and London. As the inscription on the tomb states: 'He built unshakeable dwellings, constructed synagogues . . . . In Jerusalem, the Holy City . . . he sent offerings, and he brought his benefaction . . . entire scrolls would not suffice to contain the story of his feats.'[8]

He also subscribed two-thirds of the cost of the David Sassoon General Hospital, dedicated to taking care of people of all races and creeds, the 'suffering poor of Poona'.[9] Captain H. St Clair Wilkins designed the original building, which still survives. Within it is a portrait of David Sassoon, festooned with a garland. His other major benefaction was the David Sassoon Infirm Asylum, founded in 1862. The impressive residence in Poona, Garden Reach, still stands and is still privately owned, now by a Parsee family.

At an 1863 meeting to mark David Sassoon's considerable contribution to a Poona hospital, Sir Bartle Frere (himself one of the shapers of the city and erector of many of the great buildings that remain to this day) remarked:

You have shown, Sir, the sense you entertain of the blessings you received under the British Government by training your children after the fashion of those classes to which her Most Gracious Majesty and the British nation habitually look for the men to be trusted in public as well as private affairs. It is not every one of the native gentlemen of Bombay, even in these days of general prosperity, who can follow your example by purchasing an English estate [Ashley Park] and enrolling himself among the landowners of England; but there are many who can do as you have done, in sending a son to an English school and college, there to learn not only what English gentlemen know, but what they feel and think on subjects of more permanent interest and importance than how the wealth of modern commerce is accumulated and distributed . . . . I could not refrain from noticing the prominent and prevailing feeling of sympathy which you have ever manifested with the British Government and the British people.[10]

Elsewhere he said more bluntly of the Baghdadi Jews: 'They are, like the Parsees, a most valuable link between us and the natives – oriental in origin and appreciation – but English in their objects and associations, and, almost of necessity, loyal.'[11] The Parsees, in India since the eighth century, and the Baghdadi Jews had a similar commitment to commerce and philanthropy. A Parsee industrialist and David Sassoon built the most famous landmark in the city, the Gate of India, the symbolic entrance to the city and Continent. But the Baghdadi Jews were even more closely identified with the English than the Parsees, making it more difficult for them to remain to any significant extent in Bombay after independence in 1947. However they might be regarded by others, they considered themselves English even before so many members of the family came to live in the country itself.

The marks of the Sassoon family remain vividly present in India. Although their firms continued to function until after the Second World War, today they are no more, either there or in England. Except perhaps for a cousin or two, no Sassoon still lives in India. Increasingly, from the 1870s on, the life of the family focused on England, where Sir Albert, Philip and Sybil's grandfather, made his home. England became their country.

2   *England: Becoming English*

The Sassoon brothers arrived in London in the second half of the nineteenth century and rapidly established themselves. The English in general, and the upper classes in particular, have a tendency to react to such advents in the ways that give them greatest pleasure and enjoyment. They have little objection to money. The English aristocracy has rarely hesitated to marry money, never more so than towards the end of the nineteenth century when American heiresses had come on to the market for the plucking. While recognizing the power of money and what it can do, the English wouldn't dream of allowing their semi-acceptance of those such as the Sassoons from preventing them from making nasty remarks about the *nouveaux riches* and in this case, giving a further dimension of pleasure, Jews as well. Anti-Semitism is certainly present in England at all levels of society, but its nature is hard to define. It rarely resulted in segregation, as happened elsewhere. Over the years, like other non-Anglicans, Jews had been admitted to the various institutions of society. But that did not mean that the Jew was not frequently regarded as not quite 'one of us'. Rarely this would result in an adverse action; far more often it might cause quite vicious remarks. At the time that the Sassoons were establishing themselves in England, racism was at its height. Many regarded Jews as a race, not merely Judaism as a religion. The Jewish stereotypes tended to be rather contradictory, and both were despised. The Sassoons did not fit into the radical one – Jews as prone to be revolutionaries – but they were in greater danger of being seen as greedy capitalists, overly interested in money. Philip in his magnificent extravagance exposed himself to the charge of vulgarity.

Sassoon David Sassoon had been dispatched to England in 1858 to supervise the ever growing activities of the flourishing family business. He arrived the very year that the first Jew (not surprisingly, a Rothschild) was allowed to take his seat in the House of Commons as the Christian oath was modified. This so-called Jewish emancipation meant that Jews were no longer excluded from the heart of the establishment. It was also, significantly, the year after the Indian Mutiny; David Sassoon may have felt that a greater presence in England would be desirable.

Sassoon David Sassoon died at the age of 35, in 1867. That same year his brother Reuben came to London, and eventually four more brothers would move to England. Three of the

Sassoons, Albert, Reuben and Arthur, became central figures in the social life of the time. Or, to be more specific, they joined other rich Jews, such as the Rothschilds and Sir Ernest Cassel, in becoming members of the Marlborough House set, the circle around Edward, Prince of Wales. Of the three, only Albert devoted much time to the business. As *Vanity Fair* remarked in the text that accompanied its drawing of Albert in 1879: 'He has splendid palaces in India, yet he has elected to live in Kensington, and he has met with a reception in London which cannot fail to convince him that England is the proper home of the chosen people.'

The Sassoons acquired houses not only in London but in Brighton as well. Arthur leased a shooting box, Tulchan Lodge, in Strathspey, Scotland, a fine place to invite royals, particularly Edward and his son, George. All of the Sassoons of this, the second generation, were devout. But they were much less active in the Jewish religious world in England than they had been in Bombay and other places in the East. On one occasion, when Edward was staying with Arthur at Tulchan on the Day of Atonement, the family fasted and prayed rather than devoting themselves to their guests. The Prince not only raised no objections, but expressed concern about how they were managing, probably finding it hard to imagine a day without food.

Reuben Sassoon, also a great friend of the Prince of Wales, acquired a major collection of Jewish religious art which was displayed in London at the large Anglo-Jewish exhibition of 1887. The Sassoons may have had to make some religious compromises in the entertaining of gentile royalty and others but they appeared to be completely comfortable in their Jewishness. In this generation, the first to reside in England, there was no thought whatsoever of abandoning the practices of their faith.

Arthur's wife, the charming Louise Perugia, having grown up in Trieste, was more accustomed to Western ways than her sisters-in-law and captivated London society. The Indianborn wives of Albert and Reuben were more reclusive but that caused no problem in the male-oriented society of the day. The three brothers had a splendid time in the circle of the Prince of Wales, entertaining him, providing him with food and drink and cigars, going with him to the races. Their way had been prepared by the Prince's fondness for members of the Rothschild family who presumably introduced the Sassoons to the Prince. There was a small price to be paid in the rather ugly verses in the sporting paper, *The Pink Un*: 'Sir Albert Abdullah Sassoon/That Indian auriferous coon,/Has bought an estate called Queen's Gate/And will enter upon it in June.'[1]

The connections with the Rothschilds became closer with the marriage in October 1887 of Albert's only surviving son, Edward, born in 1856, to Aline, born in 1865, a daughter of Baron Gustave de Rothschild who ran the French bank jointly with his elder brother. Her grandfather was James de Rothschild, founder of the French branch of the family. Her mother, Cécile Anspach, was a formidable and intellectual lady, part of Proust's world. Sybil remembered seeing Proust several times at her grandmother's house: 'Nearly all the people who are in his books used to come. So I mean one was very much in that atmosphere.'[2] Also in 1887 Leopold de Rothschild, a member of the English branch, married Marie Perugia, whose

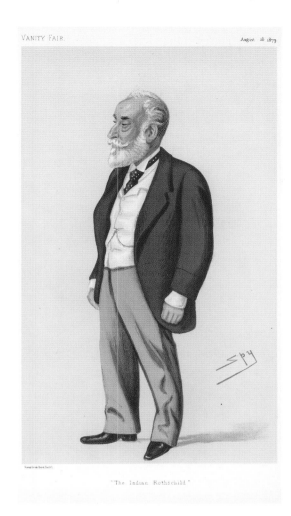

"The Indian Rothschild"

3. Spy (Sir Leslie Ward), *Sir Albert Sassoon,*
Vanity Fair, 16 August 1879.

sister had married Arthur Sassoon. He was particularly close to the Edward Sassoons and their children. The Rothschilds were expanding their marriage pattern to include other prominent Jewish families. The Sassoons had also tended frequently to marry relations up to this point, keeping the money within the family. It was not until the next generation that they married non-Jews. Then, most notably, Alfred Sassoon – son of the first Sassoon to settle in England, Sassoon David Sassoon, of Ashley Park, and the first Sassoon to be born in England – married Theresa Thornycroft and produced three sons, including Siegfried, the poet. Subsequently he abandoned his wife and died young. He was disowned by his devout widowed mother, although his brother and sister kept up with the children. Yet Alfred's mother eventually did relent and visited him on his deathbed, although she had already declared him dead on his marriage. The three sons of the marriage received enough Sassoon money, £600 a year, to be English gentlemen.[3] In any case, the Thornycrofts were fairly well off as manufacturers and Theresa's brother Hamo was a prominent and successful sculptor.

4. Aline Sassoon, 1888.

5. Sybil (on the left) with three cousins at her grandparents' château in France, c. 1897.

Aline de Rothschild and Edward Sassoon's wedding was performed in Paris by the Chief Rabbi, with the chorus of the Paris Opéra entertaining the 1,200 guests. Edward presented Aline with a pearl necklace worth £9,000. (Their son, Philip, inherited the pearls and frequently kept them warm, in a rather Turkish fashion, by fingering them in his pocket, pointing out that such treatment was good for their health.) Edward's namesake, the Prince, named a yacht in honour of the bride. Aline Sassoon later became well known for her collection of emerald, sapphire and gold jewellery. She was also deeply interested in the arts and was a talented amateur painter and sculptor.

Philip Albert Gustave David Sassoon was born in Paris at his mother's family home on the Avenue Marigny on 4 December 1888. (Philip's middle names paid homage to his grandfathers and great-grandfather.) He could choose whether to be French or English; at the age of 18 he chose to be English. Sybil Rachel Bettie Cécile Sassoon was born in London on 30 January 1894. (Her third and fourth names were those of her Rothschild great-grandmother and grandmother. Rachel was a Sassoon family name.) Both children were bilingual and spent much time in Paris at their grandparents' mansion at 23 Avenue de Marigny and at the Château Laversine near Chantilly. Sybil received a great deal of her education in France, being tutored privately with her cousins in languages, music and drawing. She also attended classes at Miss Wolfe's on North Audley Street in London.

Violet Asquith, the daughter of the prominent Liberal politician, visited Aline and Sybil in France in November 1904, when she herself was 17. She had this to say:

> Sybil and three other little French girls with Sarah Bernhardt waists came down & did some plays & dialogues – really very well .... I wish I wasn't so bored by what ought to amuse me .... On the whole I had a delightful morning marred only by the thought that poor Sassbags [a nickname for Lady Sassoon!] was bored with me; we have so little in common – it is hard to find anything to talk about .... Tomorrow we can taste the joys of freedom & stringy meat & a vagabond life in the Quartier Latin free from Semite patronage & hot rooms, constraint & orchids & champagne! ... We lunched with Sassbags in her palatial house at 23 Avenue Marigny teeming with Greuze, Van Dycks & priceless furniture. Conversation flagged at lunch. I always feel tongue tied in that atmosphere of almost oppressive kindness.[4]

This may be just the reaction of one young woman, but it is suggestive of how rich Jews were viewed by much of English society: willing to accept their hospitality, but not totally comfortable, not at ease as one might be with 'one of us'.

A photograph of 1904 of friends of Edward VII survives. It depicts a house party for his set given by Mrs William James. Edward is in the centre, with his mistress, Mrs George Keppel, standing behind him. Aline is there, rather charmingly with a dog on her lap, and Edward Sassoon, comparatively short and already with a white beard, stands in the row behind looking rather cold.[5] They were almost at the centre of Edwardian society, but, as Jews, at a slight remove. Aline was active in Jewish charities and a good friend (but apparently not quite a member) of that famous group, known as the Souls, who mixed high society, wit, and an interest in ideas. It was the generation beyond the Prince of Wales's Marlborough House set and made mock of its frivolity. It was also far more intelligent and wittier, although its members were from a similar world and mixed with that group as well. It included the rather rogue figure of Margot Tennant, shortly to become Asquith's second wife. Another member was the Lord Curzon who hoped, ultimately in vain, to be Prime Minister. Among the Souls Aline's greatest friends were Ettie, Lady Desborough, Margot Tennant and Frances Horner.

A.J. Balfour, soon to be Tory Prime Minister, was a member of the Souls and a friend of Aline's. But he did complain about a boring dinner party in Brighton with Arthur and Louise Sassoon: 'peopled with endless Sassoon girls – I believe the Hebrews were in an actual majority – and tho' I have no prejudices against the race (quite the contrary), I began to understand the point of view of those who object to alien immigration!'[6] It was Balfour whose letter to Lord Rothschild during the First World War established that the British would promote a Jewish National Home in Palestine, a development which many prominent English Jews opposed. But in 1905 Balfour as Prime Minister had supported the Alien Bill that in effect restricted Jewish entry from Eastern Europe. As he remarked: 'A state of things could easily be imagined in which it would not be to the advantage of the civilisation of the country that there should be an immense body of persons who, however patriotic, able and industrious, however much they threw themselves into the national life, remained a people apart, and not merely held a religion differing from the vast majority of their fellow countrymen, but only intermarried among themselves.'[7] This sort of remark was to be made about Philip, even though he may have had, like some other established Jews, mixed feelings about the influx of poorer Jews seeking a better life and fleeing the pogroms of Russia.

The Edward Sassoons moved in 1897, soon after Sir Albert's death, to 25 Park Lane, which would remain Philip's London house for the rest of his life. They had lived previously in Sir Albert's substantial house at 25 Kensington Gore, near the Albert Hall. After Edward's marriage, Sir Albert had left the family mansion in Kensington, moving to Eastern Terrace at Kemp Town, Brighton on the front. At the end of the garden there he constructed a mausoleum, a handsome building looking rather Indian with a copper dome in the style of the Brighton Pavilion. In the *Buildings of England* it is described as a 'curious little building, square with a pagoda roof and Indian details, Royal Pavilion inspiration, but here used for a serious purpose and by a man who could claim connection with India, which the Regent could not'.[8] Albert and his son Edward were buried there but in later years Philip did not think it suitable and had their remains moved to the Willesden Jewish cemetery in London. He sold the mausoleum and it was for a while a furniture depository. Now known as the Bombay Bar, it serves as a function room for the adjoining pub.

The new, much larger house on Park Lane had been built in 1895–6 by T.H. Smith and C.E. Sayer for Barney Barnato, a South African Jewish diamond and gold millionaire. He had died, a probable suicide, on a ship on his way back from South Africa to take possession. The mansion had a four-storey-high marble staircase, a conservatory, a winter garden and a ballroom. Barnato had remarked: 'I shall have the finest entrance hall, stairs and dining room

6. 25 Park Lane, *The Builder*, 10 October 1896.

in London.'[9] The house was indeed huge. Aline spent three years furnishing it with purchases and by acquiring objects from her parents' Paris home. It was a great venue for entertaining that Philip would use extensively.

Marriage with a Rothschild allied the Sassoons with the world's wealthiest Jewish family. Aline's great friend, Bernard Berenson, considered her the most aesthetic of the Rothschilds. She effected in 1906 what was to be financially the most important introduction of his life, to Joseph Duveen, the great art dealer, allowing him to make a lot of money authenticating pictures but also somewhat clouding his reputation.[10] Berenson had met her at St Moritz in 1904 and had a rather ambivalent reaction: he enjoyed her telling him 'a great deal about her world, all of the Rothschilds of course – Rosebery [married to a Rothschild], the Balfours, the Asquiths, etc. . . . She paints, plays, she sculpts, she has read everything . . . . Her curiosity is quite genuine but she has all her life been so overstuffed with golden opportunities that she has profited by none, at least nothing like one expects.'[11] She made an annual trip to Italy and was a visitor to I Tatti, Berenson's villa outside Florence, to the disapproval of the young John Maynard Keynes when their visits overlapped. He remarked in a letter to Lytton

Strachey in 1906 that Berenson had 'gone off in a motor car to flirt with a foul woman called Lady Sassoon'.[12]

For some years she may well have been the most important woman in Berenson's life, although he treated her with some disdain. After another motor trip in 1907 with Aline, his wife, Mary, recorded in her diary, reflecting to a degree her devout Quakerism, what Berenson thought were his feelings about Aline. They may not have been too reassuring for her, although she was accustomed to her husband's interest in other women: 'Falling in love hasn't anything necessarily to do with the desire for physical intimacy – quite often that would never be thought of if there wasn't a convention to that effect . . . . Of course, a spiritual, even intellectual intimacy is far more interesting but this requires character and brains.' In a letter at the same time to Mary, Berenson wrote rather meanly that Aline was 'a cipher which has gained value as ciphers do by numbers placed before it – her wealth, her training, her position – but *she* remains a cipher all the same, though the total comes to millions.'[13] Some fifty letters from Aline survive in the archives of I Tatti, declaring her closeness to him, fondly remembering previous visits, planning new ones but also chastising him for his disagreeableness. Their relationship seemed at its most intense in 1907, at least according to Mary. She wrote in her diary on 9 January: 'Marriage is so difficult. It seems so flat to be merely friendly and devoted, after romance, that one accepts it with indignation and bitterness – at least I think that is Bernhard's feeling – although he allows and encourages himself to indulge in the most romantic feelings towards Aline Sassoon.' And she continued on 26 January: 'I read a letter from B.B. to Aline Sassoon (a wrong thing to do, but I wanted so to believe him, and yet couldn't, by instinct somehow, yet I hoped the letter would be less devoted than the last one) and he said he had thought and dreamt of no one else while he was at Siena, that she must never doubt him, that he was "*tuo, tuo solo*" and so on.'[14] Aline also wrote that year to Berenson. 'Our friendship is too precious – we must not quarrel and we always make it up . . . . You must not trifle with me. I am worth something. What I hate and cannot stand are the ups and downs of the barometer of our friendship.'[15] In an undated letter she wrote about a trip they were to take: 'I shall see if we take a friend or Sybil who might be a proper chaperone – Philip would stay with Edward in Rome – he hates coming and Sybil would be much better.' About another expedition she wrote that she 'can't leave Philip and Edward too long. Let us say five days.' In one letter she thanks him for writing and saying that she is always in his thoughts, and in another she complains about coming to see him, presumably in Paris: 'I cross in a gale only to be with you and you say disagreeable things.' She certainly unburdened herself to him: 'I am just now in a phase of hating myself and I hope to get over it as it is so inconvenient to live with a person one dislikes [presumably herself and not Edward] and I can't understand how anyone could care for me – console me and help me get accustomed to my shortcomings and mistakes.'

On a visit to London in 1906 Berenson had spent fourteen of his sixteen days there lunching or dining with Aline.[16] In one letter she jokingly remarked that she hoped that he wouldn't become the Comte de Montesquiou's lover and in another wrote 'B.B. Mio, I am awake since early dawn and you have been *so* near me – did you feel it? . . . I think of you in the past, present, and future.'[17] At the time of her death, her sister sent him a telegram from Paris: 'Our dear Aline passed away peacefully.' He wrote about her death to his great patron, Isabella Stewart Gardner: 'You did not like Lady Sassoon but poor dear she was one of my familiars and life will be much poorer for her loss. But I feel far more the death of Rembelinski [a Polish count and a collector] . . . . Him I shall never replace, for he was a wonderful combination of so many qualities I love in a man.'[18]

Aline passed on to her children a far stronger interest in art than the Sassoons had ever had. The Rothschilds were great collectors of French decorative art and Philip continued that interest. She and her children were much more involved, comparatively, than either the Sassoons or Rothschilds in contemporary art. This was most evident in the close connection between them and the pre-eminent painter of the rich of the period, John Singer Sargent. By 1906 he had become sick of portraits and would paint them rarely. He was tired of 'doing mugs', being 'Vanity's Butler'. He had been a painter of the aristocracy and the plutocracy, quite often Jewish, most notably in his great series of portraits of the Wertheimer family. Was he a snobbish painter or a witness to the levelling power of wealth: that all could be admitted to the world of high society on the basis of money without reference to origins? In a sense, for the Wertheimers – and for the Sassoons – such portraits were part of acquiring an English provenance, as would be Philip's collecting interests, and his purchases of Gainsboroughs and Zoffanys.[19]

Certainly one of Sargent's finest portraits was that of Aline Sassoon, painted in 1907. Her family was not, at the time, totally pleased with the picture and Sargent then made his famous remark: 'It seems there is a little something wrong with the mouth! A portrait is a painting with a little something wrong about the mouth.'[20] Evan Charteris, a good friend of Philip's and the biographer of Sargent, remarked about the portrait that the painter was 'confronted with a highly strung temperament, features of exceptional distinction and refinement, and a personality kindly, alert – even to the point of restlessness – and instinct with pride of race'.[21] The portrait was a sensation at the Royal Academy in May 1907. Wilfrid Scawen Blunt went there with Francis Meynell, who informed him that Sargent hated painting women – this portrait was an exception – and that he 'paints nothing but Jews and Jewesses now and says he prefers them, as they have more life and movement than our English women'.[22] As in the later portraits of her daughter, there is in the depiction of Lady Sassoon a look of bemusement combined with a slight smile, almost provocative. Sargent remained on very close terms with Lady Sassoon and in later years with Philip and Sybil.

Edward Albert Sassoon was a less dramatic figure than his wife, but he played a solid role in the history of his children and of the Sassoons. Edward had come with his father to England and studied at the University of London. He then spent two years with David Sassoon & Co. in Shanghai from 1878 to 1880. He was a major in the Duke of Cambridge's Hussars and remained with the regiment for fifteen years. After his father died in 1896 (hailed in obituaries as a 'Prince of Commerce'), Edward became chairman of the family firm, David Sassoon & Co., which transformed itself into a private limited company some years later, in

1901. In the company, the dominant figure after Edward's death in 1912 was Edward's uncle Frederick (who died in 1917), the youngest son of David Sassoon. Edward's father had been less active in the business than his father and that pattern continued, although Edward took his involvement seriously. In the reorganization in 1917 a cousin, David Gubbay, became chairman until his own death in 1926. He and his wife, Hannah, also a cousin, would become very close to the Sassoons, particularly Philip. Indeed, Hannah Gubbay, second only to his sister, was no doubt the most important woman, perhaps person, in Philip's life. Born Hannah Ezra, she was a member of a Baghdadi Jewish family that had settled in Calcutta. She was also a granddaughter of Sir Albert as was her husband and first cousin, David. They had married in 1911. She herself became a great acquirer of English furniture, porcelain, and needlework carpets. Her extensive collection is now to be found at Clandon Park, a National Trust property near Guildford. Also there is a Sargent drawing of David Gubbay as well as a charming small portrait of Hannah by Rex Whistler.

Edward Sassoon became increasingly interested in a career in politics, which claimed more and more of his time. He had first stood unsuccessfully for office as a moderate candidate, in 1898 for the London County Council, for Bethnal Green, part of the East End and thus, if elected, he would have served as a representative for a Jewish area. The next year, 1899, he stood for Parliament in a by-election at Hythe in Kent, a constituency that had been represented by Meyer de Rothschild from 1859 to 1874. The area had strong Rothschild connections. Edward's in-laws had owned property there since early in the nineteenth century, using it as a staging point for couriers and carrier pigeons for their communication system with the Continent. The Rothschilds themselves gave £12,000 annually to the Liberal Unionist party; Sassoon put £3,000 a year into the constituency for party organization and local causes.[23] He faced a hard-fought election as his opponent was a local figure, also Jewish, Sir Israel Hart. After his election, he became active locally, becoming Deputy Lieutenant for Sussex, buying a property in the district, Shorncliffe Lodge in Sandgate and seeing something

7. (*facing page*) John Singer Sargent, *Lady Sassoon*, 1907.

8. Hannah Gubbay at Trent Park, early 1930s.

9. Spy (Sir Leslie Ward), *Sir Edward Sassoon*, *Vanity Fair*, 1 February 1900.

of his near neighbour there, H.G. Wells. Some undated letters from Aline to Wells survive, one asking him to 'send me your lecture on journalism & literature & the one you are giving at the Fabian Society'. In the same letter she offered to help him find a French translator for some of his stories. In another she invited him to come to dine with Arthur Balfour and his reputed mistress, Lady Elcho.[24]

Edward was an unexceptional backbencher in Parliament. He was a member of the Reform Club rather than the Carlton, virtually the only remaining difference between being officially a Liberal Unionist rather than a Tory. He commented in Parliament on Indian matters, strongly supporting the improvement of telegraphic communication with India (which he made his main cause) and spoke in favour of tariff reform and the Channel Tunnel. His election brought to nine the number of Jews in the House of Commons. In 1900 he received the accolade, as had his father, of being caricatured in *Vanity Fair*. His briefer text read in part: 'he has houses in Park Lane, at Brighton, Sandgate, Poona, and Bombay . . . . He is rich.'[25]

Early Years

Edward's son, Philip, received the education appropriate to his station. In the spring of 1902, after preparatory school, he entered Eton and lived in Tatham's House. His father wrote to him just before he entered Eton:

> Mr Abrahams has sent you a nice book on Jewish Life in the Middle Ages – Very prettily bound. You must thank him very much for it .... Mr. Tatham writes to say he *has* a vacancy for you in April so you will go to Eton & to his house after Easter, wh will be nice. Goodbye, my dearest boy, & let me entreat you to pay special attention to yr. studies during this, the last term at Farnbro! You will be able to pass yr. Entrance Exam at Eton, *creditably* .... It wd mean great encouragement to persevere with yr. studies at Eton so as to gain distinction in life. You will find diligence in studies particularly helpful when you join the Debating Society at Eton, an institution in wh. excellence means a brilliant career in Parliament later on.[26]

It was a famous time at Eton. Ronald Knox was the Captain of the School. The period acquires a glow from a sense of elegiac sadness; so many pupils of the time would be killed in the First World War, among them Billy and Julian Grenfell, Charles Lister, Patrick Shaw Stewart, and Edward Horner (son of Aline's great friend Frances Horner). Philip's housemaster, Herbert Tatham, was a young Apostle and classicist from Cambridge.

Philip had a less difficult time at his public school than one might have imagined. Eton rather loves its exotics. But schoolboys are extremely conformist and no doubt made mock of this 14-year-old with his dark face, heavily lidded eyes, French accent, and something of a

10. Philip Sassoon as a boy, by Elliot and Fry.

lisp. He was at Eton until 1907 and did fairly well both academically and socially, although his Jewishness may well have made him something of an outsider. He had quite a few cousins there but didn't seem to see much of them. He won, not surprisingly, French prizes. He did well in his drawing lessons and was taught by the leading Etonian aesthete of the time, H.E. Luxmoore. He didn't like 'character building' team sports, but enjoyed racket games such as fives and tennis as well as the strenuous sport of beagling. He was a fairly successful 'wet bob', rowing in his House boat and on the Fourth of June he was on the river in *Monarch*, a social triumph. He knew well Billy Grenfell, son of his mother's and later his close friend Lady Desborough. (He also knew his older brother Julian less well.) He was very fond of the House Dame or Matron, Miss Skey, who mothered him and whom he remembered in his will, along with his secretary and butler. Raymond Asquith, the son of the Liberal leader, reported that once, when dining with Edward and Aline Sassoon, a telegram came from 'little Philip' about a fire at Eton: 'to say that he wasn't hurt, but that there had been a smell in his room and he had poured a bucket full of eau de cologne over the floor and made it alright again'.[27] It was said that the first thing he read in *The Times* was the Court column (perhaps to keep current with family news, since his great-uncles Reuben and Arthur Sassoon consorted with the King).

When Philip was more senior in the House, Osbert Sitwell became his fag (his schoolboy servant). They got on very well and he visited Sitwell at his family house, Renishaw. Sitwell remarked about him in his autobiography: 'I enjoyed being fag to Philip Sassoon, very grown-up for his age, at times exuberant, at others melancholy and preoccupied, but always unlike anyone else – as he remained, I am thankful to say, all his life.'[28] Sitwell feared that Tatham's might be too philistine but he found that the housemaster encouraged the boys in the house to read widely and was always ready to discuss their reading with them.[29] (This rather contradicts Sitwell's famous entry in *Who's Who*, that he was educated during the vacations from Eton.) Philip was very sophisticated, with his knowledge of the world, ranging from art to bridge, likely to impress and possibly infuriate his contemporaries.

Two years ahead of him at Tatham's was Denys Finch Hatton, a son of the Earl of Winchilsea who achieved fame as a trader and adventurer in Africa and as a lover of Karen Blixen (who wrote as Isak Dinesen). A golden youth at Eton, he was the President of Pop, the grandest Eton society. He charmed everyone and he befriended Philip. He protected him from bullying. Once when Finch Hatton was ill, Philip brought him a pair of diamond cufflinks and a set of ruby shirt studs. Philip's extraordinary over-the-top munificence began young. Denys was allegedly offended by these gifts and threw them into the grate, only to retrieve them after Philip left and to give them to his older sister. Years later Philip would lend him a plane when he needed one to fly in Africa.[30] At Eton Philip was, as he was to be all his life, immensely generous, giving presents and buying food for all. But there is always that issue, which was to plague Philip all his life. What do the recipients feel about the person who showers gifts upon them? Is friendship being purchased? Is one liked for oneself or for material reasons?

Only one letter to Philip's father survives from his time at Eton, and it conveys a sense of his somewhat precious personality: 'How can I thank you sufficiently for the charming letter

I received this morning .... We are having at present perfect spring weather ... already the primroses are peeping their small yellow heads from beneath their thick leaves & all nature seems to awaken .... Your very loving boy Philip.' Letters from his father had a much more practical tone, with no talk of primroses, urging him to work hard and to take care of himself. 'The weather keeps cold & you take care not to loiter about after taking exercise but come home at once & change your things.'[31] Philip seemed to remember Eton with affection. During the First World War he attended a Fourth of June dinner for seventy at Montreuil, General Haig's headquarters. 'Oh those fourths of June – with their buttonholes & their bands, their blancmanges & their boatraces – with the chickens tied up in House Colour ribbons and ones "people" down & fireworks and a splitting headache the next morning .... What fun it all was.'[32]

The next step in his progression was Christ Church, the most opulent of the Oxford colleges. Although it had produced more prime ministers than all the Oxford colleges combined, intellectually it was not particularly strong. It was known as the home of the *nouveaux riches* and had a greater number of students who took no more than pass degrees who were presumably there largely for the social experience. At the time, the House, as it was called, was more welcoming than other colleges to grand international figures, princes such as Paul of Serbia and Sergius Obolensky and the heir to the Maharaja of Kapurthala.[33]

There were few Jews at Oxford. One way or another an occasional Jew had attended Oxford in the nineteenth century, but admission did not become easy until the University was opened to non-Anglicans in 1871. Even so in the years before the First World War there were seldom more than about twenty-five Jews at a time among the approximately 3,000 undergraduates. Certainly there was anti-Semitism at the University; for instance, in 1911, a man who would become one of the greatest historians of the century, Lewis Namier, and who was recognized as the strongest candidate, was not elected a Fellow of All Souls because he was Jewish. Some of Philip's relatives had gone to Oxford before him: two of his cousins, sons of Sassoon David Sassoon, including Alfred, Siegfried's father, had attended Exeter College in the 1880s but hadn't taken their degrees.[34] Philip may have wished, as did his golden contemporaries, to go to Balliol but had failed to be admitted. His mother had written to Berenson: 'Philip says he is working hard – I hope it is true and that he will pass his exam for Balliol in March'.[35] During his years at Christ Church (1907–11), he studied history, with particular attention to the eighteenth century. It was seen as a field in which students would learn something about the problems that they would cope with in later life. This interest would continue throughout his life and be a major formative influence on his aesthetic concerns.

He spent the summer after his first Oxford year in Munich in order to work on his German. There he saw a great deal of Gertrude Atherton, the then well-known American novelist. She has left a vivid recollection of Philip that conveys a sense of his frenetic energy and his determination to act as he wished. He did not change his personal style in order to be accepted by English grandees. In Munich he shared his quarters at the house of a German baron with Lord Lambton, the heir to the Earl of Durham and four years older than he. Although Lambton was much more subdued and rather disapproved of Sassoon, he had more of, in Burke's phrase, 'the unbought grace of life' that was the hallmark of the English aristocracy. As Gertrude Atherton wrote about Sassoon, 'he was as active as Lambton was lymphatic; he might, indeed, have been strung on electric wires, wanted to be doing something every minute'. In Munich there was a reproduction of the Loggia di Lanza of Florence. Once, after the opera, Sassoon, Lambton, Mrs Atherton and her niece Boradil went there.

> Sassoon and Boradil began to dance on the platform before the Loggia .... Sassoon in an excess of high spirits kicked off his hat and played football with it [and] he [Lambton] was highly offended. Despite his lazy good nature he could be haughty and excessively digni-fied, and all his instinct of caste rose at the liberty! But young Sassoon was irrepressible. Hauteur and aristocratic resentment made no impression on him. Moreover, he too was well spoilt. His mother was a Rothschild, his father an immensely wealthy Parsee [sic]; no one had a better position in English society. And it amused him to worry Lambton .... As he dined at my apartment a number of times I suppose he thought he must do something to show his appreciation. When he left Munich he went to Paris, and thence sent me a present. It was a green silk petticoat! For Boradil he enclosed two immense artificial roses, more suitable for a dowager than for a girl not yet eighteen.[36]

Back at Oxford, Philip spent a fair amount of time hunting with the Bicester, enjoying him-self, and being a lavish host. He was also mocked as being too much of an aesthete, most notably when Julian Grenfell chased him around Tom Quad in Christ Church, snapping an Australian bull whip at him and chanting 'Pheeleep! Pheeleep! I see you!' Using the French pronunciation of his name, Grenfell displayed his hatred at that moment of foreigners, among whom he included his fellow old Etonian. Nevertheless, Philip's friends at Oxford were the bright athletes of Balliol, whom he had known at Eton, and the aesthetes at Christ Church.

One letter from his father, in the tradition immortalized by Polonius, deserves quotation. It may have been written at the beginning of his Oxford career and perhaps his father was more serious since he wrote from the family firm, at 12 Leadenhall Street.

> I wish to send you my best thoughts on yr. approaching Birthday & we pray that as you grow older you will be impressed with the sense of what is owing to yourself in the way of studies & preparation for the life that is to open out before you. Sports & leisure are very well in their way but they must not be allowed to displace or to encroach upon the essential object for wh. you are at Oxford. Imitate the example of those who are perme-ated with the truth of this rather than that of those & I fear they are by far the most numerous who wile away the most precious time of their youth in senseless dissipation & equal disregard for work. We are placing to yr credit fifty pounds as a Birthday present to enable you to pay all yr. bills. I notice you have already overdrawn £20! Wd. it not have been possible to wait 3 or 4 days?![37]

His father thought he should have a commission in the East Kent Yeomanry. There was some confusion about doing his training while at Oxford, and his father drafted a letter of apology for him to send to the Colonel. 'You *must* attend the maneuvers in Sept. I think they only last a week, & you will have to be careful to answer letters as it wd never do to be asked to resign. You will find the E. Kent a nice Regiment & useful in other ways later on.'[38] On 17 December 1907, he received his warrant as a 2nd lieutenant in the Royal East Kent Yeomanry, Duke of Connaught's Own.[39] He took a second-class honours degree in the Modern History School.

His mother died of cancer in Paris on 28 July 1909 and was buried in the family tomb in Père Lachaise cemetery. It was a devastating blow for the family and perhaps most of all for Sybil who was only 15 and mourned her mother for the rest of her life, naming her one daughter after her. 'I absolutely worshipped her'.[40] As Sybil remarked when asked if she were upset at her mother's death: 'Upset isn't the word. Then it has gone on just the same until today. But she was a most wonderful woman. Great artist too, she was a sculptor and a painter .... It is very rare in England that a foreigner makes their mark to that extent. Everybody loved her. And liked her and admired her. All these very clever men, very fond of her. When she was so desperately ill and dying in Paris they all used to come over just only for the day .... Just to see her.'[41] Touchingly, still preserved at Houghton, presumably as a text of consolation, is a small *Psalms of David*, signed Sybil Sassoon and dated 16 September 1909.

Soon after his mother's death, Philip received a letter from her dear friend Frances Horner: 'You return [from Paris] to a country that *loved* her and will *always* love her children, & it *is* yours, as it had become hers.'[42] In her autobiography, Horner wrote: 'Aline Sassoon was a brilliant hostess and a very constant friend; she died young, taken away from a life full of glitter, and of all the world could give of its joys and possessions. I went out to Paris to see her when she was dying, and her great anxiety was for the two children she was leaving .... On them, even more than their parents, the gods heaped their gifts: youth, beauty and riches.'[43]

After his wife's death, Sir Edward spent much of his time in Cannes in order to recuperate. There in 1911 he had an automobile accident that hastened his own death on 24 May 1912 at the age of 56. A letter of condolence survives, from Frances Horner to Philip: 'You have both been so familiar with grief & suffering these two years [that it] must have [made] a deep mark on your youth'.[44] Philip and Sybil's maternal grandfather, Baron Gustave, died in 1911 and his wife in 1912. (Much of their furniture and other objects were bequeathed to the Sassoons. Philip had spent time in Paris cataloguing them before they were sent to 25 Park Lane.) He was to enter upon his inheritance sooner than he wished or expected. Philip and Sybil were without parents and grandparents at quite a young age.

The Baroness Gustave had apparently tried to guide Sybil shortly before her own death. A letter to her brother, written when Sybil was recovering from chickenpox, conveys a good sense of her vivacity in the face of her grandmother's irksome attentions:

Nothing can alter Gdma. We have all begged her to leave me alone & she *can not* so I am going to Brussels [presumably to stay with her mother's sister, the Baroness Lambert] as soon as I am well & there I shall be able to work well. There is a wonderful philosopher greatly recommended by le grand Bergson who has *consented* to give me lessons & I shall at least be calm. I am much better but am not yet allowed to get up . . . . I amuse myself by phoning to my friends . . . . Do write to B.B . . . . & tell him I asked you to write because I have chicken pox & I loved his nice letter & am sorry he's been so ill & send my love.

Two letters, written in the period between her mother's death and her marriage, give a sense of her personality and the world in which she and her brother moved. In one she reported on a lunch at Tring, a Rothschild house. 'Evan [Charteris?] & I quaked together in a corner & decided we were more frightened by the servants than by the hosts. They all look like Reynolds ancestors & the look of withering scorn they gave Evan when he arrived clutching a gripsack (as he was going to London) was truly epic. I had great fun at lunch between Harry Dalmeny [eldest son of Lord Rosebery and his late wife Hannah Rothschild] & Tony [?] both quite drunk & in very good form. I like Harry so much, even when he is gurgling down 100 yr. old Madeira.' In another letter written in, I believe, 1912 on 17 December, she writes to her brother: 'Darlingest . . . Our dinner went off splendidly – A.J.B[alfour] was in wonderful form . . . . Roger Fry had taken him to the Grafton Gallery in the morning & tried to explain the beauty of the pictures to him [the second Post-Impressionist Exhibition] but Mr Balfour seemed to have dried up every one of his arguments . . . . I had great discussions with [name unclear] about the relative values of Degas & Sargent . . . . The wedding was too frightful. The whole of the afternoon service tacked on & they recited the Kaddisch five times which added to the gloom.'[45]

Aline had been very close to and influenced by her mother, but Sybil was determined not to be confined by the Rothschild inheritance. Although she was, I believe, quite comfortable with being Jewish, even if not particularly observant, she was less comfortable with being a Rothschild. She admired their cultivation but felt that they were anxious to keep her within their orbit. The Rothschilds wanted their money to stay in the family. Sybil was very aware that they expected her to marry someone whom she referred to metaphorically and perhaps literally as a 'cousin from Frankfort'. One reason for her early marriage might have been to escape from this situation. When she was 16, shortly after her mother's death, Charles de Polignac fell in love with her and asked her father's permission to marry her when she was of age. This was refused with indignation. A threatened duel with Philip never materialized. Sybil was apparently engaged to Neil Primrose, a son of Lord Rosebery and a Rothschild on his mother's side. She wasn't in love with him, although she felt that she might become fonder of him. She gave him up at the request of Lady Victoria, a daughter of the Earl of Derby, who was much in love with him. He was killed in the First World War.[46]

There was talk that she might marry James de Rothschild of the English Rothschilds. There would appear to have been some correspondence with Philip about this possibility. An undated letter, written before 1912, from Paris from a friend or relation to Philip states:

I can most heartily reassure you that Sybil is quite aware of J's intentions & is totally against any such marriage & indeed any marriage at all . . . . To me it is a nightmare of horror to even think of it in the abstract. Sybil's behaviour is *perfect*. She is quite natural & friendly & apparently regards him as an amusing cousin . . . . She is at the stage of disillusion about men & is down on them & their laziness, trivial lives of pleasure seeking in their demi-monde. French life is to her appalling. She admires you so much because you don't fritter your life & health & sanity in such pursuits . . . . Surely Papa is not for Jimmy? He will have to manage Sybil very carefully & not be too frightfully strict with her.

In another letter from an older relation there is talk of finding her a companion.[47]

The question of her possible marriage and her Jewishness were intertwined. Sybil felt that the Rothschilds disapproved of almost everyone but themselves and hardly let anyone in the house other than relations. They were certainly not willing, in her view, to mix with less affluent Jews. When asked whether it was difficult to marry, as she would, a gentile, she replied 'It never *gêned* [bothered] me because as I have said to you before, the Rothschilds never wished us or anybody else to have Jews in the house. The only Jews that were ever there were Rothschilds. If they thought we must marry Jews, then their business was to invite Jews. Instead of which there was not one single Jew who ever passed the door. Never. We used to go once or twice a year to the synagogue, very rarely.'[48]

In the family papers preserved at Houghton, there are notes of a talk Sybil gave to a Jewish girls' club in the East End, an interest she had inherited from her mother. In the talk she takes a rather conventional view of the female sex. 'We are not the *strong* sex, some people have called ours the wrong sex! We cannot obtain perfection in one thing so we must divide our strength to make it best meet every occasion. We have the qualities of our defects. We may not be geniuses but we can at least be *useful*, & I think we can even make ourselves *indispensable*.' She then went on to give her views on Zionism: 'If it is meant to serve as an opening for our poor co-religionists in Russia who have to suffer so much injustice, I am all for it – but personally I do not believe in the "regeneration of our people in their ancient lands" – *We* need not chafe for the freedom of tomorrow while we are enjoying the freedom of today – We cannot be sufficiently grateful to our countrymen for their sympathy & friendly feeling – Our religion does not prevent us from being loyally English! God is within us & everywhere; we will find Him if we seek Him & remain faithful to our principles & belief . . . . Your lives will ever make us proud of you, both as Jews & as English girls.'[49]

Friends of their parents took a special interest in the children, particularly Ettie Desborough, Frances Horner and Margot Asquith. They 'invited us as though we'd been absolutely grown up, and naturally sorrow is a great forcing house and one did suddenly become quite old'.[50] She and Philip would go to large weekend parties at the Desborough house, Taplow Court, on the Thames near Windsor. This was a magical place full of young men, most of whom were in love with Diana Manners. 'We used to have these big parties at

Lady Desborough's. She had a lovely house on the river. And every weekend during the summer ... we were about twenty young people .... I could rattle off to you, about fifteen, every single one dead. Holocaust.'[51]

As orphans, it wasn't thought quite right that the brother and sister should live together and Philip, just down from Oxford, took up residence at 25 Park Lane, the family home in London. Sybil moved to Albert Gate, near to the family's first house in London, for just over a year, with Mrs Arthur Sassoon, Aunt Loo, who was widowed that year. Sir Edward, in his will, had made her Sybil's guardian. Nevertheless 'I kept on seeing my brother as often as I could, naturally.'[52] They remained extremely close; their lives were intertwined. Despite her parents' death, Sybil continued to live the life of her class. She was a débutante of the 1912 season, many said the most beautiful of the year; the next year she would marry. But the strictures of mourning kept her from going to many balls that season. In an interview years later, gliding effortlessly between French and English, Sybil said, '*J'étais tout le temps en deuil! D'abord mon grand-père, ensuite ma grand-mère, ensuite ma mère, ensuite mon père, tout ça en deux ans. Et comme j'avais des habitudes françaises, j'avais le vrai deuil* .... I was always in mourning, so that the idea of going to a ball never occurred to me.'[53]

Edward's estate had a gross value of £758,853 16s. 2d. He left the bulk to his children, three-quarters to Philip and one-quarter to Sybil. His two major English properties, 25 Park Lane and Trent Park, were put into trusts. Sybil was to receive an income of £6,000 a year and the principal when she either married or turned 30. He left £3,000 to his niece Hannah Gubbay who was already playing a central role in his family's life, citing 'her affectionate care and devotion to me in my severe trial and sufferings'. The sum of £500 was left to his butler Garton, who would continue to serve the family until Philip's death thirty-seven years later. His son was to have an income of £12,000 until the age of 30, and then come into his inheritance. Contrary to what happened, he suggested that his children live together until one of them married, 'avoiding all extravagance or gambling ... devoting some part of their time to benevolence'. He stipulated that the shares in David Sassoon & Co. were not to be sold. 'I impress on my said son the desirability of attending to the interests of the business of the said David Sassoon & Company Limited so that its reputation and standing so laboriously built up by his Ancestors for close on a century may not be tarnished or impaired by the possible neglect or mismanagement of outsiders AND it is my special wish that my said son shall maintain some connection with my Parliamentary Constituency of Hythe.' Perhaps Edward felt somewhat guilty for neglecting the firm to a degree himself, and Philip would not be particularly active in it. In the next stage it was run by Frederick Sassoon, the new chairman; David Gubbay, Hannah's husband; and a non-Jew, Cecil A. Longcroft. (Though not Jewish, he wasn't regarded as an outsider as he had worked in the firm all his life, starting as a junior clerk.) Two separate bequests of £1,000 each were made to charities in Bombay and Baghdad. Edward left nothing to charities in England, as a protest against death duties. The executors of the will were Philip, Longcroft, and Aline's brother-in-law, the Baron Leon Lambert of Brussels.[54]

It would be necessary to move quickly if Philip were to have the parliamentary seat. He was only 23 and had very little political experience. He had not been particularly active politically as an undergraduate. It might have been better for his political training if he had had some period of apprenticeship rather than being thrust into the House of Commons. As they are today, by-elections were held very shortly after a seat was vacated and a decision would have to be made whether this youth who, if elected, would be the youngest member of the House of Commons, should have the nod. On 26 May 1912, two days after Edward's death, Arthur Steel-Maitland, chairman of the Unionist party, wrote to Andrew Bonar Law, the head of the party. He had submitted to the constituency two names: Philip, and Sir Arthur Colefax, who had lost his seat in 1910 in the last election. By one of those splendid coincidences, not necessarily significant, that seem to happen more in England than elsewhere, his wife Sibyl was one of the most famous hostesses in Britain and in the future would see Philip frequently. Colefax himself, unlike his wife, was well known as a bore. Someone remarked that his services could be used to create the tunnel under the Channel. Whatever he was, Philip was not boring and that was likely to give him an edge in being selected. Steel-Maitland was not pressing the constituency organization to adopt one of them in particular. He did write, however, 'It is a seat that has nearly always been held by a Rothschild or a relation, & they have a long standing connection with the place.' Steel-Maitland had heard some negative things about Philip. But the possibility that he might not be adopted had deeply distressed the Rothschild family, considerable contributors to the party. To compensate for some bad reports, Steel-Maitland had also been told that Philip had given 'a quite remarkable good little speech at Folkestone & had impressed people considerably'.[55] Sir Edward had spent £3,000 a year on the constituency and his son would keep up that standard.

It was at this point that the Liberal Unionists were being completely absorbed into the Tory party. Sir Edward had run as a Tory in 1906, the year of the great Liberal landslide, and had won easily with 58 per cent of the vote. In the January 1910 general election he had won 65.7 per cent of the vote and in the December election that year he had been unopposed.[56] Whomever the Tories selected was almost sure to win. The constituency organization selected Philip. His Liberal opponent was Captain Samuel Moorhouse, a local man who had fought in the Boer War. *The Times* reported that 'the short contest is being waged very keenly'. It was quite a lively election, as much attention was paid to the great issue of the day: free trade versus tariffs. Sybil and his aunt, Mrs Arthur Sassoon, assisted Philip in the campaign. The national organizations on both sides set up offices in the constituency, although Philip's was notably more efficient. He had the support of the fishermen, who were unhappy that France had duties levied on their fish while there were none on French fish sold in Britain. On their masts they flew Sassoon's colours of orange and purple. He also campaigned against Welsh Disestablishment, Home Rule, and Lloyd George's new Insurance Act, but said that he favoured social reform in the form of better housing and agricultural co-operatives. He claimed that the Tories did more for the working man than did the Liberals. He was, perhaps surprisingly, in favour of women's suffrage. On 9 June he received a letter from William Waldorf Astor, a Tory MP, disagreeing with him on the issue: 'We will all be delighted to see you in the H. of C. But why on earth have you promised to support these damned suffragettes? I am distressed about that. They've got no following in the country & it's only by bluffing new candidates that they ever get any support at all. Your promise about the Reform Bill means adult suffrage, & an entirely new electorate at the greatest crisis in our history.'[57] But it might have been a gesture to thank the militant suffrage organization, the Women's Social and Political Union, for opposing Moorhouse, as the Liberal government had so notably failed to support women's suffrage and had so badly treated women who had been imprisoned for the cause. Polling was on 11 June. Sassoon won comfortably, with 3,722 votes to his opponent's 2,004.[58]

Philip remained an active member of the House of Commons until his death in 1939. (In effect he owed his seat to being a grand Jew – benefiting from the Rothschilds' contributions to the party and their connections with the constituency.) An Act had been passed in 1911 authorizing an annual payment of £400 for Members of Parliament. But as a proper English gentleman, Sassoon never accepted a salary. In 1913 Max Beerbohm did a drawing of Sassoon sitting in the lotus position in white tails on a bench in the House of Commons, looking bemused and exotic, while on either side of him two Tory Members in top hats and morning coats are shouting.[59]

He made his maiden speech in the debate on the Irish Home Rule Bill on 7 November 1912, a great moment in a parliamentary career, perhaps particularly at a time when the House of Commons was considered by many to be the most powerful club in the world. He began coyly: 'I can claim a privilege which is not shared by all the Members of the House, and that is that not one of my former speeches can be brought up against me.' He attacked the financial aspects of the bill. 'These financial clauses are the most involved and contradictory part of an inconsequent and incoherent Bill.'[60] He seemed to be doing well, but what Cecil Roth has called his 'palpable diffidence' struck the members of the House of Commons.[61] He was not an effective speaker. The Tory wheeler-dealer, Max Aitken, later Lord Beaverbrook, the Minister and press baron, snottily remarked that Philip's maiden speech produced, as was fairly common,

> floods of notes of congratulations – not because he had made a good speech but because he had big houses and even bigger funds to maintain them .... He was a brilliant gossip and an habitual flatterer, indifferent to the status of his subjects. At my house in the midst of a large company I was asked, 'Where is Philip?' I replied: 'Flattering somebody somewhere.' From behind a pillar nearby Sassoon cried: 'Not you, Max!' . . . [He] gathered the aged, the beautiful, the clever and over all the powerful at his dining room.[62]

It appears that he was determined to convince the House that, despite his youth and wealth, he was a serious young man. In his speeches before the war he concentrated on financial matters, a practical man of business who, as a Sassoon, should have a sense of such questions. In May he spoke on the Budget and against an increase in the income tax. Sassoon spoke again the following March on housing for the poor and the inadequacy of the Local

11. Max Beerbohm, *Philip Sassoon in Strange Company*, original drawing, 1913.

Government Board to deal with the issue. He would appear to be in the Tory tradition of supporting government subsidies for housing. On 1 July 1914, he made a serious and detailed speech which drew upon particular Sassoon areas: the question of taxes on tea, and contrasts between the India and the China markets. He hardly tried to hide the traditions of his family. 'England has done a great deal for China, mostly at the expense of India. By an act of vicarious generosity she has sacrificed the whole opium trade of India to the moral regeneration of China.' He cited the fact that the cultivation of poppy seeds in India had gone down from 500,000 acres in Bengal in 1905–6 to 200,000 in 1911–12.[63] Within a week, he attacked Lloyd George for, in his view, attempting to cut short a discussion, thereby 'hazard[ing] the liberties of the United Kingdom'.[64] It was his last speech until after the war.

In August 1913 his sister Sybil married the Earl of Rocksavage, the heir to the Marquess of Cholmondeley. Sybil had met him through Philip. George Horatio Charles Cholmondeley was born in 1883. He had a very unhappy childhood and did not get on at all well with his father, the 4th Marquess. He briefly attended Eton from 1896 to 1898 and then enlisted while under age to fight in the Boer War as a lieutenant, first in the 3rd Battalion of the Royal Sussex Regiment. He then joined the 9th Lancers. He also served as an ADC to Lord

12. Bassano,
Lord Rocksavage, 1908.

Minto when he was Viceroy of India from 1905 to 1910. (Sybil always thought that Lord Minto had hoped that Rocksavage would marry one of his daughters.) On his return from India he was part, as was Philip, of the wider circle of Lady Diana Manners's 'Coterie'. She wrote about him, quoting from her own letter: 'There was the most beautiful of all young men of his day, Lord Rocksavage. "We saw a lot of Rock. I think he is probably Apollo – anyhow some god." He was proud and aloof and loved to dance the one-step.'[65] Probably because of all the recent deaths in Sybil's family and the mixed religions, the wedding was a small one in a register office (which also suggests that the decision was taken that neither bride nor groom would convert). It was attended by family only. Her pious great-aunt Flora, who had moved to London after running the business in Bombay, did object to family wealth going into non-Jewish hands and her son regarded it as 'another nail in the coffin'.[66] Cecil Roth wrote, 'On the day of the wedding, scientific observers might have discerned slight seismological disturbances in different parts of the earth's surface, for the pious founders of both families had turned in their graves.'[67] Although there was no formal break, in fact Sybil and Philip, after the wedding, saw practically nothing of their Rothschild relations, despite going frequently to France. The Rothschilds may also have been intensely irritated that her mother had left to her, and hence out of the family, the famous Rothschild emeralds. On her death many years later Sybil directed that they were to be sold on behalf of a family charity. Easy terms with her Rothschild relations were not really resumed until after the Second World War. Except for some of their Sassoon relations – above all their first cousin, Hannah Gubbay – they kept up with very few Jewish friends or relations.

She said later about her husband: 'I really loved him very very much but nothing to what I loved him afterwards because I got to know him so well, I knew everything about him, and I saw him in front of my eyes, developing so much. He never knew before about building, about china, about books about a hundred and one things that he learnt and taught himself.'[68] More than likely, the change in his interests owed a lot to her.

Although Sybil had not converted to Anglicanism for the wedding, she did so eventually but not until after the Second World War. She talked about this question in the interviews she had for the film about her made by her grandson, where she places her conversion earlier. But she is probably reflecting that between the wars she attended church with her family. 'I changed because I thought that – I had my children, and I thought it was better for them to belong to the religion of the country . . . . I don't think that [my family] thought very much of [my oath of conversion]. First of all a great many of them were not there any more, either had died or were far away . . . . My family was not at all what they call orthodox. But we went naturally to services but we never kept very much to the religious things.'[69]

To mark the wedding two extraordinary portraits were painted of Sybil. A half-portrait of Sybil by John Singer Sargent still hangs at Houghton Hall. She had come to know Sargent well through her mother, taking rides with him in the Bois de Boulogne and playing piano duets with him. He did three charcoal drawings of her, in 1910, 1912 and 1920. (The last drawing he did before his death in 1925 was of her daughter, Lady Aline Cholmondeley.) Although Sargent had grown tired of doing portraits, he would paint one for special occasions and did this portrait as a wedding present. (His previous painting that year was a birthday portrait of Henry James, also a present. It achieved the dubious honour, for no apparent reason, of being slashed by a suffragette in May 1914 while being displayed at the Royal Academy.) He inscribed the portrait 'To Sybil, from her Friend John Sargent'. Wrapped in a cashmere shawl that the painter had given her, Sybil looks rather bemused and quizzical, and quite beautiful.

Sargent was of her parents' generation and part of their world. The other portrait was by quite a different artist, but one who also achieved great success as a society portraitist. William Orpen, born in 1878, was sixteen years older than Sybil. He did not feel that the age difference was a bar to his being in love with her; nor that in 1901 he had married Grace Knewstub, the sister of a leading art dealer. By 1913 their marriage had cooled. As a middle-class Irish Protestant who had made his career in England, he was fascinated by Sybil and

13. John Singer Sargent, *Sybil Sassoon*, 1910.

14. John Singer Sargent, *Sybil Sassoon*, 1912.

15. (*facing page*) John Singer Sargent, *Sybil Sassoon*, 1913.

her aristocratic world. Sybil remarked ambiguously to Orpen's biographer, 'Orpen made me an offer. Nothing came of it.'[70] He had already painted that year a conversation portrait of Philip and Sybil in the large drawing room in Park Lane. His portrait of her, still with the family, is, in my view, a masterpiece. Sybil, in a dress by Fortuny, won't let the viewer out of her gaze, as she looks even more bemused and quizzical, with charmingly arched eyebrows, than she does in the Sargent portrait. Perhaps she is amused and a little taken aback by Orpen's presumption. Painting the portrait had been his idea. The picture was then purchased by Sir Joseph Duveen, who presented it to Sybil.[71]

They remained good friends, Orpen sending her quite splendid illustrated letters over the years. He made a great deal of money as a portraitist; this very picture did a lot to establish his reputation. After the war, Sybil acquired one of his most striking pictures, still to be found at Houghton: *The Play Scene from Hamlet*, which he had painted in 1899. Its models were figures from his somewhat bohemian artistic world: the Augustus Johns and the William Rothensteins. It won a summer prize at the Slade School of Art, where Orpen had studied, and where it hung over the staircase. During the First World War the painting was put at risk by a bomb blast and in 1918 Sybil bought it for £1,200, a considerable sum. The money was used to establish a scholarship in Orpen's name.

Sybil had married into one of the great families of England, the Cholmondeleys, and became deeply involved with them and their house, Houghton Hall in Norfolk. Her husband, then using his romantic courtesy title, the Earl of Rocksavage, was among the handsomest men in England. The family traced its ancestry not quite as far back as the Sassoons: there are records of it having occupied the same site in Cheshire since Domesday Book.[72] (To keep the English and others on their social toes, the name is pronounced Chumley.) They became earls in 1706 and marquesses in 1815. The 1st Marquess remodelled Cholmondeley Hall in Cheshire in the gothick fashion (influenced by his great-uncle and mentor Horace Walpole's Strawberry Hill) in 1805, renaming it Cholmondeley Castle. It has remained officially the family's primary residence. The 3rd Earl of Cholmondeley was an active politician in the eighteenth century; no doubt his political career was helped by his marriage to Mary Walpole, the daughter of Sir Robert Walpole, Britain's first Prime Minister.

It was through the Walpoles, a family prominent in Norfolk since the fourteenth century, that Houghton Hall entered the Cholmondeley family. To mark his arrival at the pinnacle of political success, Sir Robert tore down the family house and built a new classical one (considered the finest Palladian house in England). Houghton was magnificently furnished, and Walpole amassed a great art collection (most of which was later sold in 1779 to Catherine the Great to help to pay off the debts Sir Robert had accumulated in the building of the house). His genius as a politician was to transform England's financial system and enable it to support the country's greatly enhanced position in the world. He also profited considerably from the state, but far from enough to cover his huge outgoings on the house and its contents. In the history of the house its two greatest shapers were its builder, Sir Robert, and

16. (*facing page*) Sir William Orpen, *Countess of Rocksavage*, 1913.

then two centuries later, Sybil herself. As her grandson remarked: 'When she died in 1989, my grandmother had been chatelaine of Houghton for just over seventy years and every room in the house bore her unmistakable imprint.'[73]

Walpole began to build his glorious new house in 1722. It was planned by James Gibbs and Colen Campbell, and William Kent was responsible for the decoration of the main floor. Walpole created it to display his wealth and power and as a place to hold great gatherings for the purposes of intense political discussion, disquisitions on classical literature, and heavy drinking. Sir Robert's eldest son succeeded him in 1745 as owner of the house, then his son came into possession. He never married and was succeeded by his uncle, the third son of Sir Robert, Horace, the writer. On his death in 1797 the property went to the 4th Earl and the 1st Marquess of Cholmondeley and has remained in that family ever since. In the wonderfully complicated nature of these matters he inherited because his grandmother Mary was the one daughter of Sir Robert. Having come into possession of Houghton, the Cholmondeleys' other recent acquisition, then known as Trent Place, just outside of London, became too much for the family to manage: money from its sale was necessary to purchase Houghton's furniture. (It was a nice coincidence that the Cholmondeleys would become reconnected with Trent through the Sassoons in the twentieth century.) This Cholmondeley also brought further distinction to the family through his marriage to Lady Georgiana Bertie, co-heir to her brother, the 4th Duke of Ancaster. He was the hereditary Lord Great Chamberlain of England, one of the most important members of the royal court, the sixth great officer of state, whose primary responsibility is to be in charge of the monarch's Palace of Westminster, the seat of Parliament. As the Duke of Ancaster did not have a male heir, the position of Chamberlain descended through his sisters and hence the Marquess of Cholmondeley is the co-hereditary Lord Great Chamberlain of England. He was made a Marquess in 1815 to mark his having that post. After much litigation, it was decided that the holder of the Cholmondeley title should serve in the post every other reign. (The descendants of the two other sisters – the present Lord Carrington and Lord Ancaster – take turns in the post after each Cholmondeley occupancy.) The 5th Marquess, Sybil's husband, was Lord Great Chamberlain for Edward VIII and Elizabeth II, as was his son, the 6th Marquess. On his death in 1990, Sybil's grandson, the present Marquess, inherited the position.

The Cholmondeleys made several unsuccessful efforts in the nineteenth century to sell Houghton, the first to the Duke of Wellington. The Prince of Wales almost acquired it around 1860 but instead bought the neighbouring estate of Sandringham. Although the contents of Houghton were kept, and the Cholmondeleys used the estate for shooting (for which Norfolk was famous), the house was comparatively neglected. It had a series of tenants until 1916, when it was reclaimed by the family and became the residence of the Rocksavages. Rock's father gave the newlyweds the house at the time of their marriage, but they didn't take up residence until 1919. Even then, between the wars they spent much of their time in London and elsewhere. Rather unusually, when his father died in 1923, the 5th Marquess, Sybil's husband, rather than moving to Cholmondeley Castle made Houghton his preferred residence. His mother, in effect, used the Castle as her dower house.

In the two years between Sir Edward's death and the outbreak of war the brother and sister began to lead separate lives. Philip became more active in the world of art and architecture. For instance, he became a patron of Glyn Philpot, an up and coming portraitist, who was only four years older than Philip. Upon seeing Philpot's work at an exhibition in 1913, Philip purchased several of his works: his *Head of a Negro* (now in Tate Britain) and a drawing of *Billy*, a preliminary study for a painting. That year Philip also bought Philpot's portrait of Nijinsky in *L'Après-midi d'un faune*. (Philip, like so many others, was smitten by Diaghilev's Ballet Russe when it performed in London before the First World War.) His admiration for Philpot led him to commission a portrait of himself, completed in 1914. There Philpot shows a young man both vulnerable and rather supercilious, sharing with his sister in the Orpen portrait a rather quizzical bemused look, but hers is more attractive. Some years later, in 1917, introduced by Robert Ross, Philpot painted his best-known portrait, of Philip's cousin Siegfried, although the cousins had not yet met.

17. Bassano, *Sir Philip Sassoon*, 1913.

19. Sir William Orpen, *The Drawing Room at 25 Park Lane*, 1912.

Upon the death of his father, Philip became wealthy in his own right and a considerable property owner, though he would not fully enter into his inheritance until his thirtieth birthday. He was officially the senior member of the family, despite his youth, as the direct descendant of David Sassoon's eldest son. His holding of property was somewhat complicated. Trent Park, thirteen miles from the centre of London in New Barnet, was on leasehold that his father had acquired in 1908 from the crown. Philip did not pay particular attention to it until after the war. He occupied 25 Park Lane, a vast mansion in central London, as the tenant for life of a family trust, which, for the moment, he left untouched. After the war he would undertake extensive changes in that house as well as at Trent. Orpen's conversation piece of Philip and Sybil in the drawing room at Park Lane showed the room as it had been decorated by their mother.

18. (*facing page*) Glyn Philpot, *Sir Philip Sassoon*, 1913.

But even before the war, elaborate entertainments took place at Park Lane. Edward Marsh, active as a patron of poetry, particularly that of Rupert Brooke and Siegfried Sassoon, and Winston Churchill's secretary, recalls vividly, in a letter to Brooke, one disastrous occasion in June 1913:

I arrived late [at Park Lane], and after being kept a few minutes on the landing was admitted into a place like the Black Hole of Calcutta. The door was shut behind me, the light which it admitted having shown for a second the flash of stars and tiaras, revealing the fact that all the Ambassadors and Duchesses in London were present .... Poor Mr. Balfour said, 'I'm deaf myself, but I'm sure that even people who *can* hear can't hear this.' The play was Maeterlinck's *Death of Tintagiles*. If you know it you will realize that it is not the sort of thing to hold the attention of a fashionable London audience after a superb dinner. There was the most fearful fidgeting and bumping together of Guardsmen at the back of the room struggling for a little air to breathe. I stood next Sybil Sassoon who was in despair, and kept whispering, 'You can't imagine the anguish I'm suffering' – and 'Never again will I ask a soul inside the house.' Afterwards there was a little play by Masefield .... I felt very sorry for the Sassoons, who had got Granville Barker to produce [i.e. direct], Norman Wilkinson for the scenery, Vaughan Williams for the music, Lillah [McCarthy], Maire O'Neill, Arthur Wontner etc. to act and must have spent thousands – but it was very ill-judged.[74]

Before the war, Philip also built a new house for himself in his constituency. He sold his parents' Shorncliffe Lodge in Sandgate and purchased a grand site of 270 acres near the village of Lympne, overlooking Romney Marsh as well as the Channel (France is visible on a clear day). In 1912 he commissioned Herbert Baker to build the house and it was ready the following year. Although Baker was from Kent, it was a somewhat odd choice. Baker had made his considerable reputation in South Africa, where he had been Cecil Rhodes's architect. He built Rhodes's residence, Groote Schuur, and Rhodes's memorial, as well as quite a few other major buildings. At the time of the Sassoon commission he was out of the country a good deal of the time, collaborating with Sir Edwin Lutyens on the building of the great Viceregal buildings in New Delhi.

Philip saw his house as a country retreat where he would spend much of August and September and entertain extensively. The house, built in the shape of an H, was done in Baker's South African style, known as Dutch Colonial, with its echoes of the seventeenth century, in russet-coloured brick and with Dutch gables. It appears comparatively modest, and Philip considered it a cottage. Yet it has four reception rooms, two libraries, thirteen principal bedrooms, eight bathrooms, as well as seventeen staff bedrooms with five bathrooms. The balustrades in front of the house incorporate Philip's initials, in an Elizabethan style. The property included two further houses – the French House and Danehurst – as well as two lodges, a cottage, and a separate garage building with four bedrooms. Baker was away in India most of the time, and much of the work was actually done by his local associate, Ernest Wilmott. The house was called Belcaire at first, but Philip changed its name to Port Lympne after the war, echoing Portus Lemanis, Lympne's ancient name as a

20. Port Lympne.

Roman fort against the Saxons, built in the third century. It had served as a post for Roman legions.

Although the house itself was completed before the war, the grand finishing touches, particularly in the grounds, were executed after 1918 under the guidance of another architect, Philip Tilden. Work on the gardens, however, continued during the war. Sybil and Rock visited Belcaire then and wrote to Philip: 'The rose garden is excellent .... I have never seen the Marsh look more lovely than it does tonight, very brilliant with multicoloured fields in front, & mysterious distances .... The peace of it all, with this bloody war raging so close .... I went into Folkestone to pay some calls – for which I hope you give me a good mark!'[75] Baker himself felt that the project quite quickly got out of hand:

> The 'cottage' of which he first spoke grew into a fair sized house. At either end it had two projecting curved columned 'stoeps'[verandahs] as we called them .... I was at the time away in India for many months in the year, and Sassoon, eager and impulsive, with a keen artistic imagination, which lacked a sense of proportion, employed artists to decorate the rooms of the house, and overweigh the garden with heavy stone fountains, terraces, and temples in a manner which he had admired in Paris or in Spain. The scale of Versailles and the Escorial did not fit the English home![76]

It was also here that Philip first commissioned an artist to paint a room for him. José Maria Sert, a Catalan, had an established reputation as a muralist and set designer in France and Spain. He was at the centre of French artistic life on the basis of his reputation and as the lover then husband of Misia Godebska Natanson. (She was painted by Renoir,

Toulouse-Lautrec, Bonnard and Vuillard.) Sert himself was a friend of Gide, Cocteau, Colette, Claudel and Proust. He is best remembered for his murals at the Cathedral at Vich near Barcelona, commissioned by the King of Spain, which he executed in 1927. They were destroyed in 1936 in the Spanish Civil War but he repainted them in 1938–45. He also was famous in his time for his murals for the Waldorf-Astoria in New York, and, in 1930, for murals in Rockefeller Center to replace those of Diego Rivera that had been deemed politically unacceptable.

Sassoon may have been attracted to him through the French connections, an association with his mother's world (Sert had done colourful murals for the French Rothschilds). He probably also came to Philip's attention through his sets for Diaghilev's Ballet Russe (he was the first non-Russian to design for the company), which had captivated both Paris and London before the First World War. However, Sert's grandiose works were rather out of keeping with the more restrained English style. They were fantastic on a grand scale. (Osbert Lancaster called his style Curzon Street Baroque.) As Misia's biographers wrote: 'The walls of the rich began to luxuriate with hundreds of Sert's elephants, camels, and mules, dwarfs and Herculean giants, acrobats and blackamoors, nude gods and goddesses under palm trees and parasols, popes, bishops, and cardinals, mythological and biblical scenes, lanterns and billowing curtains: all the trappings of Tiepolo, Veronese, Goya, and Velazquez – but alas, without their quality.' He was known as the 'Tiepolo of the Ritz'.[77]

Sassoon had done his dining room at Lympne in a Ballet Russe style, with lapis lazuli walls, an opalescent ceiling and gilt chairs with jade cushions. Sert's room for Sassoon at Lympne was executed in 1914–15. The topic was appropriate: France, a female figure, defended by the Allies in the form of children, being attacked by German eagles. That group was over the windows overlooking the terrace. Much more dramatic were two elephants with riders over the fireplace. Were they meant to represent India coming to the aid of France? The mural was executed in Sert's high style, with sweeping sepia and brown figures against gold, combining the pseudo-baroque with suggestions of the oriental. The central part of the ceiling was left empty. Sassoon was dissatisfied with the result. Despite his criticism, he employed Sert again, this time for elaborate murals in a room in his London house.[78] In any case, the Port Lympne murals no longer exist, as Sassoon had them painted over in the 1930s.

He wrote amusingly about them, providing a good sense of the high style of his approach, during the war, to Sir Louis Mallet, a great friend:

Sybil has just been to Lympne for a week-end & says she is very pleased with the progress in the garden & that she likes the room Sert has decorated for me. Personally I think it monstrous. Of course ingenious in imagination & drawing – but so frightfully heavy that although the room is beautifully proportioned you feel impelled to throw yourself down on your belly & worm yourself through the door as the only alternative to battering out one's brains against the ceiling – & from being a light sunny room brighter than the inside of an Osram bulb it is now so pitchy that you have to whip out a pocket electric torch even

21. Mural (detail) by José Maria Sert, Port Lympne.

at midday or you're as good as lost. And an awful cooked-celery colour which gives you a liver attack before you can say knife. Unless Sert can alter it past all recognition it will have to go. I want Baker to buy it for Delhi. I should have thought some of Sybil's black friends [from India whom she had met on her honeymoon there] would snap at it. What is the use of having ruined her complexion on an Indian honeymoon if she can't take this off my hands now for one of the Rajahs' harems?[79]

There is independent testimony about the house and the murals from the Prime Minister, Asquith, who visited it in March 1915 and felt very free to give his opinion, particularly as his host was not present. He had motored over from Walmer Castle, a residence bestowed upon him as Warden of the Cinque Ports, and wrote about the expedition to Venetia Stanley with whom he was thoroughly infatuated. (Her engagement and marriage that year to the Liberal politician Edwin Montagu and her consequent conversion to Judaism were causing him much distress.) He went with Lady Desborough, Mrs Sassoon (presumably Philip's Aunt Loo), and Sir John Simon, at that point Attorney-General. 'My own darling . . . I went in the motor this afternoon with Ettie & Mrs Sassoon & the Impeccable [Sir John Simon] our usual drive thro' Dover & Folkestone to Lympne, and then we extended it to Belcaire, wh. was happily untenanted, so we went in. Neither Ettie nor Sir J.S. cd. find words to describe their horror & disgust. It is unchanged since you & I were there, except in one room (in wh. we used to sit) the undefiled white wall is now covered with a glittering surface of highly burnished mustard-gold, on which are frescoes of a darker shade, representing elephants in different attitudes.'[80]

Both siblings' lives had connections with India and empire just before the war broke out. Philip employed Herbert Baker to build his grand house at the same time that the architect was working in New Delhi. Sybil and her husband decided to celebrate their marriage by a six-month honeymoon in India, leaving London in November 1913. Rock was revisiting the scenes of his earlier days when he had served the Viceroy, Lord Minto, as an ADC. As a wedding present, Philip gave them a white Rolls-Royce in which to drive around India (they called it *la vièrge*).

Sybil kept a diary of the trip. Their first stop was Ceylon where they were met by the car and a servant from the Sassoon office (they had a maid and a chauffeur with them as well). They arrived in India itself on 1 January 1914. Part of her time there included learning about horses; Rock was a devoted polo player, as was Philip, and he planned to buy some horses on the trip. At one stable she wrote: 'I had to walk around listening to the doings of every blooming mare & foal (some of it very improper).... It was terrible. I don't know a horse from a donkey & just brought out any old phrase I had heard Rock use on the chance of its being alright.'[81] She also went on shooting expeditions; all her life she would be a crack shot. Some days later they went on to Poona, a place that had many Sassoon connections. Sybil found the town rather oppressive. 'Poona is an awful place. We drove around saw polo grounds race courses & gardens but everything looked baked & hideous. The name Sassoon was everywhere. S. Docks [perhaps confused with the famous Sassoon Docks in Bombay] S. Hospital. S. Mausoleum (one of the features of the place near the Synagogue.)' They then went on to Bombay.

> We had heard so much of the Taj Mahal Hotel we were very disappointed with our rooms & the food is disgusting .... It is so full of contrasts, this place I've read so much about! Beastly suburbs made up of usines & chimneys as dree & grimy as Manchester with every sort of mill & works & suddenly you turn down a side track & find yourself in a coconut grove with a few mud huts, & black babies & monkeys rolling about. It might [be] in the most un-european part of India. Then over one of the great bridges past the horrible *Towers of Silence* with the unspeakably disgusting vultures waiting for a Parsee burial, to the quartier d'elite: Malabar Hill where all the rich people have their villas & gardens overlooking the bay. It is very beautiful here & there are some quite fine houses .... I went round to Sassoons & saw Meyer Nissim an alert pleasant sharplooking man our manager. I told him I wanted to see some pearls & emeralds & he said he wd send some merchants round to see me at the hotel.

Early in her life she indicated her selectiveness about whom she would see, a refusal to be overwhelmed by the grand, while conveying the opulence of the life that she led. 'This evening a huge bouquet arrived from Aga Khan he wants us to stay with him – not us.

We have now moved into a palatial suite facing the sea which is much better. Ld Brassey has just appeared in his yacht the old Sunbeam, presumably to visit his daughter Lady Willingdon whose husband is Governor of Bombay. I shall avoid them anyhow. The yacht looks minute from my room & ancient as a trireme. The old boy must have taken a year to come & is here for life as he surely will never risk his 80 year old frame on it for the return journey. The Wiborgs are here. 3 flashy girls who did the season at home last year & a truly amurrican Poppa & Momma. They left tonight so R. hasn't spoken to them. hooray!' They bought two Arab horses and at the stables 'I then spoke about Sassoons of Baghdad & they all knew the name & family well.' They did, in fact, spend some time with the Aga Khan, who flattered the beautiful and young Lady Rocksavage. 'I could see R. pricking up his ears when Aga made any particularly fatuous compliment .... The Aga is taking us to the Burning Ghats this evening – a grisly sight it must be but perhaps interesting.'

Some days later they were in Jodhpur where Sybil especially enjoyed the jewels on display in the Fort, although she commented that they were suffering from not being worn. She also noted that 30 January was her twentieth birthday, underlining the figure three times. While there she saw 'my friend' Herbert Baker and Edwin Lutyens who were in the midst of designing, with great difficulty and increasing disagreement, the great Viceroy buildings in Delhi. Baker went around with Rock and Sybil: 'I enjoyed B's company immensely.' Some days later she visited, with Baker and Lutyens, Raisina Hill in Delhi, the proposed site of Government House and the subject of endless disputes. 'They are busy on their new Delhi & full of brilliant ideas but Ld. H[ardinge, the Viceroy] pours sarcasm & cold water on their most charming schemes – and he has the obstinacy which goes with extreme stupidity & is ignorant as a coot .... The site of the New Delhi is fine & if the 2 architects carry out their plans will be a fine thing. But I doubt if the money will be forthcoming – it is a task that requires a big man like Rhodes to push through.' She had had dinner with Lord and Lady Hardinge which wasn't much fun. She was the guest of honour and sat on the Viceroy's right. 'His conversation was a long eulogy on himself & his masterly treatment of every question. How trying blowers of their own trumpets are! Fatiguing too as he never once turned to his other neighbour nor I noticed did Lady Hardinge who was having a high old time with Rock & waggling her Benares work earrings at him in a most engaging manner – after all he is a cousin! The food was fair but there was a tip top band which I greatly enjoyed.' She noted about a later occasion, although she was kinder about the Viceroy, that 'dinner was inexpressibly boring tonight & there was a ball afterwards. We scandalised everyone by dancing 1/2 a dozen dances together. R. & I & then went to bed – much to Ldy H's vexation as she told R. "I *sent* for you to dance with me but you had gone off." Sent indeed – Ld H. took me to his own room to show me the Baker-Lutyens plans & was v. amiable. I am thankful we are off tomorrow, I hate all this pomp.'

She wrote to her brother about her time in Delhi in even stronger terms:

We were bored stiff at Delhi & found the Hardinges very tiresome. He is nul and so conceited without the slightest sense of humour & poor Baker is in despair about him. The plans are really so fine & this fool of a H. will botch the whole thing as he only thinks of L S D [pounds, shillings and pence] & won't float a loan which is the only way to get enough money .... Rock ... had to take her [Lady Hardinge] into lunch & dinner *every* day! ... Rock only danced with me and we had great fun, quite like old times (only without the previous heartburnings!) ... I have bought two emerald drops .... I think very cheap but I shan't dare shew them to you in case you disapprove .... We tossed [with the merchant] for them in the end & won so he had to take off nearly a £100 .... [She had been given a white bullock] I can't tell you how divine the bullock is. About the size of a large collie .... I shall drive it about the park .... The car has been & is the greatest blessing it is a source of neverending joy admiration & comment & *we could not* have lived without it, even when in the train it is immediately behind us & we can see it wrapped in its nightshirt bumping along. This has been a lovely trip & we should have had much greater fun had you been here, but I am immensely looking forward to my summer at Trent between you & Rock & Hana. It will be *perfection* (as R. says).[82]

She had time to shop for a present for Philip. 'I bought two curious brass perches with odd crystal parrots on them for Phil – they came from a temple in Tibet & the expression on the parrot's face is very comic – but the price was *very* stiff – close on £200 I think. I hope P. will like them.' The diary ended on 3 March, when they left Benares. They returned to a Europe that was about to go to war.

3 *Philip and Sybil Serve Their Country*

Philip

Philip Sassoon was at the centre of events during the First World War. From December, 1915 until March 1919 he served as private secretary to the Commander-in-Chief of the British Forces, Sir Douglas Haig. Although for the rest of his life he was a significant though not first-rank politician and frequently entertained prime ministers, leading members of the Cabinet and members of the royal family, his position was never again quite so central. He preserved so few of his papers, except, significantly, for the period of the First World War – one reason that Philip remains so elusive. As for so many of his generation, the most memorable part of his career perhaps was when he was very young. He may have also set a pattern of subordinating himself to others which is likely, ultimately, to have hindered his political development.

He gained even more privilege from his role as a Member of Parliament. He dealt with, met and corresponded with the most important figures in the country as well as with France's leaders. Yet he wasn't a decision-maker or strategist, or a military adviser; he was primarily an arranger and an observer, 'an attendant lord'. His was an odd position, its importance hard to gauge. To a limited extent, his correspondence reflects and illustrates the pattern of the war. The years of 1914 and 1915: excitement, almost exultation, as in the poetry of Rupert Brooke and Julian Grenfell: 'If I should die, think only this of me . . . '. The terrible battles of 1916 and 1917: despair and stalemate, marked in the poetry of Robert Graves and Philip's cousin, Siegfried Sassoon: 'O Jesus, make it stop.' And then in 1918: bitter resignation, as in the poetry of Wilfred Owen: 'What passing bells for these who die as cattle?' The generals who made the decisions that led to these results were at their headquarters behind the front lines, and so was Philip. Serving them, he reflected the war experienced by the troops, but at a distance.

One does not know what Philip felt about being in a staff position rather than in the front line. He rarely said. There couldn't be a more dramatic contrast than with the front line and ultimately much more famous career of his cousin, then unknown to him and to the wider world. Siegfried Sassoon spoke for the trenches and attacked the staff officers who wore the red tabs on their caps and epaulettes: 'scarlet Majors at the Base'. Northcliffe, the great newspaper owner, once complained, perhaps rather tactlessly, to Philip: 'There are beyond question an immense number of officers at the War Office who ought to be combatant. The lunch time procession of red hats in Pall Mall is not good. Another complaint is that there are too many red hats on the Staffs in France.'[1]

It was likely to be a little disconcerting, even awkward, when so many of his contemporaries and acquaintances, particularly the golden youth in the 'Coterie', the circle of Diana Manners, were serving and dying in the trenches. The following October, Geoffrey Robinson, editor of *The Times*, tried to reassure Philip: 'I do trust you're not going to worry because you're not living in a rabbit-hole. Sir D.[ouglas] could never find anyone to do for him quite what you're doing, & I feel that its one of the chief evidences of his wisdom that he picked you out for a place *in which you must certainly stay*.'[2] In a way the ambiguity of his position was suggested in a letter that the Prime Minister, Asquith, wrote to Philip some time in January 1916 about his son Raymond, who was serving in the trenches:

Raymond is home for a few days leave. He is, as you know, in the 3rd Batt. of the Grenadiers, and has been a good deal in the trenches since he went out. He has no desire to be removed, and likes his regiment & his work. I cannot help thinking that it is rather a waste to use a man of his brains and knowledge for this kind of job, which so many, who are in these ways not so well endowed, can do quite as well. Sir D. Haig & I had a little talk on the subject when I was last out at the front. Naturally I do not wish to move in the matter, and I have a strong opinion that these things should always be left to the unfettered judgment of the Commander in Chief. Raymond himself has expressed no wish for any kind of change, and does not know that I have written.[3]

Raymond in fact was killed the following September at the front. As Lord Stamfordham, the King's private secretary, wrote to Philip: 'Everyone feels for the Prime Minister and Raymond Asquith's was a life of such promise.'[4]

Philip's commission as a second lieutenant in the East Kent Yeomanry was activated on 5 August 1914. Philip remained with his regiment until February 1915. He was home on leave during that month and the painter Philip de Laszlo did a romantic oil sketch of him in his uniform. Recognizing his skills, the Army then seconded him to work at the Staff level, first transferring him to the staff of Field Marshal Sir John French.[5] French was an unsuccessful Commander-in-Chief of the British Expeditionary Force in France, a position he kept until he was dismissed and replaced by Sir Douglas Haig in December 1915. (Some years later, in 1921, when Philip saw French again he compared him to Haig in a letter to Lord Esher: 'I thought him so attractive – easy to get on with. He certainly has more *heart* – if less brains than D.H. I shd say!'[6]) Before French was dismissed, Sassoon had left him to work with General Sir Henry Rawlinson, who commanded the IV Corps. Maurice Baring, the writer and a friend of Philip's, wrote to their mutual friend, Lady Juliet Duff, suggesting something of Philip's style. 'We had luncheon today with Philip's A.D.C. General Rawlinson. Philip is very good to him and very pleased with the way Rawlinson is doing.'[7]

His early feelings about the war are captured in some surviving letters to his mother's great friend, Lady Desborough. On 20 November 1914, he wrote: 'It will be a very broken world for those that are left. But to be out here & see the way the men face the – one would think – unbearable hardships & horrors – their indomitable courage & cheerfulness . . . . The weather rivals Greenland – deep snow and ice. I *can t* imagine how those poor brutes in the trenches stick it out. I simply hate myself for sleeping in a bed in a warm (not so warm) house.' In a long letter to her on 17 February 1915, he claimed to be having a fine time in France. 'It is so splendid being out here. The weather is foul – the climate fouler & the country beyond all words *& nothing* doing – but it is all rose coloured to me.' He went on with a detailed description of the nature of the front and a successful battle that 'shows that by close cooperation between Art[iller]y & Infantry worked out carefully beforehand in every detail we can take German defended localities without undue loss to the infantry'. The letter was somewhat indiscreet, retailing his belief that there was a German manufacturer committing fraud as so many of the German shells were defective, and that Winston Churchill was creating a dummy fleet. 'The spirit of the troops is excellent. You never hear a grouse & they are all desperate keen to get at the Germans but situated as we are in mud & water it is impossible to move. But in the Spring we shall be busy when the mud goes & the new army comes . . . . Everyone from Old Joffre downward is very confident that the war will be over in the summer.'[8] Like almost everyone else, he was optimistic, even callow.

On 23 June 1915 Philip wrote a letter of condolence on the death of Lady Desborough's elder son, Julian, whom Philip had known at Eton and Oxford. It begins: 'I have tried to write to you every day since Julian died – but have been fumbling for words.' He cites Julian's 'compelling vitality & high courage which have cheered him through all these bitter months & makes his death into a rite . . . . Such deaths as his strengthen our faith – it is not possible that such spirits go out . . . . I have expressed myself badly & clumsily but I am *so sorry* for you – so sorry.' Julian had died on 30 April of wounds. *The Times* announced his death and on the same day published his poem, 'Into Battle' which celebrates dying for a great cause. Its best known lines were: 'And he is dead who will not fight;/ And who dies fighting has increase.' It became one of the most famous poems of the war. Later, like Rupert Brooke's poems, it came to be seen as inappropriately sentimental. But it told how many felt at the time.

Philip wrote again on 10 July, reporting on how much he had enjoyed his leave and how funny Curzon and Sargent had been at his dinner party. He also mentioned her younger son, Billy, whom he'd known better than Julian, reporting that 'I am going to telephone to Charlie [Lord] Castlereagh today & arrange an expedition with him to visit Billy – how badly the latter has behaved, not a line to me since his arrival in Flanders.' He reported that Sybil, prevented by a bad cold, was jealous that he had had an opportunity to see Lady Desborough. 'Well she may have been – because I did have a wonderful time with you – but

22. Philip de Laszlo, *Sir Philip Sassoon*, 1915.

I wasn't able to get out any of the things I wanted to somehow – Sargent thinks that a bust or statue of Julian would be much more satisfactory than a painting . . . . Do have a statue not a bust. I always regret that the age of memorials is past . . . . In Julian's case I should like something very living & *vital*.'

On 9 August Philip had again to write a letter of condolence, this time for the death of Billy. 'It was only about a fortnight ago that I had a letter from him saying that he was so bored at being out of the line & aching to get back into the salient . . . . Please, dearest Lady Desborough, *please* let those who loved & admired Billy & Julian be of some support to you – lean on them a little – not because it can be of any comfort or consolation to you but because it would be *such* happiness for them.' The next day he wrote again. 'I wrote you such a bad inarticulate letter yesterday . . . . I hear – what I did not need to hear to know – how wonderful & brave you are. These glorious deaths have left you a very tangible radiance . . . . It is for all of us I grieve & not for them.' Sybil wrote to him about this death: 'It really is a tragedy about Billy. I can hardly imagine how Ettie will live through her awful grief.'[9]

There was a strikingly ironic sequel of the relation between Philip and Julian in a episode during the battle of Loos some weeks after Julian's death. One reason Julian had cracked the whip about Philip's head at Oxford was his disapproval of his luxurious style of life, of his 'Oriental and cushioned "digs"'. Now, similarly, there was a contrast between the staff and the trenches. While Philip was still with General Rawlinson. L.E. Jones, a somewhat older con-temporary of Philip's at Eton and Oxford, recounted that a

Yeomanry Regiment stood saddled up, night and day, in the grounds of General Rawlinson's château, ready to gallop though the 'gap' which our optimistic leaders still believed could be opened by the infantry through the immense tangle of pit-heads, slag-heaps, canals, trenches and barbed wire. After a sleepless night spent attempting to get some shelter under juniper bushes from the incessant rain, we were gazing, chilled and red-eyed, at the noble entrance of the château from which we expected our order to come forth, when a very slim, very dapper young officer, with red tabs on his collar and shining boots, began to descend the steps. It was Philip Sassoon, 'Rawly's" A.D.C. I have never been one of those who think that Staff Officers are unduly coddled, or that they should share the discomforts of the troops. Far from it. But there are moments when the most entirely proper inequality, suddenly exhibited, can be riling. Tommy Lascelles, not yet His or Her Majesty's Private Secretary, but a very damp young lieutenant who had not break-fasted, felt that this was one of those moments. Concealed by a juniper bush, he called out 'Pheeleep! Pheeleep! I see you!' in a perfect mimicry of Julian's warning cry from his window when he had spied Sassoon, who belonged to another College, treading delicately through Balliol Quad.[There seems to be some question whether the incident took place at Balliol or Christ Church.] The beauteous A.D.C. stopped, lifted his head like a hind sniffing the wind, then turned and went rapidly up the steps and into the doorway. Did he think it was Julian's voice from the grave? Or had he merely remembered some more pressing errand for his General? We shall never know. But the incident cheered up the dripping Yeomen. There is irony in the thought of how much, had Julian lived, he would have found to like and admire in the sagacious and gifted Minister of the Crown into which the young A.D.C. eventually blossomed. Both had a passion for beauty, as well as for getting things done.[10]

That first year his war experiences are also reflected through his meetings with Mrs Belloc Lowndes, the novelist. She remembered that 'he drove himself, in a small two-seater car, so we were alone, and perhaps because I had learned that his mother was French, I felt much drawn to him. In those days he was like an open-hearted boy, bubbling over with the joy of life.'[11] He didn't seem to object that her brother, Hilaire Belloc, an even better known writer, was an anti-Semite. Mrs Belloc Lowndes wrote in her diary on 26 January 1915 about another meeting with Philip: 'I was much interested to hear him say that his French relations all believe the War will end in May. He did not himself seem as cheerful about it. He seemed to have the curious opinion that the Germans would have to be driven back from trench to trench till they reached the frontier.'[12] In an undated letter he wrote to her: 'I am off again to the front tomorrow. Will you be *very* kind & write to me sometimes & give me some titles of books old & new.' On 8 September, presumably in 1915 as it is written from Rawlinson's headquarters, he wrote:

It is a relief to turn to books as a reaction to this hideous war. I have read with intense pleasure [W.S. Maugham's] Of Human Bondage . . . . We are all full of quiet hope & sober confidence out here & though the end of the war does sometimes seem like mirage in the Libyan desert . . . . It is much the best thing to be out here as England is too full of professional pessimists at present to be a pleasant place. I have been doing a lot of flying too which I had never done before. It is glorious going up to a height of 10,000 feet – one has never really seen a view before – the fields stretch away like an endless parquet flooring with great tracts of cubism & one gets up into a cottonwool world of cloud over which you can see the English coast in the distance which makes one feel quite homesick. Oh how sick I am of the war aren't you. But we must go on till we have made those devils pay for the ruin & havoc they have caused.[13]

On 20 December 1915 Sassoon was appointed private secretary to Sir Douglas Haig, who had just become the Commander-in-Chief for the British Expeditionary Force in France and Flanders. Robert Blake commented in his edition of Haig's diaries: 'Haig did not talk much himself but he enjoyed gaiety and wit in others, and he appreciated conversational brilliance. This partly explains his paradoxical choice of Sir Philip Sassoon as his private secretary. Aesthete, politician, millionaire, that semi-oriental figure flitted like some exotic bird of paradise against the sober background of GHQ. He was not liked by the others in Haig's entourage, but he amused Haig and helped him in relations to the political world.'[14] Haig had served in India and would have known the Sassoon name, and he shared Philip's passion for polo. He was also very close to the court, although George V's court was quite different from his father's where the Sassoons had been so welcome. He and Philip had a great mutual friend in Leopold de Rothschild. He was Philip's cousin and had married the sister of Philip's favourite aunt. The connection through Leopold may have been a major factor in his appointment. Leopold was assiduous in sending over to Haig and his staff via the King's Messenger special foods as well as supplies such as gloves and barometers. Philip sent a series of fulsome letters of thanks which occasionally contained bits of military news and a few political comments, most particularly railing against Churchill.

Haig's headquarters were at Montreuil most of the time. Philip frequently went with him when he visited the French commanders at Chantilly. His French Rothschild relations had their château there, which helped provide provisions for Haig. This 27-year-old MP – a first-generation Anglo-French Baghdadi Jew – found himself designated to deal with the greatest in the land. F.E. Smith, the Tory politician, reported to Winston Churchill that there was much criticism among soldiers of the appointment, as did Churchill's mother, Lady Randolph, citing the same reaction among people at home.[15] Yet he fitted in, for better or worse, with the sort of figures Haig liked to have about him. Shortly after his appointment, Churchill saw Philip at GHQ and wrote to his wife: 'Philip sits like a wakeful spaniel outside the door.'[16] Undoubtedly most of his colleagues were quite a bit older. Yet Philip had little difficulty in rapidly establishing himself in the job. In January Raymond Asquith com-

23. Douglas Haig and Philip Sassoon during the First World War.

mented sarcastically to his wife: 'I hear that Philip writes to his friends offering them battalions and brigades with the most Oriental profusion.'[17]

Philip was brilliant at managing Haig's schedule, his relations with the press, and other problems that would arise. He corresponded extensively with newspaper owners and editors and entertained them when they visited. He arranged visits for dignitaries such as the King, the Prince of Wales (who wanted to serve at the front but was not allowed to do so and with whom Philip became quite friendly at this time), Arthur Balfour, Lord Jellicoe, the naval commander, and many others. He drafted appropriately fulsome letters for Haig, such as one to the King thanking him for his visit. He stage-managed conferences with French generals as well as visits to Paris. He went as Haig's emissary to sound out the French leaders, such as Clemenceau. He described one meeting with Briand, Joffre, Foch and Poincaré on a train, in a letter to Lord Esher on 1 June 1916: 'We all sat at little tables for lunch in the wagon restaurant. I tried to believe I was on my way to Monte Carlo.'[18] A cartoon of him in an anonymous spoof child's primer, *The Bad Boy's Book of ADCs,* presented to Haig, depicts him writing a letter. The doggerel on the page goes: 'Courteous Philip writes to thank/ The maiden lady and the crank. / He sometimes telephones for fun/ To say that lunch will be at one.'[19] He was almost continually at Haig's side at meals and trips and at the end of the day. In a biography of Haig, John Charteris, his Chief of Intelligence, described the typical evening: 'At 8 o'clock he dined. After dinner, which lasted about an hour, he returned to his room and worked until a quarter to eleven. At this hour he rang the bell for his Private Secretary, and invariably greeted him with the same remark: "Philip – not in bed yet?" He never changed this formula, and if, as did occasionally happen, Philip was in bed, he always used to say to him next morning: "I hope you have had enough sleep?" '[20]

Philip also corresponded with Haig's wife, frequently about applicants who wanted photographs of the General. (Philip saw Lady Haig quite frequently in London. She never became particularly fond of him. Towards the end of the war, on 16 June 1918, Haig wrote to her about Philip: 'I expect you are right, viz., that he "talks in a mechanical society way," and that he wants to be "shaken!" All the same he is a good-hearted soul – I fear it is not given to many to be "natural and sincere." So we must be patient with those who fall short of our ideals. All the same I am told that the war has greatly improved our Philip! I find him very useful as Private Secretary.'[21]) In one such letter about photographs, on 7 September 1916, he wrote to her about visits that Lord Derby, at this point Director of Recruiting, and then Asquith made to Haig. 'Lord Derby is always very welcome & his cheery roundness makes his presence very agreeable. Now his place has been taken by the P.M. The old man is in great form. At dinner last night he kept showing his empty brandy glass [he was known as a heavy drinker which earned him the nickname, behind his back, of 'Squiff'], to try to attract Sir Douglas' attention but in vain! And he was at last reduced to asking for some more! We told the Chief that he had been very unkind & had quite obviously turned a blind eye on purpose.'[22] (Sassoon enjoyed repeating this story; Derby reacted to it: 'You amuse me very much by what you say about the Prime Minister. I can see the scene at dinner and can see your child's delight in tantalizing the poor old man. I am very glad that his views are sound . . . . But all the same I think he will want watching.') But most important, given his standing as a Member of Parliament and a baronet and an officer, he corresponded with the great but not necessarily the good in order to ensure that Haig, the 'Chief', would be in the strongest possible position.

In December 1915, Philip started a voluminous correspondence with Reginald, Lord Esher. He was perhaps the greatest British behind-the-scenes figure of the late nineteenth and early twentieth centuries, although he had also been an MP and held public office. He felt that one was more effective working privately rather than publicly and had thus made his mark as a courtier, helping to modernize the monarchy. Esher then helped to reconstruct the Army, playing a crucial role in reforming the War Office, supporting the significant changes that Richard Haldane had made as Liberal War Minister before the war. He was an important member of the Committee of Imperial Defence. He adored being a go-between and served in this role between the monarchy and the politicians and now had something of the same position in relation to Haig and the world of King and ministers. He was in his early sixties, and he and Philip were a perfect combination. Although their correspondence continued until his death in 1930, it was never as intense as it was during the First World War. Esher also wrote to Haig – it is striking that some of those letters are preserved in Sassoon's papers – but there were limits to how much he could write to the 'Chief', and writing to Philip assured that his ideas and concerns would be communicated.

Esher's biographer, James Lees-Milne, misunderstands Sassoon, believing that he had little ambition and was content merely with leading a luxurious life. He takes him too much at his word, citing some lines he wrote to Esher comparing the heroic life, identified largely with the arts, with his own. The letter begins with what might be interpreted as a rather startling apparent assumption of homosexuality. No evidence has survived of Philip's sexual activities, although his style would certainly support the idea that he was a homosexual, and many assumed he was. 'To have slept with Cavalieri [Michelangelo's friend], to have invented wireless, to have painted *Las Meninas*, to have written *Wuthering Heights* – that is deathless life. But to be like me, a thing of nought, a worthless loon, an elm-seed whirling in a summer gale ....' Lees-Milne comments, rather underestimating, in my view, Philip's looks:

Regy made great friends with a spirit who was more congenial to him than any other whom he had come upon during his war duties. Sir Philip Sassoon ... with his bent nose and rather shapeless mouth, filled with prominent teeth he was not handsome. Clever, talented, French-speaking, a connoisseur of the arts, darling of London society, and very good company, he relished harmless gossip .... Moreover, there was not a shadow of romance in their relationship .... Regy was enchanted by this odd, sophisticated, self-indulgent creature who was the very antithesis of the type of serious, callow youth by whom his paternalistic soul was moved. Philip stood no nonsense, spoke his mind, was from the beginning on an equal footing, and played the fool with him. Besides, Regy was impressed by Philip's surprising efficiency, usefulness to his boss, and his physical courage.[23]

The spirit of their correspondence is summed up in a letter Esher wrote to Sassoon much later, on 8 July 1918: 'My dear, you ask me to criticise the Chief and all of you! Never. The thing is not possible. When there is some small and yet important thing that a little concession can put right, I mention it. But that is not criticism .... I see nothing but merit in my friends. I would not care a jot for friendship on any other terms. You may have foibles dear Philip. So may D.H.[aig] – but no faults! Otherwise a quoi bon the legend that the God of Love flew about with bandaged eyes? I leave criticism to the Stracheys of the world .... Tell me all the scandal.'

When their correspondence started, on New Year's Eve 1915, Esher was spending much time in Paris. As was his wont, he had no official position other than as a member of the Committee of Imperial Defence. In effect, he ran his own intelligence network and had been instrumental in securing French's dismissal. Now, Philip wrote to Esher to thank him for helping him secure an appropriate position in France:

I have never forgotten how kind you were to me this time last year when I was trying to get out here again & have been meaning to write to you on many occasions since then .... I have come here as Private Secretary to Sir Douglas & that I hope you will let me know if I can ever do anything for you. You will be glad to hear that Sir D.H. gets on quite admirably with the French. We have already been twice to Chantilly [the French headquarters]. It means so much to Joffre to be able to talk *direct* to the English C. in C. & not through an interpreter as heretofore & there is no doubt that the relations between the two HQs will be very different to what they have been.

On 2 February he reported on a visit of Bonar Law, Lloyd George and F.E. Smith to headquarters. 'The latter came out without a pass or any warning, forced the sentries & was eventually arrested! If Cabinet Ministers expect to be treated as Cabinet Ministers they must behave as such.' In response Esher remarked: 'I should detest being at G.H.Q. with all your swell visitors! Keep as many away from the C in C as you can!'[24]

The battle of Verdun, launched by the Germans, began that month and lasted until June. Sassoon wrote to Esher on 2 March that the news wasn't good, but by 18 March he felt the situation was better, since the French had lost less than expected while the Germans had suffered considerable casualties. But this optimism was quite misguided, as John Keegan has noted: 'About twenty million shells had been fired into the battle zone since 21 February [by 23 June], the shape of the landscape had been permanently altered, forests had been reduced to splinters, villages had disappeared, the surface of the ground had been so pockmarked by explosions that shell hole overlapped shell hole and had been overlapped again. Worse by far was the destruction of human life. By the end of June over 200,000 men had been killed and wounded on each side.'[25]

Verdun was followed in the summer by the great battle of the Somme. There were considerable British losses. Haig had hoped to shell the Germans into submission and in this he failed. Keegan writes: 'The Allies had certainly lost over 600,000, the French casualty figure being 194,654, the British 419,654 .... To the British, it was and would remain their greatest military tragedy of the twentieth century, indeed in their national military history .... The Somme marked the end of an age of vital optimism in British life that has never been recovered.'[26] Nevertheless, at the time, the battle was seen – at least by some – as a triumph for Britain and for Haig. It was not until after the war that his reputation plummeted and many still regard him as a butcher. John Keegan sums up one current view that Haig 'managed to ignore the casualties and to be untouched by the suffering. He was a strange man, a very cold fish. A good general but a defective person.'[27] Others would not grant him the good generalship.

Sassoon had to put the best possible gloss on events. A sense of what he did is provided by a letter Raymond Asquith wrote to his wife in the middle of March during the battle of Verdun when he had a talk with Philip, 'who was very civil and talkative. He and Haig were down at Chantilly holding Joffre's hand most of last week. The French seem to have been in a pitiful state of nerves when the offensive began, and thought it was all up with them whether Verdun fell or not, owing to the losses in men which they would suffer either way.'[28] Even so, as some of the correspondence indicates, the terrible casualties did cause concern. Sassoon and Haig's other supporters needed to interpret events in ways that cast a favourable light upon him. George Dewar of the *Saturday Review* wrote to Philip in a rage about the attempt to damp down enthusiasm about the battle of the Somme. Rather, one should 'appreciate the cool skill and the splendid success of the British offensive on the Somme against a tremendously strong enemy .... Nothing in the history of England, so far as I have studied it, has been more splendid than the British soldiership & the leadership upon the Somme.'[29] Subsequent assessments of Haig's leadership have not been as generous. So many were killed and so little was accomplished.

Haig was happy with Sassoon's work. In his diary for 17 June he recorded that Joffre had presented the Legion of Honour to Sassoon as well as to other members of his staff. 'The old man gave the decoration to Alan [Fletcher, his senior ADC] and Philip because he thought it would please me. Very kind of the old man.'[30] The honours weren't published in *The Times* until the following 11 December, along with decorations given to three other staff officers as well as numerous lesser French medals given to British soldiers. Philip's acquaintances found the honour a little much for someone who was serving on staff. Cynthia Asquith recorded in her diary that she was 'screaming with indignation at Philip Sassoon having been given the Légion d'honneur'. So many young men in Philip's circle would die on the battlefield: Raymond Asquith, Patrick Shaw Stewart, Edward Horner, George Vernon, Charles Lister, Julian and Billy Grenfell. Cynthia Asquith also reported that a friend had seen Philip in a restaurant in France and had gone up to him and 'genially exclaimed: "Hullo, Monsieur le Décoré!" Upon which, Philip, purple in the face, rose and without a word rushed out of the restaurant.'[31] During the war he received two other medals from the Belgians and was mentioned in dispatches twice. After the war, he was made CMG (Companion of the Order of St Michael and St George) as well as being awarded two further French medals.

In January 1916, there was some talk that Members of Parliament who were serving officers should be sent back to England. Philip opposed this vehemently. He had written to the mayors of the two principal towns, Hythe and Folkestone, in his constituency the previous October, stating his belief that he should continue to serve but saying that he would be guided by his constituents. As far as I know, they gave no contrary advice. He did have a chance to visit his constituency in late January 1917, where he made a speech on the issue of whether he should return to London but also on general political matters such as public health, Ireland, and economic questions.[32] He indicated his identification with England in his remark: 'We have got the finest army our race has yet produced.'[33]

Philip made no specific mention of consulting his constituency in a long letter, dated 21 December 1916, to *The Times*, published a week later. There he gave three reasons why he felt serving MPs should not be forced to choose between Parliament and the front. 'They consider that they are performing useful work; they are setting the right example; and they are taking their share with the rest .... In London, under present political conditions, their [the constituents'] member would be wasting his time nine days out of ten. In France, he is not .... In these circumstances to thrust upon Service members the alternative of resigning or of returning to Westminster would be to my mind a real injustice both to the members and their constituents.'[34]

He wrote to Northcliffe, the great press lord, on 23 December about this:

I hope the idea of ordering Service Members home to their Parliamentary Duties will meet with the fate it deserves. They are not wanted continuously at home & the C. in C.

has definitely ordered that they can go over whenever they are needed & stay as long as is necessary .... It would be a monstrous injustice to force ... [them] to resign their seats if they refuse to remain permanently kicking their heels about at Westminster .... It is an agitation which has been raised purely by those members who do not wish to remain serving abroad & who desire to find in a general rule an excuse for returning home for good. It would indeed be humorous for a body of men who pass conscription for others to claim exemption for themselves.

Sassoon did return to Westminster from time to time. He sent a quite intriguing long letter to Haig about one secret session of Parliament: 'In this so-called Secret Session everyone (even that stormy petrel Winston) seems to have been more moderate in their tone – more guarded in their facts than in any open Debate!' The topic was the failure to recruit enough troops. One of the themes in Philip's correspondence was that Haig would have been able to do more if he had enough troops. One could reply that the problem was that his campaigns had killed so many of them. Philip was deeply concerned about the lack of trained men, and was in a peculiar but potentially helpful position in that he would also participate in this issue as a Member of Parliament. Conscription was introduced but recruitment was still a contentious issue. 'There has of course been a lot of dissatisfaction in the House & we had two stormy meetings [presumably of Tory MPs] under Carson where many khaki-clad members (speaking as usual for the men in the trenches!) demanded the instant break up of the ministry (which could have been effected had Carson persisted in his resolution as it would have brought our members out of the Cabinet). But saner if less robust counsels prevailed & I do believe that a dissolution now might be disastrous, fraught with dangerous delays & no one has any definite thought of what is to follow.'[35]

In April 1916 Esher went to Paris, where he would remain the rest of that year and the next. He and Philip consulted continually about Haig's standing and how it was affected by the politicians and the press. In August Esher noted to Sassoon that 'Northcliffe is *enthusiastic* about the Chief.' And in a letter later in the month he commented rather brutally: 'No combination of Churchill and F.E. Smith can do any harm, so long as fortune favours us in the Field. These people only become formidable during the inevitable ebb of the tide of success .... If Lloyd George does not behave himself, and if he tries to run the Army in the field on "business lines" through his old Munitions cronies, he may have to be killed. He is profoundly ignorant, but hitherto has been teachable.'[36]

One of Philip's primary obligations was to deal with the press. As ordinary political life was severely curtailed and contentious debates in Parliament were rare, points of view in the press more than ever shaped public opinion. In Sassoon's papers there are letters from H.A. Gwynne, editor of the *Morning Post*, George Dewar of the *Saturday Review* and Geoffrey Robinson, the editor of *The Times*. But undoubtedly Philip's most important correspondent among the press was Lord Northcliffe, who owned *The Times*, the ultimate establishment journal, as well as the more popular *Daily Mail* and the *Evening News*. He saw himself as the greatest power behind the scenes (unlike Esher, he commanded the press). He launched a campaign to dump Asquith as Prime Minister and substitute Lloyd George, who had become Secretary of State for War in July 1916. Northcliffe instructed his editors to publish photographs of a tired-looking Asquith with his alleged motto 'Wait and See' under them in contrast to pictures of a lively Lloyd George.

That summer the main issue was, in Northcliffe's view, Churchill's attempt to destabilize the government. He was in disgrace because of the failure of the Gallipoli campaign. At this point he was out of the government and was commanding a battalion in France. In some sense he was under Haig's command, but this did not prevent him from still being very politically active. As Sassoon wrote to Esher on 11 August: 'Churchill has a personal grievance against D.H . . . . He is feverishly anxious to get back into power on any pretext . . . . I believe both Churchill & Smith to be entirely discredited in the country at large.' That January he had written to Gwynne, about Churchill: 'Winston is hanging about here but Sir D.H. refuses to give him a Brigade until he has had a battalion several months. It wouldn't be fair to the others & besides does he deserve *anything*? I think not, certainly not anything good.'[37]

Sassoon wrote to Northcliffe on 11 August 1916:

We have heard all about the Churchill Cabal from the King & his people who are out here this week. As you say it is not worth worrying about as I cannot believe that the carpings of a discredited & embittered gang will find credence among any honest men . . . . Sir F.E. Smith [at this time Attorney-General in the government] also has a grievance against the C. in C. because the Adjutant General – very properly – had him arrested out here once when [he] was touring about in search of Churchill without a pass or permit of any sort! No doubt he considers this a quite sufficient reason to wish to disturb the balance just as the scale is definitely swinging in our favour. I am amazed at the lack of patriotism of these people. But so long as people like you are aware & watching they stand little chance of doing harm to anyone except themselves. It would be disastrous if Churchill were to come back to power at this juncture with his wild cat scheme & *fatal* record. The King's visit is passing off very well & we have got Poincaré [the French President] – Joffre & Foch to meet him at lunch on Saturday – all that does good & makes for smooth running & consequently helps to beat the Boche . . . . Lloyd George is coming to dine here Saturday night . . . . I do trust that he & Carson will be made to realise how damaging any flirting with an alliance with Churchill would be for them. Do you think they realise this? *Sufficiently?*[38]

A few days later Robinson wrote to Philip: 'Do by all means write to me when I can be of any service to the C in C . . . . The very weakness of the Government makes them unusually responsive to public opinion, and public opinion is infinitely sounder than it has ever been before.' Presumably Robinson felt that the paper had done much to bring that situation about and that at this point Lloyd George and Carson were being helpful in defending Haig while Churchill in his questions about casualties was not. Churchill's reputation was low: 'The simple fact that he left for the trenches amid the applause of an emotional House of

Commons, and was back again in politics almost before there was time to turn round . . . .
The attempt to get the best of both worlds as soldier and politician was absolutely characteristic of a thoroughly unstable character.'[39]

Lloyd George came out to see Haig in September and Sassoon wrote about the visit to
Northcliffe on 14 September:

> You will be sorry to hear that the visitor we were expecting did not make a favourable
> impression either on the British or the French Army. After lunch he & Reading [Rufus
> Isaacs, at this point in his career Lord Chief Justice] got hold of Foch & asked him why
> our own artillery was so much inferior to theirs. Why we took so many less prisoners than
> they did. Why our casualties were more than theirs & what he thought of a lot of our gen-
> erals. Foch was absolutely scandalized & very properly refused to express any opinion . . . . If
> *this* is the man some people would like to see P.M. – I prefer old Squiff any day with all
> his faults! *He* left a very good impression after his visit – saw everything that he ought to
> see & took such an intelligent interest in it all – was perfectly charming to D.H. & to all
> he met . . . . [Lloyd George] has done himself nothing but harm out here. Of course as you
> know Sir D.H. is much too broadminded to mind anything of that sort but I could see
> that he was terribly disappointed in him. He hardly had more than ¼ of an hour private
> conversation with the Chief & it is my private opinion that he has neither liking nor
> esteem for the C. in C . . . . No doubt Churchill's deadly poison has done its deadly work.
> Luckily D.H. has the unlimited confidence of the whole Army as a slight counterpoise![40]

Lord Derby, the Under-Secretary of State for War, thought that Philip had exaggerated the
lack of success of Lloyd George's visit. He wrote to Philip on 18 September: 'When he [Lloyd
George] came back everything connected with G.H.Q. was so much "couleur de Rose" that
I had hoped all had gone well. Of course, what you tell me only proves that with all his cleverness – it won't make up for his not being a gentleman. But I honestly think you are wrong
when you say he does not appreciate your chief, and that Winston's poison has done harm.'[41]
In a letter two days later he makes it clear that he thinks of Philip as part of his own world.
Talking again of Lloyd George he writes: 'You must remember that he is not a soldier, and
that his antecedents are not likely to make him view things as we view them.' Derby was the
head of a great patrician family.

Some months later Derby wrote about Edwin Montagu's appointment as Secretary of
State of India. It would appear that Derby either didn't realize that Sassoon was Jewish (and
had strong Indian connections) or thought he wouldn't mind, or would be flattered, to be
written to in this way. 'The appointment of Montagu, a Jew, to the India Office has made, as
far as I can judge, an uneasy feeling both in India and here, but I personally have a very high
opinion of his capability and I expect he will do well.'[42] Montagu was part of the
Samuel/Montagu/Franklin Jewish banking clan. Herbert Samuel had been the first Jew in
the Cabinet in 1905, Rufus Issacs the second in 1912 and Montagu became the third in 1915.
Philip had participated in the gossip about the marriage of Venetia Stanley, so adored by
Asquith, to Montagu and her conversion to Judaism in 1915. He commented in a letter to

Louis Mallet: 'People say she has sold her Lord for 30 pieces of silver – but I should have said it was for a much larger sum!'[43] But, as far as I know, there were few contacts between this Anglo-Jewish family and the Sassoons. Despite Philip's Indian connections, some years later he wrote to Esher, on 28 July 1918, about his difficulties in understanding Montagu's famous reforming report on India. 'Personally, I cannot follow all the intricacies, society, religion, caste, political that go to make the Indian cauldron. It almost makes the Irish problem seem easy. But how much more interesting – it instantly carried you back to the matrix of history.' His first reaction, eleven days before, had been more succinct: 'They [Montagu's schemes] struck me as pure Bolshevism.' Despite frequently being called 'Oriental', Philip took pains to distance himself from the East.

In an undated letter, likely to be of mid-September 1916, Northcliffe wrote to Sassoon about Lloyd George's complaints. '1. Too large staffs in France. 2. Too large casualties in proportion to the results gained. 3. Lack of provisions for transport of coming [sic] great output of shells and guns. 4. The corruption of the Clothing Department .... 5. Our artillery inferior to the French.' Northcliffe reported on the efforts he was making through his newspapers and by other means to dispel these criticisms. 'You will not find something in the papers every day. Very often I shall be doing things that will not be in the papers at all.' He also defended Lloyd George in the letter. 'George is an excellent man – keen to win the war, but he has a habit of rushing in where angels fear to tread, as for example, when he accused the whole of the British working class of being drunkards, which, to my own personal knowledge, is absolutely untrue.' There is a notation on the top of the letter signed D.H. and dated '23 Sept 16': 'The G.S. [General Staff] shd supply arguments agst these 5 criticisms.' It is made clear that writing to Sassoon was a way of writing to Haig.

On 19 September Northcliffe wrote that his object was 'to dispel the idea that our victories are accompanied by great losses'. The Somme was perhaps technically a victory as there was a slight advance, but the losses were so huge that, eventually, even Northcliffe couldn't hide them. But on 2 October he still regarded the Somme as a battle of which the British could be proud. He noted that Churchill was being given credit for the first use of tanks in the battle, even though in fact they had been too few to make any difference.

You may have noticed that directly the 'tanks' were successful, Lloyd George issued a notice through the Official Press Bureau that they were due to Churchill. You will find that unless we watch these people they will claim that the great battle of the Somme is due to the politicians. That would not matter if it were not for the fact that it is the politicians who will make peace. Personally I dread a peace made by these tricky people. If they are allowed to exalt themselves they will get a hold over the public very dangerous to the national interests. As far as lies in my power I do not intend that they shall have that hold over the public, and having [sic] let them know definitely that whatever influence I possess is with the Army ....

Northcliffe felt that he should run things because the politicians were not to be trusted and the military were too naïve to protect their interests at home. On 18 October he wrote a long letter to Philip about his activities. He had tried to warn Lloyd George not to interfere with the Army (although he was the Cabinet member responsible for it!). 'Either he was afraid to see me, or he was really away.' Northcliffe instead saw Lloyd George's personal secretary, J.T. Davies. 'I said plainly that I shared the national gratitude for Mr. Lloyd George's energy in shell matters and his attempts to settle Home Rule: that I had given him a personal hint in conversation and several hints in my newspapers that I could no longer support him if further interference took place with Sir William Robertson [the Chief of the General Staff] that if needed I was going to the House of Lords to lay matters before the world, and hammer them daily in my newspapers. This may seem a brusque and drastic thing to do, but I think I know the combination I am dealing with better than you folks who are so engrossed in your splendid and absorbing task.' On 30 October he wrote to Philip about Waldorf Astor, who controlled the *Observer*. Apparently it was about to attack the Army over the battle of the Somme. 'Now that almost everyone has lost someone in the war, it is very easy to arouse criticism .... We ought to mobilise the Press against the Politicians. Unless we are careful the politicians will mobilise a little of the press against the Army. That is why I ask you or anyone who knows him to drop a hint to Major Astor .... I find a great many gloomy people about. Their feelings can easily be worked upon.' On 1 November Robinson contradicted his employer and urged Sassoon to do no such thing, objecting to Northcliffe having on placards for the *Daily Mail* and the *Evening News*: 'Astor's Whine'. 'This sort of thing is an outrage and does harm. William Waldorf A[stor] is one of the best & most patriotic people in the world & the article (with which I personally don't agree) is an able one.'

Two days later Northcliffe wrote: 'My view is that, the Government having given the Commander-in-Chief power over the Army in France, it is their duty to maintain that Army to the utmost and to leave the conduct of affairs and the appointment of officers absolutely to him, and I KNOW that if they don't I can raise the country against them .... Please let me know in advance when you are in England as I will come to town for the purpose of discussion.' Derby, in any case, thought that Lloyd George was doing well in relation to the Army, and showed an unusual degree of trust in the Welsh Wizard. He wrote to Philip on 5 November: 'I think you may be assured that you will have all the men, & all the guns you want next year .... I am convinced that D.H. has the *absolute* support of Ll.G. and Winston & Co. have had no effect whatever on him.' In a reference, presumably, to Lloyd George's indiscreet questions to the French, Derby remarked in the same letter: 'The more I think of it, the more I am convinced that he never *meant* anything against D.H. in what he was supposed to have said to the French. I am sure you can trust him. Personally I do, completely.' Derby did not convince Sassoon, who wrote to Esher on 15 November: 'I have no doubt in my own mind that Ll.G. is out to down or reduce D.H. if he can .... I hear Northcliffe is out to be P.M.' Sassoon seemed intent on damage control and wished to minimize the casualty figures. Robinson wrote to him on 6 November: 'Your casualty figures are valuable, and I shall take an early opportunity of using them. But you will see that I constantly make the point about the relative lightness of our losses.'

In December 1916 Lloyd George became Prime Minister, replacing Asquith. Northcliffe, despite his negative remarks about Lloyd George, had worked very hard for this change. Lloyd George would be a much more dynamic leader. Although one might have thought that this change would have caused apprehension at Haig's staff headquarters, the contrary was the case. Philip was in London during the crisis and Haig wrote to him on 8 December: 'It is very satisfactory that L.G. has been able to form a Govt. I only hope that old Squiff will now play the game & support him for the sake of Old England . . . . I hope you found your sister better, and that you are enjoying yourself notwithstanding the political crisis & backbiting gossip.'[44] A letter two days later indicated why it was useful for Haig to have Philip as his secretary, as he expected him to have some influence on the government. 'I am anxious lest our new Govt. make a fundamental error by sending more troops to Salonika . . . . On no account send more troops there: rather bring them away to reinforce this front! . . . The new Govt. is splendid and should devote all its energies to mobilising the resources of the Empire as soon as possible but having decided the objective viz beat the Boche, it must leave to the General Staff & the Sailors the decision as to how & where to employ the troops & ships to attain that end.' Philip kept him abreast of developments in London, writing, 'I think by now all the appointments & disappointments have been arranged . . . . I think Derby's is a very good appointment. Northcliffe said "That great jellyfish is at the War Office. One good thing is that he will do everything Sir Douglas Haig tells him to do"! . . . I think the whole week has been satisfactory. Balfour at the Foreign Office & Walter Long at the Colonial Office are blemishes.'[45]

Philip also performed more mundane tasks, having a watch engraved as a gift for Charteris and worrying about where Haig might take some leave. Housing may have been one way that Philip had drawn himself to Haig's attention when he had been on Rawlinson's staff. The previous November, just before joining Haig, Haig had written to him: 'I fear I shall not be able to take advantage of your kind offer of your house near Folkestone when I go on leave this next time . . . . But I trust that when the Spring comes, you will again ask me, as I sh. love to spend a few quiet days on the Littlestone links. Sent in a letter about your General's promotion & hope it may do some good.'

Just as Sassoon had been in touch with Haig when working for Rawlinson, he did not neglect the latter when with Haig. General Rawlinson wrote to him on Christmas Day to thank him for watches for himself and for his wife. 'It is just what I wanted as my old wrist watch is nearly worn out . . . . 1917 will be a great year full of momentous events on which the fate of Millions will depend – I am confident that we shall smash the Boche, but we cannot accomplish that end without damaging ourselves.'[46] The flurry of letters between Haig and Philip in December apparently ended in an exchange of compliments. Philip tended to be fulsome, but as far as I know his letter to which Haig replied hasn't survived. Haig wrote:

> Just one line to thank you *very*, *very* much for your charming letter. It is a great satisfac-
> tion to get *your* opinion because the Private Sec. must never mislead his Chief! At the
> same time, I must confess, that when I reflect over what I personally accomplish as com-
> pared with the tremendous results achieved by my Staff, the Commanders of Armies,
> Corps etc. & the incomparable British Soldier, then I feel how very small indeed and how

insignificant is my share in it all, and also feel how much I owe to all my generous, & most loving helpers about me. To them I owe all and to you particularly, Philip, I must express my whole hearted thanks for the way [you] have helped one in the past year.

Sassoon wrote to Esher about his time in England. 'It is hateful leaving home & hateful coming back – two quite distinct & equally bloody sensations! . . . I thought people much less depressed than I had been told – but all suffering from an exaggerated idea of what the Americans are likely to do this year.'

While in London, Philip had time to enrich his literary life. Writing to the novelist Mrs Henry Dudeney, whose work he admired, out of the blue on the strength of their mutual friendship with Mrs Belloc Lowndes, he invited her to lunch. 'I am such a great admirer of your books that I know it would be the greatest pleasure to me to talk to you. Would you not think it impertinent of me to introduce myself in this manner & to say how much I hope you may be able to lunch here next week – either on the 11th – 12th – or 13th. I am only home from the front on leave for a week.'[47] In twenty novels, most of them set in Sussex, Mrs Dudeney wrote about relations between the sexes in a perceptive and interesting way. Then she was quite well known; now she is virtually forgotten. For this first meeting she came to tea at Park Lane on 12 December. 'The double doors fling back. A butler – pompous, discreetly pot-bellied: "Does Sir Philip expect you, Madam?" . . . I inform him that Sir Philip *does*! And sailed past 2 rather flabby looking footmen in the background. His sister, Lady Rocksavage there; also a nice middle-aged man, Sir Louis Mallet. I enjoyed it so much . . . . Oh I'd like to be rich for the mental leisure it gives. At the last, Sir Philip gave me a bunch of carnations: "Mrs Dudeney, I shall write to you" (and *did*).'[48]

He seemed able to reveal himself to a degree to lady novelists of a certain age (Mrs Dudeney was about to turn 50). Apparently he had solicited her advice on renaming Belcaire, his house in Lympne. Her suggestions did not seem to be particularly imaginative or perhaps he or she was joking. Also in the letter he mentions his standard excuse for not marrying despite being one of the most eligible bachelors in England. He wrote on 1 February:

I thought all your names charming – but none will suit my house. 'Hope in the Valley' is lovely but I am on a hill & have no hope! 'Five Chimneys' is exquisite – but I have only 4! I love 'Comforts' Place' but the visitor would alas find no basis of fact! 'Skiff Corner' – charming, but a solitary barge on the canal at the foot of the hill cannot justify this tempting extravagance . . . . Didn't you like my sister? She is the most charming person in the world. I love her so much that I can never marry. She has set me too dizzy a standard . . . . Would one ever have believed before the war that one could have stood for one *single instant* the load of pain & anxiety which is now one's daily breath? I find that altho' I can study the casualty lists without even seeing a name I know – for *all* my friends have been killed – yet nevertheless one feels as much for others as for oneself – just a great blur of grief & one wakes up every morning feeling one can hardly bear to live through the day. Yet these splendid fellows out here set one an example of happiness that one follows in spite of one's heart. Are you going to dedicate your new book to me? I hope so. You have many worthier, but no greater, admirer. Please write again at once.

A few days later she recorded that Philip had requested that she lend him a copy of her 1915 novel *Secret Son* and that he would be sending a King's Messenger to pick it up and bring it to him in France. 'He's a splendid and captivating sort of young man. What a queer affair it all is!'[49]

In the new government, Lord Derby replaced Lloyd George as Minister of War, but the position was downgraded and placed outside the small War Cabinet of five. Derby was seen as more pliable than his predecessor. Haig had said of him that 'like the feather pillow he bears the mark of the last person who sat upon him'.[50] In the previous coalition ministry that Asquith had formed in May 1915 Derby had been Under-Secretary of State for War. (Sassoon approved of this appointment, writing to Esher on 16 July: 'Eddie Derby left this morning in the best of form. He is a tremendous asset & I hope he will keep the Goat [Lloyd George] straight.') Derby wrote to Philip on 23 July 1916 during the battle of the Somme: 'I wish we were not having such heavy casualties. As I told you people in this country judge everything by the amount of casualties – and there is no doubt there is a great uneasiness. However if we get through all this will be forgotten – if we don't I am very much afraid of a halt being called. This is for your own eye – not D.H.'s – it would only bother him . . . . We know if we get through – the price is none too large, heavy though it be.' He went on to comment on Asquith's position: 'Asquith has long lost his hold over the country, but has kept it in a marvellous way over the H. of C. This week that hold collapsed [over the issue of Ireland].' In his next letter, a week later, he remarked that 'Haig's star is in the ascendant . . . . [Asquith] is quite the weakest man I have ever come across. He has quite lost his hold on the H. of C. and the end of the present Govt can't be long delayed.' On 6 August he reported to Philip on the good effects of his staying on the right side of Northcliffe: 'Northcliffe's treatment by you has borne real good fruit . . . . I hear that in all his letters home he praises Haig and his staff to the skies. All the other papers are writing about him, and the result is the complaints about numbers of casualties have absolutely ceased – and people see how that although the amount of ground actually won may not be very large – the effect of our offensive has been very great.'

By the following February, it was rumoured that Northcliffe was in continual touch with Haig, which Philip thought was an exaggeration. On 3 February 1917, he wrote to Northcliffe: 'I hear the "on dits" in London are that you are constantly over here & that whenever there is a rumour about my Chief or otherwise I am always rushing over to see you! This is very amusing – as you have been over here *twice* altogether, & I have only been home 3 times in 8 months, once on leave & twice on duty with D.H.'

Arras was the next major battle for the British, from 9 April to 4 May. It was the comparatively successful part of what turned out to be a disastrous French offensive. On 13 April Philip wrote to Esher: 'Don't you think it has been a fine victory when one thinks that it was never meant for anything else but a subsidiary attack. Of course it is only Mount Pisgah but perhaps the French attack will give us the Promised Land! ... We are living in a squalid little village & next week I fancy we are to move into a derelict village near Arras.' Derby wrote on the 19th to Philip: 'I cannot tell you what an excellent effect Haig's victories have had .... Given a free hand there is nothing he and his troops cannot do.' Ultimately the French offensive, under General Nivelle, was unsuccessful, resulting in mutinies among the French troops and Nivelle's replacement by Pétain. This gave Haig greater freedom and seems to have stopped Lloyd George's antagonism for a while. And Haig had a firm ally in the King.

The following month Sassoon went back to London for a parliamentary session and reported on it on 14 May to Esher:

> I ran over for the secret session. Winston made a *most* mischievous speech. The leitmotif was that we should sit down on our hunkers & do nothing until the Americans were ready, 'these measureless millions, untrammelled as we are by orthodox military opinion' – we excuse this kind of talk in the French who as you say have never been able to understand the Sea – but in a man who has been First Lord of the Admiralty it is surely a capital offence. Ll.G. made an excellent speech & absolutely demolished Winston's arguments. He showed that to stop the offensive now would give the Germans the opportunity to adopt one of 4 courses (1) to annihilate the Russian resistance (2) to clear up the Balkans (3) to attack Italy or (4) to stay still & prepare so that when America was ready, Germany would be still readier!

In reply Esher wrote rather interestingly about Churchill: 'The degree in which his clever but unbalanced mind will in future fulfil its responsibilities is very speculative. He handles great subjects in rhythmical language, and becomes quickly enslaved by his own phrases. He deceives himself with the belief that he takes broad views, when his mind is fixed upon one comparatively small aspect of the question .... The power of Winston for good and evil is, I should say, very considerable. His temperament is of wax and quicksilver, and this strange toy amuses and fascinates L. George, who likes and fears him.'[51]

The third battle of Ypres, known as Passchendaele, took place from 31 July to 10 November 1917. It was perhaps the emblematic tragic battle of the war, with casualties of approximately 250,000 British troops. Five miles were gained but the battle was a disaster. Given this and that Lloyd George had opposed the battle, it was amazing that Haig survived as commander. But survive he did, even though certain leading members of his staff, such as General Charteris, Haig's Chief of Intelligence and notorious for his unfounded optimism, lost their positions, very much as Derby wished, despite Haig's objections. Derby wrote on 6 December 1917: 'There is a feeling in this country of despondency which I sincerely hope is not felt in France .... That man [Charteris] has been the curse of the piece and if anybody could bring D.H. down it would be him. I am all for being optimistic but he has preached optimism to a degree that is dangerous in the extreme and gives D.H.'s opponents a real handle .... There are certainly some people who have lost confidence in D.H. I have not in the very least.' Philip, as was more or less his obligation, seems to have shared this rather mindless optimism, having written to Esher on 4 October: 'Things are going well with us, if only we can keep the politicians straight .... Our advances now are methodical, cheap & completely successful.' Haig's supporters in London were beginning to have their doubts.

In November Esher shared some of the pessimism about how the war was going, writing in some despair to Philip on two successive days in November. On the 14th: 'If I were L.G. I should get myself ejected from office, and let some one else lose the war. We are heading hard for that disaster .... Why don't you all go home and play golf? I am going home for Xmas! In disgust!' And the next day, 'We seem to be heading for a catastrophic peace all right .... The people in the streets [presumably in Paris] think that only L.G. stands between them and the complete loss of the war. It shows how lamentably wanting the French are in leadership that they are forced to look to that little man.'[52] Haig was in increasing difficulty on the home front. On 1 December Lloyd George had seen Esher in Paris and not only denounced Charteris but Sassoon as an intriguer against him, 'conspiring with Asquith and the press'.[53] Esher demurred.

Sassoon was becoming more aware of the problem. The battle of Cambrai from 30 November to 3 December was a failure; nothing was gained. Philip was also busy distancing himself from Charteris's optimism in a letter to Esher on 7 December: 'The War Cabinet are beginning to give tongue .... As you know I have never agreed with these foolish optimistic statements which Charteris has been putting in D.H.'s mouth all the year *but* what they ought to realize is that morale is a fluctuating entity & there is no doubt that events in Russia & Italy have greatly raised the enemy's spirits.' On 18 December he commented to Esher on Charteris again: 'Rightly or wrongly he was an object of odium & his name had become a byword even at home. I hear that he has been heading a faction against *me*! for developing the position of Private Secretary too much. I am diverted. I went to see D.H. but you know the length of my material ambitions! & I would not stay on a second longer than I was wanted.'

Northcliffe had also now turned on Haig. On 13 December he wrote very strongly to Sassoon:

I ought to tell you frankly and plainly, as a friend of the Commander-in-Chief, that dissatisfaction, which easily produces a national outburst of indignation, exists in regard to the Generalship in France .... In the few hours I spent at Boulogne, on the leave ship and on the train, I heard something very like mutiny spoken by officers .... My knowledge of the temper of the people ... shows me that they are at the end of their patience. There is the memory of a dead man or the knowledge of a missing or wounded man in every house. Outside of the War Office I doubt whether the Higher Command has any supporters whatever. Sir Douglas is regarded with affection in the army, but everywhere people remark that he is surrounded by incompetents.

The inconclusive results of the battle of Cambrai, Northcliffe felt, had caused great disillusionment.

Esher was staunchly for Haig. He wrote to Sassoon on 15 December: 'You cannot depreciate the authority of D.H. without destroying the unity of the Army .... We are heading for a French C in C and those who most detest the idea will have brought it on themselves .... And yet, *we alone* stand between Germany and the mastery of Europe. *Our* victories are the only ones that have counted at all .... You may think this all balderdash. I know your sceptical mind. But I feel strongly that we are at the parting of the ways of "victory" and defeat.' Esher felt that Northcliffe had done a great deal of harm; on 19 December he wrote to Philip: 'Quite cheerfully I would pull the string of the guillotine for Northcliffe.' And on the 23rd he remarked to Philip that he was being attacked in London. 'You are a clever little thing, Philip, and fortunate in so many ways. All such favourites of the Gods are envied. But you are sometimes deluded by these plausible visitors, who suck up to you, and afterward turn and rend. Dirty devils.' Haig was apparently quite unflappable. At the end of December, he wrote to Philip 'Would you very kindly take a box for 6 at one of the Pantomimes on *Friday afternoon* .... Better *not* the box in my name. I wish you a bright & happy New Year, my dear Philip, and I thank you a thousand times for all you have done to help me in the year that is ending today.'

On 17 January 1918 Northcliffe made it clear how much he had changed his mind, calling for more civilian control by such figures as Sir Eric Geddes, who at this time was First Lord of the Admiralty.

> The stories of Passchendaele and Cambrai have made a very bad impression .... I am rapidly coming to the opinion that Sir William Robertson will unseat the Field Marshal .... You know I have no sympathy with any politicians who intrigue against Generals. Unfortunately, there are Generals who are playing into the hands of politicians by not resigning Commands for which they are obviously unfit. In my opinion, the War Cabinet will take the matter into its own hands. I believe it will have the support of ninety-five per cent of the people. The fall of [Admiral] Jellicoe has not produced a murmur of disapproval, and Parliament [and] public are in a mood that will not brook the support of incompetence. Please convey my warm regards to the Field Marshal.[54]

On the other hand, on 8 February Geoffrey Dawson, the editor of *The Times* (because of an inheritance he had changed his name from Robinson), wrote to Sassoon that Lord Milner, about to replace Derby as War Minister, had said: ' "It is the greatest possible mistake to suppose that L.G. is an anti-Haig man. He is nothing of the kind." I really think you may absolutely dismiss from your mind the notion that there is even any speculation about a possible substitute, or anything but the most complete confidence .... I must stop now. If you will write to me fully, I will reciprocate by giving you all the inside news I know.'[55]

The last year of the war is captured vividly in the extensive correspondence between Sassoon and Esher. On 23 March Philip wrote of the great German offensive, in which they advanced forty miles, trying to put the best face on it. 'This is the biggest attack in the history of warfare I wd. imagine. On the whole we were very satisfied with the first day. There is no doubt that they lost very heavily & we had always expected to give ground & our front line was held very lightly. We have had bad luck with the mist, because as we have got the supremacy in the air, fine weather wd. have been in our favour.' He also sought refuge in the common Haig theme of not enough manpower. 'The enemy has got the men & we haven't. For two years Sir D.H. has been warning our friends at home of the critical condition of our man power .... We are fighting for our existence.' He wrote to Esher almost every day in this time of crisis, commenting on 25 March, in the midst of the worst days of the battle, 'D.H. is a great man & I am a mouse but we have a quality in common that in crisis we are incurably cheerful. It is the small worries of life that we *cannot* stomach.' On the 29th he wrote: 'This is the 9th day of the attack. It feels like 9 *years*. There have been times *in every day* when one might have thought the game was up .... King came round this morning – we tried to cheer him up.' Despite continued troubles he wrote on 30 March: 'I have a sort of feeling that somehow all the same the end of the war is not too far off.' Sassoon reported that on 6 April he had gone to Beauvais with Haig to see Foch, Pétain and Clemenceau, as well as Lloyd George and General Henry Wilson, a close adviser of the Prime Minister's. The battle picked up again on 8 April. In part in response to the German successes, Foch was named supreme Commander-in-Chief, technically superior to Haig, on the 14th. But it meant for Haig the possibility of French assistance. Sassoon felt that Lloyd George and the French would attack Haig when the battle was over. He concluded his letter, 'Here the Spring is come, leaves flowers – birds – but all bloodstained & this is the 4th Spring running that I have missed seeing the tulips in my garden.'

The second part of the German offensive, the battle of the Lys, lasted from 9 to 29 April. Although the Germans opened a wide breach in the British lines, they were unable to take advantage of their success due to lack of reserves. The order of the day Haig issued on 11 April was perhaps the most famous single British document of the war. It was full of what would be called in the Second World War the Dunkirk spirit. Of course it has a much older provenance, going back to Shakespeare's 'We Happy Few', the spirit of Agincourt from *Henry V*. Haig's dispatch concluded: 'There is no other course open to us but to fight it out! Every position must be held to the last man: there must be no retirement. With our backs to the wall, and believing in the justice of our cause, each one of us must fight on to the end. The safety of our Homes and the Freedom of mankind alike depend upon the conduct of each one of us at this critical moment.'[56] As A.J.P. Taylor rather cynically remarked, 'In England this sentence [about backs to the wall] was ranked with Nelson's last message ['England expects every man to do his duty']. At the front, the prospect of staff officers fighting with their backs to the walls of their luxurious chateaux had less effect.'[57] It is an indication of the closeness between Haig and Sassoon, perhaps particularly at this time of crisis, that Haig gave Sassoon the manuscript of this order, to commemorate that he had handed it to him for transmission. A last sentence is crossed out: 'But be of good cheer, the British Empire must win in the End.' Philip so valued the document that he left it to the British Library in his will.

Sassoon seemed to be optimistic about how things were going and felt that Esher was being too cynical. In a letter of 22 April he praised Robertson for resigning as Chief of the General Staff in London; he was replaced by Henry Wilson. Esher was less generous in his response, saying on the following day that resignation 'is the refuge of the weak man. In all my long experience of public affairs, I never knew a resignation to have the smallest effect .... As I often told you, jump-off, and the omnibus rolls on without you.'

On 26 April he wrote that the new chiefs, the War Minister, Milner, and Wilson, were visiting. 'They are both *very* friendly to D.H. when they come. I entirely wash out all the reports that they are trying to encompass his downfall.' After the visit on 30 April he wrote: 'Milner is so impersonal, passionless & detached. Like Prospero in his cave.' In the same letter he commented on someone's engagement and remarked rather cruelly, 'I shall soon be the only bachelor alive. That will be fun.' Now almost 30, he was certainly one of the richest bachelors in the country. In a letter on 4 June he commented on Lady Randolph Churchill's third marriage, to Montagu Porch. 'Winston tells me Porch is younger than he is – much better looking & very devoted. She is a wonder. No doubt when I want to marry she will be free again & in the shop window like a ripe Stilton.'

Late in April, General Maurice accused the Lloyd George government of withholding reserves from the armies in France. Sassoon discussed the incident in the few pages of a diary that have been preserved, noting that 'it might well prove a deathblow for the Government – *if* Asquith & the Unionists really mean business'.[58] Esher saw the whole business as a terrible breach of military discipline: 'You can never get soldiers to understand that politics always has been and is a game, and that politicians are a trades union. The silly fellow [Maurice] believes that "government" is a reality and that the H[ouse] of C[ommons] is composed of upright patriots. Geese! ... I tell you soldiers are hopeless. Dear good fellows – but – thank goodness you are not one.'

It did precipitate a major debate in the House of Commons, which greatly strengthened Lloyd George and left Asquith weaker than ever. After the debate, Esher wrote on 9 May: 'Can you ever make a soldier comprehend that "Politics" is not a battle but a tournament.' Esher felt, writing the next day, that 'Whatever happens, *never* permit D.H. to open his mouth. His silence is a tremendous factor.' The day after that, he remarked: 'How that little L.G. does love polemics. He gets himself into trouble for the sheer sensual pleasure of getting himself out again. You may play this game once too often!' Sassoon assured Esher that he needn't worry as Haig himself took little notice of the debate, according to a letter of 13 May: 'These gusts of politics & personalities pass him by. He is a glacier upon which little finds a foothold & so he will not involve himself .... Notoriety, position, reputation are dust these days. Hours fly, flowers die/ New men, new ways/ Pass by/ Love stays. And the serenity of mind that *you* achieve – and real friends. It is raining.' In his diary on 12 May, he further permits himself to express disapproval of Haig.

D.H. produced an absurd opinion ... this morning that as the Americans were now coming up into the line & the Germans didn't want to kill Americans, they would now make peace. He is really incorrigible .... It is incredible how little work he does & how completely out of touch he is with everything. He never goes near the office .... He ought to spend the whole day up at the office & really get au fait with the situation – instead of making himself ridiculous by his splendid isolation & his obvious ignorance of existing conditions.

But this harsh opinion was momentary, for on 27 May he wrote: 'D.H. is wonderful. I admire his character more & more.'[59]

The military tension had abated somewhat and Esher and Sassoon were able to discuss more frivolous topics, such as what Sassoon was reading and also what they regarded as Haig's and his wife's terrible taste in the decoration of their house in England. On 6 May Philip wrote to Esher ironically or perhaps in a moment of revulsion against his usual take on style, about how he liked to live: an unbelievable moment of austerity. 'Of course the sort of house I like & pine for has no "comforts," nothing but stone floors & stone walls – moth-eaten 14th century "fragments" – draughts – and a few stiff chairs against the wall with a string attached across to prevent anyone from sitting down on them. You wd. think it easy to realise this ideal. But it isn't, and I find myself the reluctant possessor of Park Lane with its *leitmotif* of sham Louis XVI, Lympne which is Martini *tout craché* which isn't even Lincrusta [oxidized linseed oil made to look like wood panelling] – when my period is Merovingian or Boiling Oil. *Le monde est toujours mal arrangé.* What drivel I'm writing . . . . The war is too boring.' Esher responded on 11 May about furnishing and marriage. 'As you say, you may be distinguished as the last bachelor on earth. Of course I cannot imagine you wedded to a Cecil or a Cavendish or a Stanley. You would not enjoy a XIVth century wife as much as a medieval dining room . . . . Where are the "rising men"! Nothing above the horizon but grey beards. Never was Europe in such a plight. *All* the young men of genius cannot be killed.'

Sassoon had time for some relaxation in Paris, evoking its spirit in his diary: 'The chestnuts of the Champs-Elysées ... magnolias, wet nurses, spinning tops, and over all the hot smell of rubber and ribbons which is so exclusively its own . . . . We came back the next day – in an open car through the heart of Normandy. Lush green fields packed with red munching cows & the orchards & young beech trees.'[60]

In the last months of the war, the Germans seemed to be doing well but were not able to follow up their initial successes, and the Americans began to have a decisive effect. In Philip's correspondence with Esher and in other ways, different concerns started to surface. He became involved with the official war artists' scheme. Earlier in 1917 he had seen a great deal of William Orpen who had come to France as a war artist. Orpen, with his rather impulsive personality, kept getting into trouble with the authorities and Sassoon had to help him out. That year he did portraits of Haig and of Hugh Trenchard, head of the Royal Flying Corps, among others. The writer Maurice Baring, Trenchard's ADC, recognized the propaganda value of the new service and suggested to Orpen that he paint two of the Corps's aces.[61] In a letter to Sassoon, Orpen discussed his relationship with Sybil, which, at least from his point of view, was still somewhat tempestuous. 'I and Sybil are fighting again hard now – you know how difficult she is – so you can perfectly understand.' Philip probably didn't understand, as he found Sybil perfect. Orpen went on: 'Would the chief like that little interior? . . . . I could not be more hurt or angry than at being kept here [that is, not being allowed to return to the front] – surely, surely I was no trouble to anyone – and I love the work with all my heart – and was only just beginning to understand things when I came home. Oh Philip do what you can for me.'[62]

Sybil did go out to France at least once to see Rock and Philip. She was there the same time as Orpen and he and Philip took her on a tour of the battlefields. She wasn't supposed to do that. By chance they met the French commander, Joffre, and while Sassoon and Orpen spoke to him, Sybil hid under the rug in the car. She also became aware of the Muslim Indian troops fighting in France and may have felt a special affinity with them. She had copies of the Koran printed for them.[63] Enjoying the challenge of travelling around the front without authorization indeed was foolhardy. She was pregnant and the roughness of the trip made her ill. Another day, she and Orpen had to seek shelter in a bombed-out farmhouse and there she had a miscarriage, losing twins. After the fact, he looked after her well, he and his driver getting her to a hospital. She credited Orpen with saving her life. But the tragedy never should have happened.[64]

Sassoon was much more involved with the later visit of his family's great friend, John Singer Sargent, who came to the front in the final summer of the war. At first Sargent had paid little attention to the conflict; in 1916 he had left for America, where his major project was an extensive set of murals for the Museum of Fine Arts in Boston. He also worked that year on his longtime project on the Triumph of Religion at the Boston Public Library. That October he wrote to tell Evan Charteris that he might visit the front in a few months: 'But would I have the nerve to look not to speak of painting? I have never seen anything in the least horrible – outside of my studio.'[65] But nothing came of that intention. The war moved closer to him when a beloved niece was killed in March 1918 in the chance bombing of a Paris church.

He returned to England that spring, and on 12 May Philip mentioned to Esher that 'Sybil is delighted at Sargent's return. That is a terrible love affair – de longue date. I have written to him to come out here. He must do something of D.H. He is *the* only artist – now that Velasquez has died.' Sponsored by the official war artists' scheme, he went to France in July and stayed until October. Sassoon took him around, particularly into Arras. Sargent wrote to Evan Charteris on 24 July that a 'Major Uzzielli took Philip Sassoon and me [on] a joy ride in a Tank up and down slopes, and over trenches and looping the loop generally. There is a row of obsolete ones somewhere about Bermicourt that made me think of ships before Troy.'[66] Sassoon arranged for Haig and Sargent to meet several times. These occasions were quite memorable.

I had had two delightful days with Sargent . . . . He arrived in the most faultless khaki, Sam Brown belt under his armpits, puttees, etc & Saratoga trunk upon trunk filled with trousseau. He and D.H. were amusing together. Both are inarticulate. D.H. can begin his sentence very well but can't always end it, as his mind goes so much more quickly than his tongue. Sargent on the other hand can't begin it, but when he does it goes with a rush to the end at such a pace that you don't know what he has said. Between the two I was quite at sea. I asked D.H. what he thought of Sargent & he replied 'He doesn't look as if he took much exercise. He'll burst one of these days' – . . . He went for a ride in a Tank and enjoyed it like a child . . . . He said to me 'Shall I paint what I want or what I must'. I said 'What you want', & I left him painting cows in an orchard, which he might just as well be doing in Worcestershire!'[67]

Sargent was supposed to be painting a grand picture with Anglo-American significance. Much later, on 20 August, Sassoon noted that 'He has been doing lovely things of Tommies stealing apples – a broken down coupe in a ruin, Arras Cathedral etc. – but he had not attempted to embark as yet upon his big picture or even made studies for it. How he wishes he had never been sent out to do it. It hangs over him like a sword of Damocles.'[68] The posed picture of Tommies stealing apples was one of a series of innumerable brilliant watercolours he did including soldiers bathing, a wrecked sugar refinery, a crashed aeroplane. The cathedral picture was acquired by Sassoon. On 14 September Sassoon wrote of Sargent to Esher that he was the only artist 'who has not seen the war through a key hole'. His large project became *Gassed*: blindfolded soldiers, victims of a gas attack, being led across a battered landscape, a very large picture he finished in March 1919. (It is now in the Imperial War Museum, London.) A commission from the British War Memorials Committee, it replaced the original Anglo-American project. It has become a controversial canvas, one in which the war appears rather sanitized, emphasized incongruously by a football game going on in the background. One of the best-known comments on the painting came from E.M. Forster, who saw it at the Sargent memorial exhibition at the Royal Academy in 1926. For him the picture represented 'Them', who ruled those such as himself. At the exhibition, he first encountered via their portraits Lord Curzon, then Philip Sassoon himself. 'My attention was drawn by a young Oriental, subtle and charming and not quite sure of his ground. I complimented him in flowery words. He winced, he disclaimed all knowledge of the East . . . . I ought to have looked first at the clothes. They were slightly horsey and wholly English, and they put mine to shame. Why had he come from Tabriz, or wherever it was, and put them on? Why take the long journey from Samarcand for the purpose of denouncing our Socialists?' At the end, Forster looked at *Gassed*. And wrote about it scathingly. 'You were of godlike beauty – for the upper classes only allow the lower classes to appear in art on condition that they wash themselves and have classical features. These conditions you fulfilled. A line of golden-haired Apollos [an echo of Frances Cornford's famous lines about Rupert Brooke] moved along a duck-board from left to right with bandages over their eyes . . . . The battlefield was sad but tidy. No one complained, no one looked lousy or overtired . . . . It was all a great war picture should be, and it was modern because it managed to tell a new sort of lie.'[69]

Some years later Sargent painted, on commission from the South African financier, Sir Abe Bailey, for presentation to the National Portrait Gallery, a not very successful group portrait of twenty-two British generals. Such large mural-like pictures were what Sargent wished to be remembered for. But they were far less effective than his portraits and landscapes. In 1921 he painted two war murals for the staircase of the Widener Library at Harvard University, *Death and Victory* and the *Coming of the Americans to Europe*, in memory of the

24. John Singer Sargent, *Ruined Cathedral of Arras*, 1918.

Harvard men who had died in the war. Hence, in effect, he completed, but in separate works, his Anglo-American task. Nevertheless, his most successful wartime pictures were the oils and watercolours that he did largely on the spot, while being looked after by Philip.

Haig was appreciative of what Philip did, even if he may have been slightly ironic about it. On 21 June Sassoon wrote to Esher: 'He made a charming speech to me saying how grateful he was for all I had done for him etc . . . . [his ellipses] "Many men have been ruined by their Private Secretaries" etc. The tears came into my eyes like John Brown when the Queen gave him a copper plated coffee pot, "faithful creature"!' Philip then moved on to a discussion of the recently published *Eminent Victorians* by Lytton Strachey. Philip had, perhaps surprisingly, a fair amount of time to read. 'If you haven't, you must read Eminent Victorians by Strachey. The essay on Flo. Nightingale *riveting*. Also I think Nails by Mrs Dudeney will please you & Hearts of Controversy by Mrs Meynell .... At present I am deep, in my spare moments, in Stonewall Jackson & Harry Lauder's book on the War! ... I meant to show you a beautiful chair I had got in Paris with a wonderful Louis XIV inkstain on it – on par for interest with the blood of the Young Princes in the staircase of the Tower!'

Esher responded on 23 June. 'I have read 3 of the "Eminent Victorians". The book has a certain cleverness but does not merit the Asquithian puff it received. The man has no real vision, and his writing, sometimes brilliant, is *vulgar*. It is journalese, and not literature .... Perhaps the ineffable Strachey would find something to ridicule in the relation between you and the Chief. *I* see nothing but devoted service both to D.H. and what is even more import-ant to England. So you can safely stow away his words, halting as I guess they were, in your livret d'or.'

Philip became less enthusiastic about Strachey, perhaps under Esher's influence. He wrote on 24 June: 'I quite agree about Strachey's litter of 4 – I had only read about Flo. when I wrote – & had been blinded, by the pleasing discovery of such robustness in her character, to his hard & twisted nib. He has no inspiration & the mind of a Green Room dresser but a certain vocabulary.' And he continued on the 27th: 'Why has Strachey's book caused such a sensation? ... A dead hand of irony *is* fatiguing. All the same he does galvanize all those dead bores into life – perhaps only a travesty .... Nevertheless the book is riveting, enthralling. I wd. not have liked to miss a line.'

Esher assumed he was primarily negative about the book, replying on the 28th, 'It is delightful to find that you modified your view of Strachey. The cleverness of the book is justly praised, but the vulgarity here and there, and the cynicism throughout, put me off .... Of course the writer belongs to a mutual admiration Society of Bloomsburyites.' It is intriguing that Esher should have been aware of the group so early, but he had probably heard a fair amount about them from his daughter, the painter Dorothy Brett, later known as Brett and a very close friend of D.H. Lawrence. On 28 May Esher had written about her. 'My elder girl, the artist, is here [at Esher's Scottish house, Roman Camp] fishing. She wears high boots, breeches, and a bright blue surcoat. Imagine the amazement of the dour Scots at this vision from the Ottoline Morrell world of which they are in benighted ignorance.'

During the summer the war seemed rather far away in the little bit of diary that survives. In it, and in his correspondence with Esher, Sassoon referred to the Billing case. Noel Pemberton Billing, an MP, had published his view that the war was being lost because of the 47,000 members of the ruling classes in Britain who were homosexuals. During the summer the actress Maud Allen was suing him, unsuccessfully, for libel for calling her a lesbian because of her involvement in a production of Oscar Wilde's *Salomé*. Sassoon commented in his diary:

Since the Billing Case all attention is diverted from the Battle of the Aisne to the Battle of the Anus. It will have a very bad effect this scandalous case .... I always liked it when the Sultan came over & was given a ball and was asked by the Master of Ceremonies how he had enjoyed himself & what he thought of the English beauties replied 'Lady Dudley est exquise & Lady Granville est ravissante et Lady de Grey c'est une femme parfaite – mais pour le vrai plaisir donnez-moi Lord Downe.'[70]

In late July and early August there was at the front a characteristically British squabble about religion. Haig had been interested in having an ecumenical service of Catholics, Anglicans and Nonconformists. Philip wrote a rather impersonal note about this issue. 'We have in one stroke been carried back through many troubled centuries & are plunged in the very limbo of mediaeval controversy . . . . The Chief had set his heart on having a great combined service in commemoration of the outbreak of the war.' But the sects began to fight. As an Anglican bishop was scheduled to come, the Presbyterians felt they were being outranked. The Catholics distributed a pamphlet, much to Haig's fury, about why they couldn't participate. Haig lectured the chief Roman Catholic chaplain: 'It was well known, alas, that the Pope & the Holy See were pro-German . . . . "And I" ended up the Chief with visible emotion "who had always looked forward to a great Imperial Church – a golden age of religion upon earth." . . . The only out seems to me for each denomination to hold a separate service in each corner of the Ecole Square & for the Chief to sit on a revolving piano stool in the centre giving his impartial attention to each in turn.'[71] The service that was finally held was for Anglicans and Nonconformists. Haig allowed his fury to enter his diary, writing there: 'The attitude of the R.C. clergy over this service should open our eyes to what the R.C. religion in our Empire really is. They must be R.C. first, and English afterwards, if their Church discipline permits.'[72] Haig was not a Scottish Presbyterian for nothing.

The battle of Amiens took place from 8 to 11 August. The British used 450 tanks and advanced eight miles. Sassoon's sensibilities about numbers of casualties seemed to be rather blunted by the brutality of the war. He wrote to Esher: 'We scored such a nice success & so cheaply (12,000 casualties) that I had hoped we would stop & consolidate & fight again somewhere else – but Foch is all for pushing on for the moment & hopes to finish the war this year. I hope he may be right.' Sassoon's chief concern was for Haig's reputation. He wanted Lord Stamfordham, the King's private secretary, to persuade the King, who was visiting France, to say 'something personally appreciative of D.H. in his message when he leaves France.' In his next letter on 22 August he remarked that 'the whole policy of the Press & the Government has been to completely suppress D.H.'s name . . . . They all take their cue from the Prime Minister.'

Earlier in the month, on the 10th, Esher had asked him about his fellow Sassoon, Siegfried. His famous protest against the war and its conduct of course was an attack on Philip's boss. His passionate anti-war statement had appeared in July 1917 and he had published *The Old Huntsman*, which contained powerful anti-war poems. Raised in Kent, Siegfried was deeply devoted to the countryside, riding and cricket. His earlier poems were heavily pastoral; a crucial part of his autobiographical writings was his commitment to being English. The cousins moved in somewhat parallel worlds, and at this point they had never met. He shared friends with Philip, such as Osbert Sitwell and, later, Rex Whistler. They had both been painted by Glyn Philpot. Philip liked literary figures. But throughout his life, Siegfried had virtually no connection with his Sassoon relations. His grandmother (her pious husband, Philip's grandfather's brother, had died) had disowned her son when he had married 'out' and her children could only see their late brother's three sons on the sly. Over the years the cousins had practically nothing to do with one another, hardly surprising, considering that Siegfried attacked what Philip was doing and those whom he served. Several other Sassoon cousins were serving in the war but there is no indication that Philip had any contact with them. Although he himself is mentioned in the *British Jewry Book of Honour*, published in 1922, he hardly identified with the approximately 60,000 other British Jews who fought in the war, of whom 2,324 were killed and 6,350 were casualties.

Esher wrote to Philip: 'By the way, *who* is Siegfried Sassoon? . . . He is a powerful satirist. Winston knows his last volume of poems by heart, and rolls them out on every possible occasion. They are very grim . . . . I should think they are very popular with the "thin red line of 'eroes." ' He complained on 24 August: 'You never answered my question "Who is Siegfried S." I really want to know.' Finally on 31 August Philip replied, putting a fair amount of distance between himself and Siegfried: 'My Wagnerian antonym is a distant relation, the grandson of an old aunt of my father's.' This was literally true, but they would seem not so distant if one thought of them as both being great-grandsons of the founder, David Sassoon. This aunt was the widow of Sassoon David Sassoon, the eldest son of David's second wife. The cousins were also very close in age, Siegfried being just two years older. Philip continued, 'I have never seen him – except as portrayed by Philpot. His verse is robust & good & he is a great protégé of Eddie Marsh – that Maecenas of the Georgian era.' Apparently Siegfried's volume of poems, *The Old Huntsman*, had arrived at Haig's headquarters but Philip ignored it and gave the impression that they weren't related, at least according to Stanley Jackson.[73]

In his diary on 24 August Philip recorded his feeling that the war was going well. He allowed himself to fantasize, in a heterosexual way, about what he would be doing when it was over. 'I think I will start by St. Moritz where one skates & skis all day under a tropical sun & where the fairest women in the world offer you nightly a panting sacrifice. Then I will drop down over the Alps – same way as Napoleon went – to Venice, where after bathing in the broiling sea I will listen to the serenades in the moonlight from the balcony of my palace on the grand canal. Then I think on to Algiers and gallop over the desert on fiery Arab mustangs and watch veiled houris doing the stomach dance in the Bazaar at Biskra. Oh dear all this is nonsense.'[74]

Virtually nothing has been preserved that indicates anything of Sassoon's personal life during the war or indeed before or after. He seems to be quite a solitary figure despite his great genius as a host and his closeness to his sister Sybil and to his cousin Hannah. He had a wide circle of friends and acquaintances. There is barely any evidence of any closer relationship with a man or a woman. A personal touch does survive in copies of two notes Philip kept that he may have sent to a fellow officer, Jack. Is it just badinage with a close friend or something more significant? One doesn't know, but it is striking that he should have preserved these fragments. One is dated 21 August.

> So you waited all the day & all the evening to ring me up until Game [?] was in your room! Charming. But I'll be even with you. *I'll* ring you *up* tomorrow morning – very early – before you receive this warning letter – before even the rosy fingered dawn has caused your white pyjamas to blush – before you have been able to refuse some (now slightly high) grouse for yr breakfast. I will wait until you are weak unwoken & at my mercy. You!

The second note, dated 22 August, reads:

> Good morning. What sort of a night have you had? Did you, according to the acrobatic adage, fall asleep before your head touched the pillow, not to stir again until your plump servant let in a flood of morning sun? Or did you (perish the thought) – after tossing on a restless couch till the Castle Clock boomed 3 a.m. fall into a troubled snooze, only to wake again at 4 – and spend the remainder of the night wide-eyed mid the crunch of chocolates and the fume of Gold Flake [cigarettes], smiling wanly over the pages of Trivia [by Logan Pearsall Smith]. In any case I don't think you rang me up – for, altho' I lay slumbering in my green goggles under the honey coloured rays of the harvest moon – I would have heard – as the black lips of my telephone receiver dangle close to my ear.

This Jack may be the same person with whom Philip travelled in the 1920s to Spain. He also copied out a letter he wrote on 31 January 1919, to Jack, picturing him at a very grand dinner party in London. 'I can imagine the hum of delighted chatter – the savoury odours of succulent fare – the reckless outpourings of rare wines. How dreary will seem to you, by contrast, the exiguous repasts in Avenue Malakoff served by the clumsy Jules. How ineffably boring the dull meals in the blue dining room at Lympne .... You know that far away though I am – across many miles of boundless ocean – I shall be rejoicing in your triumph.'[75]

Sybil

Undoubtedly, Philip's closest personal connection was with his sister Sybil. Philip urged some of his correspondents to call on his 'little sister' and of course he saw her when he was in England. She wrote to Philip on 15 May 1915: 'My darling Philippo, I feel more depressed than I can say. The news is bad, everyone is dying or dead. The Government are awful, I have lost all confidence in Asquith, L George, French & everyone else. There are strikes every where .... Do you think we shall have some form of conscription. It *makes* me boil to see all these loafers .... Not a soul realises the magnitude of our fight or the chances against our winning.'[76] Much of her correspondence with him was about family matters. That 21 July her topic was the anniversary of their mother's death. She had gone on previous anniversaries to her mother's grave at Père Lachaise, but the doctor had told her that she was not well enough to travel and in any case a trip to Paris was not easy in wartime. 'One feels such a close happy & intimate feeling of reunion somehow on that day & in that little place – it isn't at all a macabre mausoleum is it? It is *six* years fancy, since that awful nightmare & I can see her as plainly as if I had parted from her y'day. *How* much we miss her . . . . I am sending a box of Trent Rosemary to you to the Ritz & it will still be fragrant on the 28th & all my prayers & thoughts will be with you *both*.'

Much of her life was not all that different from what it might have been if there weren't a war on. Curzon seemed to be conducting a small flirtation with her. As she remarked to Philip in a letter: 'A bit fresh eh?' She maintained her artistic interests, lunching with Sargent, seeing Philpot and going to the studio of Charles Sims, a painter well known at the time. (In 1922 Sims painted a portrait of Sybil and her son, and he did some decorations after the war for Philip's London house.) Sybil looked after Philip's aesthetic interests, visiting Lympne and observing the progress of the garden. Rock was with his regiment in France.

In May 1916 she had her first child, a daughter, named Aline after her mother. As Philip wrote to Lady Desborough on 13 October in a letter thanking her fulsomely for the memorial book about her sons, 'If you ever go to London will you be angelic enough to go & see Syb who has the great joy of being able to call her baby after my mother.' (In his diary he expresses some doubts about the memorial book in a remark that may well reflect his own thinking about self-revelation: 'The war has torn away the veil from what used to be considered sacred & Lady Desborough has set the fashion for making public what one used to consider private.'[77]) In an undated letter Sybil wrote to Philip about his niece and her visitors, first Margot Asquith. 'She thought Aline a dear – she does look very intelligent & has perfectly formed features instead of lumps of unbaked dough insecurely pressed on to the face. Louis [Mallet] on the other hand was unfortunate in arriving (unexpectedly) when she was looking like a horrid little Chinese idol, her face convulsed with rage & one eye screwed up this owing to a pain in the tummy.' She discussed the war with Mrs Asquith. 'I confess I am very despondent, not of ultimate victory, but I don't see how it can be over next year & the price in lives of one year is so appalling to contemplate.'

But the dramatic event was her becoming fully involved in the war as, in effect, the founder of the WRNS, the Women's Royal Naval Service, or at the very least the originator of the idea. In an undated letter early on in the war she had written to Philip: 'When do you come home? It must be early in Dec. as once I start on my work (I am seriously thinking of the Intelligence job at the Admiralty as Bridget's cousin says they want people like me.) I shall not be able to get away. The hours are dreadful 10 to 7 & only one day off a week but as social life has ceased one must do something & there is no voluntary work I wd. care to do (like Hannah's). The Admiralty is *paid*.' Apparently, nothing came of this idea.

There were women in various semi-military roles during the war but a naval component wasn't established until late 1917. The idea for it originated in a conversation Sybil had with Eric Geddes. He was one of the businessmen whom Lloyd George had brought in to help with the war effort, in his case from the railways. In 1916 and into 1917 he was in charge of transport both at home and in the war zones. Then, in July 1917, he became First Lord of the

Admiralty. Sybil knew him socially and at one point she suggested to him that there were many jobs that women could do in the Navy that would free a man to go to sea.

Sybil herself was only 23 at the time and she could hardly run such a service. Eric Geddes's sister, Mrs Chalmers Watson, was head of the WAAC, the army women's service, and undoubtedly that was an important factor in making him sympathetic to the idea. As Geddes indicated at a lunch with Katharine Furse on 11 November, he wished to give the service a parallel name, the Women's Auxiliary Naval Corps, to be known as WANKS. Fortunately that idea did not prevail. The alternatives were the Women's Naval Service, WNS, the Women's Auxiliary Naval Service, WANS, the Royal Naval Women's Service, RNWS, but in the end the Women's Royal Naval Service, WRNS, was selected. Katharine Furse was a natural choice to head the new service. The young widow of the painter Charles Furse and a daughter of John Addington Symonds, the historian, she had been chief officer of the VAD, the Voluntary Aid Detachment, the largest women's volunteer service connected with the war, designed to help with the military sick and wounded. It was affiliated with the Red Cross and she had just resigned her position because of a dispute with that organization over the living conditions of the VAD volunteers and the unwillingness of the Red Cross to co-ordinate with the Women's Army group. She met Mrs Chalmers Watson as well as various other grand figures in the Admiralty including the Second Sea Lord, Sir Herbert Heath, who would have special responsibility for the new service. As a result, the Women's Royal Naval Service was established in November with Katharine Furse as Director. Recommended by Geddes, Sybil also became an important figure in it, attaining the rank of Assistant Principal. Furse was very pleased to work with her, noting in her memoir: 'She was one of the most delightful and amusing people I had ever met and she rose on my horizon of war work like a scintillating star, helping to satisfy hunger for the cultural side of life'.[78] According to Philip in a letter to Esher on 4 June 1918, 'She is now in uniform & holds the rank of Rear Admiral.' He was exaggerating her rank. The WRNS held equivalents; Furse herself as Director had a rank equivalent to a Rear Admiral; Sybil was not at the same level.

The WRNS received the Royal Assent on 28 November. Its motto was 'Release a man for sea service.' Ultimately there were 7,000 members who enlisted for twelve months or the duration of the war which, coincidentally, turned out to be the same length of time, although actual demobilization was not until 19 February 1919. Quite rapidly recruits were typing, cooking, waiting on tables, painting, repairing mine-nets and servicing seaplanes. Furse wrote, 'There were all the domestic and clerical duties, and our officers replaced Paymasters as Secretaries to Admirals and also as coders and decoders. We replaced writers, telephonists and telegraphists or signallers and also storekeepers and draughtsmen.'[79] But they did not serve at sea. Officers were trained from January on. The service was very successful during the war, but it was rapidly disbanded afterwards, despite petitions to keep it in existence. Katharine Furse remarked: 'It will be one of the greatest regrets of my life that we may not continue in the WRNS, but there is no room for women in the Navy in peacetime.'[80]

Sybil would not play a public role again until the Second World War, when she returned to the WRNS. In contrast to Philip, hers was primarily a private life. But both moved in the world occupied by those who ran the country. Was it unusual for Jews to be so important? Undoubtedly there were several other Jews who were as, if not more, important, but few at their level of glamour. And their isolation from their community was comparatively rare.

The Future

In the last months of the war, Philip gradually became more concerned with Haig's position in the future. Or to put it more bluntly, what would be his reward for having been Commander-in-Chief, the single most visible and important British military leader during the war, particularly after the death of Kitchener? He was on terrible terms with the Prime Minister, Lloyd George. Yet Lloyd George was the most important person in determining what would happen to Haig next.

On 9 September Esher wrote to Sassoon: 'There are rumours that he [Haig] has accepted a "Peerage." Is there any truth in them? Were I he, I should refuse. It would be wonderfully chic *not* to join the humiliated band of "Viscounts" [the rank Esher held himself, but by descent].' In reply on 14 September Sassoon wrote, apparently referring to a previous offer as well: 'D.H. has not been offered a Peerage again & I know he wouldn't accept it. What he wants is a Grant. "What's the use of being a peer & having to live in hotels" he says.' Esher wrote on 22 September: 'It will be wonderful if D.H. . . . sticks to his resolve not to accept a peerage. Such a delicious embarrassment for other aspirants. I wish the nation would purchase Bermersyde and present it to him. How can this be managed? There is the precedent of Stratfield Saye [the Duke of Wellington's house presented to him by the nation]. Exert your ingenious mind. He would require a "grant" to maintain it. In a very few years time "hereditary honours" will be a memory. Everything tends that way.' Bermersyde was the Haig ancestral house in Scotland; Haig was descended from the second son of the 17th laird. The direct line had ended in three unmarried sisters who transferred their rights to a cousin, also descended from the 17th laird. In 1921 he sold the house to Haig, as Esher proposed, for a sum gathered by subscription. Haig could then live there as the 29th laird.

On 26 September Sassoon wrote: 'I don't think there is any question of D.H. being offered a Peerage – in any case I will see he doesn't accept it. It wd. be foolish from *every* point of view. I hope if he survives his enemies (– & I know he will) we will get him a grant . . . . When one thinks what Wellington managed to scoop out of an hostile Government!' Esher replied on the 30th: 'I would take *nothing* from any of these people. A "grant" is in a different category, because it has to be the free gift of the House of Commons. There is a distinction here. But I feel very doubtful whether D.H. can stand up against an offer from the King, for that is the way the thing would be put! I pray that he may have the courage to remain F.M. Sir Douglas Haig the designation under which he practically won the war on the Somme in 1916 and has by his tenacity and indomitable courage led his troops over and over again to the most substantial victories of the War.'

On 11 November 1918, Philip accompanied Haig to the signing of the Armistice in a railway carriage at Compiègne. Immediately after the war ended, Philip came down with the flu. It wasn't a serious case, since he continued to attend to his duties. Philip was lucky: the great flu epidemic of 1918 killed more people than the Great War itself. On 18 November he wrote: 'I am submerged with telegrams. We have had 200 in 2 days & my brain is empty and used up. I feel none of that exhilaration I should feel – why is that?' Lloyd George was calling a general election almost immediately, and Sassoon continued: 'This election is weighing on me. I think I shall lose my seat to a Labour Candidate who has been working like a beaver & promising them everything. Well tant pis.'

The next day he wrote: 'Are the politicians thinking *at all* about making peace – it seems to me they are merely electioneering? *Quite entre nous* L.G. wired D.H. today that he had "the honour to inform you that His Majesty on my recommendation has been pleased to approve that the dignity of a *Viscounty* be conferred upon you in recognition of the signal services wh. you have rendered to the Empire." – D.H. wired back saying that he "hoped he wd. allow all question of reward for me to stand over until he has been able to fix the allowances for disabled officers and men as well as a batta [a bonus for having served in the field] for all ranks of the armies under my command." Don't you think it a blooming insult .... He surely ought to accept an Earldom or nothing – he must get a grant & they will try to side track him with only a peerage.' On 22 November Esher replied:

If he is wise – which I think he is – he will remain Sir Douglas, for there is no finer name in our annals. The day has gone by when a 'Peerage' means anything except to a Brummagem plutocrat .... The House of Lords is as dead as Queen Anne .... Let his renown stand, as the indomitable, modest, self-abnegating head of the greatest army our country ever sent into the field, who refused to go one step beyond the share and share alike of honours and rewards with his men, in due proportion .... He would be insane to allow himself to be swabbed off with a Viscountcy. I am against any peerage. It is certain that neither L.G. or Parlt will ever *endow* an Earldom.

On 1 February 1919, Esher wrote again about the topic after commenting on what Philip might be up to in Paris 'Are you joining the band of revellers at the Hotel Majestic in Paris? Or starting a liaison with Megan [Lloyd George's daughter] in the Rue Nitot? ... The proposed parliamentary "grants", are ludicrously inadequate. Fancy insulting the Chief with an offer of an Earldom and 30,000£. It *is* ludicrous. Nothing under 100,000£ is possible: *and* the Garter. This is the minimum. Think of the war profits.' Haig did not receive the Garter but he did become a Knight of the Thistle and a member of the Order of Merit.

The matter climaxed on 18 February, when Philip went to see Lloyd George in London in order to negotiate with the Prime Minister about Haig's future. The original statement written by Haig on 16 February for Philip to take with him to guide him in his discussion with Lloyd George is now at Houghton.[81]

With reference to statement by the Political Correspondent of todays *Sunday Times* that in the coming week the Leader of the Ho. of Commons will make an announcement regarding a reward & honour to be conferred on me, Sir Philip Sassoon will please see the Prime Minister and tell him that my wishes are as follows:

1st All questions put in the House regarding a reward for me, are made without my wish or approval.

2nd I am well satisfied with the ranks & honours already conferred on me. I only want a sufficient pension to enable me to live in a simple way without monetary anxieties for the remainder of my life.

3rd If the Govt. wish at this time to make a grant of money, I could not accept it until the new Pensions Ministry have really accomplished something. Reports of many sad cases still reach me. . . .

4th As regards conferring a peerage on me. Unless an adequate grant is made to me to enable a suitable position to be maintained, I must decline such an honour.

D.H. 16 Feb: 19.

Published in Haig's diaries are Philip's notes (dated 25 February) of his interview with Lloyd George. The first point referred to a question asked by an MP on his own. Without consulting Haig, Philip took action himself. 'It turned out that the statement in the papers referred to a question put down in the House by Sir S. Scott, which he subsequently withdrew at my request.' As regards the second point, Lloyd George said that pensions would take a long time to straighten out and, as memories were short, it was important to have the grant settled sooner rather than later. 'He mentioned vaguely £100,000 for the F.M. He then went on to discuss a Peerage. I said I did not think the Field-Marshal desired a Peerage; but that were he desired to accept such an honour, he must receive a sufficient grant to enable him to maintain a suitable position, otherwise he would have to decline . . . . What did I think would be a sufficient grant? I suggested £250,000 . . . .'[82] In August, Haig received a grant of £100,000 and two months later, an earldom. He felt he had made his point as strongly as he could that the disabled must be assisted. He thought it would be ungracious to refuse a gift from his Sovereign, to whom he was close, and his reluctance was holding up a parallel award to the Navy, in the person of David Beatty being made an earl.

Lloyd George, even though he was at this point quite estranged from Haig, was so impressed by Sassoon that he would, a little more than a year later, make him his parliamentary private secretary. This interview, conducted by a young man of 30, relaunched Sassoon's London-based political career after its interruption by the war. (By an odd coincidence one of the last issues he would be involved in was the controversy over the memorial statue of Haig in Whitehall.) The negotiation was a triumph for Philip. Esher commented to him on 25 February: 'I wonder how you were received on your return to G.H.Q. It seemed to me that you went back with the plumes of Talleyrand and Metternich flowing from your red hat.'

On 13 August 1919, Philip wrote Haig a letter of congratulations although he felt that the sum of money was far from enough. 'I do not know whether the extremely slender material and temporal reward bestowed on you by the Government in recognition of your great services – or the *manner* of its bestowal – is a matter for congratulation . . . . If the official munificence has been niggardly – & we always knew it would be – you have that which is in the gift of no one – that which no one has ever received in so supreme a measure – *the respect – gratitude and love of all your fellow countrymen.* That is your unalterable possession.'[83]

He was also involved with arranging for the issuing of Haig's dispatches from December 1915 until March 1919. As early as January 1919 he was in correspondence with the publisher J.M. Dent and was in charge of the arrangements. Probably Sassoon himself had made a considerable contribution to the writing of the dispatches. When they were published later in the year they were edited by Lieutenant-Colonel J.H. Boraston, identified as Haig's private secretary for at that point Sassoon no longer held the post. Sassoon is thanked in the last dispatch as a member of Haig's personal staff, along with many others who held various positions. By error in his citation in the index he is promoted from Major to Major-General.

Philip's other preoccupation at the end of 1918 had been the hastily called general election. Held on 14 December, only a little more than a month after the end of the war, the so-called Khaki or Coupon election was a triumph for the Coalition Liberals, led by Lloyd George, although the MPs who supported him were mostly Tories. There was a rumour that Siegfried Sassoon might run against his cousin but nothing came of that. Philip was worried that his Labour opponent, Robert Forsyth, a member of the Folkestone Town Council, would do well. He was concerned that his war duties would keep him away from the constituency – on 16 November a rally was held on his behalf even before he had arrived. On 18 November Esher wrote him a quite splendid letter about the situation:

Absolutely nothing is thought of but the Election. No one remembers the war, or cares twopence about the peace terms . . . . What are your plans after you have beaten your Bolshevist candidate? . . . I cannot form any conception of what D.H. will do. Is he likely to have a Roman Triumph through the streets of London? . . . Or, will he go quietly back to the golf course at Kingston? Does he mean to sit on an office stool in Whitehall, or join the Fabians? How fortunate was Napoleon to be chained to a rock in mid ocean, so that no one but the sea gulls noticed the decay. Now for you. You like the H of C, do you not? . . . You very humanly feel no exhilaration. How should you? An exotic life for four years, then a plunge into the foggy air of our island, amid grey souled people . . . . The pagan Gods have endowed you with antennae which is the damndest of damn bad luck. There is no solution for you except to fall desperately in love, and steep yourself in the only folly which is profoundest wisdom. Do not waste any time. I am sure that your beloved little sister would agree, although she will be hideously jealous.

Since he ran as a supporter of the Coalition, led by Lloyd George, in his speeches he had to devote himself, much as it may have conflicted with his relation with Haig, to praising the Prime Minister and making the argument for a national government to be led by him. The election was a triumph for Philip; on 14 December he secured 8,809 votes to his opponent's 3,427.[84] Even so there was a whiff of anti-Semitism. Despite his being an army officer, his relationship with the Rothschilds, with their German name, was used to suggest a lack of patriotism and he was accused of being partially responsible for the government not having interned enough Germans. Sassoon now called himself a Coalition Unionist.

He wrote to Esher: 'My Election was a great strain because I had not got over the effects of my flu & developed House Maids knee early in the proceedings! But I thoroughly enjoyed it. I became quite a good speaker at the end. Syb came down to help me & won all hearts. She made a superb speech to 3,000 people at the last meeting – & the results of the poll far exceeded our most sanguine expectations, as I had been away so long & my opponent had been working *very* hard for a long time – making extravagant promises & abusing me like a pick-pocket!' Each candidate claimed that his party would do a better job in the reconstruction of the country after the war. A fellow councillor in an introduction to a speech by Forsyth called Sassoon 'a kindly gentleman ... but the working classes felt that it was time they were represented in Parliament by a man who knew the people, rather than by a millionaire – by a man who knew the facts and sufferings relating to the poor.' In reply the *Folkestone Herald* on 23 November, in supporting Sassoon, pointed out that 'the well-being of the nation and the security of their great Empire – never so great as in these glorious days – will be promoted not by setting class against class and stirring up strife between rich and poor.'[85]

Sassoon returned to France after the election. He was demobilized at the end of February, having rendered his last service to his chief. On 11 February he mentioned to Esher that he hadn't yet told Haig his intentions, adding: 'There is something corpse-like about Montreuil – the ashes of last night's fire.' And on the 27th he wrote: 'I think I am right to go, although the severing of ties, especially such pleasant happy ones as these have been, is always heart sickening. I shall never be sufficiently grateful to D.H. for all his kindness to me.' He would keep in touch with Haig until the latter's death in 1928. Over the years, Haig wrote him to thank him for gifts and letters of congratulation, to invite him to play golf, and to say that he would come to lunch with his children. It wasn't quite his world; he noted in his diary for 2 July 1919: 'In the evening we dine with Sir Philip Sassoon. A very fashionable gathering of mostly uninteresting people – Churchill and Tavish Davidson [who had been on his staff] were the exceptions.'[86] Quite a few years later in an undated letter Philip wrote to Esher: 'D.H. is a rum cove, but always was. He is no longer actively in my life – which I deplore but can see no means of remedying.'

At the end of February 1919 Sassoon wrote to Mrs Dudeney, beginning his letter: 'I hate all seasonable things – & only care for skating if it comes in June or asparagus in December .... If it had not been for the sickening consciousness of casualties I shd. have been very happy during the war – soldiers are so delightful – & hard work & continual interest & away from all the rumours & intrigues of the Home Front! But – I shall certainly not be happy in peace – & in the H. of Commons with those 700 mugs to look at – ugh!! Worse than any prison.'[87] He had begun the war with a sense of exhilaration. He felt the death of friends, but as a staff officer he was protected from the rigours of the front. He served his chief well. He moved in the world of the great and identified with the powers that be. He did not have the searing experience of his cousin Siegfried but in a sense he shared his wearied resignation, when Siegfried returned to the front after his failed protest, to the continuing course of the war. In his public career after the war, Philip became active in the question of military pre-paredness. In his style of life, as he could well afford, he committed himself, on a grand scale, to the aesthetic and country pursuits of the English gentleman.

His official date of demobilization was 1 March 1919. Philip resigned his commission on 1 January 1921, with the rank of Major. His army career was over.

4   *Becoming a Politician in the 1920s*

Philip relaunched his political career, now that peace had come. Through being on Haig's staff, he had met practically everyone who counted in the political world. The December general election gave a decisive victory to the coalition led by Lloyd George. The Liberal party under Asquith was in disarray with only 26 Members of Parliament; the Labour party had 59 MPs. There were 339 Coalition Unionists of whom Philip was one, as well as 136 Coalition Liberals. In January, even before Philip was demobilized, Lloyd George formed a new government, one that was in effect Tory, with an official Liberal Prime Minister. It was of this Parliament that Stanley Baldwin famously remarked that it consisted of a lot of 'hard-faced men who look as if they had done well out of the war'.

Esher wrote to Philip on 16 January 1919, particularly struck by the appointment of Churchill as Secretary of State for War. '*What* a Government. Winston's appointment is, of course, a gamble . . . . You have been strangely reticent of late. What are your plans, and ideas, and comments? I suspect you are demoralized by the cessation of static warfare, or are you in love. I don't know which is the worst! I shall have to write to the sister in order to get authentic information.'[1] (Alas there is no record that Philip answered the personal question.)

Churchill was also responsible for the newly formed Air Force. (Lord Rothermere, Lord Northcliffe's brother and also a press lord, had preceded him in that post, but outside the Cabinet. The previous spring, Rothermere had had a controversy with Trenchard, Chief of the Air Staff, because of what Trenchard regarded as excessive interference by Rothermere. Trenchard knew of Philip's interest in air matters and also felt that he might be an influential ally or, to put it another way, might influence those, such as Winston, who had power. In any case, he sent Philip a series of letters about the fight, concluding: 'I resigned because the Secretary of State preferred any opinion except my own.'[2] Rothermere and Trenchard both left office over the dispute.) The Royal Flying Corps had been created in 1912. In a move strongly opposed by the other military arms, in April 1918 Lloyd George had established the Air Ministry and the Royal Air Force, the first time that any state had set up its air force as an independent military entity. The war in the air had received a lot of attention during the First World War, most notably through reconnaissance and duels in the sky. There was also a growing awareness of the importance of air raids. In fact, the first bombing on British soil had been in Sassoon's constituency in Folkestone and Shorncliffe on 25 May 1917; 286 people had been killed or wounded. German daylight raids on London in the summer of 1917 caused much concern. The first one killed 162 people and injured 432. The government set up a committee, chaired by Jan Christian Smuts, that recommended the formation of the Royal Air Force.[3] It amalgamated the Corps, run by the Army, with the Royal Naval Air Service. The Air Force would not have its own sole representative at Cabinet level until Sir Samuel Hoare became Secretary of State for Air in Bonar Law's government of 1923.

In November 1919, Eric Geddes, the Minister of Transport, appointed Philip as his parliamentary private secretary, his first official position. Geddes had become a minister three months earlier; the main charge of his new position was reorganizing the railways. Questions of transport had been part of Philip's remit during the war as Haig's secretary. Geddes had been in charge of transport in all the theatres of war and their paths had intersected then. And Sybil knew Geddes when he was First Lord of the Admiralty through her involvement with the WRNS. Haig was pleased at the appointment, writing to Philip: 'I am so glad to hear that you have really got some serious work on hand. The Transportation Dept is now so v. important that you must feel satisfied to be *in it* . . . . What a lovely Stilton you sent me.'[4] Transport doesn't sound like Philip's natural *métier*, but he was presumably pleased to have some sort of official political post, suggesting that he was marked for advancement.

He did not speak much in Parliament in these early years. In June 1919 he asked about the price of telegrams to China, reflecting a traditional area of Sassoon interests. On 21 November he participated in a debate on housing, pointing out, perhaps thinking of the work he was doing on his own houses, that 'we have to-day no Merlin who can create houses for us by merely waving a magician's wand'. He urged that public authorities and public utility societies be given more help by the government in order to build new houses. A few days later, on 1 December he spoke in favour of a Premium Bond scheme.[5] I can find no indication that he played a role, despite his office, in the great railway strike of September 1919, which Lloyd George settled in the workers' favour.

Once he was settled back in London, Philip began to entertain. Among those he invited to his Park Lane mansion was David Lloyd George himself. The other guests that night in late November included Eric Geddes and Frances Stevenson, Lloyd George's secretary and mistress (she reported in her diary, 'Miss Ruth Draper recited'). On 11 December Stevenson, who was becoming very fond of this young man, recorded: 'Philip Sassoon has just dropped in for a chat. He has been very attentive lately. I think probably because he wants to get an Under-Secretaryship, or something of the kind. Nevertheless he is an amusing person, & as clever as a cartload of monkeys.' Later in December he played golf with Lloyd George, which was a great success. She recorded: 'Had a very jolly day. He is quite good company. Very ambitious though, which he admits. D. has asked him to come to Paris with us after Xmas purely D. says because he has been nice to me! He certainly has, & very attentive – almost embarrassing, in fact. He seems to be fabulously rich, but is clever also, & can be most amusing. But one of the worst gossips I have ever come across.'[6]

Sir George Riddell was also in the golfing party. He was an intimate of Lloyd George and a great press power as the owner of the *News of the World*. After golf, he went and had tea with Sassoon at Park Lane. 'He is a very intelligent well-mannered Jew with ample means.' He was rather startled by Sassoon's statement: ' "In this huge house I occupy only four rooms. Sometimes I ask myself whether the state ought not to take the rest of the house for those who cannot otherwise secure houses." This may have been said for effect, but it is a sign of the times, that such an idea should have entered a millionaire's brain.'[7] Yet this was a passing moment. Even if he might have doubts about Park Lane, he was certainly still enjoying Port Lympne. In a letter to Lord Esher on 26 December he rhapsodized about its recuperative powers:

> The magic of Lympne has worked its usual miracle & I am my own sweet self again! How lovely it is here – The sky thick smooth blue – sheer turquoise & against it the trees are outlined with that unbelievable precision that you only see in Sir Raphael Tuck's Royal Xmas cards. The stairway up the hill with its ancillary temples is near completion & look so terribly Greek that you expect the next second to see Pericles & [?] to emerge from the top, come tripping down hand in hand – *and* the beauty of the Marshes – far more beautiful in their austere winter kit than even under the flaming summer solstice or in the overcomeliness of Autumn.[8]

In February 1920 Frances Stevenson and Lloyd George were further entertained by Philip at Park Lane and at Trent. They enjoyed being in small parties with the Prince of Wales and two of his brothers, and it seemed to flow naturally that she should ask him to serve as the Prime Minister's parliamentary private secretary. The appointment went through that month; despite the growing closeness of the two men, it was considered astounding, since Haig and Lloyd George had been such enemies during the war. Philip was establishing a pattern of serving the great that put one next to political power but was not necessarily the best way to secure it for oneself. It made one a dependant, rather than an independent power with a constituency of one's own. Cecil Roth felt that one reason he was appointed was that Lloyd George was philo-Semitic.[9] He was close to Rufus Isaacs and although he didn't subscribe to it he might have found both attractive and amusing the idea that the Welsh were the lost tribe of Israel. Both Lloyd George and Sassoon were in some senses outsiders. The appointment fed into stereotypes of Jews controlling events from behind the scenes. In 1921, a nasty cartoon appeared of a very Jewish looking Philip Sassoon as the puppetmaster pulling the strings that made Lloyd George move.[10]

In March 1922, there was a curious episode on the Jewish theme, recounted in correspondence between Beaverbrook and Lloyd George. Beaverbrook was going to run an excerpt from a book by T.W.H. Crosland stating that Lloyd George was too favourable to Jews. He wrote to Lloyd George with his customary hyperbole: 'I would in the same issue publish a refutation of the charges made – pointing out that in reality you knew less [sic] Jews and more Christians than any previous Prime Minister and that the Jews you do know are such nice ones – like Philip Sassoon. I allowed Crosland to attack me in an article on the Jews in the *Sunday Express* of last week in the most unbridled style – simply because it was good journalism and good fun.' Lloyd George did not want him to go on with the issue in the paper, and left a message for Beaverbrook, 'It is gratuitously offensive and libellous. It is grossly unfair to the Jews, and I resent very strongly his attack on the Welsh people'.[11]

Crosland's book, *The Fine Old Hebrew Gentleman*, is quite offensive and anti-Semitic. Chapter XII, the section Beaverbrook referred to, does manage to insult both the Jews and the Welsh, opening with the statement: 'It has been suggested, on what grounds I don't profess to know, that the Welsh are the lost tribe of Israel. Many Welshmen certainly possess a Semitic cast of countenance. They have the Jew glitter of the eye, the Jew nose, and a tendency to psalmody, chaffering and rapacity which strikes one as being eminently Hebraic.' Crosland accuses the Welsh of coming into power in underhand ways similar to those used, he claims, by the Jews. He depicts Lloyd George as surrounded by Jews, although he mentions only Rufus Isaacs, Alfred Mond (who believes in 'Vales for the Velsh'), and Philip Sassoon, 'a rich and gaudy youth'. Crosland also disapproves of Lloyd George being entertained by Jews. He quotes a piece from the *Morning Post* of 14 January 1922, objecting to Lloyd George staying with Jews when abroad and Aristide Briand staying with Sassoon in England. 'We must not be taken to associate these financial schemes in which the Prime Minister interests himself with the Semitic entertainers who so hospitably minister to his comfort, but we are bound to say that we think it would be more appropriate if the Prime Minister, when he goes abroad upon official business, would live in a way less open to misinterpretation.'[12] Here Jews are attacked as plutocrats; elsewhere, they are stigmatized as Bolsheviks. This book, by a fairly well-known author and published by a reputable press, shows how prevalent, indeed acceptable, anti-Semitism was.

At a young age – he was now only 31 – Philip was yet again at the very centre of power, sending out letters from No. 10 Downing Street to his friends as well as making arrangements for the Prime Minister. A few fragmentary notes survive in the Lloyd George Papers of descriptions Sassoon supplied for his chief of debates in the House of Commons, presumably when the Prime Minister couldn't be there. In addition, Lloyd George enjoyed Philip's hospitality, and Philip thrived on being used. It must have rankled a little, nonetheless, that Lloyd George actually issued invitations to Philip's occasions, as when he asked Bonar Law and Beaverbrook down to Trent to dine.[13] At times Philip's parties could become a little too much even for Lloyd George, at least according to Frances Stevenson's rather idealized picture of him. In May 1921 she wrote about a visit to Trent: 'There is always such a spirit of restlessness about Philip's houses – always a crowd of people trying to be bright – & D[avid] loves peace & quietness.'[14]

As Lloyd George's parliamentary secretary, Philip was back in his element. He wrote to Esher from 10 Downing Street on 24 June: 'Here the coal strike continues, the Polo cup has been lost & the London season is at its height – all reason for blue black depression.' Lord Derby, now out of the government, sent him his views to be passed on to the Prime Minister. Still a great power because of his political influence in Lancashire, Derby was particularly eager to impress upon Philip his thoughts about the distribution of honours in his area.

Philip still did not participate much in parliamentary life at this point. Although he was very anxious to have a successful political career, he was never really at ease in the House. As he wrote in 1921, probably to his friend Mrs Dudeney: 'I am ... quite *dead beat* after a series of all night sittings in the House of Commons, and there the dawn is not rosy-fingered but yellow-thumbed; and the blue-faced bipeds that throng that academy make me feel like a very old sardine in a very old tin – or a jigsaw puzzle that no one will ever piece together (and just as well, perhaps!)'[15]

He did ask a question on 10 May, of Sir Alfred Mond, whose position, First Commissioner of Works, Philip would occupy at the end of his life, concerning Hampton Court. Why did it open so late on Sundays, at two, and why the fountains did not start to play until that hour 'in view of the fact that Sunday is the only day of the week when it is possible for the great majority of the sight-seeing public to visit Hampton Court and other places of interest of a national character?' This revealed good attention to detail and expressed his wish that the working class might be able to share in the aesthetic aspects of the state. Mond claimed that there wasn't sufficient demand but 'I will, however, consider whether it is possible to meet my hon. friend's wishes in regard to the fountains of Hampton Court, subject to a sufficient supply and pressure of water.'[16] On 7 June Philip objected to the inconvenience for his constituents in Folkestone of the need for passports to go to France, and he was told that special arrangements would be made for excursionists.

At this time he also became involved with the Prince of Wales, whom he had come to know during the First World War. Philip could be useful to the Prince as an influence upon the Prime Minister, helping him to mitigate what he regarded as the excessive demands made by his father, the King. David, as he was known among his friends, got on famously badly with George V, resenting being told what to do. At this time, he was immersed in an affair with Freda Dudley Ward, whom he had met in 1918; Philip frequently entertained them both. The Prince hated being parted from her as he had been during a long tour of Canada. He regarded that situation as 'abnormal' for a young man of 26. Then to his irritation he was back in England for only three months (three weeks to be spent with his parents in Sandringham) before being sent to New Zealand and Australia for seven months. These tours proved to be great successes, a fact the Prince regarded as rather a mixed blessing. On his travels to the Antipodes he sent a long series of very friendly letters to Philip. His hope was that through him Lloyd George could be pushed to persuade the King that the Prince be allowed to remain in England on his return, at least for a year until 1921, instead of being immediately dispatched to India, as was the plan.

He began his correspondence with Philip most fulsomely in March 1920 with a letter of gratitude: 'How much I enjoyed the marvellous week ends at Trent and your delightful "intime" dinner parties at 25 Park Lane. You have absolutely spoilt me & to crib what you said its *all* made all the difference to my life too!! ... Again all my most grateful thanks for everything (particularly the watch).'[17] He wrote about the visit to Trent to Freda: 'I nearly go crazy when I think of ... Trent, my beloved one, though if I remember rightly we were sad

25. Philip and the Prince of Wales
at Trent Park, 1920.

that night as I was such a thleeply [*sic*] and we both cwied [*sic*]!! Still those marvellous week-ends are so so divine to remember & to think about; I suppose you are down at Lympne this weekend to look at the cottage Philip is going to lend you for the summer & which alas I've never seen, which I resent!! Then as you know I hate Philip doing all these things for you sweetheart while I can do nothing of material use.'[18]

He wrote full accounts of his travels to Philip, including a report on his stopover in southern California. He was in a foul mood as after three weeks without mail he did not have the expected letters from Freda. Now he wouldn't receive mail for more than a month. 'The only letter I did get was from Philip, a charming letter & he gave me news of you sweetheart but I don't count anything but YOUR letters!!'[19] In another letter the same day he wrote to her, 'All I have to console me is Philip's letter & he does give me a few lines of news of you mon amour ... so he dined with you the evening I left sweetie & it produces fresh sobs sweetie when he says "she was terrible miserable!!"' There is a possibility that Wallis Simpson may have met the Prince for the first time in San Diego, either at a dance or at a presentation on the USS *New Mexico*. She denied that the dance meeting took place and makes no reference to an earlier onboard meeting.[20] The Prince was particularly concerned at not hearing from Freda because of his excitement at the possibility that she might be pregnant by him. Commenting on the evening to Philip, he went on: 'There were quite a few movie stars at the Coronado Hotel tho. such awful women as one has never seen . . . . It's quite amazing how men particularly officers of either service can take an interest in the most awful looking women, & generally without the least idea of sleeping with them as there isn't time as a rule for them to do all they want to on these 24 hr. visits.' He then went on to apologize if he had said too much to Lloyd George about not wanting to go to India and had caused problems with his father at 'Buckhouse'. 'Still I'm keener than ever for India to be postponed till Oct. 1921 & wish you & the P.M. all success in your efforts on my behalf for which I'm ever so grateful to you both!!' He went on to thank Philip for all the books he had lent him. On 11 June he wrote from Melbourne:

> The doctor wanted me to be out of doors all day to rest my '*brain*' as he calls it (tho. there's so little of it) . . . [Freda] says Lympne is too marvellous for words & how I'm longing to see your wonderful house in Kent. How I wish I could write marvellous & amusing letters as you do Philip but I just cant . . . . It is so good of you to have had him [Bertie] & Harry to Lympne & they loved Trent almost as much as I did tho. it wldn't be possible to love it as much as I do!! . . . I'm also glad the cigarette box reached you only please don't ever smoke!! Give my love to Herbertpooroldman [Philip's chow].

Although the Prince hadn't yet been to Lympne, Philip was intent on making both it and Trent more attractive for him. The Prince was very fond of squash and he wrote to Freda on 27 June 'Philip writing 2 or 3 letters by each mail saying he's building squash courts both there [Trent] & at Lympne so that I can play when I stay with him for weekends!!' By this point, whether he went to India had become less of an issue since Freda had apparently written to him saying that their affair was over, for the sake of her two children. He now felt it might be good in that case if he were out of England. On 30 June he wrote to her again that he had received a cable in code from Philip saying that he was hopeful that he could prevent the visit to India, although the Prince doesn't see how he could do that, considering that Lloyd George wanted him to go. 'I've just had a cable from him & in our code sweetie (which means that you must have worked it out for him from our little unicode book) . . . . Am I to tell Philip to abandon his efforts or encourage him? And yet why do you let him continue with them or anyway why don't you put the brake on if you think I ought to go!!' But by mid-July she had changed her mind, much to his delight. On 5 July he wrote to Philip that he was enjoying Sydney more than Melbourne, but he was fed up with the press entourage on the trip, a 'bunch of the completest shits that call themselves pressmen'. He was concerned that they might have complained to Riddell who would have told Lloyd George. 'You can tell the P.M. that you've heard from me & that I've told you what impossible shits our pressmen are . . . . The biggest shit of the bunch is *Keith Murdoch* of the Times.' Murdoch had written an article entitled 'The Unpunctual Prince'. But the Prince may well have exaggerated because of his depressed and exhausted state. At this point he had had virtually a complete breakdown; there was no question that he was being made to do too much. The King finally did become concerned about his health and the schedule was pruned.

On 23 July he reported to Freda that Philip had cabled again that he hoped that he could postpone India and that Lloyd George would talk to the King about it. On the 27th he heard from the King that the Indian trip had been put off a year and he told her how grateful he was to Philip. 'Good old Philip; I bet I owe more to him than to anyone else for this postponement & how grateful I am to him!!' On 3 August he wrote to Philip himself. 'What a big debt I owe you my dear Philip I cant possibly write all I feel about it wait till we meet thank *you* thank *you* thank *you* thank *you* . . . . The joy of the thought that instead of a short month I'm to spend a whole year in the Old Country! . . . [Freda] tells me she is going to spend Aug and Sept. in the cottage at Lympne with her babies which will be divine for her & so good for her too!! . . . By the way do you ever see the "Duke of York" [the title had just been bestowed upon him] nowadays? I'm afraid old Bertie is getting rather pompous. You mustn't let him do that & anyway I'll knock it out of him what I get back!!' He felt, however, that Bertie might go to India in his place, where, as he wrote to Freda, 'it's all apparently so pompous as he's rather pompous himself!!' On 9 September on the way back home, he wrote to Philip complaining that his father

> makes me laugh a lot when he writes a lot of balls, how he has postponed it [the trip to India] on the *advice* of *his* ministers!! . . . I'm in for some very difficult days when I first get back (to Buckhouse, I mean) as I'm taking this 7 months' absence & slavery as an excuse to change things there & to show them that I'm not going to be wetnursed or interfered with any more!! . . . And what is more Philip I've *got* to win & come out on top or it'll be the end of me . . . . Of course all this is naturally *terribly private.* I've no doubt written some curious things but I write them to you because you understand & have been nice enough to take an interest in me (just as I do in you) & have become a real friend & help & confidant!! . . . I'm thinking of nothing else but of you & *Freda* & her babies down at Lympne all this time; oh! I mustn't forget Herbert . . . . I'm longing to see that marvellous place [Port Lympne] & now so *famous* for the conferences held there . . . . I see snaps in the paper of you playing polo . . . . By the way Philip I've never yet thanked you (except by cable) for those perfect onyx & diamond links which I love & wear very often alas I broke the glass of your marvellous flat watch at Brisbane . . . . You absolutely spoil me Philip.

Philip had given the cufflinks to the Prince as a birthday present; as he wrote to Freda 'how that man does spoil me'.

While he was on his tour he was quite close to Philip, pleased to hear from him about the state of play on the Indian trip and news of Freda. When the two men actually met again in England, the Prince was less loving. Before leaving, he referred to Sassoon, in a letter of 28 December 1919, as 'the Turk'; he also mentioned that Philip had 'sent me a most lovely Xmas present, a vurry vurry ancient snuff box'. Back in England, in a letter to Freda on 22 December, he wrote: 'What a bore. Philip is getting huffy because I didn't say goodbye to him, though it's our fault or perhaps more mine for having got into this state of daily communication with him! We must try to somewhat loosen the ropes with which he has bound himself so tightly ... though of course we'll keep in with him & make use of him to a certain extent!! I like a little of Philip very much but not too much.' On Boxing Day he wrote to Philip from York Cottage on the Sandringham estate, where he was cooped up with his parents. (His grandmother, Queen Alexandra, still lived in the main house.) 'What a nice quiet Xmas you must have spent at Lympne with Hannah & David [Gubbay]; it's quiet here but oh! How boring & even irksome at times. Thank you again ever so much for all your lovely Xmas presents Philip; I don't deserve this spoiling *at all* or all the wonderful help you've given me over my room in London.' The Prince had moved out of the family home, Buckingham Palace, although the King had felt it was big enough for a father and an unmarried son. The Prince now had his own place, a wing of St James's Palace. Philip advised him on the decoration of his new quarters. In an undated letter to Esher, Philip remarked: 'The young Prince is madder than ever about decoration – his dinner party was very well done – & he made a charming host – bachelors do, don't you think?' On 28 December the Prince commented about a clipping he had been sent that contained anti-Semitic remarks about his friendship with Philip. He did send it on to Freda, remarking that it was 'a very unnecessary thing to have written & which I naturally entirely disregard!! But I sent it as it will amuse you though it's foul & not at all true.' Philip continued to send him objects for his new quarters. On 26 June 1920 the Prince wrote to him: 'Thank you ever so much for your *marvellous* present – you are far too kind to me but I cant tell *how* pleased I am with these priceless prints & the match box too – *The* very things I wanted & I'm hanging them (not the match box!!) in my bed room today.' In January 1921 Philip arranged for the Prince to sit for a drawing by Sargent. The Prince wanted to have the sittings while Philip was away 'so as not to be worried by Philip!!'

Yet Philip certainly continued to see him on very intimate terms, writing to Lord Esher on 27 March 1921, 'I had a little dinner ... just Freda & Hannah & the young Prince & George Carpentier [the famous French boxer]! It was marvellous fun.' On 28 April he wrote again to Esher about his coming to dinner: 'my divine sister and Hannah & the young Prince will all be there to greet you'. The Prince was very fond of Hannah Gubbay, whom he would visit and gossip with on the phone, at one point frequently calling her twice a day, sharing with her his intense irritation at having to spend time with his parents at Sandringham.[21] On 4 March 1924 Philip dined at Hannah's house; the only other guest was the Prince. The relationship between the Prince and Philip was sufficiently informal that Philip could dash away in the middle of dinner upon receiving a message that he had forgotten that he was to dine elsewhere. The next day, Philip recorded, the Prince telephoned Hannah at their Aunt Louise's, where she was having lunch. Aunt Louise rather meanly remarked: 'I wonder what he *can* have to say to you.'[22] Some years later, in 1929, Philip put him in touch with a merchant who might supply rugs for his country house, Fort Belvedere. The Prince commented in a letter on 10 November that he hoped 'that his wares are really as cheap as you assure me they are. The trouble is that your's and my ideas of cheapness dont always quite tally.' The Prince largely used Philip for his own purposes – helping to postpone India and providing hospitality for him and for Freda – but he also enjoyed sharing his social life with him.

26. John Singer Sargent, *The Prince of Wales*, 1921.

As Lloyd George's parliamentary private secretary, Philip also provided divertissements and luxuries for the Prime Minister and his mistress at Park Lane, Trent and Port Lympne. Lloyd George enjoyed coming down frequently to play golf on local courses. One Easter Philip went with him to a local Baptist chapel. Philip was quite without religion himself, although he maintained his formal synagogue membership. He was, however, very superstitious and had for good luck a replica of a cobra on all his cars and aeroplanes. This may have been a vestigial memory from India, where the cobra has sacred implications.

Philip's homes provided places where the world of politics could go forward, with special attention to the diplomatic situation. The Paris Peace Conference had finally officially concluded on 10 January 1920, and was succeeded by a series of meetings to consider similar problems, most usually Germany's failure to live up to the terms of the Treaty, particularly over questions of reparations. The aim of British policy was to help in the reconstruction of

Europe and also to attempt to hammer out some form of better Anglo-French co-operation. Lloyd George established international conferences as a distinctive way of pursuing foreign policy.

In March 1920 the Germans requested permission to enter the Ruhr, allegedly to subdue a Communist rising. On 3 April the Germans went into the Ruhr and the French retaliated by occupying Frankfurt and Darmstadt. This put the British in a difficult position, as the French were acting unilaterally. The problem was discussed at San Remo in April 1920 with Philip in attendance. Also, at its very end, that conference ratified the Balfour Declaration and transformed the administration of Palestine from a military to a civilian one. Herbert Samuel was appointed the first High Commissioner. Chaim Weizmann had come to San Remo and was quite miffed by Sassoon's lack of interest in Palestine. As a matter of fact though, from Weizmann's point of view, it was probably just as well, because if Philip had been active on that issue it probably would have been as an anti-Zionist. Philip had no interest in Jewish issues. Weizmann had arrived late in a furious state, pointing out to Philip Kerr, Lloyd George's secretary, that earlier that month in Palestine there had been the first pogrom that had taken place under British rule: three days of riots that in his view the British authorities had done little to curb. Weizmann did not quite understand the niceties and thought that Sassoon, like Kerr, was a civil servant. Weizmann remarked: 'The only man to ignore the whole business [of Palestine] was Philip Sassoon, another of Lloyd George's secretaries, – and, as it happens, the only Jewish member of the British delegation.'[23] The French and British did declare their unity at San Remo on issues of disarmament and reparations.

In May the first meeting between Lloyd George and the French Prime Minister, Alexandre Millerand, took place at Port Lympne and put Philip's house at the centre of the news. The French and the British were not getting on well and needed to be on better terms in order to deal effectively with the Germans: forcing them to pay reparations, to follow the disarmament clauses of Versailles and to deliver coal to France and Belgium. Port Lympne was conveniently close to France, and Philip was a superb host, providing splendid food, Rolls-Royces to go about in, and Charlie Chaplin movies at Sybil's suggestion to break the tension. Philip refurbished the Octagon Library as a venue for the signing of treaties. The French felt that they were not receiving enough from the Germans and were not mollified by the gathering. Maurice Hankey, the Secretary to the Cabinet who was at the meeting, regarded this conference as a failure.[24]

In its 26 May issue *Punch* remarked that Philip, through his lavish hospitality, was paying for the equivalent of the Field of the Cloth of Gold. At the time of the conference, Oswald Mosley attacked Philip in ways that might have whiffs of anti-Semitism. (At this point he was a Tory MP; in October he joined the Labour party and later became the leader of British Fascism.) Mosley described Lloyd George at Port Lympne during the conferences as living in the 'state of a Roman Emperor . . . regaled in the evening with the frankincense of admiring friends . . . [and] liberal applications of precious ointment from the voluptuous Orient'. According to Mosley, Sassoon 'was rather a joke among the younger generation for serving

27. Rex Whistler, *Vignette of Octagon Library, Port Lympne*, 1930.

Lloyd George as Private Secretary in peace directly after he had served during the war in the same capacity to General Haig'. In the 1930s, when Mosley was the most famous anti-Semite in England, he and Philip were nevertheless polite to one another when they met at the table of the famous hostess, Lady Cunard, when she was entertaining the Prince of Wales and Wallis Simpson. Was this an example of Philip's willingness to accept the intolerable, or did it illustrate that English social conventions, for better or worse, were such that Philip and Mosley could easily dine together?[25]

Despite Hankey's misgivings, the May meeting was more successful than the follow-up; this second so-called Hythe Conference was held on 19–20 June, again at Port Lympne. At that time Greek–Turkish relations were on the table. Lloyd George was almost alone in being pro-Greek in contrast to his Cabinet colleagues and the French, and his pro-Greek policy failed. The French and British also attempted, without great success, to co-ordinate the position they would take when they next met the Germans. A photograph survives of the June meeting, with Sybil and Hannah there as hostesses, as well as Herbert, the dog, directly in front of Lloyd George. Also present on the French side were General Weygand and Marshal Foch and on the English Austen Chamberlain, at this point Chancellor of the Exchequer, Sir Henry Wilson, Chief of the Imperial General Staff, and Hankey.

These conferences were preliminary to the meeting the French and British held with the Germans at Spa from 5 to 16 July 1920. Philip kept a diary account of that event. Occasional diaries do survive in the Sassoon Papers; one doesn't know if he kept many that were lost or

28. Lloyd George and Sybil at Port Lympne, April 1921.

29. (*below*) The Second Hythe Conference, 19–20 June 1920 at Port Lympne. From left to right: Philip Sassoon, Maxime Weygand, Ferdinand Foch, Henry Wilson, Sybil Rocksavage, David Gubbay, Lloyd George, Herbert the chow, Philip Kerr, Hannah Gubbay, Alexandre Millerand, Austen Chamberlain, two unknown gentlemen and Maurice Hankey.

wrote them only when he felt he was participating in events that were particularly important, or wished to keep a journal of a trip. There is no question that if he had left indiscreet
diaries, they would have been extremely valuable and amusing. One yearns to know what he
thought of the great and famous among whom he moved. How much satisfaction did it give
him that through his skill and money he was able to help move the great enterprises of the
state forward? It gave him pleasure to serve men such as Haig and Lloyd George and it certainly put him at the centre of the world of power. The comparatively few pages of fragmentary diaries that remain contain little of his celebrated wit and hardly live up to Frances
Stevenson's characterization of Philip as a gossip. Perhaps Spa was not a suitable place for
such talents. The issues there were Germany's failure to comply with the disarmament
requirements of the Versailles Treaty. This was the first time that the Germans had nego-
tiated directly with the French and the British, and to the irritation of Parliament and the
press in London, they proved very difficult.

Philip went to Spa with Lloyd George, Lord Curzon the Foreign Secretary, Wilson,
Hankey and others. He described the arrival of the party at Ostend in a long letter to Lady
Desborough written on 6 July: 'The Quay was lined with Belgian Girl Guides carrying flags
and cardboard laurel wreaths & as our good ship drew alongside 37 men in 37 bowlers played
37 verses of the German National Anthem (by mistake, by the force of habit).' In the same
letter he went on to describe the hotel in Brussels. 'It was supposed to have a bad reputation
– so we were disappointed to find that we were all to dine in a private room & have no
chance of inspecting the Promised Land.' Lloyd George was unhappy that he was not to be
able to observe the women in the dining room; Philip was unsuccessful in his attempt to
have the location moved. He also felt that the Belgians, including the chambermaids, were
complaining too much about how they had suffered during the war. In Brussels Lloyd
George met individually with the French, the Belgians and the Italians to discuss the proportion of German reparations due to each.

En route to Spa, the party had lunch at Waterloo. Philip remarked in the diary: 'It is all
very Lillyputian after the battlefields of the Somme & Flanders – & makes me realize that the
warfare of Waterloo was nearer akin to Thermophylae than to Neuve Chapelle.'[26] In his letter
to Lady Desborough he wrote: 'There is something very dramatic about this Conference.
The Germans coming on their knees to this place which was their G.H.Q. when their hopes
were highest. This hotel was the office of Ludendorf & Hindenberg and it was in the room
next to mine that the Kaiser abdicated. The villa where the conference is being held was his
last abode before his flight into Holland.'[27] In his diary, he is critical of the French for dressing comparatively informally in order to do down the Germans. On the 5th the Germans
pledged to fulfil the terms of Versailles, yet the next day claimed that they were unable to
reduce their forces by 100,000 because of the need to cope with the Communist menace.

On 10 July the question was discussed of how much coal the Germans could supply. A
crisis arose on the 12th as Millerand, the French Prime Minister, said that he must return to
Paris for Bastille Day. Lloyd George replied that he would have to tell Parliament that
Millerand could not stay and, Philip noted in his diary pages,

that the Conference had had to break up without any definite result because Mons. Millerand insisted on going to Paris so as to stand in the sun for 4 hours without his hat on. Surely there was some colleague of his who could take his place with fatal results to him & consequently advantage to himself (L.G. had told us at breakfast that if he were similarly placed he wd. send Winston.)

On 13 July the group went for a picnic, buying German beer and sausages and having 'a succulent lunch in a very beautiful little ravine by the side of a river . . . . Which simple pleasures proved a great relaxation to [Lloyd George]. He has had to do more fighting at this Conference than ever before. That is where the American defection is bad because they wd. have stood by him on all these questions, as it is always hard to fight the French single handed.' The Germans were being unco-operative about coal. The conference was suspended on 14 July. On the 15th possible military action against Germany was discussed. Foch was for occupying the Ruhr. The idea was that the Army would enforce the importation of German coal to France, Belgium and Italy. But an agreement was reached that satisfied France and Britain on the issue of reparations, although Henry Wilson felt that the Germans would not honour their promises. They eventually accepted it, under the threat of military action. Lloyd George was pursuing a policy of moderation that alienated the more hard-line Conservatives. He was also antagonizing the French whom, according to Hankey, he compared to Shylock in their attitude to the Germans. One doesn't know what Sassoon thought of the comparison. Nor is there any mention of the Jewish Walther Rathenau being a member of the German delegation – whose reasonable attitude towards reparations led him to be labelled by Hugo Stinnes, the other highly prominent German industrialist present at Spa, as a member of an alien race.[28]

On the return to England, there was a third Hythe conference in August about Polish issues. Further meetings at the house in April 1921 discussed the possibility of harsher sanctions against Germany. Philip was happy to supply venues for whatever the Prime Minister wished. Rather incongruously, in October his London house was used as the location for a secret meeting between Lloyd George and the leaders of the miners in order to attempt to settle a strike. (Perhaps it was the last place the press would expect to find union leaders.) Park Lane was also where De Valera and Lloyd George had met to discuss the Irish treaty in privacy. Similarly in September 1922, in the midst of the great crisis over Turkey and Greece, issues were discussed over a 'sumptuous' dinner at Park Lane with only Lloyd George, Churchill, Hankey and Sassoon present.[29] And at Lympne Churchill and Lloyd George spent New Year's Eve, 1920, as well as the weekends of 9 and 29 January. On New Year's Day Lloyd George asked Churchill to move from the War Office to the Colonial Office. Churchill wrote to his wife: 'We picknicked on the slope of that big hill by the chalk pit amid the sunshine wh heralded spring, & the popping of Champagne corks wh heralded a sumptuous repast.'[30]

The Genoa Conference, to which the Russians came, in the spring of 1921 raised the question of reconciliation with Russia. Sassoon wrote to Lloyd George about Churchill's fury at the possibility: 'He is *fulminating* against Genoa & says there is seething public indignation against it – but I fancy that these lava streams are chiefly in the crater of his own breast.'[31] Sassoon's criticisms of Churchill did not prevent him from being a frequent guest at Port Lympne and at Trent. Entertaining was a central role for Philip and it fitted in with what is generally seen as a saving grace of British politics: it is very rare for political controversy to interfere with social life. Churchill wrote to his wife about a dance at Park Lane that both Asquith and Lloyd George attended: 'The old boy [Asquith] turned up at Philip's party vy heavily loaded. The P.M. accompanied him up the stairs & was chivalrous enough to cede him the banister. It was a wounding sight. He kissed a great many people affectionately. I presume they were all relations.'[32]

At his three houses Philip entertained 'everyone' who counted as well as a few who did not. He would only invite those he wished to invite; he once declined to ask Lloyd George's daughter Megan when it had been suggested to him that it might be a tactful step. He was certainly in the know and at the centre of events. His career was undoubtedly helped by his entertaining and there were bound to be satisfactions. Whatever some of his guests actually may have thought of him, they saw no reason why they should not take advantage of the hospitality so freely given by this charming and amusing man. Although his sister or his cousin frequently acted as his hostess, the lack of a wife made the atmosphere more infor-mal. And his bachelor state probably made little difference to his political career, nor did the suspicion of some that he might be a homosexual. An unconventional private life, whether hetero- or homosexual, generally did not cause problems as long as it remained resolutely private. Public scandal of any sort would be devastating for a political career. Did being Jewish curtail his political career? Philip didn't take his religion seriously and he could only hope that others would not see it as a bar. Some thought he was a Parsee; as the number of prominent Indians in Britain was so slight at the time, there was no particular prejudice against them. On the other hand, anti-Semitism was quite prevalent in British society. Some Jews had attained Cabinet rank earlier – Samuel, Reading, Montagu – but comparatively few in the inter-war period, other than Alfred Mond in the early 1920s and Leslie Hore-Belisha in the late 1930s. In Britain, Jews were certainly not totally integrated into the dominant society. Were they a separate race? Racism was a very powerful force in British society. Most Jews, and certainly middle- and upper-class ones, did not look different from the rest of the population but for some this might make them even more disconcerting as a potential force of disarray, even more dangerous because unnoticeable.[33] Philip with his dark looks, his exotic nature, his Eton, Oxford and military background, and his great wealth, could not more clearly have been an 'outsider' as 'insider'.

A letter that Philip wrote to Lloyd George in 1921 shows that he did have political ambition:

You know that my interest in politics is much more than a passing fancy or the desire to enjoy such privileges as a seat in the House may give. My interest is indeed very deep and it is for this reason alone that I am presuming to write to ask that when changes are made in the Government you will give me a friendly thought and if possible obtain for me the chance to shew in some minor office that in course of time I may become worthy of bigger things. You know that I have now been almost 10 years in the House of Commons & that for the last six years I had had the good fortune to see a great deal of the inner workings of both the military and civil machines . . . . I am really very anxious to get a chance to make a start in politics [in] a more responsible, though possibly less interesting, position than I have yet held.[34]

He shared his ambitions with others. Later in the month Churchill wrote to Lloyd George recommending Sassoon to him for promotion: 'I promised to mention Philip Sassoon to you. You can judge better than anyone else. Personally I should like to see him given an opportunity and I think he would do well.'[35] In April 1922, when Lloyd George and his mistress were occupying Danehurst, a house on the Port Lympne property, Philip asked Lloyd George to give him the position of Chancellor of the Duchy of Lancaster which Lord Peel had vacated. 'The PM had been kind & faltering and promised nothing.'[36] And indeed nothing happened.

The rest of his time with Lloyd George was largely devoted to the question of how long Lloyd George could hold on to office. At the end of 1921 he had resolved the Irish issue through the creation of the Irish Free State. While there was no end to warfare in Ireland itself, it was now largely an Irish problem. Sassoon advised Lloyd George to try to maintain his power by gaining the support of the central group of MPs, the moderate Tories and the moderate Liberals. He wrote to his master about the endless ins and outs of politics, who would do what, and what various figures, most notably Churchill, were thinking. In the Lloyd George Papers some fragmentary notes survive, impressions of events and reports of discussions in the House of Commons. Apparently Philip also maintained his independence to a degree. In August 1921 he voted, according to Austen Chamberlain, the Chancellor of the Exchequer, against the government on one unspecified issue. Chamberlain sent Lloyd George a note: 'Prime Minister Please ask your Private Secretary to be careful not to get in the wrong lobby again.'[37]

The Prime Minister had the responsibility to decide when to ask the King to call a general election. There were endless calculations as to when that event should take place to be the most advantageous for the party in power. On 19 December 1921, Sassoon wrote a thirteen-page memorandum entitled 'The Political Situation'. In it he cited the economic depression as the reason for the growth of support of the Labour party, which was in the process of replacing the Liberals as the party of opposition. He also felt that the voter could not follow the fights that were going on between the various sorts of Liberals and Tories. It would clearly be better to call an election when trade had revived and the workers would be in a better mood and state. Sassoon pointed out what he saw as the achievements of the government: the making of the peace after the war and the Irish success. He believed it was important to be able to choose the time of the election and not to have it when Parliament was forced to dissolve in a year's time. He advised an election as soon as possible on the basis of the need to reconstitute Parliament after the Irish agreement, the recommendations of the committee chaired by Sir Eric Geddes to make economies, and the settlement of international questions. Sassoon concluded that 'there should be a general election at the earliest practicable moment; and that in any event the dissolution should not be postponed beyond Easter'.[38] However, this did not happen.

The following March he wrote a letter to Esher analysing the political situation. He now felt that it was time for Lloyd George to resign:

I feel in my bones that Ll.G. ought for his own sake to go at once. No patch up will avert the coming smash – & he has a chance of jumping clear. But Winston (whose views are always personal) advised him to hang on – *because* Winston does not want to give up his job. I am sure he means to join the Tories at the earliest possible moment. I hope Ll. G. will do something for me in any event, but I am not counting on it too much – for I know his nature. It is all thrilling & heart breaking at the same time. How right *I* was when I urged the January election. Ireland was an asset *then* & was *bound* to become a liability.[39]

That month Edwin Montagu, the Secretary of State for India, resigned in protest over Lloyd George's pro-Greek and anti-Turkish policy and also because of Montagu's indiscretion in allowing the Government of India to object to a British foreign policy decision. Lloyd George wasn't pleased, remarking in a letter to Frances Stevenson that 'Montagu is a swine of a sneak. When I come back I'll recircumcise him.' In the same letter he also wrote: 'Tell Philip I am very pleased with his letter .... I entirely agree with him in his estimate of Winston.'[40] Sassoon actually felt that the situation was now even more difficult. Lloyd George was endangering his support by moderate Liberals and moderate Conservatives.

His advice was not taken, and the general election did not take place until November 1922. The month before the election, Lloyd George was disowned by his Conservative followers in a famous meeting of Conservative MPs at the Carlton Club. That gathering, on 19 October, marks the birth of the modern post-war Conservative party, which would be in power for so many of the remaining years of the twentieth century. It was expected that the Tory MPs would come to Lloyd George's support; instead they rebelled and Bonar Law was willing to become their leader. The previous June Derby, perhaps one among many, had written to tell Sassoon that Lloyd George had made a serious mistake by going off to so many international conferences and neglecting the political situation at home. This was, in his view, a major reason that the Coalition was bound to break up. Sir George Younger, the chairman of the Conservative party organization, believed that the Coalition should contest the election as such. But at the Carlton, the Tory MPs, by a vote of 185 to 88, decided to fight the election, unlike the 1918 one, as an independent party – that is, to leave the Coalition.

Stanley Baldwin, the President of the Board of Trade, made the most notable speech of the day, denouncing Lloyd George as 'a dynamic force ... a very terrible thing', someone who would smash the Conservative party, as he had the Liberal party. Sassoon was at the meeting as a Coalition Unionist. When he rushed out of the Club looking green in the face Mrs Baldwin, who was sitting in a car outside, knew that her side had won and Lloyd George would no longer be Prime Minister.[41] Mrs Baldwin apparently reported several versions of the colour of Philip's face. In her own account she manages to denigrate in two sentences Philip, his car and his chauffeur. 'Opposite our car was stationed a rather unwholesome-looking Rolls-Royce car with a small but "bookie"-looking chauffeur with a snake about to strike as its mascot [this was Philip's good luck cobra]. Suddenly there burst through the crowd a yellowish-white drawn face and the slight figure of a man who jumped into this car and was off in a flash.'[42]

Philip rendered both Haig and Lloyd George considerable service. It would be hard to imagine two men who were not only enemies but were more different in temperament and values: the stolid unemotional Scot and the mercurial Welshman. Sassoon displayed adaptability and skill, and it sheds light on his character that he could get on so well with such different leaders. Probably Lloyd George was more enjoyable to work for but with Haig he participated in even greater events. He remained on good terms with both men but after their official connections were over they rarely figured in Sassoon's circle or he in theirs.

Bonar Law replaced Lloyd George as Prime Minister and Sassoon was not part of the government he formed. He did receive an honour on Lloyd George's resignation, a GBE, Grand Commander in the Order of the British Empire. Esher remarked to him in a letter of 24 October, referring yet again to what would appear to be an imagined heterosexual love life: 'I suppose you have settled to remain a Commoner!! Anyway, do not marry. It is so un-chic in these days.' Lloyd George was notorious for selling honours in order to build up his party treasury. But Philip was much too young to receive a peerage and in any case he realized that he could have more of a political career in the House of Commons. Indeed it would be after Bonar Law's brief ministry that Lord Curzon expected to be the next Prime Minister rather than the man he regarded as 'insignificant': Stanley Baldwin. A major reason for Curzon's failure to achieve that eminence was his membership of the House of Lords.

Lloyd George spent the night of the election, 15 November, at Sassoon's house in Park Lane. Sassoon had installed ticker-tape machines to record what turned out to be the crushing defeat of the wartime Prime Minister and many of his political followers who were running for election. Sassoon himself was unopposed in his constituency. Lloyd George was not to hold political office again in the course of his long life; he died in 1945. The Conservatives easily won the election. William Orpen was at Sassoon's that night as well, and wrote a bit of doggerel verse: '... Then the little band [of ticker tape]/ Ran smoothly out in Philip's hand. Curling, curling like a snake/Till Philip's hand began to shake/ Impossible!'[43] During Bonar Law's short-lived government (he resigned in May 1923 and shortly thereafter died), Sassoon loyally offered up Park Lane as a headquarters for Lloyd George's followers. In October when there was a possibility that Curzon might become Prime Minister, Sassoon's London house became the base for his supporters. However, when Baldwin became Prime Minister Sassoon began to switch his allegiance. In the not too distant future Baldwin would be enjoying the hospitality of Trent Park, not only as Philip's guest but at times having the house for the sole use of himself and his wife. The powerful were not reluctant to take advantage of his generosity but it earned him little credit. He did not have a political base in the party and hence had little support that he could bring to the table. Prime ministers did not strengthen their position by appointing him to office.

The tradition of the Jewish grandees was that they did not, on the whole, pursue Jewish causes, so that was not a possible political base, even if Sassoon had been interested. There has almost been an implied contract that in return for the right of political participation Jews would not pursue identity politics. Zionism was becoming a more important issue and Jewish politicians might feel increasingly strongly on the issue, either for or against. But Philip had little interest in the future of Palestine.

In 1923 C.K. Scott-Moncrieff, the translator of Proust, wrote a poem, privately printed and published anonymously, that reveals the sort of abuse Philip had to face. I know of no reason why Scott-Moncrieff should have been abusive about Philip, particularly as one might have thought he would have been sympathetic to Philip's Proustian world. Nor does one know why this bit of verse should have been preserved in the papers of Eddie Marsh, the literary patron and Winston Churchill's secretary. Philip did make himself useful to the powerful, and he ran the risk of being seen as obsequious. This bit of doggerel was called 'A Servile Statesman' and some of its lines ran:

> Sir Philip Sassoon is a member for Hythe
> He is opulent, generous, swarthy, and lithe,
> Obsequious, modest, informal and jejune . . . .
> The houses he inhabits are costly but chaste
> But Sir Philip Sassoon is unerring in taste . . .
> Sir Philip Sassoon and his sires, it appears,
> Have been settled in England for several years
> Where their friendly invasion impartially brings
> To our Cabinet credit, and cash to our Kings . . . .
> Sir Philip was always a double event,
> A Baghdadi banker, a yeoman of Kent
> But now in four parts he's appearing at once,
> As a lackey, a landlord, diplomatist, dunce.[44]

One might almost think that Philip was better described, although obviously T.S. Eliot did not have him in mind, in some of the famous lines of 'The Love Song of J. Alfred Prufrock', published in 1917.

> . . . Not Prince Hamlet, nor was meant to be;
> Am an attendant lord, one that will do
> To swell a progress, start a scene or two,
> Advise the prince; no doubt, an easy tool,
> Deferential, glad to be of use,
> Politic, cautious, and meticulous;
> Full of high sentence, but a bit obtuse;
> At times, indeed, almost ridiculous –
> Almost, at times, the Fool.

Philip was certainly intelligent but in a sense his role, in his lavish entertainments of the great, had some similarity to that of the court jester. And although he did not organize the finances of his employers, in his great outlay of expense on their behalf he was somewhat in the continental tradition of the Court Jew, even harking back to his Baghdadi ancestors.

Scott-Moncrieff brings to mind a letter preserved in the family archives at Houghton, where comparatively little has been saved other than material from the First World War. It is an undated letter from Marcel Proust to Philip. Proust was familiar with Philip's grandmother's Rothschild circle; they had a mutual friend in the composer Reynaldo Hahn but they had never met. Philip had sent Proust three volumes of *A la recherche du temps perdu*, via the wife of José Maria Sert, the famous Misia, to be signed for an unidentified lady friend. The situation is positively Proustian.

> I would like to reply to your most gracious request in the most gracious manner. But I do not know the 'female admirer.' If she is unknown to me and benefits from the honor of your friendship, naturally I will not permit myself a mere dedication but above my signature I shall copy out an entire page to give the book a special value. If on the contrary, she were an enemy of mine using your name to obtain from me what she could not ask for herself, even my simple signature would seem too much and I would prefer to send you the books unsigned. A third case could present itself and that's that the lady imagines that the book was written by Marcel Prévost . . . . If ever I should see you . . . I should tell you what a delightful pastiche I wrote about you about one year ago . . . . For a long time I heard nothing from you save a watery murmur. I was dining at the Ritz (where often I took a room for several hours in order to avoid those in the dining room) and thinking I had no neighbor, I explained to a waiter who had undertaken the role of Sosie [a character from Molière] for the Conservatory the gist of the Molière play . . . . Presently menacing sounds nearby made themselves heard. I became aware of a true deluge near to me and I did not doubt that to punish my irreverent explanations Jove was throwing his thunder. But no, I was told it was Sir Philip Sassoon, taking a bath. There, sir, an even worse deluge of explanations, and for a trifle.[45]

Philip spent some time on foreign travel in the period between the fall of Lloyd George and his return to office in November 1924. His trips were that of a rather conventional well-connected and rich young man. Even before the fall of the government he took a trip to Spain and Morocco in March and April 1922. He went with an unidentified friend named Jack (perhaps his fellow officer from the time of the war). They went to Madrid, Toledo, Seville and once they had to spend the night in their car on the road as they ran out of petrol. In Gibraltar Philip won £32 at the Casino and was quite irritated when a lady remarked to him, 'They always do say that those that don't need it usually win.'

They sailed over to Morocco on a British destroyer, visiting Casablanca, where they lunched with Lyautey, the great French pro-consul. They then went on to Rabat, where Philip had an eye for the ladies. 'Over the balcony that divided us from the adjoining room we caught sight of a ravishing peach – but alas on seeing us she retired hastily & banged the window – thus dashing our hopes.' The wife of their host that night 'turned out to be an old flame of mine – a dream of beauty & very nice. Jack says I talked to her the whole evening & did not do my duty by the other members of the party . . . . We dressed chicly for dinner in our evening clothes which consisted of flannel suits and bedroom slippers.' On 26 March they went from Rabat to Fez, admiring 'the beautiful gate leading into the Sultan's gardens – so well described by Loti'. At a dinner there he remarked that 'two of the ladies were as bright as buttons – one of them – a bride of 2½ months had a kittenish charm – so of course Jack monopolised her & left me to the mercies of the other one who because of the scarlet setting to her blue porcelain teeth, we instantly christened Red Gums.' They had an accident when their car hit a camel while going at 70 miles an hour. 'It was like going into the side of a house. Our car was completely telescoped & ended up in the ditch – the camel however got up & trotted off like a Derby winner.'

They then returned to Spain, where Philip particularly liked Granada; the Alhambra and the Generalife gardens provided 'a lot of ideas for Lympne . . . . .The Alhambra . . . must remain for all time the crowning glory, the seal, the apogee, in a word the supreme consummation of Moorish Art!' There they attended Andalusian dances arranged by a man who was apparently also something of a pimp: 'A large bed in the corner was conveniently placed should we prove anxious to play a more active part than that of mere spectators – but we resisted the allurements of the sirens.' At Granada they read Washington Irving out loud. Madrid was the next stop; Philip enjoyed a bullfight there, except for how the horses were treated. There were problems about their French visas and with difficulty they arranged for the British Ambassador to write them a note on a Sunday and found him, Sir Arthur Hardinge 'a very good example of our Diplomatic Service – wooly [sic], garrulous, incompetent & kind'.[46]

At the beginning of 1923 Philip embarked, with his old friends Sir Louis Mallet and Lady Juliet Duff, on a more ambitious trip, to Egypt. He wrote a series of letters about it to Sybil; in 1924 they were privately printed as a book of eighty pages. They are pleasant, if not outstanding, travel letters. The account begins in Rome on 31 January, as he remembers his previous visit when he was a schoolboy. 'Were you in Rome when I was here with Mama? I can remember nothing of it except a flirtation with a Mademoiselle Blanc, and an attack of influenza, which I managed to prolong by putting the thermometer in the tea, thereby delaying my return to Eton.' He also wrote to Lloyd George from Rome:

What an awful mess everything is at home & abroad . . . . I hear that it is impossible to realise that Geo. Curzon has been at Lausanne. He has insulted the Turks in every way . . . and yet I hear he fully expects to be Prime Minister in May! . . . [In Rome] the drains run into the soup & all the ugly women are so amorous! I am going to Egypt tomorrow to muck abt among the tombs & see the latest Pharoah woken up . . . . Mussolini seems popular here & if the House attempts to shew any lip he brings up *his army* & they soon shut up![47]

In his last letter to Sybil from Rome, on 2 February, reporting on his sightseeing as he did in his other letters, he also mentioned that he went shopping. 'There are marvellous things and some not expensive. I bought, among other things, an ancient statue, a side table of Egyptian Empire, supported by four god Tutankamens, an ivory mirror, two porphyry vases.'

He did not visit the Pope, Pius XI, on this trip as he did another time in Rome, when he wrote about it in an undated letter to Esher: 'Yesterday morning I spent with the Pope & the afternoon with Mussolini! The Pope was *charming*. I was with him alone for over an hour . . . . He was exquisitely dressed in white flannel & sapphire & rocked with laughter at all the things I told him. I don't believe he likes Catholics at all.' Perhaps this was his visit of April 1928 when, according to *The Times*, they discussed 'the development of aeronautics'. He did write about that visit to Mrs Dudeney; this time the account is a little less sober.

Flew all over the country in all the Italian machines with their star pilots – & had private audiences from the Pope, Mussolini & the King – all frightfully interesting in their different way. But the Pope's is much the best *show* & he is really *the* Great Swell in Rome. He never enjoyed himself more than when I was with him. I think he was so thankful to be with a heathen & not to talk *Shop*. He was exquisitely dressed in white moiré & sapphires & kept me over an hour – with 50,000 Easter Pilgrims waiting to see him pass in front of them. The Swiss Guards are quite the *chicest* thing I have ever seen & all his lackeys wear old red cut velvet![48]

The letters to Sybil are written in that jocular tone of travellers making mock of their companions, with Philip joking about Louis and then Louis writing to Sybil about the exaggerations committed by 'Phil'. In Cairo they had lunch with Edmund Allenby, who had been made a peer and Field Marshal in 1919. At this point in his career he was special High Commissioner for Egypt, having the previous year secured its recognition as a sovereign state. Philip was not much impressed by either him or his wife. In the morning they went to the museums and in the afternoon to the Pyramids.

The party continued on to the Valley of the Kings at Luxor. There was great excitement there as just the previous November Lord Carnarvon had discovered the tomb of Tutankhamun. The search had gone on since 1915, and the world was convulsed with interest. There was the romance of the alleged curse: Carnarvon died in April. Philip wrote that their hotel, which was full of the English, 'reminds one of the Granville Hotel at Ramsgate, dull respectable-looking English people, with a large contingent of Press in connection with the Tomb'. Philip mentions the peers and peeresses present: Lady Ribblesdale, Lady Ludlow, the Swaythlings, the Granbys and the Angleseys.

Philip was pessimistic, believing that neither Carnarvon, who was away at the moment, nor Howard Carter, his famous associate, would let them into the tomb. In the meantime they had a fine time sightseeing: the Temple of Luxor and the Colossi of Memnon. On 13 February, they did see Tut's tomb itself: 'I must say it does give one rather a thrill . . . . They have taken out nearly all the things now, and the only things left are a couch, slung between two elongated lions – all brilliantly gilt – rather pantomime but rather Lympne-ish.' A letter of 15 February to Sybil from Louis Mallet printed in the collection remarks, perhaps with a touch of irony, 'never Pharaoh drove the chosen people to their daily task with more unrelenting and concentrated ferocity than Philip drives us to the daily round of sight-seeing'. Mallet was hopeful that they would see more of the tomb itself, as Juliet Duff was Carnarvon's cousin, although at first Carnarvon was very uncooperative. He had recently made exciting discoveries and on 22 February took Juliet and Philip to see them; Mallet unfortunately was ill. Philip wrote to Sybil: 'I must say it gave me one of the biggest thrills of my life . . . . You cannot imagine what one feels looking at that sarcophagus that has lain here hidden for three thousand years – brilliant – glittering as if it had been completed only yesterday.' (Over the next ten years everything from the tomb except the coffin and the sarcophagus went to the museum in Cairo.) Philip wrote to Sybil from Cairo on the 24th: 'I am still gloating over all Carnarvon showed us in the Valley of Kings. We were very lucky as *hardly any one* has seen the new room in the tomb and storeroom.'

On his way home on 3 March he wrote again to Sybil:

My trip to Egypt has been an unqualified success! I have seen the Temples of Luxor, Karnak, Medinet Habu, Ramasseum, Gurnh, Komombo, Esna, Edfu, and I have sailed round Phylæ. I have visited the Tombs of the Kings, the Queens, and the Nobles, and been shown the innermost secrets of Tutankhamen's Sepulchre. I have slept in Cairo, Luxor, Assuan, Alexandria, and on the Nile. I have marvelled at the Pyramids and have looked at the Sphinx and the Colossi with awe. The Museum at Cairo is one of the most wonderful in the world. I have ridden a donkey in the Libyan Desert, a camel in the Sahara, and a horse in the Nubian Desert . . . . Whenever we come across anything tawdry, trashy, or vulgar or hideous, Louis and Juliet with one breath say that it would be just the thing for Lympne![49]

Philip would travel to other places, including the United States, but this was his best-documented unofficial trip. It shows him as a lively and interested tourist, with some concern for the political situation. He spent several days in Italy on the way back, and he noticed how brutally Mussolini's regime treated those who disagreed with it, calling it a 'White Terror'.

He was not very active politically for the rest of 1923. Perhaps it was an awkward situation: to make a mark in Parliament while his party was in power, but he himself was not in the government. Another general election was called that December, and Philip ran unopposed. Once Labour came into office in January 1924 as a minority government, Philip felt the time had come to play a more prominent public role, perhaps to assert a claim to office in a future Conservative ministry. In a brief diary entry for the end of February he gives a vivid picture of the debate on the new suffrage bill which stipulated that women could now vote at the same age as men. 'Lady Astor made the usual Friday afternoon scene – screaming, swooning, & shaking her fist at the Speaker when he called Hugh Cecil before her.'

Political life was not a total pleasure. He could not face going to a reception at Londonderry House. In early May he had a terrible time at the annual Royal Academy Banquet. 'A ghastly evening . . . . There were hundreds of speeches – all long & dreary – only comfort that neither the Speaker or the Archbishop of Canterbury were called upon

.... I rushed away as soon as possible.'[50] On 14 March he spoke in the House in favour of a bill which reinforced the Act of 1913 that allowed unions to collect money for political purposes from their members but stipulated that union members had to agree to contribute the additional sum rather than paying it automatically. According to Sassoon, 'The Bill was neither more nor less than a measure of common justice to which many thousands of men and women were looking to restore to them the liberty of thought and action which was the birthright of every Englishman.'[51] On 1 April he attacked an unofficial builders' strike that was impeding the opening of the British Empire Exhibition at Wembley Stadium. He blamed the strike on the indulgence of the Labour government towards unions. He predicted, rather extravagantly, that it 'will end, unless the Government change their attitude, in mob law and a total overthrow of the social system of this country'.[52] On 9 April he duelled to a degree with his old boss, Lloyd George, over the ratification of the Treaty of Lausanne. Sassoon supported it, objecting less than Lloyd George to its acceptability to the Turks; indeed it was seen by the Turks as the beginning of their existence as a modern state. While on his travels to Egypt Sassoon had rather made mock of Curzon's participation in the Treaty, but now was in effect supporting him. Two days later, on 11 April, he participated in a debate on British Summer Time, attempting to secure a more permanent basis for it. This was out of family loyalty, as his father had been its major proponent, chairing the Select Committee in 1908 to which the question had been referred. On 13 May he spoke passionately in favour of preserving tariffs and on 18 June in favour of Imperial Preference. He feared that the Labour government might sacrifice the interests of the Dominions in order to continue to receive the support of the few Asquithian Liberals who were still committed to free trade. (Although their opposition to free trade had been a major reason why the Tories had done badly in the general election.) He compared that attitude to the Boy Scout who, having forgotten to do his good deed for the day, got out of bed and fed his brother's white mice to the cat. He also revealed his somewhat hyperbolic style, claiming that a vote against Imperial Preference might be 'an action which may be more full of harm, and more pregnant with disaster, than any action taken by any Government in the last 150 years.'[53] He also paid attention to the needs of his fishermen constituents, asking a question on 23 July about the problem of the discharge of oil into the sea.

Philip had been quite fascinated with the Air Force since the First World War. He spoke several times on air issues, building a claim for office in that area in the future. On 11 March 1924 he argued that Britain must maintain a strong air force for both military and civil reasons:

The first people to bear the brunt of an attack upon the security of these islands will be the man and the woman in the street, going about the round of their daily business. It will be ordinary peaceful citizens whose lungs will be the first to be affected by poison gas [presumably from the air], whose body will be rent, and whose home will be destroyed by the bombs of the invader .... A strong, active, civil air industry is vital, not only to act as a reinforcement of the military arm in case of need, but also for the usages and for the general purposes of such an Empire as ours. We have been told that in Iraq the aeroplanes have been able to take the place of 24 battalions of infantry. That shows what vast economies can be effected when aeroplanes discharge the military burdens of Empire.

On 28 May he spoke to a thin House on the Air Estimates and the projected building of airships, accusing with some eloquence the Labour government of doing a bad job, saying that Socialism meant that 'the greatest sum of money is spent with the least possible result'.[54]

Ramsay MacDonald's Labour government couldn't hold on for long without a majority in Parliament, so another general election – the third in twenty-four months – was called for October 1924. (Sassoon had been unopposed in the elections of 1922 and 1923.) This time, he easily beat back a challenge from a former president of the Oxford Union, Constantine Gallop, as the Conservatives swept back into office. Like other members of his party, in his campaign he played the easy card of anti-Communism, inspired by the Labour party's alleged sympathy with the Soviet Union. 'They had seen the Prime Minister in a new light, in a lurid light, in the light of red revolution, flaming across the sky with mendacity.'[55] His opponent claimed that the best way of suppressing Communist aggression was through a loyal and constitutional Labour government, although he did defend Labour's treaty with the Soviet Union. It was a hard-fought campaign, with packed meetings. Sybil played a major role in speaking for him and he had to defend the integrity of the voters against the allegation that his 'millions' had influenced them. But in the end Sassoon won handsomely, receiving 12,843 votes to Gallop's 3,936.

As Stanley Baldwin set about forming his government, Philip was rather discouraged about his prospects. He may have been too closely identified with Lloyd George and then Curzon. He wrote to Esher in an undated letter in 1924, 'I am sorry not to have been able to get even the meanest of jobs, after 12 years slavery in the House – but I did not expect anything or *ask*.' He noted in an occasional diary: 'There is no chance of my getting office – there are too many hungry (and *vocally* suppliant!) mouths to feed – I am not letting it worry me!'

But in fact he was asked to join the government. Baldwin formed his second ministry in November 1924, appointing Philip as Under-Secretary of State for Air. It would be perhaps his most important and certainly his longest-lasting political activity – far longer than he may have wished. Philip occupied this eminent position of sub-Cabinet rank for eleven years in two terms, from 1924 to 1929 and after the hiatus of another Labour government, from 1931 to 1937.

His superior was Sir Samuel Hoare. Hoare had been Secretary of State for Air in Bonar Law's government from 1922 but outside of the Cabinet until 1923. That year, and then again in Baldwin's government of 1924 to 1929 he had the same position. He and his wife, Lady Maud, a daughter of Earl Beauchamp, were acutely aware of the special challenges he faced as the first minister of Cabinet rank of the 'fledgling' service. The Air Force, with stories of air duels and such, had played a comparatively romantic role in the First World War. But what would happen in the future? There was a risk that it would be identified more with its engineering side and become unfashionable. The Air Force also had to be careful not to become *outré*. In the 1920s there were, particularly in Italy, connections between the Air Force, Futurism and Fascism, which were not yet dangerous from the British point of view. But one had to proceed with a certain amount of care, and not allow air power to be associated with the radical right. How could the Royal Air Force acquire the social standing of the Army and Navy?

It was not necessarily a trivial concern. Many believed, with good reason, that the Air Force would be the most important military arm in the future. (It also had the appeal of being less expensive than the Army and Navy in these years when Britain was in bad financial shape.) Samuel Hoare recognized from the beginning that the position of Under-Secretary of State for Air needed someone who had a certain social cachet. Both the Duke of Sutherland, Hoare's under-secretary during the first Baldwin government, and Sassoon were able to entertain properly for the new service. Hoare himself wrote that Sassoon was extremely adept at the 'social presentation of the *débutant* service ... Philip Sassoon's extreme sensibility responded at once to the novelty and romance of flying. The conquest of the sky, the young pilots who were the *conquistadores* of the newest world, the romantic mentality that ignored time and space, made an irresistible appeal to his artistic intensity.'[56] Years later, reviewing Hoare's memoirs, Sir Michael Howard commented:

> The Hoares set out to make the Air Force smart .... Lord Templewood [Hoare's eventual title] chose for his associates in the Air Ministry the Duke of Sutherland and Sir Philip Sassoon, whose hospitality, enthusiasm and social position made aviation a huge social – and therefore popular success. By 1939 it was at least as smart to go into the R.A.F. as into a good county regiment, and that, in twentieth century England, was an astonishing achievement .... England in the Twenties still depended very largely on the Whig tradition of independent wealth and bizarre unconventionality to keep her institutions – as she did her arts – flexible and progressive.[57]

Sassoon would do this in a number of ways. The most obvious was through entertaining, especially at his country houses at Trent and Port Lympne; his parties became well known for the smattering of air force officers who were there. The receptions he gave at Trent were particularly notable, giving officers and their families the chance to meet royal dukes. The children present would leave with £5 notes. At Lympne, officers could stay in the bachelor quarters that Philip Tilden had built around the Moorish courtyard in the house. A conscious effort was made to have the graduates of leading public schools enter the Air Force, and Philip gave talks at such schools in order to persuade them to join.

Another social-cum-military aspect was the establishment of an air militia. In October 1924, when Philip was at the Air Ministry, Parliament passed the Auxiliary Air Force and Air Force Reserve Act, creating what was called Trenchard's 'Territorials of the Air'. Chief among the units formed as a result was No. 601, a squadron of light bombers, nicknamed the 'City of London'. Headed by the daredevil Lord Edward Grosvenor, a son of the Duke of Westminster, it was mostly made up of his friends from White's Club. The 601 won the Esher Trophy, given by Philip's friend, a bronze figure of Perseus by Sir Alfred Gilbert, as the best squadron in 1926 and 1928. They became known as 'The Flying Swords' as well as 'the millionaires' mob'. When Grosvenor died at the age of 37 in August 1929, Sassoon succeeded him the following October as commanding officer, with the rank of Squadron Leader, a position he couldn't hold when in the government. (After he re-entered the government he became Honorary Air Commodore of the squadron.)

In 1919 Philip slightly expanded the small airfield at Lympne, the oldest airfield in regular use in the country. It was one of the attractions of the annual summer camp he held there for two weeks; his fabled hospitality and the swimming pool also made it a pleasant interlude for the airmen. Grosvenor was famous for his high spirits and practical jokes and the traditions of military messes made for some rambunctious times at the headquarters on Kensington Park Road in London. At the Lympne airfield, the squadron developed a game of towing someone in a hip bath as quickly as possible by car. However, at Philip's country house itself, they might have been somewhat subdued by the grandness of the other guests in attendance. They, for their part, had the chance to meet and be impressed by representatives of the newest service. When Philip became the commanding officer, he gave the squadron a three-seater biplane. In 1934 the 601 became a fighter squadron, reflecting the change in thinking about the Air Force in that decade.

Shortly after his appointment, Sassoon had an exchange of letters with Churchill. On 17 November 1924, Philip wrote Winston a reply to his letter of congratulations the previous day on his appointment. That letter itself is lost but Philip copied Churchill's letter out: 'I was relieved & delighted to learn that all was well with you. I am sure you will do yr work extremely well & it will be singularly interesting in a department wh is broadening out & playing an even larger part in national defence. You will be well posted at Lympne to watch developments & inspect various Stations. In fact I think you must have built your house there upon a prophetic inspiration.'[58] Philip replied: 'Nothing could suit me better than being here – as I love the work & consider myself Extremely Lucky to be working under such a nice fellow as I am. It is marvellous that you should be at the Exchequer & that we shd be all together – it is a jolly Troupe .... What a good friend you have been to me all my life. I am so happy.'[59] They were exchanging letters even though Winston, between houses in London, was staying with him at Park Lane.

The relation between Winston and Philip had its elements of tension: Philip was perhaps somewhat jealous and Winston somewhat patronizing. Churchill had made the transition from being a member of the Coalition and being defeated in the election of 1922 to returning to Parliament, with some difficulty, in 1924 and becoming, rather improbably, Chancellor of the Exchequer. He had run as an unofficial Conservative candidate in Westminster against an official Tory candidate. Whatever doubts Philip might have had about Churchill, he helped him in his successful campaign. Churchill now officially became a Tory as Baldwin had renounced the tariffs that had driven him out of the Tory party originally. Philip noted in an occasional diary: 'He's [Churchill] going to be a damned nuisance to our party .... He is going to get a group of opportunists round him & try to hold us up to ransom.'[60] Philip was both a confidant of Churchill's, supportive of his plans to return to Parliament, and highly critical of him. In a letter to Esher he remarked: 'Winston is lucky isn't he. He just ratted in time – but I am sure he will do well & I hope will reduce our income tax.' As Churchill himself remarked, as this was a return to the Tory party, it takes genius to rerat.

In the 1930s Churchill became the major proponent of rearmament. But his role now, as Chancellor of the Exchequer, was to limit the estimates, including those for the Air Ministry. As the threat from Nazi Germany grew, air power turned into a central issue as part of Britain's defence, but in the period from 1919 to 1934 a primary responsibility for the Air Force was as an imperial police force. For instance, in 1922 it took over from the British Army the obligation for policing Iraq; in the process, Philip became a central figure in controlling the country, under a British mandate, that his family had fled. The success was spectacular as, thanks to aeroplanes, the desert no longer provided a refuge for rebels.

Sassoon threw himself enthusiastically into his new role. He kept a diary from 21 November 1924, until 15 January 1925. He began with his pleasure at the appointment:

1 because it is the lone live & expanding service 2 because I prefer to work under Sam Hoare to anyone else 3 because I know all the chiefs in the Ministry so well from the War. The Prince rang me up to say he wd. drink a cocktail on the strength of it. My speech went down very well at Folkestone .... Had very nice letters from everyone especially Austen [Chamberlain] Winston Curzon – I owed my job to Sam Hoare having asked for me. Geordie [the Duke of Sutherland, who had had the position in the previous Unionist Ministry] very sick – but very nice about it.[61]

Most of the diary is an account of his social life, with conversations with Winston and Trenchard also noted. On 4 December he recorded the special character of the previous day, when he took his seat in the House of Commons for the first time as a member of the Ministry although not in the Cabinet. 'I am 36 today. Yesterday I took my seat. The Speaker told me that he had personally been down to see my room in the House to see if it was comfortable & had had special pictures hung in it for my benefit .... This afternoon sketching estimates with Sam Hoare.' He was increasingly active in Parliament, speaking and answering questions about the Air Force. Trenchard, whom he had known from the war, was Chief of the Air Staff from 1919 to 1929. He was dedicated to air superiority over other countries through building up the number of bombers, hence neglecting air defence. Misguided as the policy later seemed to be, it had some fortunate consequences; Britain was not as encumbered with obsolete fighters later on.

Philip's years in office were full of activity: he established Sassoon Cups within the Air Force: one was for the highest score in the Annual Inter-Squadron Pistol Competition. He presented it and other prizes at Cranwell to those being trained; another was for races of 100 miles between single-seater fighters and another for map reading; he inspected schools for air force mechanics; he opened the London Aeroplane Club; he presided at a lecture on Air Communication with the Middle East and announced there the commencement of an air service for goods and mail between Cairo and Karachi by way of Baghdad and Basra; he gave a toast at a dinner celebrating the Japanese airmen who had flown from Tokyo to London; he delivered a lecture in French to the Belgian Aero Club in Brussels. There, he had a long conversation with the King.[62] As he wrote to Esher, 'I could not bear to come back by train & sea again, so got an aeroplane to come over to fetch me – & it is very pleasant flying over the old haunts in Flanders & to see how the scars of war have disappeared .... My lecture went off very well .... The King was very kind & very boring.' He noted the considerable reduction in the number of planes between 1918 and 1925. 'We hoped that, like us, other nationals would reduce the number of their military aeroplanes; but our hope has failed.' He pointed out that during a disturbance in Iraq planes had carried 300 men and 20,000 cartridges in eight hours: ordinarily this would have taken 4½ days. Long flights, of which Lindbergh's the following year was the most famous, captured the public imagination. In Parliament on 17 March 1926, he gave news of a British flight that was going from Cairo to the Cape and back.

But as his chief was in the Commons, he did not perform the Ministry's most important parliamentary obligation: the presentation of the Air Estimates, the entire budget for the Ministry. The smaller tasks were left to Philip – speaking innumerable times and answering questions put in the House to the Ministry. Hoare was considerate in thanking him for what he did. In March 1925 Philip wrote to Hoare, 'I must quickly seize my pen to thank you a million times for much the nicest letter I have ever received. I only wish it were even a little bit deserved .... I think yours was *much the best estimates speech ever delivered* – because it was so riveting and amusing quite apart from yr absolutely excellent delivery.'[63] In an undated letter the same year, Philip addressed his superior in a similarly elevated fashion while making it clear that he wished to go further up the political ladder:

> When I look back over my political career I am so profoundly conscious of the fact that I owe *all* my appointments & the interest they have brought, to you alone. I shd. like to feel that you think I have been able to make some use of these opportunities & have been able to achieve something at the Air Ministry & with the Air Force. You know how wrapped up I am in that show & therefore the hope of promotion in that sphere wd. of course be an immense joy .... If you can do anything for me in other directions I shall be *deeply* grateful.[64]

Hoare was genuinely fond of him and felt that he did an excellent job. He also much enjoyed visiting Trent, where he and Philip had well-matched, very competitive tennis games. Philip played excellently and was generally the best player present, except for the pro.

The most dramatic event of 1926 was the General Strike of 3–12 May. Reflecting the government's careful planning ahead for industrial disputes, Sassoon had been asked as early as 17

December 1924 whether he would be Civil Commissioner for the Eastern Division, if there were major labour unrest.[65] (England and Wales were divided into ten divisions.) On 1 September 1925, W. Mitchell-Thomson, an MP who was head of the Civil Commissioners, asked Sassoon to pay a visit to the Eastern Division headquarters in Cambridge and to speak to the officials already in place there. 'While impressing upon them the necessity of a due measure of reticence in public, they should be encouraged to discuss difficulties with each other and with the Chief Assistant.' Two days after the General Strike actually started, Philip wrote to Hoare, full of praise for Winston's production of the *British Gazette*, the news-sheet that replaced the non-existent regular press. 'The publication of the Government newspaper is the finest thing that cd. have happened .... I have got my organization working all right & everything is very quiet in the area except for the electricians coming out at Bedford & Yarmouth & a certain amount of trouble at Ipswich .... Everyone is glad that the Govt are being so firm. Winston must be in his element .... Things are not going so well at the Docks – I suppose you may have to use troops.' On 9 May he wrote about the possibility of receiving food from Holland at King's Lynn and Yarmouth and remarked that 'I am sending up [to London] large detachments of undergraduates for special constable work.'[66] Most Oxford and Cambridge undergraduates (with notable exceptions, such as Hugh Gaitskell) were notorious for their mindless opposition to the strike and for regarding it as a great lark.

Soon after the strike ended, Sassoon received a letter of thanks from the Prime Minister, and in turn he sent one to Cambridge University, the location of his headquarters, for the help that its undergraduates had given. The strike became well known for its elements of jolly class warfare, most famously in the football game played between the police and the strikers in Plymouth. He also received a letter of thanks dated 15 May from Mitchell-Thomson: 'Your Eastern Division was one of considerable importance from the point of view of food supply and a breakdown there would have had very serious consequences for all of us. Though you have no very large industrial towns you had a very awkward situation to deal with in Ipswich and I quite understand the anxiety it must have caused you.' The episode meant much to Philip; the letters about the General Strike are among the few that are preserved in his archive. His cousin Siegfried, although believing that the strike would be ineffective, rather meanly enjoyed contemplating the possibility that Philip's Park Lane house might be burnt down although he lost his enthusiasm for that idea when it occurred to him that the strikers might move on a few streets and destroy his beloved Reform Club.[67]

Philip had slightly more authority at the Ministry when Hoare was out of the country. In February 1927 he accepted on Hoare's behalf Churchill's insistence – ironic in terms of Churchill's later views – that the Air Estimates be cut from £16 million to £15.5 million. Even so, he was in constant contact with Hoare by cable while the latter was on a trip to India, resulting in his book *India by Air*. Sassoon was particularly fervent in his letter of thanks for 'the most lovely book in the world. I am enraptured with it. If you had tried 1000 years you could not have found anything that I could like half as much .... It will be invaluable to me

.... I have been to see the Prince three times this week & each time he has told me how much he enjoyed his talk with you & how much he likes you. So you have the entire House of Windsor at your feet.'[68]

In April 1927 Philip presided at the International Conference for Air Navigation attended by sixteen foreign delegations. The proceedings were private but it was reported that Sassoon had remarked that the considerable increase in the number of women pilots was an indication of the great growth of the popularity of flying and its acceptance as an ordinary thing to do. This popularity might also help make commercial air companies begin to be successful operations.[69] Later in 1927 he went on an official visit to the United States and Canada, discussing in the Dominion the possible developments of airships, the R100 and R101, that were under construction at this time. There was a passage of arms about them in Parliament on 7 December when some MPs were concerned about press photographs of the ships. Issues of security were raised and Sassoon handled the situation ineptly. He gave the impression that he would not trust the MPs to visit the construction site, that they would be less security conscious than the press. One Labour MP remarked that their position as Members of Parliament should be enough to assure their probity, another asked if his low opinion of MPs had been formed when he was on Haig's Staff during the war, and another, the radical David Kirkwood, one of the vehement Clydesiders (although he ended his life as a baron) shouted at Sassoon: 'You are insulting us; you are no Briton; you are a foreigner.' The Speaker attempted to calm tempers by stating there was no reflection on anybody's honour.[70] Kirkwood's invective, in effect xenophobic and anti-Semitic, was reported in *The Times* but interestingly was not preserved in the official *Parliamentary Reports*. Otherwise the accounts are the same in content although the language differs considerably in small ways. The *Parliamentary Reports* are edited for grammar and the speakers can make corrections within certain limits but obviously there can be cases where editing can misrepresent what was actually said or, as in this case, result in an omission.[71] The British development of airships ended in 1930. The R101 was destroyed by fire in France, killing Lord Thomson, who had been Air Minister in the Labour government in 1924 and again in 1929.

It seems that Kirkwood particularly riled Sassoon and he was mentioned in a sketch that Ellen Wilkinson wrote of Sassoon in 1930. She was a radical Labour MP, and ultimately a minister in the great Labour government of 1945. She wrote of Sassoon with a certain affection, yet with an emphasis on his 'otherness'. David Low did a vivid drawing to go along with the piece.

Sir Philip Sassoon seems to have been wafted into the House of Commons on a magic carpet and to look around with a detached air as though wondering at the strange animals the Fates have brought him to see. If he would tuck up his legs and sit on the Big Table behind the Mace, with one finely carved hand on each brass box, he would make an appropriate Eastern altar-piece. The Asiatic students who are always in the galleries would feel quite at home .... He has the habit of standing on one foot as though just waiting for a breeze to take him to the clouds. An atmosphere of luxury and mystery surround him .... What does he think about behind that ivory mask? I should like to know just what went through his mind during a speech by David Kirkwood the Downright. Has Sir Philip, in that fascinating lisp of his, ever committed himself positively even to the fairly safe assertion that two and two make four? ... He is almost too refined, too fastidious, too perfectly conscious of what is the best in life, and with his wealth far too able to secure it. Sir Philip makes one want a revolution just to see him for once in an environment that had not been planned with perfect taste, but alas! even if the Westminster Soviet made him carry coals, he would do it with a delicate air.[72]

Sassoon had to fulfil various ceremonial tasks such as speaking at a luncheon of the International Commission for Synoptic Weather Information and at a dinner for the Ramsay Memorial Fellowships where he celebrated the progress of chemistry. As *The Times* reported, summarizing his speech, chemistry had 'opened a new horizon for the agriculturist, and put new powers in the hands of those who worked in metals'. His speech was greeted with cheers but one doubts how much he enjoyed such occasions.[73]

In the general election of 1929, he won easily at Hythe against two women candidates. He received 12,982 votes while the Liberal Hester Holland received 6,912 and the Labourite Grace Colman 2,597, losing her deposit.[74] The *Folkestone Herald* firmly supported him in an editorial on 18 May:

> As a member of Borough of Hythe for seventeen years, Sir Philip Sassoon has proved himself a capable and earnest administrator, one upon whose services to the State great value is placed, and one who has had some considerable share in the development of that great new service of the air which to-day is the pride of the great British nation. He has not allowed these duties, onerous as they are, to overwhelm the requirements of a constituency such as the Borough of Hythe. In all movements locally he has shown the greatest interest and he has never, for one moment, lost that sense of personal interest which the electors of every constituency have the right to expect from their Member.

Sassoon attacked the Liberals (and their leader, Lloyd George) as advocating unlimited borrowing to finance their social plans – indeed their platform reflected the thinking of Keynes – and in any case he viewed voting for the Liberals as a waste as they could not possibly secure a majority. A vote for Labour he regarded as a vote for 'a social system which has brought ruin, misery, and disaster wherever it has been tried'.[75]

Kent on the whole was firmly Tory but Sassoon was helped by an excellent local organization and he was particularly adept at arranging for cars to bring the voters to the polls. However, Labour won the election, although still a minority party, and the Conservative government resigned. Baldwin wrote Philip a letter of congratulations on being returned. He answered, commenting how the Liberals, who had provided many of the ideas of the election, had caused the Tories' defeat: 'How disappointing & unkind have been the results & how different to our hopes on that happy day last week when you allowed us to come over to Chequers. Sybil & I enjoyed ourselves more than we can ever say . . . . Ll. G. has really proved himself to be a national disaster & calamity. I hope we shall meet Parliament so as to put on the Liberal shoulders the onus of putting the Socialists in.'[76] Philip was pleased to be made a member of the Privy Council in the resignation honours.

He also wrote gratefully to Hoare: 'You know how happy I have been working with you & how much I appreciate all the unfailing kindness you have always shewn me. These last 4 ½ years have been among the happiest in my life & *I owe it all to you*. I hope that before very long we shall be working together again . . . . Please use Trent as if it were your own.'[77]

His political skills were limited in the sense that, even though his speeches read well, he didn't deliver them particularly effectively, either inside or outside Parliament. Nevertheless, he was certainly in the public eye and received a fair amount of press attention. He was one of the glamorous people of the time. He had style and a certain panache. He was a competent administrator. He had lots of bright ideas but on a small scale without an overarching vision that might have made a greater political appeal. He did not have a specific political power base within the party nor a group of MPs with whom he associated. Being connected with the great, such as Haig and Lloyd George, early in one's career might appear useful but it does not necessarily work to one's advantage. It makes it hard to move beyond being subservient to one's chief. His father's early death precipitated him into a constituency without any political training although he had an excellent local political organization. His great wealth allowed him to entertain and mix with the prominent. But as a young, rich Jew he was inevitably an outsider among those who had been in the political game so much longer than he. Unlike some, he did not marry into a political family. Nor did he have those qualities, the special sort of seriousness, combined with being able to sparkle, that characterized the most successful politicians. Mrs Belloc Lowndes noted that he was very conscientious in his constituency. With a sort of democratic snobbism she wrote with approval that he had the local tradesmen to lunch:

> Years later, when driving through that district, I noticed over certain shops the names of the men with whom I had then made friends. Philip took his Parliamentary duties very seriously, and there came a time when I asked the then Prime Minister [Baldwin] why Philip Sassoon had never been made Minister for Air. He told me it was because he had an indifferent Parliamentary manner. This, which was undoubtedly true, was strange, for he was a delightful and witty talker, and sometimes kept his guests in fits of laughter.[78]

During these years Philip was closely involved with other developments connected with air power in different ways: the Schneider Trophy, learning to fly, and his air trip to India. It was a period in which there was great interest in long flights – Lindbergh's flight across the Atlantic in 1927 being the most dramatic – and air competitions. It was a golden age of air, with the public captivated by heroic flights and rivalries. From 1920 to 1938 the British had an annual air display at Hendon, an airfield just on the outskirts of London. On the international level, the most important competition was the Schneider Trophy. This was founded

30. The Schneider Trophy, 1913.

in 1912 by the Frenchman Jacques Schneider, a balloonist and aviator and son of the owner of the Schneider armaments works, to stimulate the development of flying boats. The trophy itself is an overwhelming object of art nouveau style. Designed by E. Gabard and mounted on a huge marble base, it is a silver-plated casting of a woman with wings, the Spirit of Flight, kissing the waves in which appear four heads of young men: Neptune and three Tritons.

Britain won the first competition in 1914. By the mid-twenties it had evolved from a competition of flying boats into a race between float planes, a rivalry primarily between the Italians and the British. The greatest Italian triumph was in the United States in 1926. The Italians also won the race in 1919 and 1921. The United States won in 1923 and 1925, and Britain in 1922. The competition was not held in some years. Philip became involved with the event in 1927, when the British government, under Hoare's leadership, provided subsidies for the race and it ceased to be a contest between private individuals. Philip had to inform Parliament in detail of the efforts made and the expenses devoted to the competition. For the race, he travelled to Venice, arriving on 21 September. With a quarter of a million others he watched as the Italian planes failed and the British easily won. At the time, Hoare was with the King at Balmoral. At first George V was dismayed that the race had become less of an amateur sporting event but eventually he was extremely pleased by the British victory. That year, a decision was taken that the competition should be held only every other year and that the trophy would be retired if one country won it three times.

Great attention was devoted to the 1929 race in England on the Solent. Philip was now out of office but nevertheless he was a figure at the race itself, particularly as he and his sister had become very friendly with Marshal Balbo, the chief of the Italian Air Force, who came to England with the Italian flyers. Balbo had become infatuated with Sybil. T.E. Lawrence, a.k.a. Aircraftman Shaw, was also very much in evidence. The newspapers had photographs of him talking to the air minister in his enlisted man's uniform. One would think that a Labour Air Minister might think well of this, but Lord Thomson was deeply irritated and Lawrence was specifically prohibited from having anything to do with Churchill, Birkenhead, Austen Chamberlain, Philip Sassoon and Lady Astor.[79] The British won again, so if they triumphed in 1931 they would have the trophy permanently and the competition would cease.

A crisis ensued over the financing of the Schneider competition. For reasons of economy, during the worldwide depression, the government decided to stop subsidizing British planes for the race. Lady Houston, an extremely right-wing and flamboyant figure, an active supporter of women's suffrage, owner of the *Saturday Review*, and allegedly the richest woman in Britain, stepped in and offered £100,000 to pay for the British part of the competition. She sent a telegram to the Prime Minister, Ramsay MacDonald, saying that she was offering the money 'to prevent the Socialist Government from being spoilsports'.[80] The Chancellor of the Exchequer, Philip Snowden, opposed such international competitions. Sassoon was quite irritated at his successor as Under-Secretary, Frederick Montague, for his total lack of grace in accepting the contribution. He attacked him for his 'outburst of vulgarity and spite . . . . One might have thought that the duties of his office might have restrained Mr Montague from going out of his way to offend a lady who was prepared to do so much for aviation.' *The Times* conveniently published Montague's remarks, which Sassoon said he wouldn't deign to repeat:

> While wealthy industrialists demand stringent economy at the cost of the desperately poor, this lady talks about 'the paltry excuses of a Socialist Government that they could not afford the expenses of this country's participation in the race for the Schneider Trophy' and the thermal state of her blood . . . . Her wealth did not drop from the skies. It has come out of the toil of the nation for whose honour she professes such pride, and while her friends in the House of Commons begrudge a paltry shilling or two a week to the unfortunate unemployed man's child she has the bad taste to exhibit the worst sides of her political and class prejudice in supporting what she regards as her country's vital interests.[81]

Nevertheless, the Labour government accepted the money. Philip was part of a deputation to the Prime Minister urging the continuation of government support. He went in his capacity as chairman of the Royal Aero Club.

Flight-Lieutenant J.N. Bootham, flying a Supermarine Rolls-Royce S6B, won the race, attaining the speed of 340 miles per hour. Italy was the only other nation scheduled to compete. However, after arriving, their planes had difficulties and dropped out, so Britain was unopposed and acquired permanent possession of the trophy. The race did keep the public alert to what was happening in the air. The work done in perfecting the winning engines ultimately played an important role in the evolution of the Spitfire and Hurricane fighters, which made such a difference in the Battle of Britain. So it was far from wasted effort.

Now that he was out of office, Sassoon himself finally had time to devote to learning how to fly. He asked the Chief of the Air Force, Sir John Salmond, who should teach him. Salmond arranged for Flight-Lieutenant Dermot Boyle to be adjutant-instructor for the squadron as he felt he would be particularly good in training Sassoon.[82] (Sir Dermot Boyle himself would become a famous airman and Marshal of the Air Force.) Philip was a slow learner. He took his first lesson on 6 October 1929, and had forty-one lessons between then and 15 August 1931. He first flew solo on 9 April 1930. In his training period he flew a total of 25 hours and 55 minutes on dual control and 10½ hours solo.[83] Boyle said that he wasn't teaching him to fly, only to land. The Prince of Wales sympathized with Philip's difficulties, writing to him in November 1929: 'How is the flying getting on and have you got to the state of feeling you are making any sense in the air at all yet? I can assure you it took me a long time to reach that stage and am in doubt even now sometimes whether I've reached it or not. There's no doubt but that its tricky work but safer than motoring and far more fun.'[84]

In his memoirs Boyle tells a story of flying to Trent for lunch. In his opinion the field there was 'everything that a landing ground should not be. It was small, ridged and furrowed and surrounded by tall trees'. Philip wouldn't cut down the trees, saying to him: 'Boylo, you fly beautifully and trees are beautiful things.' This time the Duke and Duchess of York were at lunch and Philip asked Boyle to take the Duchess up for a spin. 'I took off out of the appalling field, my mind filled with the horrific things that might happen if the field lived up to its reputation. We flew round, watched the Duke playing golf, had a bit of a look at London.' Later there was hell to pay 'as it had come to the notice of the Air Council that members of the Royal Family [in some years' time of course to be King and Queen] were being flown in conditions quite unbecoming to their station'. Boyle imagined that this was a horrified reaction to Sassoon coming into an Air Council meeting and remarking: 'Boylo took the Duchess of York for a flight and she was delighted. She is devoted to the Royal Air Force.' Boyle also recorded that in 1931 Sassoon kindly lent him his private aeroplane so that he and his bride could fly to Paris after their wedding.[85]

Philip was a quieter commander of the squadron than Ned Grosvenor; one does not imagine him at ease in the rough house of an officers' mess. But he and his cousin Hannah became very fond of the flying officers they came to know. He much enjoyed entertaining them at Port Lympne, and photographs attest to their great enjoyment of the house's pool. Mrs Belloc Lowndes tells the most extraordinary story. Philip would come to see her in London when he was dejected, as when he felt that a speech he had given in the House of Commons had been a failure. Popular lady novelists appeared to play almost a maternal role for him. One time he called on her when a young airman who had piloted him frequently had been killed in an accident in Egypt on the way to Australia. Mrs Belloc Lowndes remembered seeing a photograph of him in Mrs Gubbay's house and Philip was clearly deeply attached to this young man. This incident may have occurred in 1922 as presumably it was the same young man he wrote about to Mrs Dudeney from Port Lympne: 'This lonely, peaceful, loved landscape has made me feel more anguished than ever, looking over the plains we used to fly over so often together . . . . I am so very miserable and see no light any-where . . . . The heart is a wretched business.'[86]

Philip came to ask Mrs Belloc Lowndes to get in touch with Sir Oliver Lodge, the scientist and President of the Society for Psychical Research, whom she knew, to arrange for a seance so that he could reach the young man. She secured from Lodge a name and address but then to her distress Philip insisted that she come to the session, an action that she regarded as inconsistent with her Catholicism. The medium spoke to them in the flyer's voice and 'made an allusion to a pair of flying-boots, which the speaker hoped Philip would find useful'. Afterwards she asked him whether he had understood the allusion to the boots. He replied 'Of course I did. I bought his flying-boots after his death.'[87]

A considerable accomplishment at the end of the decade was the publication of Sassoon's one book, *The Third Route*. The effective endpapers, drawn by Rex Whistler, explained the title. They depicted a map of Europe, Africa and India with three routes indicated: Vasco da Gama's of 1497 to Bombay, the route of 1869 through the Suez Canal to India, and now the air route from London to Karachi. The purpose of the 17,000-mile trip was to test the flying boat, to support the idea of commercial air travel and to point out that air power could be used not only to bring together the Empire but also to help control it. In fact, Imperial Airways had started commercial flying to India between Sassoon's trip and the book's publication. Another purpose was to visit British air bases abroad. He left on 29 September 1928, from Cattewater near Plymouth on the south coast, in a Blackburne Iris II flying boat, although he was also to fly in three other planes in the course of the trip. Philip was particularly pleased that Sybil came to see him off.[88] There were nine in the plane, an air commodore, Arthur Longmore, the Air Force's Director of Equipment, two pilots, four crew and a valet. The valet, Henry Hock, tended to be airsick and to a degree Philip had to look after him. They flew across France and in Marseilles Sir Louis Mallet, who was now living in Grasse, joined him for dinner. The book contains twenty-five dramatic photographs most of which Sassoon took, almost all of them from the air. The frontispiece was a picture of the flying boat itself, the *Iris*, and on the title page was a Greek phrase, stating 'How swiftly flies fleet Iris pressing forward.'[89]

They stopped in Naples, where Philip dined with Balbo who, he recorded, 'presented me in the name of Italian aviation with a beautiful silver flying trophy, executed with the art for which Italy is famous and on so magnificent a scale that I dared not add it to my luggage. It travelled home independently and now adds charm to the room in which I work in London.'[90] In a letter to Sybil he sounded less enthusiastic: 'a nude female with her toes astride a dolphin and holding a bowl . . . all in silver & enormously heavy with inscriptions galore! It was very kind of him & luckily too heavy to take on board the Iris!' He and Sybil had become quite close to Balbo, one of the major leaders of Italian Fascism and head of the Air Force, and saw him whenever he came to London. Like a number of British Conservatives, Philip may well have been rather favourably inclined to Italian Fascism, although as we have

31 (*facing page*). Rex Whistler, end paper for *The Third Route*, 1929.

32. Philip setting off on his trip, 29 September 1928.

seen he was aware of its brutal aspects. It was said that a cigarette case that Philip had given Balbo was found on his body when the Italians mistakenly shot down his plane in Libya in 1940.[91] Leaving Naples, Philip took a vivid photograph of the crater of Vesuvius. They then flew on to Athens, Cairo and the Sudan, where he noted the importance of aeroplanes to keep order. He had found time to visit the museums in Naples one morning and in Athens the same afternoon.

Philip took a photograph of one of the planes accompanying them as they flew over Khartoum, making it clear that the city had been laid out in the form of the Union Jack. While flying over the Pyramids of Gizeh, 'my engine cut out and we had to make a forced landing .... We landed comfortably in the desert.' He took it very calmly and returned to Cairo. From there he wrote to the Prime Minister, Baldwin, thanking him for allowing him to take the trip in which he could see 'in one day 3 of the Seven Wonders of the World – Parthenon – Colossus of Rhodes & the Great Pyramid – don't say when you read this "How American" – say rather "what a tribute to the mobility of the Air." '[92] He now was sharing the Western vision: 'Avenues of jacarandas, festooned with countless blue flowers, and the golden mohurs with the scarlet panicles, made the more open streets and gardens scenes of beauty. In their own way they convey a sense of oriental strangeness as vivid as do the narrow, tortuous streets and thronged bazaars of the eastern quarter of the city.' He flew over the Nile and Jerusalem on his way to Amman. Palestine seemed to have no particular significance for him.

His lack of identification was also striking when they arrived in Baghdad, for there was no mention that his ancestors had lived in the city for centuries. But for those who knew of his connection he made, like Disraeli, a claim for greater distinction in pedigree than that possessed by his fellow English. 'Romance must have departed from Baghdad with the Caliphs. Today it is a disappointing place, and is more like a great overgrown village than the capital of the land where civilisation had its birth.' Yet the charm was not totally gone. 'As one walks at night along the roads leading to the city among the avenues of oleanders with which they are set, the reflections of the lights of the city mingle with the mirrored stars upon the slow-moving waters of the Tigris and recall to mind the feeling and romance of earlier days.' He was also very busy inspecting air stations. He made a point of trying to raise the morale of the ordinary troops. One letter written years later recounts the experience of an airman of a visit by Sassoon to Iraq.

> Morale could get really dented, and when one had to set to for an annual visit [Sassoon made several such trips, but not on an annual basis] of the Under Sec for Air with all the 'bull' it could bring life didn't seem to have its usual appeal. However Sir Philip was a man in a million. After his inspection it was his practice to leave the Officers Mess 'just for a walk around to relax'. Strangely enough it always seemed in the direction of an Airmans Billet, which he would enter on his own and unannounced. He would sit on the edge of a bed and enter into the general 'nattering'. Bring out a comment such as 'lighting not too good in here' which usually brought a pithy answer from some Airman . . . . Within a few weeks anything he spotted was sorted out. He raised morale as much as if one of your relations had dropped in.[93]

Sassoon reacted powerfully to Iraq, but without mentioning his family connection with the country. 'Iraq takes you by the throat the moment you enter it, saturated as it is with history and legend, religion and fable . . . . I went to see King Faisal. He was very charming.' He anticipated that with the development of Imperial Airways and of bridges, hotels and railways Baghdad would be transformed. It was a crucial point in the air link to India and the Far East. 'Then it will be as thronged as are Cairo and Luxor by visitors drawn by the discoveries of the excavators, by the strange charm of an oriental city and the delights of a perfect winter climate.'

He summed up the romanticism of it all in a letter to his sister on 10 October from Baghdad. 'Darling Syb, I left this morning the Land of the Pharaohs & arrived this afternoon at the City of the Caliphs – flying from the Valley of Kings at Thebes over the Birthplace of the King of Kings at Bethlehem over Jerusalem & Jericho & Bashan & over the Nile & the Jordan & the Tigris & the Euphrates – all rivers seem wretched after the High Nile – Jerusalem is a pale city scattered over pale mountains.' He wrote the next day: 'Baghdad is not really romantic at all – it is rather like a squalid overgrown native village – full of dust & debris & one looks in vain for the glamour of Samarkand.'

The next stop was Basra, where he expatiated on the glories of Nebuchadnezzar and of Babylon. He then travelled to Karachi, the official destination of his air trip. He spent a little more than a week in India before starting on the way back. In the text he did not make any reference to his own personal connection with the subcontinent. He did mention it, however, rather casually to the family. On 15 October he wrote to his cousin Hannah about being in Karachi where the Sassoons had an office. 'Darling Hansie ... How amused David wd have been to think of me here.' Presumably David Gubbay would have been amused that he had taken an interest in the business. On his return to Karachi on 24 October he wrote to Sybil: 'I forgot to tell you that I went to the office yesterday .... Large crowd – I was garlanded & given a silver replica of the Taj Mahal.'

His chapter about his visit to Jodhpur is called 'Plane Tales from the Hills', a play on the Kipling title. In light of its abandonment two years later, he was unduly optimistic about the airship programme. He inspected the airship shed and mooring-mast there: 'the airship is destined to be in the near future a most important factor in the development of the Empire's air communications'. Air was a much faster and less tiring way than train of getting around India. His travels included flying up the Khyber Pass, which he photographed, and peering into Afghanistan. It was not all smooth going, as all along the trip there were a series of minor mechanical difficulties.

After Jodhpur the party went on to Delhi. In the text he praises Baker's and Lutyens's great and still incomplete project, although he does mention that it will be softened when it is more in use. In a letter to Sybil he was less enthusiastic: 'The Secretariat buildings of Baker's are really very fine – but the rest looks rather like the White City [the exhibition buildings in Shepherd's Bush, London] The new Viceregal Lodge is immense & with no room inside it – everything passages – a dull flat garden – not in the least Mogul as it sets out to be. The legislative assembly is rather a low round building & looks like a gasometer – which it is!' He then took a train for Simla, the summer capital where the Viceroy Lord Irwin (later Lord Halifax) was in residence. He saw the Irwins, and went shopping with Lady Irwin. To his sister he was succinct ('lousy shops'), but in the text he mentioned that since there were too many English in Simla the goods were both shoddy and expensive. He commented to his sister in his letter of 19 October: 'We had great fun choosing colours for the ball room at the Viceregal Lodge .... The Irwins were really too charming & I think E.[dward] was pleased to gossip with someone from home.' He then went on to Lahore and savoured, as he wrote to his sister, the great gun, *Zam-Zammah*, on which Kim sat against municipal orders in the first lines of Kipling's novel. He toured various stations and commented on the efficiency with which the Air Force could police the area.

At the tiny station of Miramshah, ten miles from the Afghan border, he met T.E. Lawrence. Over the years he saw much of Lawrence, one of the most fascinating as well as more enigmatic figures of the period. Officially at the lowest level of the hierarchy in which Philip was virtually at the top, Lawrence mixed with the grandest in the land, while maintaining, for complex psychological reasons, his position in the ranks. Philip seemed comfortable in his dealings with him. In the book, Philip wrote that 'he seemed thoroughly happy in his self-chosen exile and pleased to think that he had got himself taken on for another five years of peaceful and useful obscurity'. To Sybil he commented 'I had a long talk with Lawrence who is an aircraft hand – the lowest rank. He wants to sign on for another 5 years – & is quite happy there, miles from anyone. He is still suffering from the complex that everyone is gossiping about him – but that is because he is so frightened of being turned out of the air force.' As Philip noted in the book, shortly thereafter when a rebellion started against the Emir of Afghanistan, Lawrence had to be removed as it was reported in the press that he had masterminded it.

Lawrence was in touch with Sybil the next year in April about subscribing fifteen guineas to the private edition of *The Seven Pillars of Wisdom*. 'You won't read it, you know. Nobody has yet . . . . It is very long, very dull, very technical, rather hysterical: but it means well, & is truthful: or as truthful as I can make it.' (In later years its truthfulness became a matter of great debate.) One doesn't know what Sybil thought of his remark in the letter: 'Your connection with the only Siegfried is a great thing in the eyes of this generation.' She may well, at this point, not even have met her famous cousin, the poet. A few weeks later in mid-May Lawrence wrote Philip an acute letter about *The Third Route*:

The strongest impression the Third Route conveyed to me was *freshness* . . . . Here you write like a man out of prison on his first day, seeing everything with a pair of new eyes; and you have written it down exactly as you saw it in your own words . . . . Your book feels easy, as if you had written it easily. Curious, since fortune made you complicated! Natural ease is not very admirable, but ease of this kind, which comes only with very hard work, is well worth its difficulty . . . . You glide too lightly across the ancient world. Also you miss the foreground, the life *inside* the machine. You were too often looking over the edge. That's the pity of being not crew, but a too carefully guarded officer-passenger.

At the end of this letter Lawrence refers to his new posting at Cattewater and sends a message – as an airman – that Sassoon is to give, should he see him, to Trenchard, the Chief of the Air Staff: 'I'm perfectly suited at Cattewater, & being very good.'[94] Some years later he was thinking himself of writing such a book as *The Third Route*. He wrote to Philip in 1933, but it is hard to tell how seriously, that he would like 'to do a long flying-boat voyage and write a log of it. I have the ambition to compete with you there.'[95]

After the visit to Lawrence, Philip started on his return journey; there were various difficulties with the plane and the authorities in Persia. Sassoon and his companions made it to Bushire which he enjoyed, without alluding to the fact that his grandfather had lived there as a young boy, as well as in Basra, where he would go next. Because of the necessary repairs to the *Iris*, which was to catch up with them, he not only completed his inspection of bases, but also explored the Sumerian excavations at Ur, shown them by Leonard Woolley, their discoverer. He called the chapter recounting these events 'Cradle of Civilisation'. There was no deliberate claim for the antiquity of his own traditions, but it was implied. 'I found myself fully ready to accept his [Woolley's] estimate of the cultural debt which the Western civilisations of our own day have inherited, through the channel of Jewish writings and

Greek learning, from those strange early peoples of Sumer who, until some thirty years ago, were forgotten as though they had never been.'

They then went back to Baghdad, where Philip distributed sports prizes at the air force base and stayed with the British Resident in a room overlooking the Tigris. He enjoyed discussing the problems of Iraq and of gardening with the Resident. 'Sir Henry Dobbs, like all people of real discrimination, is a very keen gardener.' He then went on to Mosul, a great source of oil, which the British had gained control of in the Lausanne negotiations of 1923. Philip was more interested in seeing the ruins of Nineveh. They moved on, via Cairo and Malta, with a stop in France to spend a night at Baron Rothschild's Château Lafitte – no mention that he was a relation. The Baron wasn't in residence and so his agent entertained them. November 13 was the last day of the flight and he landed at Calshot, comparatively close to Port Lympne. Philip had been gone a little more than six weeks. It was a trip of 17,000 miles and he visited twenty-five British air bases in Egypt, Sudan, Palestine, Trans-Jordan, Iraq, Mesopotamia, India and Malta. His purpose in *The Third Route* was to make flying more popular and to emphasize the importance of air for the Empire. 'We have got the greatest need of all nations for air communications.' The last photograph in the book shows Sassoon himself at home again, waving from the plane after it had landed on the water. *The Third Route* is an excellent travel book written in a straightforward style and full of interesting material. It fulfilled Sassoon's purpose of extolling air travel and describing the sights visited. He pursued that same theme in an article he wrote for *The Times* on 18 February 1930, highly recommending the air route to India, and the far greater comfort of flying boats and their roominess as compared to the planes that flew between London and Paris. The trip was not without its dangers, the plane being forced down twice because of engine trouble and once having to turn back because of bad weather. But in his account, he barely mentioned these problems. He also made it clear how important air power was for Britain's military role, particularly in the Empire. It was largely coincidental that the trip took him into the cradle of his family.

The prominent firm of William Heinemann published *The Third Route* in April 1929, while Philip was still in office. It received a fair amount of attention, including a good review in the *Observer*. Philip wrote a thank-you note to its famous editor, J. L. Garvin, perhaps a bit disingenuously: 'I had not sent it to you with that idea in mind! I hope you will believe that.'[96] It was also well received in the *Spectator, Country Life* and elsewhere. *The Times* reviewer, who called it 'charming' and a 'sunny narrative', was especially taken with the photographs.

> Sir Philip Sassoon is confident that soon the air route to India will be traversed backward and forward by a steady stream of traffic: the Third Route will be as crowded as the Great North Road. Yet some holiday makers rather want to get off that congested highway to-day. When the day dawns of which Sir Philip speaks so hopefully what will they do? The wilds of Regent's Park may still remain to them, or, the ruins of Nineveh spoiled for them by the familiarities of the crowds, they may seek in the solitudes of Greenland all that is left in nature to attune with their thoughts.[97]

33. Marthe Bibesco at Port Lympne, May 1921.

The next year the book was published in France, translated by his and Sybil's good friend, and also a great friend of Proust's, Princess Marthe Bibesco. She was a prolific author of novels and memoirs, including several about Proust. A Romanian aristocrat, she spent most of her time in Paris and regarded herself as a French writer. She visited Philip several times both in London and at Port Lympne, once, according to her biography, at the same time as Alfonso XIII, the King of Spain. In gratitude for her translation, he gave her a brooch of sapphires and emeralds that Napoleon had given to his mistress, Marie Walewska, to celebrate her pregnancy.[98] She was intrigued by air power and was also a very close friend of Lord Thomson, the Labour Minister for Air. In her rather hyperbolic introduction she emphasized Philip's French side, suggesting that he might well have composed the work in French, summoning up the memory of his 'exquisite' French mother. She refers to him as an

Athenian from Oxford who records the sights from the point of view of a connoisseur, saying that he writes of his trip in the spirit of Horus, the Egyptian sky god of light and goodness. In his papers at Houghton one French review is preserved, but with no indication of where it was published. The reviewer took Philip as impetuously English with the faults and virtues of his race, from time to time phlegmatic and proud, idealistic and practical, generous and diplomatic.[99]

The American edition, published by Doubleday in 1929, contained an introduction by Thornton Wilder, famous since the 1927 publication of *The Bridge of San Luis Rey*. Philip was an admirer of his work, and once when Wilder was his guest he bought multiple copies of the book for all members of the house party.[100] Wilder, who was in Europe frequently in the 1920s, followed Sassoon's trip to India in *The Times* while on holiday at Juan-les-Pins, where he also saw something of Louis Mallet. He was working on his novel *The Woman of Andros* but it was going badly and he enjoyed writing a gossipy letter to Philip, hoping that he would come to St Moritz at Christmas time. Wilder wrote to him on 10 December from Vienna. 'Elizabeth and Essex [by Lytton Strachey] is splendid. I hope to enjoy Orlando much. Will you lend me your copy of the Seven Pillars of Wisdom for 24 hours when I come to London?'[101] On 6 August 1929 he wrote to Sassoon from the Lake Sunapee Summer School at Blodgett's Landing, New Hampshire, urging him to come to Vienna and Munich in October. But the letter is mostly one of apology about the preface for the American edition. It hadn't been shown to Philip; Wilder assumed that the publisher would do this. There was confusion at the publisher's and he never saw proofs himself. 'All I hope is that you will not be disappointed; but you know already that I am not stuffed with angry literary vanities and if you find it unsuitable to that kind of book don't hesitate to lay it aside.' The short Introduction itself was rather vapid. 'It is the property of these pages – for all their author's poised understatement – to furnish endless material for wonder and for reverie .... All the liberating power and breadth that we feel from life on the sea, however brief our participation, will be multiplied for those who daily submit themselves to the currents of the sky .... *The Third Route* turns one's mind as persuasively towards the past as it does towards the future.'[102] Doubleday thought that Wilder's reputation would help sell the book. The American edition has some variations: unlike the other two it has a dedication, to his sister, the Greek epigram was removed from the title page, Sassoon whose name had appeared unadorned in the English edition, was identified as a knight, an MP and the former Under-Secretary of State for Air.

There is one other surviving letter from Wilder to Philip, written from San Francisco on 17 January 1930, referring, presumably, to the death of another airman of whom Philip was fond. 'It made me very happy to know that in the hours of fresh grief you thought of me and of some of my pages .... In such cases we grieve for what we lose in happy and sincere companionship, but we know that by some mystery brave and good men *accept* their deaths.' The decade had ended in some sadness. Although Philip was only in his early forties, his high spirits were becoming a little subdued and he was subject at times to melancholia. Politically his career was on hold during the years that the Tories were out of power, from 1929 to 1931. One of the few times he spoke in the House of Commons, on 18 March 1930, was to comment favourably on the Air Estimates as presented by the Labour government, although he felt they did not allow enough for home defence. He also modestly drew attention to his own recent experiences, extolling the usefulness of the amateur auxiliary air force squadrons and of flying boats as continuing the 'nautical tradition of the British race'. He suggested that these two aspects be combined in the creation of an auxiliary squadron of flying boats.[103]

Philip Sassoon led a very active political life during the 1920s and accomplished much on behalf of the Air Force, playing a crucial role in establishing a new armed service. He had become a very well-known politician and public figure. But it was not clear that his political career was evolving in a way that would increase its impact. He was not associated with any one group within the party nor did he seem to occupy an identifiable place in the political spectrum. He had not developed a set of political ideas. He was competent and imaginative. Part of his fascination is the ephemeral nature of his accomplishments, as if he were, as Sir John Colville remarked, a fragrance of the times. He was a supremely colourful figure, but too easily forgotten after his death. He was exotic, he was Jewish, he was rich. He had easily moved beyond being a backbencher but he did not seem to be able to rise beyond being a minister outside the Cabinet. He could not achieve the lightly worn gravitas that characterized the successful politician. Perhaps he did not seek sufficient support from the public or his party. Such was not his skill. He was rather a crucial facilitator who could make his colleagues' lives much more comfortable. At the same time that he wished to be a successful politician, he had nevertheless a certain diffidence about his own political career. His interests were far broader than many of his colleagues' but that did not help him politically. He had wide-ranging aesthetic concerns. During these same years, he became deeply involved in redoing his three houses. And towards the end of the decade, in 1928, he presented the first of ten path-breaking art exhibitions held in his London house.

5   *Setting the Stage in London and in the Country*

Philip

In the first years after the war, Philip was very interested in doing further work on his houses at Lympne and in London; some years later, renovations got under way at Trent Park. He was also dedicated to the idea of moving forward his political career, of trying to make himself indispensable to the government. His hospitality was a large part of his political role and for that his houses were a necessity. Country house hospitality was a well-established English tradition and in many ways reached its apogee in the Edwardian period, when Philip was growing up. But the lavishness of Philip's entertaining may also owe, perhaps unconsciously, something to the Baghdadi and Indian traditions of his family. Philip Tilden, the architect whom he had met through Sir Louis Mallet, was a central figure at Park Lane and Lympne, doing extensive work for him. No architect is named for the work at Trent Park but one imagines that Tilden is likely to have advised him there. (Sassoon thought sufficiently highly of Tilden to recommend him to Churchill when the latter purchased a country house at Chartwell in Kent. Tilden had also done work for Churchill's aunt, Lady Leslie, and for Lloyd George at Churt in Surrey. Unfortunately his relations with the Churchills were to become quite strained.[1]) Sassoon also highly valued Mallet's advice on architecture and decorative matters.

Mallet, whom he had known since 1909, was a close friend. Born in 1864, he was descended from a well-known Swiss Huguenot family; his father and brother were prominent civil servants. He had a distinguished career in the Foreign Office, rising to Under-Secretary of State from 1907 to 1913. That year he was sent as Ambassador to Turkey. Perhaps he was expected to be a latter-day Lord Stratford de Redcliffe who had more or less dictated Turkish policy at the time of the Crimean War; his mission was to keep Turkey out of the war or to persuade her to come into the war on Britain's side. His virtually inevitable failure turned out to be disastrous for his diplomatic career. Despite the assurances of the Foreign Secretary, Sir Edward Grey, to the contrary, Mallet was held responsible in popular opinion for not having prevented Turkey from entering the war on the side of Germany. After the war, he attended the Peace Conference as an assistant Under-Secretary of State in the Foreign Office, but his career was over. He retired in 1920.

Mallet was a connoisseur on comparatively modest means. He restored, with Tilden as architect, a fourteenth-century yeoman's house, Wardes at Otham in Kent. He had a permanent room at Philip's house in London on Park Lane. As Philip Tilden recorded, it was 'high up above the Park, where he made his London quarters, and to which he rushed in panic to avoid the crowds below'.[2] Shortly after the war, he sold Wardes to Lady Juliet Duff and moved to Bellevue, owned by Sassoon, near Port Lympne. Philip Tilden wrote about the move: 'I never could understand the reason for Louis moving from a place that suited him well to a place that really did not suit him at all, until I realized that it was after all an expression of capitulation to Philip Sassoon's selfishness. I do not use the word in any unkind sense, but mean it to express the fact that Philip needed someone of experience near him as a dumping ground for confidences, quite apart from his cousin Hannah Gubbay.'[3] Whatever these confidences may have been, they have not been preserved.

Mallet tended to favour the Jacobethan although his taste was eclectic and one suspects he helped train Philip's sense of style in seeking out beautiful objects and arranging them well. Mallet also conveyed to Philip his enthusiasm for Tilden. At the same time, Philip could be furious when someone disagreed with his aesthetic judgement. He seemed particularly to dislike old English, despite his high opinion of Mallet's taste, complaining to Diana Mosley about the style of decoration favoured by Lady Evelyn Guinness with whom they were dining. She used cow parsley and moon daisies when she could, he felt, have had orchids, and pewter when she could have had gold.[4] In his autobiography Tilden writes about Philip. 'He was, I think, above all else obsessed with things rather than with people. I do not think, either, that a more brilliant man for his age existed than Philip ... intensely amusing and amused .... His taste was sometimes exotic.'[5]

34. Sir Louis Mallet, 1920.

Philip's parents, Edward and Aline Sassoon, had moved to 25 Park Lane (its number was later changed to 45) in 1896 on the death of Sir Albert Sassoon. It no longer exists, having been torn down after the Second World War. (A Playboy club replaced it, now gone, but the same structure is now an office building. Sybil Cholmondeley met Hugh Heffner once and told him that she had grown up in the space then occupied by his club. He made her a lifetime member.) Number 25 Park Lane was the Sassoon house seen by the most people. Philip entertained there extensively, in the heart of London, and many came to the art exhibitions he held in the house from 1928 to 1938.

Aline Sassoon had transformed the interior at Park Lane but there were still aspects of Barnato's house to be removed: statues of Virtues, Flora and Father Time representing, in petrified form, it was said, Barney Barnato's creditors.[6] Many objects remained that Philip and Sybil had inherited, most notably sixteenth- and seventeenth-century pieces, some tapestries and Eastern rugs favoured by their Rothschild great-grandfather, James de Rothschild, as well as Italian majolica, Limoges and Sèvres. Philip and Sybil had a two-day sale of 213 objects on 27 and 28 November 1919, at Christie's. It also included items that they had inherited from their own parents.

Both Sybil and Philip chose to identify mostly with the eighteenth century, both in terms of England and France. This was highly suitable for Lady Rocksavage, whose country house was Houghton. Ever since Oxford, or perhaps before, Philip had been attracted to the history and art of the eighteenth century in England. At the time there was a general revival of interest in the century. But it may also have had a special significance for those who feel somewhat outside of the system. The eighteenth century was a time when status, commerce, land and new families, formed an intriguing mixture. In the 1920s, Sir Lewis Namier, an English historian of Polish-Jewish origins, was starting his work on eighteenth-century England. He concluded that the basis of its stability was the ownership of land, which he contrasted to the landlessness of his own people. Following his own logic, Namier became both an active Zionist and a devout Anglican. Despite the acres they did own, land would never be the basis of the Sassoons' wealth. Did that bar them from being 'true' aristocrats?

The differences between Philip's taste and the somewhat more ornate taste of the Rothschilds, toned down by his mother, can be sensed in two paintings of the drawing room at Park Lane. In 1913 William Orpen had depicted it with small figures of Philip, leaning against the mantelpiece, and the seated Sybil. In the 1920s, some time after Tilden had remodelled the room E. Shepherd painted the same view. The ceiling was raised and, in accordance with Philip's taste, the mirror over the fireplace is not as big nor is the chandelier. The panelling is less ornate and no longer in the white and gilt Louis XV style. Even the pictures on each side of the mirror are smaller and built-in bookcases now flank a different tapestry. Rather than a rather rococo Gobelin with a scene after Boucher, this is a more austere Brussels tapestry of the Duke of Marlborough overlooking a battle scene. (Sir John Lavery depicted the same room, in *The Red Hat* in 1925, with his wife sitting in the foreground.) Philip filled the house with French furniture, oriental and Limoges china, and tapestries. He softened Barnato's grand four-storey staircase by creating a gallery of three arches

35. E. Shepherd, *The Drawing Room at Park Lane*, 1923.

overlooking the stairs. In these were mirrors done in glass of an oyster shade darkening to black. Tilden remarked: 'I can assure you that deep red roses in porphyry vases reflected in black glass give an effect that is not without uniqueness.'[7] The six reception rooms of the house were now furnished with eighteenth-century French furniture, many pieces of the highest quality.[8] On the ground floor there was the dining room and a library. On the first floor were two drawing rooms and the ballroom. The house was 13,000 square feet.

Max Beerbohm recorded dining at Park Lane in April 1914. The room may have changed somewhat later, but his account provides a sense of what it was like:

Sargent and Lady Essex completed the party .... The rooms through which one passes into the dining room are too many and too perfect. Also the dining room itself is too big for less than 1000 diners. One little perfect porphyry table without a table-cloth; and a crystal bowl with a lid, with pink carnations floating inside it .... It takes the heart out of one – and one only wants to say 'I'm glad I'm not rich', and one can't say that, and so one is rather at a loss.[9]

36. John Singer Sargent, *The Countess of Rocksavage, later the Marchioness of Cholmondeley,* 1922.

37. Charles Sims, *The Countess of Rocksavage and her son, Lord Malpas*, 1922.

At Park Lane Philip had his most important paintings. Sargent's portrait of his mother hung on the staircase and then, in 1922, another Sargent of Sybil, a portrait that he had commissioned, much more formal and larger than the 1913 one. It is evocative of Velázquez, partially inspired by a large Renaissance Spanish jewel of an imperial eagle that had belonged to Dona Maria of Austria, given to her by Philip IV, that Philip had bought. (Was there meant to be any suggestion of her possible Sephardic background?) Her dress, by Worth of London, was from a sixteenth-century design. She wears not only her own pearls but her mother's, which Philip had inherited.[10] He remarked of it in an undated letter to Esher: 'Sargent's picture of Syb is a masterpiece – her face is like a camellia with an electric light behind it.' The painting was exhibited at the Royal Academy in April, rather in rivalry with a portrait of her and her son by Charles Sims for the title of portrait of the year. The headline for the story in the *Morning Post* read 'Mr Sims challenges Mr Sargent.' The critic of the *Daily Sketch* remarked of the sitter that she was the 'descendant of two of the richest Jewish families in the world and a very beautiful and gracious lady, who is the wife to the heir to a marquisate, a charming hostess, a cultured woman of the world, and a really fine shot'.[11] In 1925 Orpen wrote to Sybil:

> Let me tell you of the Sargents – a most wonderful Exhibition – and tho' I think the 1922 portrait of you a little sombre in colour for a portrait of you (if *far* finer than the earlier painting) its the one portrait – the one picture of all which has for me an appeal entirely on ground of pure beauty – there are others more remarkable in technique & sheer paint-brilliance & more forceful in some ways, but you alone seem to be a *real* patrician. – It is extraordinarily like you – & that air of serene melancholy – it is a thing I *do* admire.[12]

Philip also kept at Park Lane Sargent's portrait of him done the following year. (Sargent also made two charcoal sketches, one in 1912 and the other in 1921.) Other than his rather pale mammoth study of British generals, it was the last portrait he painted. One critic remarked that it had 'a slight touch of aristocratic insolence'.[13] Philip looks both superior and diffident but rather vulnerable. Philip bequeathed this portrait, along with the Sargent drawing of the Prince of Wales, to the Tate on his death in 1939. The trustees accepted the former but not the latter, presumably because they were apprehensive about adding Edward VIII to the collection so soon after his abdication.

While Philip's portrait was being painted, the American sculptor, Paul Manship, who at that time had a studio next door to Sargent's, was doing at Sargent's insistence a head of Sybil, still to be found at Houghton. Also preserved there is a charming small sketch Sargent did for Sybil of her and the artist at work. According to one account, while the brother and sister were sitting for the two artists, Margot Asquith 'would drop in and entertain with her amusing chatter, and Artur Rubinstein would play for them in his most brilliant manner'.[14] At this time, Philip gave to Sargent, perhaps in return for the portrait, a beautiful Ingres drawing of two young men that the artist had done in 1817, possibly representing the friendship between Sargent and Sassoon. Sargent treasured the drawing.

38. John Singer Sargent, Philip, Rock and Sybil at Port Lympne, August 1920.

Several Gainsboroughs – a very early self-portrait and a picture of the artist and his family – now to be found at Houghton – were in the study, as well as what was considered the most valuable painting in the house, J.F. de Troy's *A Reading from Molière*. Painted in the 1730s, it had passed into Frederick the Great's hands in the next decade and it remained at his Potsdam palace, Sanssouci, until 1806, when it made a Napoleonic move to France. (One wonders if the coincidence of its being in the namesake of the Sassoons' Bombay house might have intrigued Philip.) At the time of Philip's death, it was valued at £2,500, even though Agnew's had purchased it for 5,000 guineas in 1919 at auction. The Dowager Countess of Lonsdale, in whose family it had been since the mid-nineteenth century, had consigned it. Philip bought the painting in August 1919. In the Houghton sale of 1994 it had pride of place as the last item in the catalogue and sold for nearly £4 million.

A pair of flower pieces by Jan van Os was in his bedroom. Valued at £250 at the time of his death, they are quite charming: one depicts 25 fruits and a few flowers, a bird and two insects, while the other has 26 flowers and a nest of baby birds. They were Dutch paintings

39. John Singer Sargent, *The Marchioness of Cholmondeley and Paul Manship*, 1923.

of the 1770s; they sold for £463,500 in 1994. There were other Sargents in the house, grouped in one room, as well as Gainsboroughs, Reynoldses, Hoppners, Zoffanys and Ramsays.

Splendid late eighteenth-century rococo panelling taken from two rooms of the Palais Paar in Vienna was a comparatively late addition. Philip bought it when that house was torn down and installed and restored it in 1934, a date confirmed by particles from the *Daily Telegraph* of 29 March 1934 found in the filling of the wood cracks. The panelling may have come to him through Stéphane Boudin of the decorating firm of Jansen that had supplied a floor from the Palais to the London house of Chips Channon, the MP and socialite. Boudin may also have acted as Philip's adviser for decorating some of his rooms, as he did work for his cousins in Brussels. Philip's room from the Palais Paar is a comparatively restrained beautiful blue room and can now be seen in the Wrightsman Galleries of the Metropolitan Museum, New York, having been purchased when the Park Lane house, in its turn, was torn down.[15]

Although there was no question that the rest of the house was opulent, the ballroom, painted by José María Sert, was quite another matter altogether. In 1920 Sassoon commissioned him to do the room, despite the distress he had expressed to Mallet about Sert's earlier decorations at Lympne. He executed an overwhelming work, called *Caravans of the East*. Painted in blue and silver, some actually on silver plate (silver rather than gold was much favoured in the 1920s), Sert covered the walls with fantastic scenes of Greek temples, of camels, elephants and exotic figures on their way through a desert. When in the room surrounded by the frenetic painting, one could sit on benches along the walls, remarking on the *trompe-l'œil* pillars and the fantastic vistas: baroque fountains, palms reaching up to a ceiling that had swirling clouds surrounding a still point, an eye of a hurricane. Mirrors where the ceiling met the wall created an illusion of unlimited space. One commentator thought that the murals might symbolize the voyage of the wandering Jew looking for the promised land, as well as alluding to Sassoon's Indian connections.[16] If true, it is unlikely that Sassoon would have appreciated these points. James Knox has written: 'Sert's coup de théâtre was a masterpiece of modern Baroque. The subject matter had obvious parallels with the history of the Sassoons, a topic on which Philip Sassoon always remained silent. Only through the medium of a work of art did his alter-ego find uninhibited expression.'[17] A Spanish writer on Sert commented: 'Not knowing whether to run away or to fall in ecstasy: such is the impression that this room must have produced upon its viewers.'[18] Did Sert consciously

40. Charles Sims, *The Marchioness of Cholmondeley in the Ballroom at 25 Park Lane, c.* 1923.

make his two commissions for Sassoon more oriental than his other work or did the exoticism represent the wishes of the client? When the house was demolished, the Museum of Modern Art in Barcelona acquired the huge work.

Sassoon also had Tilden do extensive work at Port Lympne, making it what has been called the most exotic country house in England between the wars.[19] Mallet had taken Tilden, perhaps for the first time, to the house at Lympne for a weekend during the war, along with Mrs Tilden. Philip thought that Tilden would have had a better time there without his wife, although he was intrigued that she might be descended from Scandinavian royalty. He commented in his wartime diary: 'I wd. have imagined that it wd. have been more fun for him without her. The wives of one's friends being only one degree less tiresome than their mistresses.'[20]

Sassoon adored the location of the house, as he wrote to Mrs Dudeney on 17 July, 1918: 'I am on the lip of the world and gaze over the wide Pontine marches that reflect the passing clouds like a mirror. The sea is just far enough off to be always smooth and blue – and everywhere the acute stillness that comes from great distances. How altruistic nature is. And this year the wild rampage of colour seems to be on tiptoe to soothe one's wretched heart.'[21] After the war, making up for lost time, he threw himself into great schemes to shape his houses to his own vision. He had now come fully into his inheritance and had the money to do whatever he wished. He was influenced by his travels, most particularly in the early 1920s to Spain and to Egypt.

The grounds at Lympne also reflected Philip's interest in the eighteenth century. In the circular forecourt at the entrance, framed by yew bushes, thirteen caryatids representing Greek high priestesses are to be found around the fountain. Philip had purchased them from Stowe, the great house of the Dukes of Buckingham. A contemporary statue of George II, also from Stowe, stood in the grounds.

Philip now felt the Sert room at Port Lympne needed to be modified. Sargent gave advice on how to change it and suggested doing the walls the colour of a chow, presumably in honour of Philip's dog Herbert. As Tilden recorded, a colour emerged that had a 'warm, moss-borne effect, streaked with gold .... The walls were rusticated with this beautiful if gloomy material .... At symmetrical intervals around the room ... were placed high mirrors of black and oyster-coloured glass.'[22] There was a small library with silver and gold woodwork, with books bound in red morocco, and the Ballet Russe dining room. A rather Egyptian frieze of figures in black, chocolate and white by Glyn Philpot was added to it, at the top of the wall, in 1920. There is a story that Philip and Philpot spent a frantic day painting shorts on the men before a visit by Queen Mary to Port Lympne on 10 September 1936.[23] (It was a formidable visit. 'Crowds lined the streets of Folkestone,' reported *The Times* the next day.)

Tilden changed the dining room as well, panelling it with a green-blue marble effect. Philip's own set of rooms, which was on the ground floor, consisted of bedroom, dressing room and bathroom with a sunken tub. All the tubs in the house were of white marble,

41. The dining room at Port Lympne.

which presented a great danger of slipping. In front of the house, Tilden added a grand three-part swimming pool with a fountain in its centre. It was too heavy for the land and in 1919 it was reduced to its central portion. A garden on one side of the pool was laid out as a chessboard; on the other lay a striped garden. He also built a grand triumphal Trojan staircase of 135 steps, from the top of which one could see France on a clear day. This provided one entrance down towards the house. Two small temples flank the top of the staircase. They are no longer there because when Herbert Baker saw them some years later he ruled them out of character and Philip rather docilely took them down. Surviving photographs make that appear a rather sad decision.

Inside the house Tilden's most notable work was a Moorish courtyard halfway up the main staircase open to the sky. It may have been inspired by a trip Philip took in the 1920s to Fez. It has fifty-one slender columns and is paved in Swedish green marble, with shallow channels of water meeting in a central fountain. Small bedrooms were built around it. A delightful photograph shows Lord Louis Mountbatten clowning in the courtyard. Tilden also constructed a great bronze front door with a Roman-style collection of trophies above it.

Kenneth Clark came to know Sassoon well through Philip's chairmanship of the Board of Trustees of the National Gallery when Clark became the Director. Despite Philip's deep aesthetic interests, Clark thought, wrongly, that he had very few visitors representing that

42. (*above left*) Georges Carpentier, Rock and Philip at Port Lympne, September, 1921.

43. Lord Louis Mountbatten in the Moorish Courtyard at Port Lympne, August 1923.

44. A corridor at Port Lympne.

45. The garden at Port Lympne.

part of his world, and that most of the guests at his houses were somewhat maverick Tories such as Winston Churchill and Robert Boothby. Clark felt that Sassoon was at the summit of a new sort of post-war society, an 'unstuffy, new world society .... He was a kind of Haroun al Raschid, entertaining with oriental magnificence in three large houses, endlessly kind to his friends, witty, mercurial and ultimately mysterious.' Clark has left a vivid account of a tour of Port Lympne and its gardens with Philip. It began with being greeted by Hannah Gubbay. Jane Clark remarked to her on the extraordinary view over Romney Marsh. ' "It is so peaceful." "You won't find any peace in this house" said Mrs Gubbay.' They then met Philip.

He was dressed in a red shirt open at the neck and velvet slippers embroidered with PS in gold, and looked exotically out of place in the wet Kentish landscape .... In [Baker's] public buildings every proportion, every cornice, ever piece of fenestration was ... an object lesson in how not to do it. Port Lympne was no exception, and Philip's taste for interior decoration had not improved matters .... Philip, more than almost anyone I have known except for Maurice Bowra and Vivien Leigh, had an idiosyncratic and infectious *style* .... He saw the ridiculous side of Port Lympne. Going round the house we came on a particularly hideous bathroom, panelled in brown and black zig-zags of marble. Philip said, without altering his tone of voice 'It takes you by the throat and shakes you.' The point of Port Lympne was the garden. Philip's extravagance, which was such an agreeable feature of his character, expressed itself in the deepest and longest herbaceous borders, the most colossal beds of blue delphinium, the most imposing staircases of yew hedges. He told us with great satisfaction that he had heard a guide taking round a party of visitors and saying 'All in the old-world style, but every bit of it sham.'[24]

One can capture the flavour of living there from comments Philip made in letters to Lord Esher. One August, he remarked 'I am out all day playing games, bathing, making love to my constituents & reading Trollope and Meredith.' In another undated letter he says: 'I have been bathing canvassing & entertaining my usual series of August female authors.' He wrote to him one summer: 'I am receiving my usual August Lympne clientele, which consists almost entirely of architects female gardeners and authoresses!' Through Esher he had also acquired some Scottish cattle; then later a bull was added: 'Thank you so much for this young suitor for my harem of kine. Will he be able to play his part next Spring after the accouchements? ... The cows are lovely. They are well & their shaggy profiles look most effective against the background of marsh & sea.'

Philip became well known for his expressions and his style of speech. He rolled his 'r's in a French way. Cecil Beaton remarked, 'When he spoke he emphasized every single syllable with a trip-hammer tongue: "My de-ah, I couldn-dern't be more sorry." ' Beaton said that he popularized the expressions 'I couldn-dern't care less' and 'I could-dern't agree with you more.' Philip liked to use expressions with a touch of hyperbole but delivered in a deadpan manner, such as saying of a guest – Lord Berners – that he snored so loudly 'that the tiles flew off the roof like confetti'.[25]

Chips Channon has left another critical account. An American, he was determined to get to the centre of the English establishment. He had married Lady Honor Guinness and became an MP in 1935 with a family seat held previously by his father-in-law, Lord Iveagh, and then by his mother-in-law. He remarked: 'Philip and I mistrust each other; we know too much about each other, and I can peer into his Oriental mind with all its vanities .... But I admit he is one of the most exciting, tantalizing personalities of the age.'[26] Channon recorded that, at a dinner with the Duke and Duchess of Kent, 'that arch social barometer Philip Sassoon invited us to Lympne for the Bank Holiday .... Our social stock seems to be rising.' He wrote about the visit:

We left with Norah Lindsay [the garden designer] for Lympne to stay with Philip Sassoon, whom, as we arrived, we met in the road. He waved us a welcome and went on. 'Very Jewish of him', Norah remarked. We were received at his fantastic villa by armies of obsequious white-coated servants who seemed willing enough, but second rate .... The house is large and luxurious and frankly ugly. Honor said that it was like a Spanish brothel. The drawing room is a mixture of fashionable whites, distressed white, off white, cream, and even the famous frescoes have been whitewashed .... The whole affair is second rate, even the lavish lapis dining room, and especially the white coated footmen who will wait on one at tea, always a bad sign. In the evening more flying boys to dine, whilst all day their planes roar about us.[27]

Elsewhere he described the house as 'a triumph of beautiful bad taste and Babylonian luxury, with terraces and flowery gardens, and jade green pools and swimming baths and rooms done up in silver and blue and orange. A strange hydro for this strangest of sinister men.'[28]

Mrs Belloc Lowndes was much more enthusiastic about a visit she made in August 1935. 'The divine beauty of the place, inside and out, so enchants me. A very good party – Anthony Edens, Lord Hugh Cecil, the Hardinges, Lady Desborough, Osbert Sitwell – and – Rex Whistler.'[29] Max Beerbohm visited Port Lympne in the 1930s and wrote to his wife about his time there: 'This place seems very *restless* .... But it is of course beautiful to the eye. Extraordinary elaboration of Persian fantasy, controlled by Etonian good taste. Wonderful successions of gardens with flowers blazing in seemingly endless vistas. Endless steps ascending steeply between walls and towers of clipped yew. Etc. etc. How awful it would be to *own* them!'[30] An anonymous author in a 1923 article in *Country Life* was enthusiastic, stating with perhaps a touch of hyperbole that Sassoon had 'produced the most remarkable modern house in England .... He has proved that it is possible to achieve beauty, proportion and balance in modern architecture and decoration without slavish mimicry of the styles of past centuries.'[31]

Philip himself wrote a piece for the *Architectural Review*, billed as a 'Lay View' in an issue devoted to the last twenty years of British architecture. His remarks were quite generalized but one can sense his intention in his houses to achieve what might be called a modernized eighteenth-century taste. The interiors of Port Lympne wandered quite far away from that criterion and his own stated purpose but his aim was more evident at Trent Park. As appropriate for the publication, he made painting rather subsidiary to architecture, while urging its use. 'In art, the effort to create is life. Originality, however, should not be degraded into eccentricity [as some would accuse him of doing at Port Lympne]. One of the chief lessons of the past, and, in my opinion, the best guide to the future, is the power of simplicity of line and the danger of over-decoration.'[32]

With few exceptions he did not keep valuable furniture and paintings at Lympne. Only two paintings there were listed at the time of his death as worthy of exemption for tax: an Augustus John full-length portrait of a child and a Sargent of Jack Johnson, the prize fighter. When Sassoon had the Sert room whitewashed in the 1930s he hung some of his Sargents of Italian marble ruins there. He may well have redone the room around *The White Duck* of 1753, the single most famous painting by Jean-Baptiste Oudry. If so, he later moved the picture to Park Lane. Philip acquired the painting at an auction in Paris in 1936. (It was at Houghton until 1991, when it was stolen.) The whiteness of the room was probably influenced by Syrie Maugham, a very fashionable designer of the time, who was devoted to white. She had decorated Noel Coward's house nearby.

There were fifteen acres of gardens, planted very much under Philip's supervision, mostly after 1919. He was given advice both at Port Lympne and Trent Park by Norah Lindsay, Diana

Cooper's aunt and a good friend of Philip Tilden's, one of the best-known garden designers of the period, whom we have met being rude about him. She specialized in giving advice to the grand, and had made her own garden at the manor house at Sutton Courtenay into a show place. The gardens were Philip's imposition upon nature, in an Italian style, with their falling-away terraces. Norah Lindsay recreated the feel of Italy by setting herbaceous plants against dark backgrounds. She also worked out ways of softening formal terraces through using colourful flowers. There is a story that on being complimented by a lady on his gardens at Lympne, Philip replied 'At twelve noon on the first of August each year, I give a nod to the head gardener who rings his bell and all the flowers pop up.'[33] Fourteen gardeners were employed during the year, rising to twenty in August, when Philip did most of his entertaining there. In his gardens, as would also be true at Trent Park, Philip did achieve, as he had indicated in his article, a successful combination – more or less what he wanted in his life as well – of eighteenth-century taste with modern style. The danger was the element of pastiche; his rooms were more successful at Trent Park. But at both places the gardens were triumphs. G. C. Taylor wrote about the gardens at Lympne in *Country Life* in 1936, including twelve photographs, four of them, dramatically, in colour. Sassoon's garden, Taylor found, 'combines the classical traditions of the eighteenth with the ideas and tastes of the twentieth century … one of the most notable contributions to gardening art during the present century … an excellent example in garden planning of successful mastery over nature, not by any attempt to obscure or destroy natural features, but rather by emphasising them.'[34] The borders in the West Garden could be seen from the Trojan steps, providing a dramatic vista. They were about 120 yards long and some 14 feet wide, and were planted so that they made their greatest impact during August and September. He also had a clock garden and a box garden (rendered in a painting by Winston Churchill) as well as a vineyard and a figyard. Jane Brown, a garden historian, has remarked: 'This hillside garden has never been taken quite seriously in English gardening terms, and yet it is worth suggesting that Sassoon and the Medici princes had much in common in terms of desires and resources, as well as immensely high standards and a taste for the best of their own time. Port Lympne … is the nearest England can come to the Italian villa gardens in aesthetic terms.' In what is typical of the way Philip is approached, at a later point she groups his garden with others created by Americans in Britain (the Astors at Hever and William Randolph Hearst at St Donat's) as 'all a little unEnglish'.[35] Philip was generous in opening the gardens to the public, and would have parties there for his constituents, particularly wounded veterans.

The last notable embellishment to the house was in 1932, when Rex Whistler painted the Tent Room to the right of the entrance. Whistler also did work for Philip at Trent Park, smaller murals and lunettes with his initials in several of the rooms. But his most impressive work for him was at Port Lympne, rivalling his grand rooms at the Tate restaurant and his greatest achievement, the dining room at Plas Newydd for the Marquess of Anglesey. He had painted the Tate murals, *The Pursuit of Rare Meats*, in 1927, when only 22. Sassoon, a trustee of the Tate, would have been familiar with them. By 1930 he decided that he wanted Whistler to do a room for him. Whistler and Sassoon had close mutual friends, such as Lord Berners the composer

46. Rex Whistler, *The Tent Room*, 1932.

and author, and Osbert Sitwell. Sitwell gave a dinner so that Philip could meet for the second time his cousin Siegfried, who was also a good friend. Rex Whistler was the only other guest. Although Siegfried had some of the style of the Sassoons and was a country gentleman as well as a prominent poet, he tended to avoid the grand circles in which Philip moved. Years later at the time of Siegfried's death Sitwell described the dinner in a letter to Sybil in the following way: 'It could not have gone worse, though Philip was at his most delightful, but Siegfried took me on one side first and explained that there was a lot of jealousy abroad, and that Philip would have liked to write the Old Huntsman ... and Philip told me that he simply couldn't stand a book which he thought so bad.'[36] As Siegfried once remarked, 'All my life I have instinctively reacted against worldliness, only conforming to it with – as dear Robbie [Ross] once said – "the expression of an offended deer-hound." '[37] The dinner was not a success, although Siegfried wrote to Philip after it 'You see we are not as alarming as we look!'[38] They had met briefly once before, in 1925, when Siegfried had gone to Lady Desborough's at Taplow at the invitation of Lady Ottoline Morrell. Siegfried recorded in his diary: 'introduced to Sir Philip Sassoon. He looks a bit of a bounder, but has a remarkable face.'[39] He did eventually visit Port Lympne in August 1933 and had a much better time than he had anticipated.[40] In December of that year, having ended his long affair with Stephen Tennant, Siegfried married. Philip sent him a letter of congratulation, to which Siegfried replied: 'There'll always be a plate of porridge for you at my fireside.'[41] He must have enjoyed making such an incongruous suggestion.

During the Second World War, Siegfried had several friendly meetings with Sybil. Philip knew Osbert Sitwell and Lord Berners well and shared aesthetic and perhaps sexual interests with their circle. But his literary taste was more middlebrow and he did not share their high-style bohemianism.

According to his brother's biography of him, Rex Whistler had the unthought-out anti-Semitism of the time, unaware that he himself was descended from an eighteenth-century Jewish piano maker. This may have influenced his relations with Sassoon. Rex wrote to a friend on 10 September 1930, that 'His Majesty has commanded my presence down at Lympne. It is a *great bore*. But I shall be taking further drawings down with me, and I hope that *this* time the business will be settled – though there will be the *agony of saying the price*.'[42] There was an amusing coda to the question of price – Philip paid £800 for the work – considering the implication that the Christian gentleman, in contrast to the Jew, was supposed to be above such matters. Whistler mentioned the price to Cecil Beaton in the presence of Tom Driberg, the Labour politician and gossip columnist, who published the information in his column in the *Daily Express*. Whistler was profoundly embarrassed at this breach of gentlemanly behaviour and rushed to Park Lane to apologize. He found Sassoon annoyed, but willing to forgive.

Whistler followed the visit with a deeply contrite letter:

I am still so miserable about that wretched press notice of the painted room. Everyone thinks me the most loathsome swine, I'm sure; and I can hardly expect them to credit the fact (though it *is* fact) that I never for one instant thought that the information might reach the papers ... *that is the case, upon my word of honour*. The possibility even (though it was incredibly stupid of me) of that happening, did not once occur to me .... I have written to Driberg to tell him how caddish and grossly ill-mannered it was not to have asked my permission – *do please forgive* me for having unintentionally been the cause of this horrid piece of vulgarity.[43]

Whistler's painting task took him months, including five at Port Lympne; he now felt that he had not charged enough. Philip was not happy with his staying at the house after the 'season' and wanted him to continue the following year, but Whistler wished to finish the work and be paid. The room itself was a great success: a striped blue and gold tent from which various views were visible of a lady travelling by carriage from her country house. That was based on Faringdon, Lord Berners's house, with Berners himself in the foreground as a little boy with a trunk by him with a large B on it. The eighteenth-century grand lady travelled past St Martin-in-the-Fields in London, a Palladian bridge in Dublin and to Sassoon's own house on Park Lane. The murals played with *trompe-l'œil*, painted statues but real curtains, tent poles and tassels. In the centre of the ceiling there was a huge monograph of 'PS', which looked as if it were embroidered on the silk of the tent. On the wall opposite the mural on the side of the windows there was an idealized cartouche of Port Lympne and its gardens. As a neo-Georgian painter of great wit, Whistler fitted into Sassoon's affection for the eighteenth century.

The Visitors' Book records the endless number of the famous who came to Port Lympne. Sargent, Orpen and Philpot drew in it. It also contains photographs of Philip and Sybil; perhaps the most memorable depicts them sitting on the top of plinths at the bottom of the Trojan stairs. A photograph survives of Charlie Chaplin with Philip, Sybil and Hannah marking Chaplin's visit in September 1921. Chaplin remembered that there was a chafing dish in one's room containing hot soup, in case one became hungry or cold during the night. He depicted Sassoon as a picturesque personality, handsome and exotic-looking. He said of the house: 'it was something out of the *Arabian Nights*'.[44]

The novelist Alice Dudeney came to Port Lympne virtually every year. In 1917 her *Head of the Family* was dedicated to Philip, as 'P.S.' Philip wrote to her, 'When is *my* book coming out? I am sorry you did not put 'To Philip Sassoon' on the flyleaf, as I should have felt so *proud* – no one will know who P.S. is – and I should like *everyone* to know.'[45] Philip sent her presents such as a tortoiseshell bag and a fur wrap. Once when she was cold at home she used the coat to keep herself warm, remarking, 'God bless that gilded youth.' She felt that she had to buy special clothes when she went to stay. She recorded of her visit in August 1919: 'The house most lovely and luxurious. I seem to be staying with a fairy prince . . . . A Mr and Mrs Gubbay in the house, his cousins, very Indian and Jewish-ey looking.' At times she

47. Philip and Sybil at Port Lympne, 1921.

48. Hannah, Charlie
Chaplin, Sybil and Philip,
September 1921.

found it too rich for her blood but she was intensely pleased by Philip's close attention. 'If I
were young I would be head over ears in love with him.'

Philip was appreciated more by those not so high on the social scale. The grand and the
aristocratic took from Sassoon as if it were their due, with a tendency to patronize him along
the way. A remark is attributed to Churchill about Philip: that when one took a trip one
should always be sure to travel in a train with an excellent Pullman restaurant car attached.
He received endless hospitality from Philip, staying at Park Lane for long visits when it was
convenient for him. His wife, Clemmie, also was entertained at length by Philip, whether he
was at the house or not. She spent several weeks at Lympne in 1914 after the birth of her
daughter Sarah. The Churchills' daughter Mary Soames wrote that Philip was 'a man of
charm, wit and distinction, and he dispensed princely hospitality to a brilliant and varied
circle of friends . . . . Winston received much help and encouragement from Philip Sassoon,
and painted many pictures of both of his houses and gardens. Winston was always fascinated
by water and the problem of catching it, and many of his coastal scenes and seascapes were
painted at Lympne.' Sassoon lent him Sargents, which Churchill liked to copy, and gave him
outright a painting by John Lewis Brown of two horsemen that Churchill had admired at
Trent; it still hangs at Chartwell.[46]

In August 1922 Mrs Dudeney made another visit with her daughter. Although she still
adored Philip, she was then less fond of his relations:

We were met at Ashford by the Rolls-Royce which I'm always so thankful to get out of,
because it makes me feel sick. There was nobody staying but Sir Louis Mallet, the Dowager
Lady Gosford and the Gubbays of course. Mr Gubbay a dear little man, but so palpably
Oriental – the palms of his hands looking as if they were sprinkled with soot. Mrs Gubbay
handsome: in the short-necked Jewess way but . . . take off her fine clothes and her ropes

of pearls, put her behind a banana stall in the East End on a Saturday night – and there you are! Dozens of her anywhere.

But by 1925 she had quite mellowed towards her. 'I like Mrs Gubbay more and more.' In 1938 when there was a greater awareness of the risk of being Jewish and how Jews might be treated, she acquired a sense that, grand as the family was, it might still feel excluded as Jews. Mrs Dudeney had been entertained by Lord and Lady Gage of Firle Place near Lewes, whom Philip had entertained at Lympne. This impressed Mrs Gubbay, who said to her: ' "You've been to the Gages. What an honour! And they've been to you." Neither Philip nor she have ever been asked. I suppose, however rich you are, that being a Jew goes 'agin'. And probably Philip feels it, and that is the secret of his occasional insolence.' As Sybil might experience to a degree in Norfolk – although she and Rock did not choose to mix with the gentry – it was frequently the county grand, in contrast to what one might call the 'national' upper class, who were the least welcoming to those they regarded as outsiders. This might be particularly true of Jewish outsiders, even if Philip's family, through the Rothschilds and then his father, had been associated with his constituency for a long time. In the 1918 election, some still regarded them as *arrivistes*. Royals, politicians, high society, writers and artists, though perfectly capable of being snobbish, tend to be more flexible and less stuffy than the long established, less cosmopolitan old families of England. But on the whole those were not the families with which Philip wished to mix.

In 1924 Mrs Dudeney met Edith Wharton at Lympne. 'I thought her detestable.' On her return home she read her *Ethan Frome*. 'Wonderful! What a pity she's such a hateful person.' Her diaries provide a good sense of the constant activities at the house. On her 1926 visit Philip came to visit her in her room in the morning. 'Very charming, abrupt, affectionate, inscrutable in fact. He then went off flying which he does in state with an escort of two other machines.' The next day they visited Folkestone, which with Hythe was part of his constituency, in the afternoon and then after tea she was taken up on a flight. The day after she watched him play polo, and then visited the Fish Market in Folkestone, where the fishermen crowded round him.[47] Philip wrote her a charming letter of sympathy from Lympne on the death of her dog Nelson that also provides a sense of the place:

I know *exactly* how someone with yr. great depth of feeling must suffer on such an occasion .... Here is a leaf of verbena that I am pulling in from outside as I write to you from the table by the window in the little silver library with the autumn sunshine streaming in with a vigour that high summer never knew or certainly vouchsafed – what an illegally long sentence to spin to a great writer! I wish you were here & I could tell you my sympathy & affection. Certainly the sweets of life never seem to make up for its blows.[48]

W.F. Deedes, the journalist and politician, who knew Sassoon in the late 1930s, remembered a frenetic visit at Port Lympne where he was much impressed by Philip's extraordinary energy, but also by his inability to relax even when he was supposed to be enjoying himself. In the morning they played golf with four caddies so no time was wasted looking for balls, then dashed to his private beach for a swim, then lunch and a brief rest before taking a spin in an aeroplane. He was impressed with his sense of style, and he followed him in wearing black and white brogues. He felt that Philip never took enough time to recharge his batteries, that he burnt almost too brightly and never switched off. He was impressed by his sensitivity and intelligence, his quicksilver quality. He wasn't a particularly good public speaker, with a rather thin and reedy voice. As others had remarked, Deedes too felt that somehow he 'wasn't entirely English'.[49]

Philip pursued those whom he wanted to entertain who were figures of the hour. Despite his doubts about *Eminent Victorians* as expressed in his correspondence with Lord Esher, Strachey was someone whom he wished to come to his houses. On 9 August 1922 he wrote, presumably out of the blue, 'My dear Mr Lytton Strachey, I should be so pleased if I could persuade you to come down here for a night or two sometime this month. Do let me know if there is any chance of it.' He did succeed, and marked the occasion by pasting a copy of the famous Henry Lamb portrait of Strachey in the Visitors' Book. Strachey went to several dinner parties at Park Lane in the 1920s. At the first he had quite a good conversation with Winston Churchill, as he wrote to Dora Carrington: 'Winston was there and I talked to him a good deal. Do you know, in spite of everything I couldn't help liking him .... He was delighted when I said I thought his book [*The World Crisis 1911–1914*] very well done, and hardly seemed to mind when I added that I also thought it very wicked.'[50] Philip invited Strachey to visit in May 1930: 'Of course if you are going to France in Sept it is quite obvious that you shd break the journey here on your way. I will send you over to Folkestone or Dover – whichever is your port. So you must let me know later on when I may look forward to your visit.' This time he was not successful. And then again two months later, on 5 July: 'You have allowed far too long a time to elapse since your first & (up to date) last visit to this charming coast. The object of these lines is to tempt you here again this August or Sept. Will you help me to convert my hope into a reality? The garden is improved & grown up (the reverse of what happens to us).'[51]

Philip met Virginia Woolf in 1929 at a lunch at, of course, the famous hostess, Sibyl Colefax's. He would have been devastated and astonished at Woolf's very inaccurate description of him in a letter to her sister, Vanessa Bell, on 28 April 1929: 'I lunched with Sibyl – I sat between Sir P. Sassoon – an underbred Whitechapel Jew – and Harold [Nicolson].'[52] The following June he sent her a copy of his book, *The Third Route*. She recorded in her diary 'I ought to send several dull silly letters ... [one] to Sir Philip Sassoon who most unexpectedly sends me, by motor car, his book of travels.'[53] He enclosed a note with the book in which he inadvertently took revenge in a small way by misspelling her name and changing her marital status. He wrote to her: 'Dear Miss Virginia Woolfe, May I have the presumption to ask if you will accept a copy of my humble Traveller's Tale. It has one great advantage – which is that the outside is greatly superior to the inside. So you need not turn a page.'[54]

Among other visitors was Noel Coward whose country house, Goldenhurst Farm, was nearby. Coward records meeting T.E. Lawrence at Port Lympne. Lawrence was there when

49. Lytton Strachey,
Philip and Baba Curzon
at Port Lympne,
September 1922.

he was in the Air Force as an enlisted man under the name of T.E. Shaw. Coward made a joke
of Lawrence's claim to anonymity in a letter to him, using his identity number, writing:
'Dear 338171 (May I call you 338?)'[55] Nigel Nicolson was taken when very young to Port
Lympne by his parents, Harold Nicolson and Vita Sackville-West. His one memory was of
his father telling him to look at a man dressed in an airman's enlisted uniform and urging
him to remember that he had now seen Lawrence of Arabia.[56] Lawrence greatly admired
Lympne, writing to Philip about a visit in 1933: 'You are a colour artist, in your garden, your
house, and your company and the mixtures – no, not mixtures but appositions of unblended
colours – are entrancing. I asked Mrs Gubbay if you knew in what a work of art you lived.'[57]

There is another vivid description of an earlier visit by Lawrence to Port Lympne in
August 1930 written by Tom Mitford, the sole brother of the Mitford sisters. (He was killed
in the war.) The party consisted of his cousins Clementine, Winston and Venetia Montagu,
E.S. Montagu's widow as well as the Samuel Hoares and Aircraftsman Shaw. 'I am a little disappointed with Shaw: he looks just like any other private in the air-force .... Winston
admires him enormously. He said at one moment "If the people make me Prime Minister, I
will make you Viceroy of India." ' He also describes an hour's flight that the house party took
in seven planes, each with a pilot, to visit Tom's sister, then Diana Guinness, who later married Oswald Mosley, at her house, Biddesden in Hampshire. They flew in formation with

Philip at the head, Winston behind him at his left and Hoare on his right.[58] (Indeed, the first time Mosley had spotted Diana was at a ball at Philip's London house.)

Also entertained at Lympne were novelists well known at the time such as Mrs Belloc Lowndes and Maurice Baring. Among many others, there were the composer, Ethel Smyth, Philip's old teacher from Eton, H.E. Luxmoore, as well as many leading politicians most notably Winston Churchill, Neville Chamberlain, Lord Hugh Cecil and Anthony Eden. Max Beerbohm drew a caricature of himself in the Visitors' Book (he also drew one of himself in Sybil's autograph book in imitation of a glowering self-portrait of Orpen on the previous page). Osbert Sitwell, Lady Astor and three of her sons, the famous hostesses Emerald Cunard and Sibyl Colefax, Lord Duveen, Marthe Bibesco, Frances Horner were also among the visitors. The Gubbays were there innumerable times as were Sir Louis Mallet and Sybil and her children.

Although views differed on the beauty of the house itself, its interior was striking and the location dramatic. On his death in 1939 it was left to Philip's cousin Hannah, then a widow. It was requisitioned during the war as a residence for airmen (because of the airfield nearby), both British and foreign. The house was treated very badly by them. In 1946 Colonel Waite, an Australian son-in-law of Lord Austin of the motor company, bought it, and then a property company. In 1973 John Aspinall acquired it for the second of his private zoos, so it is now open to the public. In the house the Tent Room and the Moorish court are well preserved. The Philpot frieze was restored and moved to another room while other rooms on the ground floor are now devoted to animal themes. The gardens are in good shape and the location is as dramatic as ever. As the animals are kept at a distance from the house, the outside of the house and its immediate gardens are much as they were in Sassoon's day. Whatever its oddities, Sassoon created one of the most striking country houses of the century.

Although Philip would come to Port Lympne at various times during the year, and would from time to time fly from Trent to Lympne, he was most often there in August and September. His third house, Trent Park, thirteen miles from the centre of London, he visited more frequently. It was used throughout the year for weekend entertaining, most intensely in the late spring and early summer, and when he wasn't there he would lend it to others, such as the Prime Minister, Stanley Baldwin. Trent was practically a country club with its sports facilities and professionals on tap to assist guests: it had a nine-hole golf course, tennis courts, boating on the lake and a swimming pool with an orangerie. It was particularly dramatic in the early spring when there were carpets of daffodils from bulbs that Philip had put in. Baldwin wrote about the grounds in a letter to Thomas Jones, a Cabinet secretary: 'The spring flowers are a marvel. The daffodils which were put in literally by the tun .... The water garden is chockablock with every kind of colour of polyantha.'[59] He wrote a positively ecstatic note when staying there on his own in late January 1936 when he was Prime Minister. 'My dear Philip, Shod in your shoes, warmed by your wine, expanding under the influence of Sybil's Stilton, I can just rise to call you blessed. Without your bounty, I should be shoeless, chill, and empty. And then where would the country be? Answer: exactly where it is now! With grateful affection (or should it be affectionate gratitude?) S.B.'[60]

On an earlier visit Thomas Jones joined the Baldwins at Trent. He and his wife were picked up in London by Sassoon's Rolls-Royce. Mrs Baldwin said to him,

'We feel we are in the Island of the Blessed.' ... They took us round, and through the avenue of limes to a Japanese garden, and along the lake by the edge of the golf course .... At 8.0 we all met for dinner, and were waited upon by very tall men in white linen coats and blue trousers. Mrs. Baldwin drank orangeade, S.B. and I drank some claret diluted with Malvern water.[61]

Arthur Bryant, the Tory historian, visited Baldwin there at Easter 1937, and recorded that Philip lent him the house every Easter starting 'after his defeat in 1929, when he had no money and no house in London to go to .... He liked it because unlike Sassoon's other houses, it had nothing exotic in it (he agreed that Sassoon's taste was otherwise almost flawless) but was purely English. In the summer Sassoon entertained large weekend parties from London there – ladies with painted toe-nails he said – he was not there then.'[62]

With its 1,000 acres it was extraordinary to have such a splendid country house so close to London. Virtually everyone came by car, but it was not too far from the last Tube stop, Cockfosters, on the Piccadilly Line, one of Charles Holden's striking modern stations. Philip regularly opened both the house and the gardens, the latter weekly during the summer, to the public. He would also have larger celebrations for important events there, such as the coronation of George VI.

Trent's land was part of the ancient royal hunting grounds of Enfield Chase. Sir Richard Jebb, the royal doctor, in 1777 had saved the life of the Duke of Gloucester, a brother of George III, at Trento in the Tyrol. In gratitude, the King made him a baronet and facilitated his acquisition by lease of some royal land belonging to the Duchy of Lancaster. Jebb built the first house on the site, and called it Trent Place in memory of the Prince's recovery. On his death in 1787 the estate was sold to the Earl of Cholmondeley, who resold it six years later to John Wigston in order to raise funds for Houghton. The leasehold had two further owners, Sir Henry Lushington and John Coming, before being sold in 1833 to the Bevans, a family of Quaker bankers. They were at Trent Park until 1908 when Sir Edward Sassoon acquired the lease. In 1923 Philip bought the leasehold from the Duchy of Lancaster and converted it into a freehold. This, he felt, gave him greater freedom to remodel it. Francis Bevan had rebuilt the house in 1893 into a not particularly attractive building, although less ugly than many other Victorian residences. But it was not what Philip wanted. (Early during the First World War he would lend the house occasionally to young officers to recuperate and then in 1916 he rented it to Grace Duggan. In 1917 she married the widowed Lord Curzon and they gave a coming-out party for 150 guests, for his daughter Irene, which gave great offence. A newspaper headline read: 'Curzons dance while Europe burns.'[63]) In 1923 Philip tried minor modifications by installing new, more elegant windows, with smaller panes of glass, to replace the larger Victorian ones. He took the creepers off the house and removed

50. Trent Park in 1893.

the balustrade from the entrance front. In 1924 he had an auction of much of its French furnishings in the eighteenth-century style, put there by his mother.

From 1925 to 1931 he took more radical steps, devoting a fair amount of energy to the
house and grounds. The demolition of William Kent's Devonshire House in Piccadilly presented an opportunity in 1924. By a nice touch his cousin Siegfried wrote a 'Monody on the
Demolition of Devonshire House':

> ... While musing on the social gap between
> Myself, whose arrogance is mostly brainy,
> And those whose pride, on sunlit days and rainy,
> Must loll and glide in yacht and limousine, ...
> And not one nook survived to screen a mouse
> In what was Devonshire (God rest it) House.

Was he also contrasting himself with his cousin? Philip bought Devonshire House's
eighteenth-century rose-coloured bricks and stonework and used them to reface Trent Park,
except for the servants' and office wings. Through his redesign of the house, and most dramatically through the use of eighteenth-century brick, Sassoon made the house and himself
part of that century.

He did the same in the grounds. He acquired the stone lions from Devonshire House,
installing them at his entrance. He bought statuary for the park from Stowe and from Milton

Abbey, the home of the eighteenth-century Earls of Dorchester. In 1934 he acquired three columns to enhance the grounds appropriately when he lent it to the Duke and Duchess of Kent for part of their honeymoon.[64] They were married on 29 November and stayed at Trent, without Philip or other guests, from 12 to 18 December. The columns had previously been at Wrest Park in Bedfordshire where they had belonged, coincidentally, to an eighteenth-century non-royal Duke of Kent. At Trent, they honoured the title just bestowed on the newlyweds. One was a short obelisk marking the beginning of the straight carriage-way to the house. It is inscribed 'To the memory of Henry, Duke of Kent'. Closer to the entrance there was a taller column with a pineapple on the top inscribed 'To the memory of Emma Crew, Dutchess of Kent'. And finally, across the lake was a much taller obelisk as a viewpoint. Philip also owned the famous picture of a gardener presenting to Charles II a pineapple, the ultimate symbol of luxury in the previous centuries (it is now at Houghton: appropriately, since it had once belonged to Horace Walpole). Outside the house, he took down the rather heavy porch and substituted the pillared doorway from Chesterfield House. He also removed a tower that had been erected in the nineteenth century. Through bricks and statues, Philip constructed a connection with the eighteenth-century Dukes of Devonshire, Kent and Buckingham, and the quintessential figure of the century, the Earl of Chesterfield.

51. Rex Whistler, *Trent Park with Philip and Sybil*, 1934.

The house emerged as a recreation of an eighteenth-century one, but with slight reference to the original one on the site. It was as if the house had been built at the time of Queen Anne in the 1710s, had a Palladian interior of the 1720s and 1730s, and was furnished with Chinoiserie of the 1750s and 1760s as well as neo-classical furniture of the 1760s and beyond.[65]

Christopher Hussey's articles on Trent Park in *Country Life* marked the conclusion of the redesign and redecoration. Hussey, the dean of architectural writers and an expert on the eighteenth century, was editor of *Country Life* from 1933 to 1940. He wrote a preliminary article in October 1930 on a comparatively restricted aspect of the house, its Japanned furniture – that is, furniture ranging from around 1685 to 1820, from Charles II to the Regency, that English makers did in a Chinese style. Philip also possessed some objects made in China, such as a polychrome-decorated black and gold coromandel lacquer six-leaf screen. Apparently it was too sober for him, and to make it sparkle he had it gilded.[66] In January 1931 Hussey wrote two extremely enthusiastic articles on the house. 'An ugly Victorian building has been transformed into a stately yet very simple country house in the pure English tradition . . . . Without the Palladian tricks and aggrandisements with which architects, from Inigo Jones onwards, distorted the native idiom of "right building" and practical planning. Though the style is traditional, the house is essentially modern in its simplicity of form and fitness for the purposes of country life . . . an ideal example of English domestic architecture unalloyed by fashion or fantasy.' Hussey's ideal was a fusion of the classical and modern styles.

He continued to be quite ecstatic in the second article:

Philip Sassoon has been guided by tradition and exceptional tact in creating an ideal country house . . . . A building at once traditional and modern, traditional in its materials and genial proportions, modern in its concentration on essentials alone and its expression of purpose . . . . Strait is the path between the Scylla of period reproduction and the Charybdis of modernism. . . . At Port Lympne, Sir Philip Sassoon had experimented in various engaging styles within a more or less traditional shell . . . here . . . catching that indefinable and elusive quality, the spirit of a country house . . . an essence of cool, flowery, chintzy, elegant, unobtrusive rooms . . . . [He] has only succeeded in distilling it [the subtle essence of a country house] at Trent by virtue of having supervised the process himself . . . . The furniture is very much of the kind that accumulates in a country house through centuries of use, though of a rather finer quality than is usual, and arranged with distinctly more taste . . . . To create this atmosphere, this subtle sense of ease and charm and tradition, in a house that is, essentially, new has been a remarkable achievement not quite to be matched in any work of reconditioning or building that I am aware of . . . . It is rather an exquisite sense of values that has enabled Sir Philip Sassoon to make Trent what it is, and a natural artistry of that rare kind whose aim is *celare artem* [to conceal itself].[67]

Well! Through Trent, at least in architectural terms and in Hussey's opinion, Sassoon had achieved that 'unbought grace of life' that was the mark of the true aristocrat. Visiting the house today, even when surrounded to an extent by institutional buildings of the University of Middlesex, one can see that it was a triumph.

But perhaps it didn't completely work. As Stephen Doree has pointed out, visitors to the house seemed to be reminded more of the *Arabian Nights* than of an eighteenth-century world. Doree also rather interestingly mentions one of W. Somerset Maugham's most famous stories, 'The Alien Corn'. It describes the furnishing of a country house by Sir Freddy Bland, a Jewish figure similar to Sassoon, who tried to be more English than the English. As the narrator remarks, despite the great beauty of the house and its furnishings, 'It did not give you for a moment the impression of an English house. You had the feeling that every object had been bought with a careful eye to the general scheme. You missed the dull Academy portraits that hung in the dining room beside a Carlo Dolci that an ancestor had brought back from a grand tour, and the water-colours painted by a great-aunt that cluttered up the drawing room so engagingly . . . . There was beauty but no sentiment.'[68]

The University has even preserved to a degree the rooms inside, using them as meeting places with some appropriate furniture. Rex Whistler's 'PS' monograms and small murals have been restored. Through photographs, one can recapture what the house was like, with its spaciousness and elegance, in Sassoon's time, although without people the rooms are somewhat lifeless. Sassoon raised the entrance hallway through arches in the ceiling. The

52. The drawing room at Trent Park.

Blue Room had a theme of patriotism with a small mural by Whistler of Minerva and Mars. Churchill had made a painting of this room in 1934. Also, one could see from the room the Union Jack in stonework in front of the entrance. It was made of stones taken from Westminster Bridge. There was a story that once Philip had the Union Jack flying over the house hauled down as he felt that its colours conflicted with the sunset.[69] Sassoon arranged that the Library, Salon and Drawing Room – rooms from the original house of 1780–1808 – be opened up into one another, providing an enfilade, a splendid vista and ideal space for entertaining. In the Library Whistler painted Sassoon's monogram and also a mermaid mural. The pineapple painting was in that room, as well as two Zoffany portraits including one of Horace Walpole. Here Philip had his eighteenth-century conversation pictures, a genre that he had done much to make more popular. Zoffany's *The Colmore Family* was in the Drawing Room; in the Red Lacquer Room hung a Devis of the Sergison family; and a Gainsborough of the Brown family as well as another Zoffany of the Young family had pride of place in the Dining Room. Aristocrats on the outside of the house; gentry on the inside.

Philip constructed a terrace on the north front, where he could stroll out and view the lake where cranes, white and black swans, exotic breeds of ducks and geese, teals, ibises, spoonbills, and even a pair of king penguins were to be found.[70] One could glimpse the deer, some of whose antlers he had had gilded to catch the sun. In 1927 Philip sent to Churchill a pair of black swans from Trent, the origin of the famous black swans still at Chartwell. Churchill thanked him on 9 June, writing; 'the black swans arrived safely, and I conducted them to their pool .... They sing to one another beautifully, and dance minuets with their necks. I am so glad to have them, and it was charming of you to send them to me .... Could your bird man at Trent say what steps ought to be taken to look after them in the winter? Ought they to have a house to live in, and how do you teach them to go into the house?' Philip replied the next day: 'You will not need to protect them in the winter because 1 our summer weather is a very good training for the most arctic conditions & 2 these birds are much hardier than their delicate exterior wd lead one to believe. It is certainly too late I shd imagine for them to mate this year. I am making enquiries as to domestic details of their past life & will let you know.' In 1934 Philip sent him as a Christmas present some Indian Comb ducks that he had at Trent. Churchill thanked him by telegram, alluding to his own attitude towards Indian independence: 'Enchanted to receive Comb duck from India. Hope by firm government [to] make them loyal subjects.'[71]

The rest of the grounds were opulent with magnificent gardens. They were designed to be at their best for the weekends in May, June and July, but the house was used, to some extent, throughout the year as it was so close to central London. In September 1997, when I first visited Trent, I met a gardener, Alec Dale, and his wife, who had been a maid in the house. They were still living in a cottage in the grounds. They remembered Sassoon, whom they described as Indian, very fondly. Eighteen gardeners had worked there, and flowers and vegetables would be sent to Park Lane. If necessary, fully grown plants were transported to Trent to be put in at the right moment. Robert Boothby remembers a sight early one morning. He had come the night before, earlier than the rest of the house party, which would include the

WISHING YOU A MERRY CHRISTMAS AND A HAPPY NEW YEAR.

53. Christmas card of penguins at Trent Park.

Duke and Duchess of York. 'I heard the sound of cart wheels. I got up and went out in my dressing-gown to find six horse-drawn carts coming up the avenue, laden with flowers from Covent Garden in full bloom. An Army of gardeners was waiting to plant them out in borders which had been carefully prepared. By the time the guests began to arrive for lunch, they were all in.'[72] There would be parties there at Christmas (to which Sybil and her children frequently came) and Easter. The most dramatic part of the garden was, as at Port Lympne, the long flower borders. Here too Norah Lindsay gave advice. There was a pergola of Italian marble covered with vines, wisteria and clematis that Churchill depicted in one of his most vivid paintings, as well as a Japanese garden near the lake. The daffodils were planted in 1928 to greet his Easter guests. They still bloom annually to great effect.

Perhaps Osbert Sitwell provided one of the best summations of the house. It turned out that he had wandered the grounds when he was attending a prep school nearby.

It was, therefore, with a shock of the utmost surprise that, thirty years later, while passing a few days with Philip Sassoon at Trent, and living in that state of luxury, imbued with the spirit of fun, of which he was a particular master, I recognized the place .... Philip had

... [made] a kind of paradise, touching it with magic, so that, where formerly had glowered a mid-Victorian mansion of mauve brick, with designs in black brick covering its face, and a roof of mauve slate, turreted and slightly frenchified, now stood an old house of rose-red brick and stone cornering long settled and stained by time; before, too, statues, and lead sphinxes, smiling from their pedestals, and shepherds fluting under ilex groves, and orangeries and fountains and pyramids, seeming to have been rooted in the bracken for centuries, had made their appearance, and tall old trees, magnolias, and the rarest shrubs that sprung from the ground with something of the same pride with which the Swans and multicolored water birds displayed their plumage on the lake below.[73]

The major purpose of Trent Park was as a venue for entertaining, particularly at weekend parties. As at Port Lympne there was a mixture of the literary, the aesthetic, the social and the political. One of the fascinations of Sir Philip's life was how he intertwined different groups. The literary was mostly at the level of serious popular literature. The aesthetic was quite strong in that he was one of the greatest connoisseurs and collectors of his age. He was a shaper of taste. There are or were certain rewards in the English world that are hard to resist. What frequently happens is that the outsider who might cause trouble is neutralized. English high society may accept the outsider but that person changes to a degree in order to accommodate. When I asked a distinguished English historian, Sir Jack Plumb, who knew Sybil Cholmondeley well, whether it was significant that Sybil and her brother were Jewish, and what difference that made to their lives, he answered, 'There are no Jews in the English aristocracy' as in the expression, 'There are no Blacks on Bond Street'. Obviously he did not mean the statement to be literally true: but once a Jew can afford to be in the English aristocracy, or a Black can afford to shop on Bond Street, they are no longer, in one sense, Jewish or Black. Society tolerates and accepts the outsider, at a price. Who has triumphed in this situation: the outsider or society? Or is it a typical English compromise that makes for an easier but a less resolved life? Philip was warmly welcomed to English society, up to a point.

The acceptance may well be far from total and it may have meant giving up aspects of his identity. Sybil appeared to be much more relaxed than Philip; he tended to be tense and frenetic. He was flamboyant, extravagant and 'over the top'. He seemed somewhat ill at ease with being Jewish. Nevertheless, he remained his own person. He entertained on such a lavish scale that it was hard to avoid the impression that he was buying attention. Yet he loved entertaining. He entertained whom he wished from quite a range: the King and Queen, the royal dukes, aristocrats, prominent politicians, literary and artistic figures, airmen and their wives. He certainly did not move in Jewish circles but remained close to some of his relations – for example, Mozelle Sassoon was a frequent guest. David Gubbay's sister and a great London hostess herself, she was widowed in 1924 and was connected with the other family firm, E.D. Sassoon. His aunt Louise Sassoon came for weekends. And of course, Philip was extremely close to his sister and to his cousin, Hannah, who were eventually his heirs. They were continually at Trent, Hannah even more so after she was widowed. Second to Sybil, she was the most important person in his life, and also played a central role

54. Philip in the library at Port Lympne by Howard Coster, 1929.

in Sybil's life as in that of her children and grandchildren. After the Second World War, almost every Sunday she would have lunch with Lord and Lady John Cholmondeley; their son remembers vividly how funny she was.

Nowadays, and one suspects then in private conversation, Philip was frequently assumed to be homosexual.[74] Not surprisingly, I have found no evidence of his sexual activities. I do not know if he had any physical relations with either men or women. If he were homosexual and wished to conceal it, he certainly made no attempt to curb his natural exuberance and extravagance of expression that might have, given the assumptions of then and now, supported such a belief. I know of no traumas in his childhood, which conformed to the standards of his class, that might have affected his sexuality. He frequently entertained without hesitation Osbert Sitwell, Lord Berners, Glyn Philpot and, though married, Malcolm Bullock and Chips Channon, figures who those 'in the know' (and even those who were not) knew were homosexuals. If the main object of his life were to blend into the English world, he might have tried to make himself duller.[75] Through his skills, wealth and activities he had power and authority in the English world and made himself part of that world. There is an intriguing tension in English society between individualism, even eccentricity, and conformity. After 1924 Philip made his political career in a rather grey Tory party. He was seen as an exotic. In the later 1930s he did become more moody and difficult, and melancholic, a tendency he had had since Eton that became more marked as he aged. His health and spirits may have been damaged by an apparently somewhat botched operation on his tonsils he had had in April 1931. He may have been depressed by his lack of a close relationship, other than with his sister and cousin. Perhaps he had a touch of manic-depression, as he was certainly capable of unusual energy and high spirits. He wrote to a friend as early as 1918: 'I am well and happy except occasionally for those causeless depressions that are forever floating about and fastening onto somebody's heart.'[76] Perhaps he was frustrated that his political career was not developing. In July 1936 Mrs Dudeney records having lunch with him in London 'Philip was very nice – quite as of old. Mrs Gubbay and Lady Cholmondeley quite affectionate!' But then some days later she had lunch with the Cholmondeleys. 'They, especially he, told me that Philip is becoming quite outrageous in his behaviour to everybody and Lord C. can't think why people don't walk out of his house when he is in that mood. Sir Louis [Mallet] told me much the same.'[77] No specifics are provided. One can imagine that he was moody and peremptory, possibly the price of being nice and accommodating to the powerful. And he was known for his furious temper.

Perhaps the paradox of the tension between his 'Englishness' and 'non-Englishness' was at its most intense in the magnificent setting of Trent Park. There he had created in a few brief years a perfect English country house where he entertained frequently and well. The Trent Park Visitors' Books, with illustrations and photographs, are rich evidence of that.[78]

55. Queen Mary, Sybil, Hannah and Lady Cynthia Colville at Trent Park, 1938.

56. Trent Park Visitors' Book: 12 July (above) and 18 July 1925.

Queen Mary visited Trent Park regularly in the 1930s to see the flowers, including a visit on 27 May 1934 when she brought her granddaughter, 'Lillibet'. The royal dukes would often come to play golf and tennis. For instance on 7 July 1924 Prince Albert, later George VI, wrote: 'I did enjoy the games though I fear I spoilt them for Borotra [a famous tennis player], being so very much weaker than our opponents.'[79] He and his wife, Elizabeth, were back for a weekend in June 1930.

Royalty, politicians, social and artistic figures would mix at Philip Sassoon's table. He provided at Trent a location where politics could be played in a luxurious setting. He was one of the world's great hosts, a role that is bound to fade as time passes. Yet, in its way, it is a considerable accomplishment and it is striking how many of those he entertained are names we still recognize. To what purpose? To amuse himself? To move the world's business forward? To be in the swim? To provide point to his life? All these factors were likely to be present in Philip's mind.

Frances Stevenson's diary records for 12 February 1920: 'Dined last night at Philip Sassoon's [at Park Lane]. Did not know till I got there that the Prince of Wales was to be there. Just 8 of us. I sat between the Prince and Sir Robert Horne.' Lloyd George had appointed him Chancellor of the Exchequer, summoning Sir Robert to Port Lympne to offer him the post. Two days later she wrote, 'Just off to Trent for the weekend. D. says I can ask Sassoon if he would like to be his Parliamentary Secretary ....[on the 16th] Returned from Trent this morning – after a most interesting and enjoyable weekend. The P. of W. and his two brothers were there. Played tennis with Prince Henry. Prince Albert is great fun. After dinner last night we danced & were very merry.'[80] Having the Prince of Wales as a dinner guest meant that Philip's invitation to join him had practically the power of a royal command. Dorothy Rodgers, the wife of Richard Rodgers, the American songwriter, declined such an invitation for herself and her husband because she was giving a dinner party that day. Her friends told her afterwards that she had committed a social gaffe and that they would have understood and not held it against her if she had cancelled her own party in order to dine with the Prince.[81]

He would also entertain the young who might have a claim upon his affections. Late in the 1930s, Philip gave a talk to an Oxford political club, and met Earl Haig, then an undergraduate; his father had died in 1928. Over the next three years, he would see quite a bit of Philip, whom he remembers as very kind, considerate and happy to spend time talking to a young man who had lost his father when he was ten. (Philip's letters to Esher during the war had recorded Haig's intense pleasure at the birth of his son and heir.) As in Kent, Philip had an airfield at Trent and his own plane, a Super Moth, painted in the Eton colours, black with blue strips. Philip sent his plane to Oxford to pick up Haig for a weekend and when he arrived presented him with a Humber car.[82] He quite frequently sent his plane to pick up guests. Churchill's wife wrote to him from Chartwell: 'I'm lunching at Lympne today. Philip is sending his aeroplane.'[83]

Mrs Belloc Lowndes, a frequent visitor, remembered one visit to Trent for New Year in 1927:

This is a delightful house to stay in. Philip Sassoon is such a very *kind* creature – People come and go to meals, Eshers, Lee of Fareham [the politician and art patron], and so on .... A good deal of talk about the Prayer Book [the issue was whether Parliament should revise the Anglican Book of Common Prayer]. I think there is *no doubt* that the country, as a whole, is *passionately* against it. Philip had 100 letters against it, from his Constituents, to 1 for it! He did not vote, belonging to the Jewish faith, but he came into my bedroom and *talked* about it for an hour yesterday![84]

She went regularly for New Year, and nine years later she was there during the early stages of the Abdication crisis, when Wallis Simpson arrived with her husband. 'At about six o'clock "Mr and Mrs Simpson" were announced. Most of the people in the house-party did not know them and we all felt a very real sense of thrill, of interest and of curiosity.' There was the question of whether she would be given pride of place as a royal mistress at her host's right at dinner, but that did not happen. 'She was, therefore, put in the middle of the table some way from her host, while Philip had at either side the Duchess of Rutland and some other woman whose rank entitled her to be next to him.'[85]

Sybil did not wish to meet Mrs Simpson, in part because she was not particularly fond of Edward himself; in any case, Rock had asked her to avoid the new King even if he were to be his Lord Great Chamberlain.[86] The situation was much harder for Hannah Gubbay, who had become a great friend of the Prince's. Mrs Belloc Lowndes wrote to her daughter in 1938:

At one time – over years – she saw him constantly. Once he dined with her and her husband 16 nights running. She is attached to him, says he is unselfish, *always* puts the woman whom at the moment he loves, on a pinnacle. She thinks he is faithful by nature. Of late years he was bitterly enraged that Hannah would never receive Mrs Simpson .... The very last time the King and Mrs S. dined out together was at Park Lane (to see the film of his tour in Wales). Hannah, of course, was there and Mrs S. was really rude to her, speaking coldly of Hannah's friendship with the Duchess of York.[87]

T. E. Lawrence was a guest for the Christmas weekend in 1934. He had written to Philip on 18 December: 'I've long wanted to see Trent and my time is running short, so I would like to come for Friday night. Only to believe the Papers, instead of you and Mrs Gubbay I might run into a nest of junior Royalty – and I've always hitherto kept clear of them .... My present notion is to ring up Trent, then, and ask who are the inhabitants: and if all's clear may I come for the night? They say it's easy to get to, being on a Tube Railway. I suspect you of having a private station, with your lift into the house.' Philip replied: 'Royalty have fled & only the Plebs remain you will be glad to hear. I will send for you to Smith Square some time after 5:30. if you find an air force officer in the car you will know it is Squadron Leader Pope who is in the Fleet air arm'.[88] He arrived on 22 December and, as he wished, the party was not a grand one.

The visit is recorded in the Visitors' Book of that day. Others there at the time were Mrs Belloc Lowndes, Louis Mallet and Mozelle Sassoon. Lawrence, perhaps characteristically, misrepresented the visit. His version was that he and Squadron Leader Pope were the only visitors. When they were to sign the book, they noticed that the previous guests had been the Duke and Duchess of Kent on their honeymoon. As the royals had signed, correctly, with a single name, in their case their first, in parallel fashion Pope signed Pope and Shaw signed Shaw and then Shaw wrote after Pope, 'not *the* Pope', and after his own name 'not *the* Shaw', a reference to George Bernard Shaw. Then Philip, according to Lawrence, snatched the book away, accusing them of messing it up.[89] The story is untrue; no such pages exist in the Visitors' Book although Shaw's and Pope's names are there along with those of their fellow guests. Pope included his initials and Lawrence signed as 338171 A/C Shaw.

There were certainly plenty of grand visitors. Queen Mary came again on 17 May 1936, and her photograph in the Visitors' Book faces one of the two king penguins. For the weekend of 11–13 July 1936, Edward was there as King, along with Wallis Simpson and the Mountbattens. The following May, Lady Elizabeth Paget, a daughter of the Marquess of Anglesey, came several times. Philip saw the Paget family frequently; there was a link through Rex Whistler, who was painting his great mural in their house in Wales and having an affair with her sister. There are several dramatic photographs of Lady Elizabeth in the Visitors' Book. She was a woman of great beauty and bore a resemblance to Sybil. Philip may have been a little bit in love with her. But as her cousin John Julius Norwich has said, everyone was in love with her, and she would shortly marry Raimund von Hofmannsthal. That same month, the Prime Minister, Neville Chamberlain, and his wife, Anne, came, and that June George and Elizabeth, now King and Queen, visited for a weekend, along with Charles Lindbergh.

Social life was intense at Trent and Philip made sure that his guests were happy, doing what they wished, observing the great beauty of the place, and eating extremely well. The appointments were perfect, and it was even said that the cut flowers were dyed to match the colours of the curtains in the guests' rooms. (Unlike his friend Lord Berners, he did not dye his doves pastel shades.) He was amusing and witty but increasingly in the 1930s guests remarked on some decline in his high spirits. His guests were always willing to accept his lavish hospitality, but some recorded their memories of him in a rather patronizing way. Being a rich Jew had its potential problems, as the biographer of Isaiah Berlin suggests:

> Eagerness to please figured at the top of his list of vices. He always worried that a Jew should not be so emollient and accommodating. It was a central moral dilemma in his life to reconcile the sense of dignity with this eagerness to fit in. Ingratiation, he maintained, was the characteristically Jewish sin, always hoping, against the evidence, that one would 'pass'. Paradoxically, of course, this extreme sensitivity to the dilemmas of assimilation made him uniquely successful at it. He became a master of fitting in, at the price of lingering self-dislike.[90]

Harold Nicolson went to Trent in 1931, just after the completion of the transformation of the house. He knew the Middle Eastern world, having served in the embassy in Turkey as an attaché when Mallet was Ambassador and then later in Tehran.

Motor down to Trent. Philip alone in the house, a slim, Baghdadi figure, slightly long in the tooth, dressed in a double-breasted, silk-fronted blue smoking-jacket with slippers of zebra hide .... [He] is a strange, lonely, un-English little figure, flitting about these vast apartments, removed from the ordinary passions, difficulties and necessities of life. He always seems to me the most unreal creature I have known. People who care over-much for the works of men end by losing all sense of the work of God, and even their friends become for them mere pieces of decoration to be put about the room.[91]

Philip embodies the whole issue of 'outsiders' in British society, no matter how grand they might be and no matter to what extent they follow its forms. For instance, Robert Boothby viewed Sassoon as not 'one of us'. 'In so far as he can be said to have had any intimate friends outside the family circle, I was one of them. But he was curiously impersonal. You got so far; and then an invisible and impenetrable barrier supervened. He was not part of England, and whatever gods he worshipped were not our gods. Fundamentally, he was a detached and acute observer in a strange land. As such he missed nothing, but was seldom wholly at ease. As a rule he was superlative company. A favourite method of producing his effects was an astonishing power of reckless and witty exaggeration .... There were black moods, invariably replaced – without reason or warning – by spontaneous and irrepressible gaiety.'[92] Part was personal to Sassoon, but part seemed to be intrinsic to his situation as a rich Jew in England. Although Boothby claimed to be close to him, he nevertheless thought that the Sassoons were Parsees, although he also knew that his mother was a Rothschild. Despite his criticisms, Boothby made Sassoon even grander than he actually was: 'Behind the whole social scene in England, and dominating it all, was Sir Philip Sassoon, the greatest host and the greatest gardener I have ever known and, in the right mood, the best company. For ten years he shaped my life.'[93] According to Boothby, he and Sassoon went to Berlin shortly after the Nazis came to power, and Sassoon insisted on visiting Goering, who was in charge of the German Air Force.

Boothby was a considerable recipient of Sassoon's generosity, having at low or no rent French House next to Port Lympne and being a frequent visitor to Trent Park. Although he would call his second volume of autobiography *Boothby: Recollections of a Rebel,* he was well born, educated at Eton and Oxford, and had an active although ultimately not that successful political career. He had a long affair with Lady Dorothy Macmillan, wife of the Prime Minister, Harold Macmillan, and had a daughter with her; he was also allegedly bisexual. He was quite close to the notorious criminals, the Kray brothers. Yet he could quite accurately judge himself an insider, and Philip not.

Boothby has left a rich, perhaps even over-rich, description of the weekends at Trent:

His hospitality was on an oriental scale. The summer weekend parties at Trent were unique, and in the highest degree enjoyable, but theatrical rather than intimate. He frankly loved success, and you could be sure of finding one or two of the reigning stars of the literary, film or sporting worlds, in addition to a fair sprinkling of politicians and, on occasion, royalty (the Sassoons never forgot that they owed their position in this country to the influence of the Court). I remember one weekend when the guests – who included the present King and Queen [George VI and Elizabeth] – were entertained with an exhibition of 'stunt' shots at golf by Joe Kirkwood after lunch, with flights over the grounds in our host's private aeroplane after tea, with a firework display over the lake after dinner . . . with songs from Richard Tauber [whom Philip had sponsored for British nationality], which we listened to on the terrace before going to bed . . . . The white-coated footmen serving endless courses of rich but delicious food, the Duke of York coming in from golf, an immaculate Sir Samuel Hoare playing tennis with the professional, Winston Churchill arguing over the teacups with Bernard Shaw, Lord Balfour dozing in an armchair [Balfour liked the armchair so much that Philip had a replica made for him, and it was the chair in which he died]. Rex Whistler absorbed in his painting. Osbert Sitwell and Malcolm Bullock laughing in a corner, while Philip himself flitted from group to group, an alert, watchful, influential, but unobtrusive stage director . . . . The beautifully proportioned red brick house, the blue bathing pool surrounded by such a profusion of lilies that the scent at night became almost overpowering, the flamingoes and ducks, the banks of exquisite flowers in the drawing room, the red carnation and cocktails on one's dressing-table before dinner, were each and all perfect of their kind.[94]

On Philip's death in 1939, Hannah Gubbay became tenant for life at Trent. The war interrupted that plan and the house was requisitioned, appropriate in an ironic way, as a place for German air force officers to be quartered and questioned. After the war, Hannah returned but established residence in the bailiff's house, with her own important eighteenth-century collection. After various legal complications, the contents of the house, as Philip intended, went to his sister, some of them dispersed in the great Houghton sale of 1994. Following the war the Ministry of Education took over the house as a teacher training college and in 1950 the estate was requisitioned as part of a green belt, with Mrs Gubbay having a life interest in part of it. On her death in 1968, the entire estate became public and was divided between the London Borough of Enfield and the Greater London Council. In 1974 the teacher training college became part of Middlesex Polytechnic and in 1992 Middlesex University. The house itself has been well preserved. New buildings on the grounds do not look as bad as one might have feared. Philip might have had mixed feelings about one of the dormitories being called Sassoon and another Gubbay. And he would not have been amused by the recent historian of the house, Patrick Campbell, in his useful short book, remarking about the celebrations at the opening of the University: 'In a felicitous gesture that forged anew the Jewish connection, fourteen fiddlers from the university's School of Music played "Fiddler on the Roof" atop the mansion as the Vice-Chancellor raised the flag of Middlesex University, its fast-forward logo emblazoned in red and black.'[95]

Sybil

In a similar fashion, Sybil's houses reflected her life. Early on, she and Philip had shared Park Lane. Like Port Lympne, her London house was more or less her creation. (And Houghton was her Trent Park. Once owned by the Cholmondeleys, it was a much more distinguished eighteenth-century house, a house of central political importance.) The Rocksavages acquired after the war on leasehold one of the grandest of London houses in millionaires' row, at 12 Kensington Palace Gardens, at the very end of Kensington Gardens and close to Kensington Palace, near where Sybil spent the first few years of her life. The street ran parallel, although at a great distance, to Philip's house on Park Lane at the opposite end of Hyde Park and Kensington Gardens. These houses were built in the 1840s on a crown estate that had been the kitchen gardens for Kensington Palace. Number 12 remained her London house until 1980, when the lease from the Crown Estates was being renegotiated. It was far more comfortable for her when she was in her eighties to spend most of her time at Houghton. A small flat on Eaton Square became her London *pied-à-terre*. Kensington Palace Gardens had become by then largely a street of embassies. In fact, during the Cold War, her house did service to the British government as a listening post on the Russian Embassy.[96]

Robert Richardson Banks, the head of Sir Charles Barry's office, designed the house on Kensington Palace Gardens, the most distinguished on the road, in 1846 for Samuel Morton Peto, subsequently a railway king. The house is in the rather Italian palazzo style that characterized the clubs Barry, the architect of the Houses of Parliament, built on Pall Mall. Peto himself did not occupy the house until 1853. In 1861 it was sold to Alexander Collie, a cotton merchant. The well-known architect Matthew Wyatt Digby extended the main staircase to the second floor, built a new breakfast room, and most dramatically a billiard room replaced a former kitchen. The Cholmondeleys used the room as a flower room:

> a rich and glittering invention in the Moresque style, with a brightly coloured glazed-tile dado above which is a cornice carried on carved brackets. Over this is an arcade on colonnettes of marble, behind which is a series of mirrors. The coved ceiling, decorated with arabesques, is open in the centre and supports a clerestory pierced by eight-pointed star-shaped lights. The clerestory is decorated with intricate geometrical patterns based on Islamic motifs. The colours are varied and strong, and the gilding is lavish.

(By coincidence, Sybil had acquired an oriental room.) Alexander Collie lived there from 1865 to 1875 when he went bankrupt.[97] The house was more in keeping with the Sassoons' sort of money than the more countrified riches of the Cholmondeleys. The entire row of houses was occupied by *nouveaux riches* around the turn of the century.[98] They weren't particularly fashionable dwellings until after the Cholmondeleys moved in. Sybil suggested to the French Ambassador that he move his official residence there, leading to the area acquiring a new lease of life as Embassy Row.

57. 12 Kensington Palace Gardens.

The London house provided a centre for her musical interests. Sybil was intensely musical, a talent inherited by her eldest grandchild, Lady Rose Cholmondeley, as well as the present Marquess. She attended musical parties at John Singer Sargent's in London, frequently played duets with him, and at other musical events in Paris she heard and met Poulenc, Auric, Ravel and Debussy. She was at Vladimir Horowitz's first concert. Before the First World War, she had been present at the famous first performance of Stravinsky's *Rite of Spring* and the subsequent riot in the theatre. As she said in retrospect, she didn't know any better then and banged her umbrella in disapproval like the rest. She became much more progressive in her interests after the war, befriending Francis Poulenc and Georges Auric both in Paris and London, where they would dine with her after concerts.

Sybil also became close to Artur Rubinstein, whom she met in the 1920s; he practised for his London concerts at her house. He described her as a 'striking Oriental beauty'. They met at various points: at Cannes when Rubinstein was playing Brahms's B-flat Concerto conducted by Reynaldo Hahn, who was a friend of both Philip's and Sybil's through their French world. (Philip saw Hahn in Paris and remembered 'such jolly parties at Mama's and Lady Ripon's where he wd. sit down & play the whole of Offenbach by heart'.[99]) Rubinstein once crossed the Atlantic with the Cholmondeleys when Sybil's husband, Rock, was going to America to play polo. When Rubinstein married in 1932, Sybil provided a home for him to be married from as well as the venue for the reception. Characteristically, Rock was not there as he tended not to take too much part in her cultural life.[100] In the style of the English aristocracy, they did not feel the need to be together all the time. After the Second World War she was a great help to the young Romanian pianist Dinu Lipatti, who also used her London house as his English base.

There were two tennis courts at Kensington Palace Gardens, one clay and the other Cumberland grass. (This was useful for Rock as he played the Riviera tennis circuit, where the courts were clay. He competed at Wimbledon and one year reached the third round.) Great tennis figures such as Borotra and Suzanne Lenglen played there frequently. Sybil enjoyed going to concerts, opera, the theatre, dinner parties and meeting figures in politics, in cultural life and in sport, who had accomplishments of their own and were not merely prominent because of birth or money. She didn't particularly enjoy dances or the more ordinary aspects of society life, but did enjoy hosting dinner parties and small gatherings. Her style was rather low key and private. She was not one of the great hostesses of the day, did not give great balls or participate in large charity events. Nor did she give large house parties in the country; she left the more public life to her brother. In terms of houses, cars and sports, she led the life of an aristocrat – but a highly cultivated one.

Some of the royals were her neighbours, in London at Kensington Palace across the greensward and in the country at Sandringham. She was especially close to Queen Mary, with whom she shared an interest in furniture and paintings. Years later Mary's great-grandson Charles would come for talks with her at Houghton. The royals too were working aristocrats. Rock was to be a member of the Household; on the death of George V and then again on the death of George VI he became one of the most important working peers of the land, the hereditary, not appointed, Lord Great Chamberlain. For Rock too, London was a much better base than Houghton. From there it was easier for him to make trips, long and short, to pursue his interests in tennis and golf. He was a famous polo player, with a handicap of nine.

In 1936 Rock had built Le Roc, a modern art deco holiday home on Cap d'Antibes. It was very much Rock's house where Sybil was to be treated as an honoured guest. The house and its style were his idea. They both went there on holiday, but Rock tended to visit it alone for a month or more in the winter to get away from the English climate. Sybil and the children – Aline had been born in 1916, Hugh in 1919, and John in 1920 – would frequently have Christmas with Philip at Trent, although Rock was concerned about their being spoiled by their uncle.

58. Sybil with Hugh, Aline and John on a houseboat during a holiday at Key West, Florida, 1928.

The family also spent time at Houghton, moving in after the First World War, even though it had officially been their country home since their marriage in 1913. When Rock became Marquess of Cholmondeley in 1923, he did not move to Cholmondeley Castle in Cheshire, the first seat of the family. It became the residence of his mother, the Dowager Marchioness, until her death in 1939 and then home to the Cholmondeleys' elder son on his marriage in 1947. (Sybil discovered there on a back stair a painting officially valued at £5 that turned out to be Holbein's *A Lady with a Squirrel and a Starling*. It was moved to Houghton and then after her death sold for £10 million to the National Gallery.)

They were frequently at Houghton during the summer and for shooting parties from the autumn until the end of January and for other occasions. But they rarely had people to stay in the house, not even those who came to shoot, although he did entertain sports professionals who were there to train him, his children and the locals. They did not spend most of their time there until after the Second World War. Then Sybil to a greater extent turned her considerable talents to its beautification. Before the war extensive repairs were necessary: to the roof, as well as the water and electricity systems.[101] There were large indoor and outdoor staffs. In the Royal Archives there are letters from Sybil to Queen Mary, one of 19 January 1934 thanking the King and Queen for coming to visit with the little princesses, Elizabeth and Margaret, and another in August 1937 thanking her for coming to a small dance.[102] It was a place to keep their collection of Bugattis (racing them along the drives) which they also drove frequently in France. Over the years they would own thirteen. Sybil noted that although Ettore Bugatti did not have a drop of Jewish blood, he did a lot during the Second World War to save the furniture and paintings that belonged to her relations, the French Rothschilds.[103] When they stayed with the Bugattis in France, Rock provided the specifications for the cars being made for them. He and Sybil participated several times in the Monte Carlo Rally and nearly won it one year.

Lord Cholmondeley owned six villages in Norfolk: Houghton, West Rudham, Harpley and the three Birchams – Great Bircham, Bircham Tofts and Bircham Newton. He also had manorial rights in other villages. He and his wife naturally served as patrons for a variety of local activities. For instance, Lady Cholmondeley formed and sponsored the local branch of the Women's Institute. In the early 1920s she opened a Tory fête near Cholmondeley Castle in Cheshire, but most of their country activities were in Norfolk. In the 1920s Lord Cholmondeley founded a club for the locals which had a bar, a billiard and games room as well as providing films and dances, not to mention sports facilities. He organized horse trials, founded a football team and gave tennis lessons. He also organized sports days and fun fairs, culminating with fireworks, on the August Bank Holiday. These occasions ceased around 1929. In the 1930s organized physical activities took a different form, as a result of his enthusiasm for the Margaret Morris system. He had been devoted to exercise since before the First World War, and had extensive gyms in all his houses.

Born in 1891, Margaret Morris was both a pioneer of modern dance in Britain and a theorist of movement, with a particular interest in how such activities might help the handicapped.[104] Since the Cholmondeleys' daughter, Aline, contracted polio when she was eight, her parents had a personal interest in such an approach. Rock felt that the world would be a much better place if everyone did these movements. He started with the locals at Houghton, who presumably were willing to humour the local lord. And it was also enjoy-

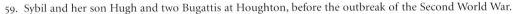

59. Sybil and her son Hugh and two Bugattis at Houghton, before the outbreak of the Second World War.

able; there was an annual sports day as part of the enterprise that echoed the earlier Bank Holiday ones. It was very elaborate with not only athletic events but a flower show, a band and rides, and ended with a fireworks display. Three thousand people attended.

Rock also arranged for the headmaster of the preparatory school his sons attended to hire one of Morris's teachers. Along with the Swiss and Swedish ambassadors, Lord Astor, the royal doctor, Lord Dawson, the Bishop of Liverpool, and Herbert Morrison, the Labour party leader, Rock became a patron of demonstrations around the country of Margaret Morris's 'Physical Education and Aesthetic Development'. In 1937 he contributed an introduction for Morris's *Basic Physical Training*, a book she wrote on his insistence.[105]

Despite Rock's tireless public promotion of the Margaret Morris system, the Cholmondeleys led a more private life than Philip. Nevertheless, Rock would be forced into a public role as Lord Great Chamberlain when Edward VIII came to the throne in 1936. Rock played this role well, but reluctantly. In contrast, Philip entered into his activities with enthusiasm throughout the decade of the 1930s in the worlds of both art and politics.

6 *The Role of Art: Making an Aesthetic*

Throughout Philip's life his houses and gardens provided large canvases for his aesthetic activities. Starting at a very young age, he was a major and very knowledgeable collector and connoisseur of the decorative arts (in the tradition of the Rothschilds), of French and English pictures, furniture and objects mostly from the eighteenth century. In their own time they were magnificent pieces and attested to the social standing of their owners, and they continued to do the same in the nineteenth and twentieth centuries. (Much of his French collection was dispersed in the sale of 1994 but many of his English paintings and pieces have remained with the family, and are still to be found at Houghton.) He was also a patron of some contemporary artists, notably Sargent, Rex Whistler, Philpot and Sert and he had purchased a David Bomberg and at least two Wilson Steers. He formed an important collection of English painters of the eighteenth century such as Gainsborough and Zoffany, specializing in conversation pieces. He followed his own aesthetic instincts. Contrary to the plutocratic taste of the time, he preferred the more domestic Gainsboroughs rather than the more popular full-length portraits. Indeed his intense interest in the conversation piece – two or more persons engaged in talk or other pursuits – was innovative for his time. He was a great collector who shared his vision with the public. The French objects tended towards the opulent, while the English were somewhat more austere. A remark that J. Ronald Fleming, an interior designer, made about his house in London might be applied to his collecting, indeed his life, in general. His house on Park Lane 'had the atmosphere of the palace of a wealthy pasha combined with the meticulous taste and connoisseurship of an artistic aristocrat'.[1]

In the 1920s and 1930s, Philip became even more involved in the art world, particularly as the trustee of museums, that area in which administration, politics, society and aesthetic concerns meet. He was also in a position, as a Member of Parliament, to bring such questions to public attention as well as being able to help the institutions with which he was connected. In March 1921, to his intense pleasure, and at a young age, Lloyd George appointed him a trustee of the National Gallery. He wrote to Lord Esher on 27 March: 'I couldn't be more pleased than I am about it. I am sure that you will agree it is a very excellent appointment!'[2]

On 29 May 1922, he spoke at some length in Parliament on the great danger of art treasures leaving the country and how this affected those who were not rich enough to travel:

I do not think it is sufficiently realised how largely our national galleries and museums in London and in the provinces that are now open to the public exist for the benefit of the poorer sections of the population, or how largely they are frequented by people who have no other means of gratifying their love for rare and beautiful things . . . . Our national galleries and museums exist for those who have no chance of studying art elsewhere and who have no opportunities of widening their knowledge or experience by personal travel, study or research. They exist primarily for the poor . . . . The community as a whole is impoverished in a sense both morally and materially [if great pictures are exported]. It is part of our civilisation that leaves us whenever one of these outstanding triumphs of human art and man's creative genius is carried away to another country.

He felt that steps must be taken for the state to acquire such treasures, specifically by means of grants from the Treasury to the National Gallery. He returned to the topic on 3 August, stressing that there were likely to be no more than a dozen works of art in the country of such importance that they could not be allowed to leave. He felt that the Treasury must do more. 'The £5,000 which the trustees [of the National Gallery] get yearly from the Treasury is wholly out of proportion with the prices that really important works of art command from foreign purchasers.' Sir Robert Horne, the Chancellor of the Exchequer, reacted favourably: 'the house will congratulate the nation on having so enthusiastic and studious a member of the Board of Trustees of the National Gallery'.[3] The following October, Charles Holmes, the Director of the Gallery, thanked Sassoon for 'the very great service you have rendered to this Gallery and to the Arts, by your efforts in the House of Commons'.[4]

In May 1923 he became a trustee of the Tate Gallery as well as the representative to its Board from the National Gallery. The Tate had been founded in 1897 and was known until October 1932 as the National Gallery, Millbank. Two years before Philip joined its Board, an issue had arisen involving the museum and his family. Although Siegfried Sassoon teased Philip, in effect, to take action on the matter, it isn't known whether he did so. Siegfried's aunt, Rachel, had rebelled (like her brother Alfred) against the family, and particularly her pious mother, by marrying a Christian, the newspaper magnate Frederick Beer. (He inherited the *Observer* from his father, and his wife bought the *Sunday Times* in 1893, and he became the editor of both newspapers.) Before his death in 1903, Frederick had acquired John Everett Millais's *Christ in the House of His Parents*, also known as *The Carpenter's Shop*. This was one of Millais's best-known paintings, in part because it had been the subject of universal derision when it was exhibited at the Royal Academy in 1850. Critics, most famously Charles Dickens, detested its depiction of Christ in what some considered mean and unworthy conditions.

Rachel Beer went mad the year after her husband died. In 1921, the administrators of her affairs, who had lent the painting to the National Gallery at Millbank nine years earlier, decided to sell it. Siegfried, who was very fond of his aunt and was unhappy that the picture might go into other private hands, wrote to *The Nation & the Athenæum* on 9 July 1921.

As a comparatively indigent member of the tribe of the Sassoons, I deplore the fact that none of my family have acquired the picture for the National Art Collection. In order to remind them of their responsibility in the matter, I have to-day placed one goldfish in the fountain in the entrance-hall of the Tate Gallery. I hope that the presence of this diminutive cyprinoid may induce some Sassoon, more affluent than myself, to come forward with the money needed to retain a pre-Raphaelite masterpiece in one of our National Art galleries.

It wasn't clear what the logic of placing the goldfish in the fountain was.

In the 30 July issue of the same journal, another letter appeared on the matter. Although signed 'An Angry Sassoon', the writer in fact was Osbert Sitwell, having a joke. He also gently appeared to be playing on the paradox of the Sassoons owning a painting of Christ, even though they had not originally bought it. One aspect of the picture was how it prefigured the Crucifixion in the pose taken by Christ as a boy. Sitwell wrote:

> It is reported that when it was first suggested to a member of our clan that the 'Christ in the Carpenter's Shop' should be presented to one of the National Galleries, he replied: 'It is a subject which does not appeal to me.' This tactful and ambiguous saying well sums up the family feeling on the subject. Capt. Sassoon should remember the fine old Norman-French motto of our ancestors: 'Sassoon à son goût.' Finally, may I say that I have examined Capt. Sassoon's gold-fish, and, in my opinion, it is not a genuine cyprinoid.[5]

Beyond this frivolous exchange, the campaign to retain the picture became quite intense. The artist D.Y. Cameron wrote to Robert Witt, chairman of the National Art Collections Fund, 'all may help to secure for this, the Heart of the Empire, this trysting place of the British Race, one of the highest notes of artistic and prophetic insight of an age and the fittest achievement by an English painter second to none in popular appeal'. The Beer trustees informed the Tate that they had an offer of £10,000 from the National Gallery of Victoria in Melbourne but they would sell it to the Tate for 10,000 guineas, that is, £500 more. The Australian gallery representative in London, Frank Rinder, felt that the higher patriotism should allow the picture to go to Melbourne, conveying the national spirit to the younger country.[6] The Tate did rise to the challenge – probably not greatly influenced by the owner's nephew's letter – and with its own funds, as well as considerable help from the National Art Collections Fund and a long list of other donors (including Sir Joseph Duveen, but not Sir Philip Sassoon), secured the painting as a permanent part of the national collection. Philip probably found his cousin Siegfried's antics a little embarrassing.

Philip attended his first meeting of the Tate trustees on 27 June 1923. The trustees generally met once a month, except in August, and the Tate's minute books record his fairly conscientious attendance. The Tate Board was not, on the whole, made up of the National Gallery's sort of grandees. It had artists on it – William Rothenstein and Glyn Philpot – and friends of Philip's, such as Lord Esher and Evan Charteris. At a meeting of 16 April 1935, the trustees agreed that a number of pictures be put at Philip's disposal, as Under-Secretary of

State for Air, to be lent to various Royal Air Force bases, as long as members of the public could see the pictures on request. One recorded action at the Tate was his purchase in 1926 of a charming oak sculpture of two cormorants by the 22-year-old William C. Graveney, on exhibit at the Royal Academy Summer Show. Philip acquired the piece and presented it to the Tate. The difficulty in further discovering Philip's contributions is that minutes of meetings are almost invariably somewhat anodyne and give no indication of the disputes that mark the history of any organization. For example, they do not record the problems that the trustees had with James Bolivar Manson, a well-known Post-Impressionist painter himself and the Director of the Gallery (where he had had a post since 1912) from 1930 to 1938. He had a serious drinking problem, turning up drunk at a trustees' meeting and once causing a public scandal, through drunkenness, at an official lunch in Paris. As a result, he was forced to resign, on medical grounds, a full month short of his regular retirement at the age of 60 (presumably, he was thus punished in terms of his pension).[7]

Philip was also a trustee of the Wallace Collection, the comparatively small and exquisite museum on Manchester Square in London. It very much reflected Philip's taste, with its emphasis on French painting and decorative arts. It also has an outstanding group of paintings by Oudry that particularly interested Philip as he had acquired in 1936 probably the most famous Oudry of all: *The White Duck*. The Marquess of Hertford had formed the collection in Paris during the nineteenth century, and his illegitimate son, Sir Richard Wallace, had added to it, moving it to London when he felt it was threatened by the Paris Commune of 1870. Although little trace of Philip's trusteeship survives in the archives of the Wallace Collection, there was correspondence in January 1925 about the use of claret for the cleaning of bronzes, and he sent over several bottles. He also donated some skins, which he had purchased in Cairo, that might be used to bind books.

No doubt his most important commitment was to the National Gallery. He attended even more of the Board's monthly meetings than those of the Tate. Indeed, he was concerned that the Board made its decisions too quickly and did not pay sufficient attention to dissident voices. Sir Charles Holmes was Director when he arrived. In the mid-1920s Philip took a close interest in the creation of the Boris Anrep mosaics in the entrance hall of the Gallery. In 1927 Sassoon and the chairman of the Board, the Earl of Crawford, a Scottish patrician and politician with a strong aesthetic bent, began negotiations with the Earl of Pembroke for the acquisition of the Wilton Diptych, the great late-fourteenth-century painting centring on Richard II that the Gallery finally acquired in 1929. Philip's first term as trustee ended in 1927; Ramsay MacDonald, the former Labour Prime Minister, replaced him. In April 1929 he was reappointed to the Board for a seven-year term.

Crawford was won over to Philip by his grand hospitality, at least for a while and in a rather patronizing way. Crawford remarked of a lunch he had at Park Lane:

What a lunch Sassoon gives! I have always had a pardonable ambition to make the acquaintance of a Grande Cocotte. Sassoon's lunch is precisely the style and manner of lunch I should expect from a G.C. Table napkins are yellow satin. Fruit for the four of us would have fed twenty people. Salad for four filled a large bowl as big as a large washing basin. The waste, the robbery of it all – and yet I derive great pleasure from a combination which makes me extremely greedy; and Sassoon himself, despite an Asiatic outlook, remains quite simple and unaffected in the midst of all this opulence .... I try to keep aloof from the rich Jew or American and I don't much want to be mixed up with Asiatics – but Sassoon is a keen and loyal colleague on the National Gallery Board, and I wish to see him often; and I acknowledge a peculiar charm in his cool friendliness, or is it a friendly coolness?

Nevertheless, Crawford could also be unhappy about Sassoon's influence upon the Board, holding him in part responsible for the growing number of appointments to it of those who really did not know much about art, who weren't really interested or had their own agendas: such figures as Stanley Baldwin, MacDonald, the Prince of Wales and Duveen. In fact, another board member, Lord Lee of Fareham, was the prime mover behind the candidacy of Duveen, whom Crawford thought had 'avowedly bought his Trusteeship'. Lord Lee, a politician and a major figure in the art world, had told Duveen there should be no problem about joining the Board if he retired and was no longer a dealer. Duveen countered that the point was exactly that: he was very eager to be a trustee while still a dealer in order to distinguish himself from other dealers! Lee did succeed in getting Duveen appointed by the Prime Minister, MacDonald, in 1929.[8] Lee was a controversial figure: there were those who thought this powerful trustee had profited from Duveen's buying art from him. The Board also witnessed feuds between Lee (known to flail around on the floor in a fit if he didn't get his way) and William Ormsby-Gore, later Lord Harlech, another politician very interested in the arts.

Meanwhile, other board members rankled the chairman. Crawford was deeply annoyed by the Prince of Wales's lighting a cigarette at board meetings (smoking was strictly against the rules), and that he and Sassoon wouldn't stop chatting during the proceedings. Sassoon 'with his raucous Syrian voice and his acute desire to "honour the King" chattered away – and between them the two made business practically impossible .... As far as I could make out, the chatter was chiefly about racing and society'. Ultimately Crawford disapproved, despite the hospitality, of Sassoon and of most of the other more public figures appointed to the Board. 'Sassoon on merit has few claims other than a position acquired through political prowess; Baldwin is a nonentity on a standing committee. Duveen and the Prince of Wales contribute nothing unless it be cash or prestige.'[9]

At the National Gallery, Sir Augustus Daniel had replaced Holmes as Director in 1928. Although one couldn't tell from the minutes, the museum was in considerable turmoil; the staff and the trustees were in a state of continual warfare with each other. According to Lee, Daniel was a disastrous Director 'without parallel for sheer incapacity and a kind of malignant timidity'.[10] Lee wanted Kenneth Clark to become Director and arranged for Ramsay MacDonald to offer him the position in 1933; early the following year, at the extraordinarily young age of 30, Clark assumed the directorship. In 1933 Sassoon had become chairman of the Board, itself a considerable honour for a man still only in his mid-forties. It was hoped that his appointment would ease the tension between the staff and the trustees as his predecessor, Lord Lee, had been quite contentious.

These changes meant that Clark and Sassoon were highly important administrative figures in the British art world, although Sassoon's position as chairman was more of a titular post. Clark became very close to Sassoon and was a recipient of his lavish hospitality. (The trustees lunched on gold plate at Park Lane before their meetings.) Clark and his family spent many days at Trent, and also at Bellevue, a house they rented from Philip opposite the entrance to Port Lympne. Philip would frequently give the Clark children rides in his aeroplane, buzzing their parents on the golf course. Kenneth Clark, like Crawford, rather patronized the world in which he now lived. He not surprisingly found it far less intellectual than anything he had experienced either at Oxford as a student, or later as Director of the University's museum, or when he was with Bernard Berenson at I Tatti. As he remarked, harshly, it had 'education without books, without information and without ideas . . . . I had a front seat at Vanity Fair.'[11]

Clark, generally supported by Sassoon, did an outstanding job, although he was deeply aware of what he regarded as his total lack of knowledge of administration, despite having been Director of the Ashmolean at Oxford. Thanks to Ormsby-Gore in his government position as First Commissioner of Works (a position Sassoon later would occupy), Clark introduced electric light into the Gallery. At the reception to celebrate the event, Ormsby-Gore as commissioner and Sassoon as Chairman had a great row as to who should receive the guests, and Clark proposed that they stand side by side so chance would decide whose hand would be shaken first.[12] The Board also, assisted by the lighting, extended the museum's opening hours, Sassoon arguing for 8 rather than 7 p.m. as people did not generally stop work until 6 or 7. One of Clark's and Sassoon's major tasks was trying to control Sir Joseph, who had become Lord Duveen in 1933. He was a great benefactor of museums – particularly the Tate, where in 1926 he donated £50,000 to fund new galleries; the National Portrait Gallery, to which he gave a wing in 1933; and the British Museum, where he gave the money for the galleries, not completed until 1939, for the Elgin Marbles. At the Tate in 1925 Duveen had paid £500 for the Rex Whistler murals *The Pursuit of Rare Meats*, in the refreshment rooms; that scheme was completed in 1927.

Was it also a matter of concern that Duveen and Sassoon were Jewish? These two Jews almost automatically roused the feeling in the minds of some gentiles, particularly their colleagues on the Board, that they were bound, by reason of their religion, to be wheeling and dealing. Duveen made no bones about being a dealer. Did the anti-Semitism never very far below the surface extend to Sassoon as well? Clark tended to worry about Duveen's activities and the young Director and Sassoon had several intense disagreements over the issue. The situation was especially awkward in the mid-1930s, when the Gallery was trying to purchase six panels by the fifteenth-century Sienese master, Sassetta. Officially they belonged to an American millionaire, but because the man had never paid Duveen for them, the museum was in effect buying them from one of its own trustees. There were unseemly discussions at the board meetings about Duveen's complaints that the price wasn't high enough. It also turned out that, in the Duveen tradition, the paintings had been very badly over-restored. Sassoon was furious at this point about Duveen's behaviour, but the pictures did come into the collection in 1934.

Three years later, Clark had a serious fight with Sassoon, who was now friendlier with Duveen, over the question of the latter's reappointment as a trustee. Clark and his supporters on the Board won and the Prime Minister did not reappoint him. Sassoon did not speak to Clark for three months but after that their friendship was renewed. Duveen had been an extremely generous donor but was not a particularly scrupulous businessman. Philip missed him on the Board, remarking to Clark in a somewhat barbed comment that 'now the meetings will be a bore: like a harlequinade without the clown'.[13]

Over the years Sassoon performed various public tasks associated with the arts. He spoke at the annual dinner of the British Art Dealers' Association in 1928, commending the Art Treasures Exhibition the organization had arranged. In 1931 he became a member of the Royal Commission on Museums and Galleries. On 1 June 1935 he presided at the opening of a picture lending gallery in London. He opened the autumn art exhibition at the Walker Art Gallery in Liverpool on 9 November 1936; there he commented, with perhaps a touch of the optimism that marked such public occasions, on the general improvement in public taste. *The Times* reported, 'At one time, he believed, those responsible for purchases for our art galleries would frequently buy some sugary Venus getting in or out of her bath, or some maudlin gorge-raising piece of sentimentalism, and would excuse the purchase by saying that it was exactly the kind of picture which the public wanted. The pictures people admired to-day were exactly those which those in position to judge regarded as great masterpieces.' From 1926 until his death Philip was also a supporter of the British School at Rome, to the extent of 10 guineas a year.[14] On 19 April 1937, he presided at the opening of an extension of the Mappin Art Gallery in Sheffield. John Rothenstein, William's son, the Director of the gallery, noted in his autobiography the difference between the elegant Sir Philip and the worthy and substantial Alderman Graves whose collection was being displayed: 'The contrast between Sir Philip, an exquisite slender figure out of The Arabian Nights, thinly disguised by a suit from Savile Row, and the raw-complexioned burly alderman was so extreme as to make them appear quite simply to be different kinds of human being.'[15]

His activities in the art world and on the National Gallery Board were also very helpful to Philip in the planning of the large annual loan exhibitions that he started in 1928 and continued to 1938, with the exception of 1935, in his mansion on Park Lane. Most of the exhibitions were very varied, displaying pictures, furniture, china, silver and other objects. They greatly benefited from being shown in a home and no doubt the public enjoyed coming into a private residence. There, and elsewhere, Sassoon played a significant role in the shaping of taste and the growth of interest in the arts of the eighteenth century. He put his vast knowledge and connoisseurship to work for the exhibitions. It was a remarkable commitment of time for someone who was so active in many other spheres, especially a public political figure. Of course, as a very rich man, he had lots of help, and his cousin Hannah Gubbay, a major connoisseur of the period in her own right, played an essential part in arranging the events. Nonetheless, Philip remained the central figure.

The exhibitions arose out of his charitable activities. He opened the gardens at Port Lympne and Trent Park – the latter weekly during the summer – for charity and he had established a free dental clinic at Folkestone. But he adopted as his major charitable activity the Royal Northern Hospital. Located on Holloway Road, it was the main hospital for northern London, but also included as part of its operations the Royal Chest Hospital on City Road, the Hospital of Recovery in Southgate and the Reckitt Convalescent Home in Clacton-on-Sea. In 1920 Sir George Lawson Johnston, the chairman of the food firm Bovril, served as honorary (i.e. unpaid) treasurer for much longer than he wished until, in January 1923, he wrote to Gilbert Panter, the secretary of the Hospital, that there was need to 'get a Treasurer who can give time to the Hospital's affairs, as my resignation must be accepted as definite'. Panter wrote to the Marquess of Northampton, the chairman of the Hospital Board, 'I think the list of names you mention is an excellent one, and if we could possibly persuade Sir Philip Sassoon to consider the matter it would be excellent as one of his houses [Trent] is in the Hospital area.'[16] Sassoon was asked and he accepted. He would occupy this post until his death in 1939.

Philip began his fund raising for the hospital in a traditional way, helping to organize balls. In 1924 he held one for the hospital at his house on Park Lane and it was a great success. The Prince of Wales, who was Honorary President of the hospital (his father was the Patron) attended, as did Prince George and, as Philip noted in a diary entry, 'all our friends plus crowds of strangers & most of the trades people I deal with . . . . The house looked all right, tho' I moved all the furniture covered in velvet. The ball room looked like a ploughed field afterwards.'[17] In subsequent years he was closely involved with the annual balls to benefit the hospital, and the committee would usually meet at Park Lane. In 1927 a tradition was founded of having the annual ball in the Royal Albert Hall on the eve of the great race meeting, Derby Day. That year the ball was graced by the presence of the Prince of Wales, and also by a short speech by Charles Lindbergh, which Philip, then working at the Air Ministry, must have arranged. That year as well he wrote a letter to *The Times* urging the public to send to the hospital the foreign money they happened to bring back from trips abroad rather than going to the bother of exchanging it at an English bank.[18]

It was in March 1928 that an art exhibition was added to the roster of annual events designed to raise money for the hospital. The first two exhibitions were for a comparatively short period of time. Even so the first one, 'Early English Needlework and Furniture', was such a success that it remained open for two weeks rather than one, as originally planned. *Country Life* called it the most comprehensive exhibition of secular needlework in England for many years. It included loans from great country houses such as Arundel, Knole and Hardwick, as well as items from dealers such as Seligman of Paris (one of Philip's major suppliers). Pincushions, book covers and falconry hoods were featured, not to mention a mitre of William of Wykeham from New College and Edward VI's coronation gloves from Alnwick Castle. Lady Horner lent the veil worn by Mary, Queen of Scots at her execution.[19] A catalogue was issued of the 574 items displayed, but with no illustrations. The hospital's annual report for 1928 thanked both Sir Philip and Mrs Gubbay and noted that £2,215 had been raised.[20]

This attention to the house on Park Lane was not totally welcome. *The Times* of 6 April reported on a foiled attempt to rob the house; the thieves, though chased, were not caught. Later in the year, on 2 July, *The Times* ran a story about Sassoon in a series on private art collections. The writer noted that the collection consisted of modern pictures in contrast to 'old masters'. There seemed to be a faint suggestion that the Sassoons lacked the ancestry possessed by grand English families in the remark on 'the absence of family portraits other than those painted for the present or last generation'. Sassoon's collection was compared to 'what we read about the collections formed by the merchant princes of the Italian Renaissance'. The article pointed out that the pictures were decorative and were brought 'into close relations with the architectural features and other appointments of the house – and the preference would seem to be for pictures with a social bearing'. The article particularly mentions the de Troy of the reading from Molière, a David portrait of a young woman, some Hoppners, Reynolds, Gainsboroughs, a Velázquez of Philip IV, and the numerous Sargents. The story was accompanied by illustrations of three of Philip's pictures: the Sargent of Lady Sassoon as well as Lady Frances Peacock by Hoppner and the earliest self-portrait by Gainsborough.[21]

In March 1929 the second exhibition, 'Old English Plate', displayed 873 items. The catalogue for the two-week show, while still without illustrations, was more substantial than the previous year, featuring a foreword by Philip. Emphasizing the importance of the event, he wrote that many of the objects were

for the first time on public view … possibly the finest and most representative collection of Old English Silver that the public has ever had an opportunity to behold. Public Companies and Colleges that ordinarily are very reluctant to allow their irreplaceable treasures to pass even temporarily out of their possession have most generously made an exception in our favour …. From XIV century drinking horn … to the end of the eighteenth century … [we see] the luxury of the table and domestic appointments of earlier generations.

The anonymous reviewer in *Country Life* felt that this display had democratic implications. 'The step from appreciating beauty in antiques to demanding it of everyday surroundings is a short one.' The objects were not as ordinary as that sentence implied; the emphasis was on gold and silver plate. There was a cup of Charles II, silver-covered furniture from Knole, as well as medieval, Elizabethan and Jacobean work. Philip found being on the National Gallery Board useful as he hired some of its warders (he was to do so for his subsequent exhibitions) to guard the exhibition; he was also able to borrow turnstiles from the Royal Albert Hall. Almost the same amount of money was raised, £2,200 (Philip raised a further £67 4s. for the hospital that year through the proceeds of a lecture he gave on his flight to India).

'English Conversation Pieces', the March 1930 show, represented a quantum leap forward in the extent, coverage and success of Philip's exhibitions. It was open every day, from 11 a.m. to 7 p.m., with an admission charge of five shillings – no small expense at the time. Students and children were admitted between 9.30 and 11 at the charge of a shilling. Running almost four weeks, it was the first serious exhibition of eighteenth-century art to be held in Britain since the First World War. There was a two-part catalogue, one a listing of the 152 pictures displayed, and the second a selection of illustrations. About half the pictures are annotated with information, mostly about the sitters. Twenty-nine painters were represented: those with the most work on display were Arthur Devis (with 15 canvases), Thomas Gainsborough (9), William Hogarth (18), George Stubbs (4), and John Zoffany (57).

The exhibition was very important for both the restoration of Zoffany's reputation and the re-evaluation of eighteenth-century British art and of the 'conversation piece'. That genre was, on the whole though not exclusively, an eighteenth-century form. (When in 1936 Sacheverell Sitwell wrote his pioneering study of conversation pieces, he dedicated it to Sassoon, 'To whom the Conversation Piece, and Zoffany, more especially, are deeply indebted'. Rex Whistler executed a pastiche eighteenth-century conversation piece as the dust jacket.) In the introduction to the catalogue of the exhibition, Philip pointed out the essential characteristics of the conversation piece. It differs from a portrait: the figures tend to be considerably smaller and there is generally some dramatic or psychological relationship between them. Unlike a genre painting, the figures are drawn from 'polite' society. 'In brief,' Philip wrote, 'the Conversation Piece stands half-way between the portrait group and the genre picture, drawing upon the qualities of both and adding one of its own, intimacy.' He observed that the type was invented by Dutch painters in the seventeenth century but reached its flowering in England in the eighteenth. French painters such as Watteau might have elements of the style but generally lack the quality of portraiture. Although there were some French examples (Philip himself had owned the great Jean-François de Troy since 1919), on the whole in France 'the soil proved comparatively sterile'. In England the style triumphed and became a way for the upper and middle classes to have themselves depicted. Sassoon ended his foreword with a plea for a return to the form. 'In these days of flats and small houses, the full size portrait is difficult to hang, and may easily become tiresome. Painting which unites convenient size and decorative charm to the interest of portraiture, which, moreover, is peculiarly an English product, ought to find ready patronage.' In the Orpen of himself and Sybil in the room at Park Lane, he already had his own modern conversation piece.

There were six pictures Sassoon owned in the exhibition: Zoffanys of the family of Sir William Young, of R.H.A. Bennett, of Horace Walpole (which had connections, of course, with his sister's house), and of the Colmore family; and Gainsboroughs of Mr and Mrs Browne, and a self-portrait with his wife and child. Hannah Gubbay, whose main interest was in the decorative arts, lent a theatrical double portrait by Zoffany and Sybil's husband, Rock, lent the Hogarth of the Cholmondeley family, dated 1732. There were ninety-nine other lenders, including the Duke of York as well as Osbert Sitwell. The latter had lent the

60. Thomas Gainsborough, *Mr and Mrs Browne of Tunstall and their daughter Anna Maria.*

John Singleton Copley of the Sitwell children. It was a particularly interesting painting because John Singer Sargent, another American expatriate like Copley, intended his famous picture of the Sitwell family of 1900 as a companion piece to the Copley. Other notable lenders were Lord Bearsted, the Marquess of Bute, Lady Cowdray, Lord Durham, Lady Edward Grosvenor (the widow of Philip's flying friend), James de Rothschild, Mrs Meyer Sassoon (who lent two Morlands), and Ronald Tree. The Foundling Hospital lent Hogarth's great *March of the Guards to Finchley*, not quite a conversation piece. (It, another Hogarth belonging to the London Borough of Camberwell, and a Zoffany owned by the City of Glasgow were the only pictures in the exhibition that were owned by public bodies.) The exhibition included Gainsborough's *Mr and Mrs Andrews*, still in the family for whom it was painted, as were several of the pictures. The Andrews were here exhibited publicly for only the second time. It entered the collection of the National Gallery in 1960, to become one of its most popular paintings.[22]

No matter how much help Philip may have had from Hannah Gubbay (given credit as a co-organizer) and his secretary, Grace Boyce, these exhibitions were formidable and considerable undertakings that required great effort on his part. It was characteristic of him that he was able to charm so many of the grand, from the royal family on down, to lend to his exhibitions, for the sake of charity. Queen Mary visited the 1930 show. He had met her in 1928, when she had shown him objects of plate and lent him some of them for his first exhibition. Philip and the Queen established a friendship based on their shared love of beautiful objects. In July 1929 she thanked him for some sofas. But, despite her reputation for loving to receive gifts, it was not a one-way relationship. On 12 March she sent him a piece of jade as a souvenir of her visit to the 'Conversation Pieces' exhibition.[23] That year too he had given her a sixteenth-century amber cup, chocolates from Paris, and late raspberries from Port Lympne, and he sent her specially bound copies of the exhibition catalogues.[24] The Queen offered to take Philip personally on a tour of Windsor Castle, writing on 15 April 1931: 'It takes nearly 2 hours to see the rooms properly & in detail which I know you like.'

The 'Conversation Pieces' exhibition created an immense stir. Christopher Hussey wrote in anticipation on 15 February in *Country Life* that Sassoon's exhibitions had become 'one of the recognised pleasures of the year'. He also characterized Zoffany as 'the Jane Austen of English painting'. The later review in *Country Life*, with five illustrations, commented: 'As a subject of an exhibition it is absolutely virgin soil. Never before has so complete a gathering of this class been seen together, and this is the more surprising when one considers how thoroughly most other branches of English eighteenth century art have been surveyed by now . . . . [This is] a hitherto almost neglected branch of English art.'[25] C. Reginald Grundy, editor of the *Connoisseur*, was also very positive, writing that the exhibition 'had never before been equalled either in comprehensiveness or in the general high quality of the works included'.[26] George C. Williamson in *Apollo* devoted seven pages to the exhibition, with twelve illustrations. He pointed out that a surprising number of the pictures were still owned by the families depicted, as were the objects to be found in the pictures. The piece is more of an appreciation than criticism, concluding, 'in all these groups we are looking as in a peep-show into the English home, and having its charms brought most vividly before us. As examples of English life these pictures are all of enormous importance; the best of the English painters delighted to paint them, the noblest of the old English families were charmed to commission them, and by their means we still see the life of the seventeenth and eighteenth centuries pictured before us, so different in its calm and quiet from the excitement that tends to mar English domestic life of today.' Two of his three full-page illustrations were of pictures belonging to Sassoon.[27]

The following year Williamson published *English Conversation Pieces* without much critical comment but including twenty-two pages of notes on the pictures. It had eighty-five plates, reproducing many of the pictures displayed. There are two photographs of the installation itself at Park Lane, of the Drawing Room and the Oval Drawing Room. Sassoon adapted his catalogue introduction to serve as the foreword for this book.

The National Gallery and the art establishment became excited at the thought that so many paintings in private hands, many now seen for the first time at Philip's exhibition, might possibly be acquired by public collections. On 21 February a letter appeared, rather anticipating the timing of the exhibition, in *The Times* from members of the Royal Commission on Museums and Galleries. It commented on the need for the nation to acquire English eighteenth-century painting. 'The remarkable exhibition of sporting and conversation pieces which is now open at Sir Philip Sassoon's house at 25, Park Lane proves how rich the store of these pictures is in England; how powerful their attraction, how quaint and delicate their charm.' In the archives of the National Gallery there is an assessment of the exhibition that expressed particular interest in a George Stubbs of Colonel Pocklington and his family that belonged to Mrs George Carstairs; a Ben Marshall of Colonel Powlett and his hounds that belonged to Lord Woolavington; and the Willoughby de Broke family by Zoffany, still with the family. Lord Woolavington was approached but had no interest in putting his picture into a public collection. There was a public appeal in *The Times*, raising the possibility that Lord Willoughby de Broke might sell, but nothing came of this. A Miss Berry did write to the trustees that reading about Zoffany in *The Times* had led her to decide to bequeath three of his paintings to the gallery. The National Gallery also approached the Earl of Normanton about his Hogarth of the Graham children but the result was that His Lordship telegraphed Philip on 10 April that the picture 'should at once be returned to Somerley'.[28]

There was one further flurry of activity at the time at the National Gallery centred on a picture of the period, but not one that had been in the exhibition. It was on the question of whether the Gallery should purchase what was then known as the Sefton Gainsborough of Isabella, Viscountess Molyneux (later Countess of Sefton) still in the family's hands. Sassoon objected quite strongly to the purchase, writing on 31 March a long memorandum on the subject. The Director and staff of the National Gallery favoured purchase, even though at the price of £35,000 to £40,000 it would use up the annual budget. Sassoon thought it was weak, as Gainsborough was not at his strongest, he felt, in a full-length portrait, particularly in his early years, and that the woman was 'plain' and 'ugly': 'The best that can be said of the picture is that it is good in spots.' Such a major purchase that 'will temporarily exhaust our resources, ought not, as a matter of principle, to be made, except by the unanimous decision of the Board'. He argued that 'the selection and purchase of pictures is one of the main functions of the Trustees and one for which, one may fairly say, they are admirably equipped'. He concluded: 'I am as anxious as any of my colleagues on the Board to see a better representation of the English School. But I do not think that this particular picture is likely to add anything to the Gallery because, although parts of it are superbly painted, it is on the whole inferior in quality and interest to the three full and two smaller canvasses (the artist's daughters) that we already possess.'[29] Sassoon was probably wrong; the picture is now regarded as one of Gainsborough's masterpieces; Liverpool's Walker Art Gallery acquired it in 1975.

'The Four Georges' was the next exhibition, running from 23 February to 30 March 1931. It was shown all through the first floor of the Park Lane house. A catalogue was issued in two slim volumes, one a listing and the other of illustrations. An innovation was a list of thanks, which included Rex Whistler for doing a poster for the exhibition, the art historians W.G. Constable and A. Yockney for their assistance, E. Beresford Chancellor for writing the foreword, various galleries such as Agnew and Partridge (who also lent to the exhibition) for their help in the collection of objects, the firms of Duveen and Knoedler for helping to bring pictures from the United States, and the Royal Albert Hall for supplying turnstiles. In his foreword, Chancellor emphasized the triumph of the eighteenth century in Britain in painting and in the decorative arts, not only Hogarth, Gainsborough, Reynolds and Raeburn but also such furniture manufacturers as Chippendale, Sheraton, Hepplewhite and the work of Kent and the Adamses. The exhibition itself was an intriguing mixture of paintings, silhouettes, furniture, objects, silver and books of the period, the last mostly lent by Lady Desborough and Lord Esher, including a book by Byron that he had inscribed to his lover, Lady Caroline Lamb. In its review on 23 February, *The Times* commented that the exhibition showed material from an age that was 'artistic, literary, humanistic, social, philosophical, satirical, poetical, sentimental or "curious"'. Queen Mary lent forty-one objects, notably from her famous collection of fans (in December, she had invited Mrs Gubbay to Windsor to select objects for the exhibition). The King and Queen visited Park Lane to be shown around by Philip a few days before the exhibition opened to the public. There was another private view on 20 February, this one attended by members of the aristocracy, Charlie Chaplin, lenders and other notables. The Duke of Richmond lent his two great Canalettos, *The Thames from Richmond House* and *Whitehall from Richmond House*. Edwina Mountbatten lent a Romney of Lady Hamilton. The Duke of Devonshire lent two Reynolds, one of the eighteenth-century Duke's wife Georgiana and another of his mistress (later wife), Lady Elizabeth Foster.

There were 348 catalogue entries in all, and some of the listings covered more than one object. Philip and his cousin Hannah each contributed ten. Hers were all of the decorative arts, including a Kent table. The Marquess of Cholmondeley lent four chairs, two made by Kent for Robert Walpole. A reviewer remarked: 'the two gilt armchairs from Houghton, which will be seen for the first time by most visitors to the exhibition, are powerful propaganda on behalf of Kent'.[30] Sassoon lent his self-portrait of Gainsborough, as distinct from the self-portrait with his family that had been shown the previous year. He lent as well Gainsborough's portrait of Sir John Briscoe, a rather simpering portrait of a lady by the Reverend Martin Peters, a Hoppner of Lady Frances Peacock, and a magnificent Reynolds of Lady North. Other than paintings, he provided from his collection a George I gilt gesso table and a George III gold snuff box that the Lord Chancellor, Lord Thurlow, had presented to George IV to mark his divorce proceedings. His objects also included a very elaborate Chippendale hanging wall cabinet in the Chinese style of around 1750 and an Old English lacquer cabinet of around 1760 decorated in black and gilt with Chinese scenes. The volume of illustrations had as its frontispiece a Gainsborough of Miss Linley and her brother belonging to J.P. Morgan and as the first illustration another American Gainsborough of Mrs Graham, belonging to J.E. Widener. The Queen was particularly pleased to see the Linleys. 'I was miserable when it was sold to America.' The work of assembling the material must have been formidable.

The reviews were very favourable. Frank Rutter in the *International Studio* called it 'the chief event of the past month ... representing the rich variety of the numerous phrases in which the art of the epoch expressed itself ... paintings ... furniture, old silver, porcelain, glass, enamels, costumes'. He was especially struck by the number of effective portraits that had come from American collectors (there were thirteen pictures from the States in the show).[31] Grundy, the editor of the *Connoisseur*, wrote two ecstatic reviews: 'A discriminating selection from works of only the highest merit, and he [Philip] has charmed from their owners masterpieces which have not been shown to the British public, and some – I refer to the important loans from America – which they can hardly hope to see again without hazarding a journey across the Atlantic . . . . [There was represented in the exhibition] the finest period of domestic art in Britain.' He commented on the almost 200 lenders and said that 'a goodly proportion of noble country seats, private collections and leading dealers' galleries have been temporarily depleted of some of their more interesting contents in order to serve as magnets in order to draw funds into the ever emptying coffers of the Northern Hospital'. As he pointed out in his second review, the chairs were of particular interest.[32] *The Times* was full of praise for the skill of the display: 'Even the flowers that have been introduced . . . seem to belong to the period. The exhibition has, in fact, itself the character of a work of art.' The annual report of the Royal Northern Hospital makes it clear that the show was far more successful than the two other annual fund-raisers, the Derby Ball and the Ice Carnival, netting almost £4,000.

'The Age of Walnut', covering the years 1660–1714, ran from 23 February to 4 April 1932, and was accompanied by two slim catalogue volumes, one of text enumerating the 476 items, and the other of illustrations. Walnut had replaced the sturdy oak as the wood of choice as the age became more elegant. This year's poster, again by Rex Whistler, depicted William and Mary. The novelist E. F. Benson wrote the brief foreword. Mrs Gubbay was the main organizer of this exhibition. Philip, who had returned to the government as Under-Secretary of State for Air, probably had less time. In addition, his energy was comparatively depleted; he never fully recovered from an operation to remove his tonsils the previous April. Mrs Gubbay lent numerous items, while Philip had seven of his pieces on display, including a Charles II two-handled gilt porringer and cover.

The emphasis in the exhibition was on furniture, ranging from baroque fantasies from the time of Charles II to the comparative simplicity of the age of Queen Anne. V. de Serbe remarked in *Country Life* that 'no more distinguished collection of English applied art from the Restoration to the Accession of George I, has been shown in London. [It presented the] age in the round more surely than by relics of public significance.'[33] But these too were in evidence, such as the 1688 document, drawn up by five bishops and twenty-two peers, at the time of the Glorious Revolution, on the loss of the Great Seal that James II, the deposed King, had thrown into the Thames. The objects were shown in natural groupings in the ballroom and in the large drawing room: pottery, glass, tapestries and silver as well as furniture. Grundy's review in the *Connoisseur* mentioned Queen Anne's repeating clock, lent by Queen Mary. As he pointed out, although walnut was used for most furniture, there were also on display fine pieces in marquetry, gesso and lacquer, as well as grand mirrors. Mrs Gubbay lent fifty pieces. Nineteen City companies (as well as the Lord Mayor and the Bank of England) contributed much ceremonial silver, such as the Seymour Salt from the Goldsmiths' Company made for the arrival of Catherine of Braganza in England for her marriage to Charles II (coincidentally, the dowry of this marriage had brought Bombay to

61. A Louis XIV ebony and brass and pewter-inlaid brown tortoiseshell *coffres de toilette (mariage)* by André-Charles Boulle, acquired by Philip Sassoon before 1923.

the English crown). There were also portraits by Lely and Kneller as well as the famous painting owned by Sassoon of the pineapple being presented to Charles II.[34]

George V and Queen Mary came to Park Lane while the public was there. But according to Lord Crawford, everyone enjoyed being pushed aside for the royal party. He also recorded the tea given in the dining room: 'I never remember such a tea .... Some wonderful grouse sandwiches arrived – the King refused them because he could not stop eating haddock sandwiches .... I suddenly realised that I was in the noisiest party I could recall .... A chocolate cake of unique and incomparable distinction was handed round in quarter pound slabs.'[35] In terms of revenue, however, the 1932 show was a disappointment, making less money than any of the previous exhibitions.

Philip's 1933 exhibition continued this downward trend, and in fact for the first time the hospital's other fund-raisers brought in more money. Nonetheless, the catalogue for 'Three French Reigns: Louis XIV, XV & XVI' featured an introduction by André Maurois, who observed that everything was designed to 'proclaim the magnificence of the King .... A bed has a sovereign attitude. A picture surpasses the individual; it is a dress, a wig, a function of the State.' Altogether 544 items were on display from 90 lenders, including 26 from the Queen. The *style Rothschild* was well represented, with nine English and French Rothschilds contributing. To that could be added the 25 items from the Earl of Rosebery, whose mother was a Rothschild. Philip himself lent 50 items: tables, bowls, dishes, stools, bureaus, candle-

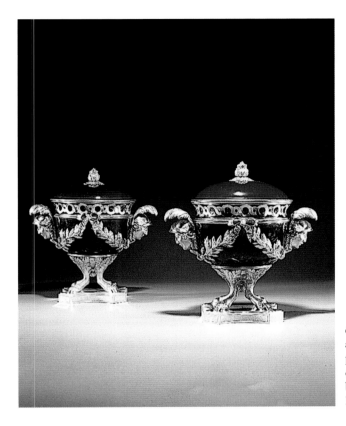

62. A pair of Louis XVI gilt-bronze and Chinese powder-blue glazed porcelain pot-pourri vases and covers, acquired by Philip Sassoon before 1927 and shown at the Three French Reigns exhibition, 1933.

sticks, fire dogs, commodes, settees, vases, chairs, clocks, tureens, Madame de Pompadour's dispatch box, porringers, dessert knives, forks and spoons, barometers, flower pots, stirrups, rugs, powder boxes, inkstands, bookcases, and a bust of Louis XIV, all of the period. His sister, Sybil, lent a necklace, eight vases, and a Louis XVI clock.

There were paintings as well, including a very grand Hubert-Drouais of Madame de Pompadour, lent by the Earl of Rosebery, as well as Fragonards, Greuzes, Roberts, Boillys, and a Largillière whose *La Belle Strasbourgeoise*, lent by François Coty, had never been seen in public before. *Country Life* found 'it a far more complete record of the decorative arts during this period than the French Exhibition of 1932'.[36] *The Times* noted on 18 February some of those who were at the private view: the Prime Minister, Ramsay MacDonald, as well as the French and American ambassadors, numerous Rothschilds, Lady Juliet Duff, Mrs Belloc Lowndes, Mr Alfred and Lady Diana Duff Cooper, Mrs Stanley Baldwin as well as Mrs David Gubbay, 'who has organized the exhibition and been responsible for its arrangement'. A *Times* editorial observed, 'The young devotees of efficiency and of adaptation to function will be so enraged by what they see there that their mental balance may be seriously disturbed.' The writer greatly admired the beauty of the exhibition and concluded: 'We have not yet made the other parts of life so much more beautiful that we can do without the peculiar gift and example left by the Three Reigns.'

The next of this series was 'Porcelain through the Ages', which ran from 13 February to 27 March 1934. It was a huge exhibition of 797 items. Queen Mary lent 25 pieces, and there were 98 other lenders. Philip himself lent 15 objects. They included Chelsea ware, quite a lot of Dresden, and Chinese work of the eighteenth century. The show did better than the previous year, raising almost as much for the hospital as the annual Derby Ball. The next year a break was taken, and perhaps as a substitute Mrs Meyer Sassoon opened her house for the hospital.

The series resumed in 1936 with 'Thomas Gainsborough' the first exhibition to concentrate on painting since the 'Conversation Pieces' of 1930 and also, apparently, the first one in England to focus exclusively on Gainsborough. There were 139 pictures on display. Philip lent three, the self-portrait, the artist and his family and *Mr and Mrs Browne*. *Mr and Mrs Andrews* returned to Park Lane. There was, as usual, a two-volume catalogue. Two members of the National Gallery staff worked on it: E. K. Waterhouse, an expert on eighteenth-century painting, supplied the facts and Martin Davies wrote the entries. The Sassoon Gainsborough self-portrait depicted the artist at the age of 19; Philip had bought it in Paris in 1914. The gallery's experts thought that the portrait of the artist, his wife and daughter (acquired by Philip in 1927)[37] had been ruined by over-cleaning but that *Mr and Mrs Browne* was in fine condition. In the middle of the exhibition, on 3 March, the King added eight Gainsboroughs, never before displayed in public other than at the Royal Academy in 1783. They were seven portraits of the children of George III and Queen Charlotte, and an oil sketch of Mrs Robinson for his portrait of her, *Perdita*, in the Wallace Collection.

Meanwhile Kenneth Clark wrote a memorandum about the exhibition, perhaps with a view of interesting the National Gallery in buying some of the pictures on display. But its primary purpose was to assess the Gainsboroughs for another show, planned for the Louvre in 1938. He picked out four landscapes as being of particular interest – one, *Drinkstone Park*, belonging to himself – and said that *The Market Cart*, belonging to Sir Gervase Beckett, was the best. Of the portraits he did single out *Mr and Mrs Andrews*. He mentioned various other full-length and half-length portraits. Clark felt that the earlier Bath period in Gainsborough's work was much better than the later London period. He didn't mention any of Sassoon's early Gainsboroughs, but he was critical of the late Gainsboroughs that were generally favoured by the plutocracy. 'It is when one comes to the calligraphic and often "stagey" late London portraits that one feels embarrassed and hesitant for Gainsborough's reputation. These are the pictures that fetch high prices at auctions and decorate the drawing rooms of millionaires. But they seldom stand up to any absolute standards as works of art.'

Nonetheless, for millionaires – and perhaps especially for Jewish millionaires – owning eighteenth-century paintings was one way to establish a claim to Englishness. At Waddesdon, the greatest Rothschild house in England, where the decorative arts were mostly French, the collection contained fifty works by Reynolds and ten by Gainsborough.[38] Clark singled out four Rothschild Gainsboroughs for particular criticism. Victor Rothschild, the heir to the title, owned three and James de Rothschild of Waddesdon owned *Mrs James Douglas*.

'The Marsham Children' is frankly a very bad picture, [*The Times* reviewer found it 'heavenly'] and the famous 'Morning Walk' a bitter disappointment. The bold rhythms and flourishes of No: 18 (Mrs John Douglas) from Waddesdon cannot disguise the fundamental weaknesses in drawing and realisation . . . . Even the 'Mrs Sheridan', the best of the Rothschild pictures – only the charm of the sitter and the pleasant general tone of dress and background redeem a 'boneless' and shallow conventionalism.

(That year Lord Rothschild sold this picture to Andrew Mellon; it is now in the National Gallery in Washington, DC.) Clark also commented on the low quality of Lord Lothian's Gainsborough. He concluded: 'But while there are these disappointments, there can be little doubt that there are at least ten or a dozen pictures in this Exhibition which do enhance Gainsborough's reputation, and would convince even continental critics that that reputation is justified.'[39] In an editorial, *The Times* praised the show enthusiastically, stating that it was 'as near perfect as may be in beauty, in size, in variety, and (let us out with it boldly) in interest of subject'. In addition, its importance is indicated by the fact that in the unillustrated *Preliminary Check List of Portraits by Thomas Gainsborough* of 1953, edited by Waterhouse, the volume of illustrations issued for this exhibition is cited as still the best source then available for depictions of Gainsborough's portraits.

Financially, reflecting the popularity of Gainsborough, the exhibition was a great success, earning £7,000 for the hospital. This was despite some controversy about attendance and the charge for admission. On 29 February Lady Cohen published a letter in *The Times* commenting sadly on how few, in her view, were attending the exhibition. On 3 March Constance Hope wrote that five shillings was a formidable price of admission. Soon after *The Times* weighed in with an editorial lauding the show, which touched on the issue, Hannah Gubbay wrote a letter arguing that the admission price was for charity and that many would not hesitate for a moment to spend the same amount of money for the cinema. 'Then, again, should not the fact that the exhibition is being held in a private house be taken into account? Have not the public been given a unique opportunity of studying art under ideal conditions?' She also observed that at this exhibition, as at the others, students and others were eligible for reduced admission, and that it was open for longer hours than most similar shows.

By what one might consider rather a natural progression, the 1937 exhibition was devoted to Sir Joshua Reynolds. Organized once again jointly by Philip and his cousin, it was opened by the Duchess of Gloucester on 9 February. That month *The Times* recorded the visits of other royals: the Duke and Duchess of Kent, who 'spent about half an hour looking with much interest at the pictures'; the Princess Royal; and Queen Mary, who, the Court Circular recorded, viewed the show the day before it opened. There were 101 pictures from 76 lenders from England, Ireland and the United States, with a single-volume catalogue with 30 pages of entries, 93 pages of illustrations and a brief unsigned introduction. Continuing an important aspect of Philip's exhibitions, many of the pictures had never been shown publicly before. Sassoon's portrait of Lady North of 1757 was included. The

Marquess of Cholmondeley lent several, including one of the 1st Marquess, painted in 1780 (before he was advanced to the marquisate in 1815), and of the Duchess of Ancaster, the mother-in-law of that Lord Cholmondeley and through whom the family inherited the position of Lord Great Chamberlain. Lady Desborough lent her portrait of the children of the 1st Viscount Melbourne. Three of Reynolds's rather saccharine well-known portraits of children – *Lady Caroline Scott as Winter,* still in the possession of the family, the Dukes of Buccleuch; *Master Crewe as Henry VIII*, then in possession of Lord Crewe; and *Mercury as a Cut-Purse*, belonging to Lord Faringdon – were on display. As with the Gainsborough show, E. K. Waterhouse assisted in putting it all together. Besides the net proceeds from the show, Philip gave the hospital additional funds that year from opening his house to the public for a day.

The last in the series took place from 15 February to 10 April 1938; it was called, rather nostalgically (perhaps appropriately so, considering that it was the culmination of eleven years of work), 'Old London Town'. There were 227 objects on view, according to the catalogue written by Martin Holmes, and royal lenders included the King and Queen as well as the Dukes of Kent and Gloucester. The King lent a tapestry depicting the battle of Solebay that some regarded as the finest piece in the exhibition; the *Art News* commented that, 'fitting exactly into a recess of the panelled wall and flanked on either side by two superb Canaletto Views of London lent by the Duke of Richmond, it makes a fine central point for the exhibition'.[40] City companies lent, as did various churches. The show covered a far longer period than its predecessors, from the Elizabethan to the nineteenth century, although as usual most of the material was from the eighteenth century. Among the famous paintings on display were William Frith's *The Railway Station* of 1862 and his *Haymarket at Night* of 1868. Sir George Sitwell lent a George Morland of the Westminster election of 1783 in which the Duchess of Devonshire, campaigning on behalf of Charles James Fox, is depicted kissing a butcher. Philip lent eleven works. Mrs Gubbay contributed thirty-nine objects. There was much china, furniture and plate. As in most of the exhibitions, there was a mixture of media, since Philip believed in presenting the whole range of art of a period. The public still liked painting best, in terms of coming to Park Lane and paying the entry fee.

While 'Old London Town' was only moderately successful, Philip supplemented his charity work that year with a display of old and antique clocks at his house in July. Over the years, the exhibitions not only had raised more than £33,000 (Philip also left the hospital £5,000 in his will),[41] but were also a way for Philip to display his wide knowledge of the arts. In the process, he had made a considerable contribution to the aesthetics of the time and to a far greater appreciation, indeed to a degree a rediscovery, of English art and decoration of the eighteenth century. Many of the exhibitions presented a rich mixture of art objects, reflecting the diversity of Philip's own interests and possessions as well as his financial ability to indulge them. He was one of the greatest collectors of his time and he showed a rare generosity in displaying his own possessions to the public as well as going to great effort to make visible many items belonging to others that had rarely, if ever, been seen before.

63. Sybil, *c.* 1926–30 by Cecil Beaton.

Sybil

Sybil was less involved with the visual arts. She was less of an acquirer than her brother and thought of herself more as a custodian of what she owned already in her own right and of her husband's family possessions. She was deeply devoted to music and poetry, more private pursuits, and continued those interests between the wars. She took a more personal interest in contemporary artists. In addition to being close to those on the French musical scene, she knew Artur Rubenstein and Arturo Toscanini well and saw them in London and elsewhere. In many ways in the 1920s and 1930s she led a somewhat independent life, further than she had been from Philip, despite the intensity and devotion of their relationship. Her husband rather resented the time that she, and then their three children too, spent with Philip. Rock may have disapproved of Philip's ostentation, and at one point he even went so far as to insist that Sybil return a particularly valuable jewel that Philip had given her.

64. Sybil and Rock.

Philip now needed her somewhat less, since, after being widowed in 1924, Hannah Gubbay served more often as Philip's hostess at Port Lympne, at Trent and at Park Lane; and the cousins worked closely together on the London art exhibitions. When Sybil entertained at her London house, Rock might put in only a token appearance or none at all. They permitted each other to lead somewhat separate lives, particularly as he was so much less sociable than she. At the same time, under his wife's influence, Rock became much more interested and knowledgeable about history and architecture, especially that of his own house, Houghton. He developed an expertise in and a growing collection of Sèvres that Philip himself did not usually favour. He also became a keen photographer and took quite splendid photographs for the Cholmondeleys' annual Christmas card.

Not only did Sybil have her own intense cultural interests, she had a string of admirers from the world of the arts. Besides the painter Sir William Orpen, these included Paul Furse, the son of the artist Charles Furse and Katherine Furse, who did a series of watercolours of wild flowers for her and the French actor Louis Jouvet. There was the Italian Air Marshal Balbo as well, who presented her with a set of the works of Gabriele D'Annunzio, each volume having a poetic inscription. Unlike her brother, her interests took shape through personal relationships. Despite his intense sociability, there was something self-enclosed about Philip. He kept to himself; she reached out. He moved in a much more public world of the great. While Sybil knew many who were eminent, she related to them in a far more personal way. In town and country she carried out the duties imposed upon her by her position but not at the cost of her private life. She had a greater interest in the odd and quirky.

She had a strikingly close if unlikely friendship with the writer and artist Wyndham Lewis, the leading figure in Vorticism, a short-lived British movement in the arts that had affinities with Cubism and Futurism. Born in 1882, he painted some of the most vivid pictures of the First World War and, with Ezra Pound, founded the periodical *Blast*, which published only a few issues in the early years of the war. *Blast* was designed to rail against what Lewis saw as the complacent values of pre-war England.

Lewis was a deeply creative figure who fought with almost everyone. He belonged to the tough and radically right tradition in letters found in its more benign form in Yeats and Eliot, and its more aggressive stance in Ezra Pound, who had established with Lewis the Rebel Arts Centre before the First World War. A trenchant critic, Lewis published another magazine in the late 1920s, the literary review, the *Enemy*. He was anti-Semitic, in the style of G. K. Chesterton and Hilaire Belloc: the Jews could be hated by both ends of the political spectrum. Some on the right despised them, accusing them of being Bolsheviks intent on destroying capitalism, while some on the left depicted them as archetypal capitalists. A figure such as Lewis, who attacked both capitalism and Communism, might well hate Jews for both reasons.

In addition, Lewis was an admirer of Hitler, although he eventually recanted that position late in 1938. He had published his book of praise *Hitler*, in 1931 during the period when Sybil saw most of him; it had appeared in a serialized version in the respectable publication *Time and Tide*. But, as is frequently true in England, his political opinions were not a significant obstacle to his social life, which was hardly conventional in any case. During the 1930s, for instance, he was also a great friend of the left-wing writer Naomi Mitchison. Lewis took pleasure in extreme positions. His views did not appear to bother Sybil; perhaps she didn't take them seriously or found them part of his fascination.

According to Jeffrey Meyers, Lewis's biographer, Sybil and Lewis met in the studio of Augustus John (Sybil knew John and his circle slightly, through William Orpen). In 1930 John presented her with a charming inscribed drawing of a nude woman. Sybil and Lewis saw a lot of each other during the early 1930s. In a 1978 interview, Sybil told Meyers that she did not find Lewis attractive and felt that he was not attracted to her. She visited Lewis in one of his London rooms in Ossington Street in Notting Hill, very close to her London house, bringing with her sixpence for the heating meter (Lewis may have been very well known, but that did not prevent him from being poverty-stricken). He talked to her about his work, and read to her from the novel he had just published, *The Apes of God*, a controversial and satiric work. He disliked coming to her house and wouldn't meet her husband. She also visited his studio in Percy Street in Soho where he drew her as one of the portraits in *Thirty Personalities and a Self-Portrait* which the artist and patron, Desmond Harmsworth, of the newspaper family, published in October 1932. The original drawings were exhibited at the Leicester Gallery in London. It was a very successful set of portraits, including Augustus John, J.B. Priestley, Edith Evans, James Joyce, Rebecca West, G. K. Chesterton, Lady Rhondda, Lord Rothermere, Constant Lambert, Noel Coward, and the aviator Captain Orlebar whom Sybil knew through Philip and had introduced to Lewis. Sybil bought the original one of her.[42]

Many of Sybil's letters to Lewis are undated, but on 1 January, presumably of 1931, she wrote, 'I was in a rage when I got your telegram but as it is a day for good resolutions, I forgive you – My only other resolution – & I doubt your finding it good – is to continue to paint my face and keep the home cheeks burning until you return.'[43] In the next letter she says how much she enjoyed their evening together: 'I do hope you will be back in June, it makes an enormous difference to my pleasure in London.' She had arranged for him to do a portrait of Noel Coward for the collection. On 7 July she wrote inviting him for lunch with Coward, who would sit for his portrait afterwards. This letter listed her efforts on his behalf in an itemized way, ending '4/ I love you very much but that is another story.' Clearly Lewis hated the idea of the sitting at her house, since in an undated note without salutation, she said: 'All right – your remarks have gone home & you shall be asked to no more luncheons. Noël and I will come to you tomorrow at 2-45 & you can tell me if you want me to stay a bit or leave you in peace.'

Because she did indeed ask him to more luncheons, he must have come sometimes. In a later letter she wrote, 'I hate not seeing you ever these days, your friendship is such an enjoyable thing in my life . . . . I feel today rather homesick for 31 Percy Street! & am off with Balbo to look at some aeroplanes.' And she was also arranging her own sitting for the portrait drawing of her. She reported to him on 30 July that 'Rock likes the drawing & is grateful to you for having let him see it. His only criticism is the shadow on the nose & the sort of twist of the nostril but you must only change what you feel like changing.' In a letter from France she discusses her relationship with her husband:

> Rock & I had one of our rare & royal rows. I was of course in the wrong & my arguments were the usual feminine ones, unreasoned & unreasonable but it made me feel very rebellious – these rows are of course a sort of mental blood-letting & should occur at intervals in all well regulated households but its just this awful punctual & regular life which at times drives me mad – I should hate to make out I was a sort of 'femme incomprise' as Rock is really a remarkable character & I'm deeply fond of him but marriage is certainly an absurd relationship. I miss my boys very much. My youngest who was relying on a timely epidemic to curtail the term writes wistfully today that 'ten boys are in bed but nothing has broke out yet'.

Sybil was reading Lewis's latest book, *The Doom of Youth*. He was sued for libel over it by Alec Waugh, whose title *The Loom of Youth* was clearly being parodied; the book was withdrawn from circulation. On 25 July she was very excited at seeing her portrait, 'very unusual for me as I have no liking for my mug'. That same letter provides a picture of her life: she was going down to Folkestone for a day to do 'some "stunts" for my brother', attending a family dinner and then giving the party after Artur Rubinstein's wedding. 'I am bitterly regretting my rash offer to him & the house will be filled with people that I spent the last 20 years avoiding but I did vaguely mention it & he seized on to it like a vice! ... Friday afternoon I can

65. Wyndham Lewis, *Sybil Cholmondeley* from *Thirty Personalities*, 1932.

come but I am pledged to my brother for dinner as it is my last night & I shant see him for months.' She also reported that she had sold fifteen copies of Lewis's *Filibusters in Barbary*, about his trip to Agadir, published in June 1932 and suppressed because of libel two years later. She tried to find him a lawyer for his libel cases whose charges would be low. She also enjoyed *Snooty Baronet*, published just three months later (Lewis had to write at an extraordinary pace in order to make some income).

Sybil was in Paris in November and early December. She wrote to him that she hoped to see him shortly in London, as she had refused to go to Houghton for Christmas. On 1 December, she reported that 'my brother was here & we went to every antiquaire in Paris & every museum & saw some grand stuff. I am enthralled by "Death in the Afternoon" by Hemingway – bull-fighting has become a very big thing for me!' She also wrote about the just published book on him by Hugh Gordon Porteus, *Wyndham Lewis: A Discursive Exposition*. She thought it was a good discussion of his work, although with some misreadings: 'His admiration & reverence are quite worthy of the subject. If only I had a bit more intelligence I should like to write a small book on W.L. from another aspect .... I look forward to seeing you more than I can tell you. Your friendship is such a very important & precious possession.' Her plan to stay in London was apparently frustrated by family obligations, and she was there only for two days just before Christmas, but hoped, in vain, to see him then. She did send him a Christmas card depicting the Saloon, one of the grandest of the state rooms, at Houghton.

She was still at Houghton when she wrote on 8 January 1933: 'My life here is entirely given up to doing things with the children, shooting & hunting (I merely follow by motor) & playing all kinds of very violent games with them.' (In a later letter to Lewis, she would describe such activities as 'occupations which have no history'.) This New Year's letter went on:

> I'm reading a lot of Walpoliana .... The Queen [Mary] has just left, after spending 3 hours here & I am much exhausted. I find that royalty make one lie so, because you tell them your best story & not seeing a flicker of interest or amusement on their face, you wildly have to start lying to improve on it. But she is very delightful & it is an enormous relief to her, one feels, to get away from 'The Court' & come here.

From the beginning of their friendship, when Lewis was suffering from the aftermath of venereal disease, Sybil was always very concerned about his health. He was ill from the end of 1932 until 1937 from cystitis, an inflammation of the bladder, triggered by an infection from the old gonorrhoeal scar. According to Meyers, this terminated for some time his many love affairs. He was in and out of nursing homes, and Sybil was anxious that he consult a doctor in Paris: she sent him the address and assured Lewis of the doctor's discretion. He had a series of operations, of varying success, paid for by patrons such as Sir Nicholas Waterhouse, Richard Aldington, Sydney Schiff and Sybil herself. She not only went to see the Paris doctor on her own to consult about Lewis but she offered to accompany him to a specialist who had treated Clemenceau. She also offered to pay his doctors' bills in Paris but he did not take advantage of this. On 13 March, around the time of his first operation, when she was at her house on the Riviera, she sent him £50, a considerable sum in those days. She was just off to see Louis Mallet, Philip's great friend, whom she thought that Lewis would enjoy meeting (this seems a bit improbable). He 'has a most exquisite old farm right up in the hills & who would be just your affair'. On 11 April she reported that she had scared off burglars from the house. In November she was enjoying his long satiric poem, *One-Way Song*, an attack on the 1930s poets, and hoped that he would read it aloud to her. In the same letter she tried unsuccessfully to secure his home address as she found writing to 'poste restante' at a safe-deposit company in London quite unsatisfactory because of the uncertainty of her plans. She continued to be concerned with his further operations but the letters seem less intense. From Paris on 30 May she wrote about her attempts to help him be published in France, having campaigned on his behalf with André Maurois. (Although Lewis did write to him, nothing came of it.) She continued to try to help, showing his drawing at Knoedler's and giving his mailing address to Lady Rhondda, the editor and proprietor of *Time and Tide*; this resulted in a lunch invitation, but she didn't know whether he had gone. (Lady Rhondda had commissioned the articles that had led to his book on Hitler. Sybil also put him in touch with the *Daily Telegraph* through the son of the proprietor, and invited him to go to the circus with Philip and Katharine Furse. She wrote that she was obliged to take a son 'for an hour to that awful Eton & Harrow cricket match'.

No letters appear to have survived beyond the early 1930s and one doesn't know to what degree they continued to be in touch. Lewis was a famously difficult man but there is no indication of a rupture. He spent the war years in Canada and the United States but returned to London for the grim period right after the war. In March 1957, Sybil attended his small funeral, along with some people she had known in Lewis's circle in the early 1930s: Sir Nicholas Waterhouse and Desmond Harmsworth. The latter had published the portfolio that included her portrait – the most lasting mark of her connection with Wyndham Lewis.

Late in the 1930s, Sybil in her early forties, became infatuated with the great conductor, Arturo Toscanini, then in his early seventies. He was a dominant figure on the international music scene, performing in the United States and Europe and, as a fervent opponent of Mussolini, playing a part in the politics of the time. Sybil preserved in the family clipping books programmes of concerts he led in Oxford on 8 June 1937 and a series in London in May 1938. She entertained him at her house in London, where he much enjoyed a dinner with the Anthony Edens. A few letters survive from this period, as well as a series of letters she wrote to him in the 1940s. On 30 June 1937, she wrote that she had been infatuated with him for two years, and found merely being 'just a "cosy friend" hard to bear'. In this letter she declares: 'My life is really dedicated to that love, it is the only good & perfect thing in it. It has blossomed for you & by you & I want to be always worthy .... I don't allow myself to think of the future – my only fear would be to ever cause you one "half-beat" of worry .... I can endure anything except not seeing you sometimes.' She is writing from Paris and she provides her schedule: she is going back alone to London for her sons' half-term holiday from school, then to Cannes and after that to Salzburg to see him conduct. 'I hardly dare to think of that but it makes my whole life golden. You will be surrounded by people all the time – I am quite prepared for that – but I shall be near you sometimes & I shall be happy & content just to be with you . . . . I must not write again like this – but I do long to know if you are rested & happy.' Toscanini seems not to have responded to her with the same intensity. He was flattered by her interest, but did not take it seriously.[44]

Sybil wrote the following October rather sadly about his having been in London for several days and not having been in touch. Her only request in that letter is permission to come to his rehearsals. She concludes her letter by sending love to both Toscanini and his wife. In a telegram on 4 November from London to Milan, she is a little more demonstrative: 'The only fog now is the unhappiness of your going away which is more lasting and harder to endure.' One other pre-war letter has been preserved, from June 1938: a rather impersonal note about a book on Rimbaud. It is written in French and, using the 'vous' form, she thanks him for the concert she heard the previous day. She did go to the United States in 1939 and saw a great deal of him, his family and circle at that time as well as hearing him conduct quite often.

There was a characteristic difference between the brother's and sister's lives. Philip lived his on a very public level, not only as a politician but as a trustee of museums and arranging large and important exhibitions in his house. Sybil was a well-known figure and was highly cultivated. In the course of her long life she had many friendships and was engaged in many activities while in London, Paris, the south of France and at Houghton. She was involved with her children, her husband, her brother. She entertained in London and in the country. She had an intense interest in music, frequently attended concerts, and her house in London provided a haven where visiting musicians, most notably Rubinstein, could practise. She was an extremely active sportswoman and the courts in the grounds of her London house were used by world-famous tennis players. She was an expert shot, unusual for a woman. But little survives in terms of memoirs, writings or personal papers to give substance to this active but essentially private life. The group of letters to Wyndham Lewis and the few to Toscanini provide an intense but not a representative glimpse of her life in the 1930s. She, like her brother, had a deep aesthetic sense. But his was more impersonal and fulfilled itself in public ways. He was one of the great collectors of his time. He was a patron of artists and had been, as had Sybil, a great friend of Sargent. Sybil's relationships with artists were much more personal and she became much more emotionally involved than Philip ever permitted himself to be. But for both of them the arts formed a central part of their lives.

7   *The Bomber Always Gets Through: Politics in the 1930s*

Air

The Labour government collapsed under the strain of the world economic crisis in 1931. To the indignation of the Labour party, Ramsay MacDonald remained as Prime Minister of the National Government. In its spirit, Sassoon had his greatest triumph in a general election, with a majority of 16,699, gaining 20,277 votes against the same Labour opponent as in the previous election, Grace Colman, who received 3,608 votes. She tactlessly remarked in some despair at a meeting just before the election: 'Really, you are very backward in Hythe.'[1] In an intense campaign of ten days, beginning at his adoption meeting with an audience of 1,500, Sassoon again played to the prejudices of his voters in conservative Kent, describing the election as a choice between 'a Government of patriots drawn from all parties and a Government of Communistic wreckers'.[2] He came out strongly for tariff protection, which he illustrated vividly at one meeting by bringing three wooden doors: one from Kent; and inferior ones from Russia and Sweden that sold for less. The Liberal, Hester Holland, decided not to run, as the Liberals were supporting the National Government. She urged her supporters to abstain from voting. The former Tory Prime Minister, Stanley Baldwin, dominated the Cabinet, although he did not actually take that office again until June 1935. Once again, Philip became a junior member of the government, returning to the position of Under-Secretary of State for Air. It may have been somewhat depressing for him as it was the same position he had held in the former Conservative government. In any case, he put a good face on it and wrote Baldwin a letter of profound thanks for the appointment.

The Marquess of Londonderry became Secretary of State for Air. His personal relationship with Ramsay MacDonald, who was a frequent guest of Londonderry and his wife, was probably a factor in his appointment. However, it was not a particularly fortunate choice, for despite the fact that Londonderry had had a prominent political career, he was seen as a rather weak politician (a reputation that to a degree Philip shared). Since Londonderry sat in the House of Lords (unlike Philip's superior in the 1920s, Samuel Hoare), Philip's position would be more important. As the principal Air representative in the House of Commons,

Philip had to speak frequently – most often, as did other ministers, answering questions put by Members of Parliament. To choose one day at random some years later, on 4 March 1936 he dealt with 'slot safety devices' in planes, the need to train mechanics, the acquisition of engine parts, speculation in aircraft shares, the number of passengers that Imperial Airways had carried in 1935 and the vexed issue of margarine versus butter in the airmen's rations – margarine was compared to axle oil and Sassoon was accused of having 'no consideration for British agriculture'.[3] (Indeed, at the time of Philip's death, one of his accomplishments mentioned was returning butter to the diet of the British airman.)

Philip also became the semi-official entertainer for the government. While Parliament was sitting, he gave a lunch almost every week for the Cabinet and other ministers such as himself who were not of Cabinet rank. Also attending were such pivotal figures as Maurice Hankey, secretary to the Cabinet, and Clive Wigram, secretary to the King. Philip may well have been the best politically informed man in Britain and as such it is a pity that he did not, except for a few stray pages, keep a diary.

The state of the Air Force had been rather rocky in the 1920s. By 1931, however, it was well established, but nagging questions throughout the decade caused a sense of continual crisis. Up until 1934 the role of the Air Force as an imperial police force was a consideration as important as military rivalry with other countries, if not more so. Sassoon recognized the significance of this aspect and took great pride in its general effectiveness as an imperial tool. These concerns were reflected in his many long tours of inspection, such as one in December 1931 and January 1932 to Cairo, Jerusalem and Iraq. The Air Force's role in policing Iraq was crucial both for maintaining its strength and, through experience, increasing its efficiency.

Philip resumed an active parliamentary life. He dealt with the range of issues that involved the Air Force, as well as speaking frequently in the House about such matters as the development of a commercial air system; this was his special charge as Under-Secretary. The issue could be tricky – a private business was receiving government subsidies, in large part for carrying the mail – and Philip did not always handle it as tactfully as he should have. Fellow MPs of his own party interested in the air criticized the subsidized position of Imperial Airways, chaired by Sir Eric Geddes, pointing out its failures and difficulties.

As the senior Air Minister in the House of Commons, Philip presented the annual Air Estimates on behalf of the government. The first time he did this, on 10 March 1932, Philip was trying to walk the tightrope between maintaining the strength of the service and the austerity, according to the thinking of the time, required by the Great Depression. In an undated letter to T.E. Lawrence he stated the problem that would plague him throughout his tenure as Under-Secretary: 'I am not looking forward to the air estimates on Thurs. I shall get it in the neck from all sides. Why not come up and see the fun'?[4] As usual, he executed his virtuoso feat of talking without notes. The estimates were £17.4 million, a reduction of £700,000 from the previous year. Economies were made through the termination of the airship programme and the curtailing of the use of large flying boats for passenger and mail services. He also reported on his trip to the Near East stations and on how the expansion of air power had meant a considerable growth of travel and trade for the British and for the Empire.

The proposed budget did not appear to raise too much concern. Less than a fortnight later, however, the Cabinet revoked its Ten Year Rule, which had mandated that planning was on the basis that there was no possibility of war within the next ten years. This decision was precipitated by the Japanese threat to the Empire in the Far East. After Adolf Hitler became the German Chancellor the following January, the issue of rearmament would come increasingly to the fore.

T.E. Lawrence wrote Philip a series of letters at this time. Undoubtedly Lawrence enjoyed the splendid paradox of an airman in the ranks corresponding on equal terms with the Under-Secretary. He had resumed his consorting with the great upon the death of Lord Thomson, who had tried to restrict his activities. At the beginning of the year, writing on 12 January from the air station Mount Batten near Plymouth, he bemoaned the fact that he could no longer work on flying boats, since, after an article in the press about him criticized such activity by one of such lowly rank, he had had to return to ordinary station duty. He also raised in the letter the possibility of being posted to Philip's squadron, the 601, at Hendon but nothing came of this. Lawrence was going through a period of discontent. On 21 March he suggested that he might quit and if so 'I should manage Lympne again in summer. Lympne, I feel, is probably your masterpiece.' Some days later, on the 30th, he wrote that his work was too routine; he was extremely ambitious about what he might do for the Royal Air Force, although it was unclear how he might fulfil his plans while still in the ranks. 'At Karachi, for instance, they let me revise the procedure of engine overhaul in the Depot . . . . In these eleven years I have learned every square inch of the R.A.F. and it seems a pity to leave so much knowledge unused. However please understand that I look back upon these eleven years with delight. I have been most happy, and owe the R.A.F. a great debt which will always make me its advocate and silent supporter. I will *not* write about it.' He was planning to leave the service on 6 April and perhaps 'do a long flying-boat voyage and write a log of it. I have the ambition to compete with you, there. We should have a collection like Hakluyt, for the air.'

As events turned out, Lawrence did not quit, nor did he undertake the trip. Two months later he thanked Philip for a position at the air base at Cowes that Philip had helped him secure. 'I am very grateful . . . . My notes on R.A.F. improvements will follow as soon as I have time to copy them out.'[5] These notes, if sent, have not survived.

In March 1933 Philip took another international tour of British bases. In July he opened an exhibition of photographs from *The Times* of pictures taken when flying over the Empire. Sir Eric Geddes, with whom Philip had worked in Parliament, chaired the event in his role as head of Imperial Airways. There were pictures and models illustrating the routes between London and Cape Town and between London and Singapore.

Philip was off on a 20,000-mile tour again in the autumn. This is probably the trip described in a fragmentary diary with only a few entries for September and October. He enjoyed swimming whenever he could ('I am very keen to get as many different clasps for my bathing pants as possible'). He emerges in these notes as quite relaxed. Dining with a governor, he remarked: 'The Governor & Mrs Caldicott are charming – both got a very good sense of humour – as they liked all my jokes.' Of course that was one of their obligations in entertaining a visiting dignitary. In Singapore he noted:

> At 8:30 I took the parade of all units & afterwards went round the whole station – raining most of the time .... Bathed in the Paga. Bathed at the Swimming Club .... I gave a dinner to some of the chaps at Raffles – then we went on to a dance place called the New World where I had great fun dancing with some of the Chinese women & having a drink with the airmen who were there .... At Karachi displeased by feeding of men & their morale .... View of the Tigris in the setting sun exercised its same witchery upon me .... Gaza stopped for lunch bathed in sea – green glass waves – very *resorty*.[6]

On 10 November 1932, Baldwin had made a statement in the House of Commons that would become famous: 'The bomber will always get through. The only defence is offence, which means that you will have to kill more women and children more quickly than the enemy if you want to save yourselves.' For a few years, a considerable body of opinion held the view that bombing of London and elsewhere would be devastating. By the mid-1930s, rearmament would occupy centre stage as an increasingly significant and contentious matter for the nation to grapple with. Before rearming, the Royal Air Force had to make a series of tough, strategic decisions. How much to spend on new planes? Should the emphasis be on building bombers, which could attack the enemy, or fighters, which could defend the airspace over Britain? To the degree that it did rearm in the early 1930s the RAF emphasized bombers, which the air staff favoured. Despite Baldwin's remark, most politicians pushed for more fighters. In the long run, the politicians turned out to be right. Nonetheless, the misguided policy of the early 1930s did mean that when the emphasis shifted to fighters, the latest models could be built without the Air Force being saddled with older fighters. Meanwhile, as Chancellor of the Exchequer, Neville Chamberlain delayed development of new planes on the basis of expense. There was considerable feeling in the country, particularly on the left, against rearmament, largely because of the horrific experience of the First World War. That feeling diminished to a degree with the rise of Fascism.

In 1934 Londonderry and others pointed out to the Cabinet the threat that Germany represented but the government was slow to react. Early that year Winston Churchill launched his campaign for rearmament, a cause to which he would passionately devote his powerful eloquence. On 8 March Baldwin pledged in the House of Commons that 'this Government will see to it that in air strength and air power this country shall no longer be in a position inferior to any country within striking distance of our shores.' A special Cabinet committee was charged with this concern. Many in Parliament, both inside and outside the government, saw Londonderry and by extension Sassoon as not adequate to deal with the problem, although they weren't replaced at that point.

The government did not take the strong steps that it seemed to be promising, struggling instead to strike the proper balance between preparedness on the one hand and disarmament on the other. It recognized the need for rearmament but it also felt committed to economy and to maintaining its appeal to an electorate that hated the idea of war. But if there were to be expansion, the Air Force had the advantage, or so the Treasury thought, of being less expensive than the Army or Navy. In that light, on 27 February 1935, Philip announced the appointment of a special committee to consider scientific means to counteract air attacks. Its members were influential scientists: H.T. Tizard, A.V. Hill and P. M.S. Blackett. Captain Balfour, a Tory MP particularly interested in air questions, asked if Frederick Lindemann would also be a member of the committee. Sassoon responded that he had been invited.[7] Lindemann would in effect be Churchill's representative; he was a brilliant scientist and an extremely difficult personality. He broke up the committee in 1936 but Tizard in particular nevertheless played a crucial role that year in bringing forward Watson Watt's invention of radar. This would eventually make it possible for the British to prevent German bombers from 'getting through' to the extent that Baldwin had envisioned.

Despite the doubts about him, Philip fulfilled his office admirably. In December 1933, 2,500 of his constituents recognized his accomplishments by presenting him with a grand testimonial book inscribed with their names in commemoration of his twenty-one years as their representative, along with a cheque that he gave to the Folkestone Hospital. That year, as before, he presented the complicated Air Estimates without using a note, a striking feat since the speech was full of figures and other highly detailed material. He operated under the considerable handicaps of not being the Minister and of being overshadowed in the House by Baldwin himself, whose statements on air questions carried more weight than Sassoon's. (The situation was further complicated by Baldwin and Londonderry not being on good terms.) The first point in Sassoon's speech was the continuing importance of economy, as reflected in what he regarded as a modest increase on the previous year: only £26,000. The estimates had been kept down by the closing of one of the four training schools and the addition of no new units. The Air Force, first in the world at the conclusion of the Great War, was now fifth. Philip spoke in favour of disarmament and expressed his hope that the International Disarmament Conference then in progress at the League of Nations in Geneva would have positive results. But he also recognized that there was a need for strength, mentioning Baldwin's bomber statement of the previous November. Sassoon felt that 'the kind of disarmament which would leave the disparity between our air strength and the air strengths of other nations relatively great as it is today does not recommend itself to His Majesty's Government'. The aim was 'to ensure, firstly, national safety at home, and, secondly, the maintenance of law and order and the protection and development of communications in more backward territories overseas. For these latter purposes, air power has finally established itself as an instrument which is at once humane, economical and incomparably effective.'

The only expansion in the estimates was for Imperial Airways, so that it could extend its services to Australia. It now served 100 European cities and had doubled its passengers from

20,650 to 41,500. In his speech he mentioned that the Air Force was the symbol of British power, as in Iraq where supplies, including blankets, were dropped for British troops who were fighting insurgency, observing that 'the work that they [units of the Royal Air Force] are doing belongs to the same order of beneficent and creative activities as those which were once carried out by the road-making legionaries of the Roman Empire'. He mentioned further accomplishments of the Air Force, including the fighting of locusts, long-distance flights and various records broken by British airmen. In conclusion, he said that 'as long as air forces exist, no Government in this country can disregard its responsibility for the air defence of our great urban populations'. Yet he would not go into any detail about military preparedness because of the ongoing disarmament conference, which made it inappropriate, he felt, for the House to discuss such issues. (Government policy aimed at an agreement by the powers to reduce their air forces.)

Hovering over Sassoon's speech was Baldwin's statement of the previous November. Neil Maclean, a Labour member, talked of the terrorism that aeroplanes represented, and their need to be controlled internationally. Churchill spoke next. He was not going to allow Sassoon to ignore the issues that he regarded as the most vital. One must not think, he said, 'that the Air Force exists to fight locusts and that it never drops anything but blankets'. This position was totally unrealistic, Churchill argued. He rejected the 'helplessness and hopelessness' of Baldwin's speech. He felt that there was no chance that the other European powers would accept disarmament. 'We have to be strong enough to defend our neutrality .... Therefore, it seems to me that the possession of an adequate air force is almost a complete protection for the civilian population, not indeed against injury and annoyance but against destruction.' In remarks at the end of the debate, Sassoon totally ignored the question of rearmament and made no mention of Churchill's speech. He dealt instead with the smaller points that various speakers had raised.[8] With neither Baldwin nor MacDonald present in the House, and his Minister in the House of Lords, Sassoon was in a weak position to respond to the most important question: how would the British Air Force react to the failure to secure disarmament? Despite his disagreements, Churchill wrote a letter to Londonderry on 15 March praising the Under-Secretary's performance: 'I thought Philip spoke extremely well and everybody liked him.'[9]

The next year Sassoon introduced, on 8 March in a speech of fifty minutes, the Air Estimates in the House of Commons in a debate that would last seven hours. He began bluntly and honestly by setting out the two widely divergent points of view: 'On the one hand, there are those who regard the Air arm as an imminent threat to the survival of our present day civilisation and would like to see all military aircraft swept out of existence. On the other hand, there are those who consider that the provisions that His Majesty's Government have made for the air defences of this Island are utterly inadequate.' He reported an increase of expenditure of approximately half a million pounds, which would support the creation of four new squadrons. He pointed out that the government had attempted, without success, to persuade other nations to pursue policies of disarmament. On the contrary, other countries had been increasing their air fleets. 'We cannot any longer accept a position of continuing inferiority in the air . . . . This does not mean that we have in any way abandoned our belief in the advantages of general air disarmament . . . . [But] as other nations will not come down to our level, our national and Imperial security demands that we shall build up towards theirs.'

There was a continuing report of the activities of the Air Force in Iraq (an intriguing theme, considering the Sassoon family's origins). Philip also dwelt on the peaceful activities of the Air Force. Clearly Churchill's attack the previous year had stung him and he echoed it now:

> Those who disagreed with me tried to 'blanket' my argument with ridicule . . . . It is not indeed by fighting locusts or dropping blankets, or even evacuating threatened civilians or carrying medical assistance to the sick and injured, that the Royal Air Force does its only work for peace . . . . In the establishment of the rule of law and in safeguarding the life, liberty and goods of the subject on the frontiers of our Empire, the policeman goes hand in hand with the philanthropist.

In his speech he paid more attention to these questions and to those of civil aviation than to military issues. Clement Attlee, then the Deputy Leader of the Labour party, attacked him for advocating an increase in arms and advocating the need for parity. In a powerful speech Churchill warned that Germany was arming fast. He urged that Parliament and the Cabinet decide to rearm and not wait for a change in public opinion. Baldwin himself had hoped for some sort of international disarmament plan.[10]

Four months later, on 19 July, Baldwin himself announced in the House of Commons an expansion of the RAF and other services. His famous remark about the bombers always getting through had put him in a difficult position: if defence were impossible, why, its opponents argued, bother? In this 1934 speech Baldwin coined another famous, and rather contradictory, phrase. 'The old frontiers are gone. When you think of the defence of England you no longer think of the chalk cliffs of Dover, you think of the Rhine. That is where our frontiers are.' That November, Baldwin pledged that Britain's Air Force would be 50 per cent greater than Germany's; at the same time he denied that the German Air Force was at that moment practically as strong as Britain's.

Sassoon and Churchill's disagreements over air policy made no difference to their social life. Philip continued to welcome Churchill as a frequent guest at all three of his houses, and Churchill was perfectly happy with Philip's providing such favours as arranging to send his private plane to Paris to fly him and his son Randolph back to Lympne at the end of a French trip in August 1934. The following autumn Churchill sent him a *bon voyage* telegram on the 19,000-mile tour he took from 22 September to 29 October to fourteen countries, including Egypt, India and Singapore.[11] He went out by Royal Air Force and returned by Imperial Air, to emphasize the advantages of civil air travel. The mid-1930s saw an effort to improve the speed of commercial trips, stimulated in part by the growth of night-flying, to the various parts of the Empire, and the shift to send all first-class mail by air.

66. Philip, Winston Churchill, Sybil, Clementine Churchill and Hannah at Port Lympne, soon after the First World War. Note Philip's initials on the balustrade.

By the time this was accomplished in 1937, the increased pace of life was on Philip's mind in other ways. The publisher Hutchinson brought out a curious volume that year by Owen Cathcart-Jones, *Aviation Memoirs including Australia and Back and Other Record Flights*. It featured an introduction by the Rt. Hon. Sir Philip Sassoon, Bart, G.B.E., C.M.G., M.P. Under Secretary of State for Air (so is he credited on both the title page and the book's spine). His brief foreword reads in its entirety:

I have been asked by Lieutenant Cathcart-Jones to write a foreword to this book, but, owing to the very short time in which it is being produced – a matter of days only – I have unfortunately been unable to read it. I gather that Lieutenant Cathcart-Jones, not content with the laurels gained by record-breaking in the air, is impelled by something dynamic in his personality to attempt records in literature also by producing his book in the short-est possible time. To the airman, speed must apparently ever be in the forefront of achievement! I trust that success will attend his efforts and that this book will prove that his ability as an author is as great as his skill as an airman.

When the Estimates were presented the following year, 1935, Philip depicted himself, vividly, as St Sebastian, who was being pierced by arrows from both those who thought that the provisions were totally inadequate and those who favoured the abolition of all armed forces. He reported that the Air Force was the fifth in size in the world, outranked by small margins by the United

States and Italy and by considerable margins by France and Russia. He recognized the need for increases in strength as the disarmament conference was not making any progress. He announced quite considerable increases: the estimates were to go up to £23.8 million; the plan was to add 41.5 squadrons over the next four years. Nonetheless, Churchill would not allow Sassoon to get away without discussing Germany at greater length. In his speech, Churchill pointed out that the Germans had more planes than the British, and claimed that their bombers could reach London more easily than British bombers could reach Berlin. Churchill's standing with his own party was weaker than it had been. He was now seen even more as a maverick, not only on the question of rearmament but also in his opposition to any sort of liberalization of Britain's connection with India. He had gone as far the previous April as to accuse Samuel Hoare, the Secretary of State for India, of political misconduct. Hoare was particularly incensed because a few days before making this accusation, Churchill and Hoare had sat together at lunch at Sassoon's house on Park Lane on apparently perfectly amiable terms.

There was great uncertainty about whether reliable figures existed for the size of the German Air Force. As Philip said in his presentation that day, 'A great many inaccurate figures have been bandied about and an unduly black picture has been painted of our weakness in the air.' Moore-Brabazon, another leading Tory MP who had himself been an air force hero during the war, shared Churchill's distress about the state of the RAF, remarking in the debate that Sassoon 'puts a glamour over a sorry story with a regularity which is almost a danger to the community'. Churchill acknowledged that the government was expanding the Air Force but he felt that it was not coping with the likelihood that the war that had ended in November 1918 would be resumed in the near future. Since the government would be attacked for expansion, he asked, 'why not expand effectively?' In Churchill's view the German Air Force was three or four times as strong as Britain's. It was a battle of figures, and in refutation Philip claimed that by ordering 1,000 more machines Britain would be stronger than Germany. He certainly recognized that 'the situation is one which does give us all cause for grave anxiety'. Sassoon had to admit that because of German activity, it was not certain that Britain could fulfil its pledge of having 50 per cent more planes than Germany. 'There has been a great acceleration, as far as we know, in the manufacture of aircraft in Germany, but still, in spite of that, at the end of this year we shall have a margin, though I do not say a margin of 50 per cent.'[12]

Churchill seemed vindicated when two weeks later, on 3 April, Hitler made the claim to two British politicians, John Simon and Anthony Eden, that his Air Force had already achieved parity. On the 9th Philip nevertheless stated in the House, in answer to a question, that the British Air Force was still bigger than Germany's, although he added that 'the rate of Germany's development is such as to cause His Majesty's Government grave concern'.[13] On 29 April Churchill wrote a powerful memorandum citing his history of warning the House since March 1933 that Hitler was building up his Air Force in violation of the Treaty of Versailles. He distributed it to various important political figures, including Londonderry but not Sassoon.

The next month, Baldwin admitted that he had been misled about German air strength. 'Where I was wrong was in the estimate of the future. There I was completely wrong. We were completely misled on the subject.' Harold Macmillan, then a prominent MP and later Prime Minister, has commented in his memoirs on the reaction to this statement in the House of Commons. Rather than becoming convinced, as Churchill wished, that the Air Force should be built up, the majority of the Tories felt less strongly on the issue than one might expect. Macmillan attributes this to the English affection for 'owning up'. Baldwin's approach had won over the House, and in any case the public supported his reluctance to rearm, as did the opposition party, Labour. In answering a question that day from a leader of the Labour left, Sir Stafford Cripps, Baldwin did point out that disarmament hadn't worked. In the last major speech of the debate he said that there was an addition of 22,500 in personnel to the Air Force, of whom 2,500 were pilots, that there were five more training schools, and increased construction of bombers. He concluded that he and the government were 'fully alive to the gravity of the situation .... A strong British airforce is the best guarantee for the peace of Europe.'[14]

Nevertheless, there was an awareness that more decisive action needed to be taken and a month later, in June 1935, Philip Cunliffe-Lister, a much stronger politician, replaced Londonderry as Secretary of State for Air. It was about time, as Londonderry was a member of the Anglo-German Fellowship and in 1938 would publish *Ourselves and Germany*, a study sympathetic to the Germans. He was also an anti-Semite, although that had not apparently affected his working relationship with Sassoon. He wrote to Ribbentrop, the German Ambassador to Britain, in 1936: 'As I told you, I have no great affection for the Jews. It is possible to trace their participation in most of those international disturbances which have created so much havoc in different countries.'[15] Londonderry was a firm believer in the racial similarities between the English and the Germans, particularly in contrast with the French.

The appointment of Cunliffe-Lister was the result of Stanley Baldwin's replacing Ramsay MacDonald as Prime Minister, thus finally occupying the central position in the government after unofficially dominating the Coalition since its formation in 1931. Cunliffe-Lister was undoubtedly a more aggressive Air Minister, although Londonderry later claimed that he had tried to expand the Air Force but that Baldwin had not co-operated. Cunliffe-Lister tripled the number of men in the Air Force. He moved the Hurricane and Spitfire fighter planes off the drawing board and into production. Meanwhile, Sir Thomas Inskip, the newly appointed Minister for the Co-ordination for Defence, urged that the proportion of fighters to bombers be increased. Throughout the mid-1930s, the production targets for both kinds of planes the Ministry promised were not achieved. It was not until December 1937 that the shift in proportion from the old rate of two new bombers for each new fighter was accomplished.[16]

Cunliffe-Lister encouraged Philip's successful activities in recruiting potential officers from public schools and established a special committee, on which Philip sat, to expand the service. In July 1935, with the new Minister in the Commons, there was another major debate about rearmament (the Labour MP Neil Maclean declared, 'We are sick to death of all this mad talk about rearming'). Frederick Guest, a cousin of Churchill's who had been Secretary of State of Air in 1921–22, and who commented frequently on air matters, said that it was particularly valuable that the responsible Cabinet member should now be in the House of Commons. That wasn't much of a vote of confidence in Sassoon.

In any event, the Air Minister wouldn't sit in the Commons for long. A general election was called for November 1935 (it would be the last general election until 1945, after the war). Sassoon was easily returned against a Liberal candidate, Richard Ellis, a local barrister, with a majority of more than 6,000 in a turnout of some 24,000 (15,359 against 8,688) although it was less than his landslide victory of 1931. Presumably Labour felt it was hopeless to field a candidate. Although Britain was far from being out of the Depression, calls for economic reforms were of little interest locally. As Ellis sadly remarked, the constituency 'rests happily in placidity and comparative prosperity'.[17] The election was also seen, to a degree, as a mandate for rearmament and Sassoon admitted in his constituency that the National Government had not done enough. (His Liberal opponent was against further rearmament.) As he stated: 'We have allowed our defence forces to decline to a level which impairs the influence which Great Britain can exert in support of the League [of Nations]. If we are at fault in that, others must share the blame .... It must be shared by those who on every occasion have urged upon us to disarm still further. We, at least, have already begun to increase the strength of the Royal Air Force.'[18]

Cunliffe-Lister went to the House of Lords the same month as Lord Swinton, on the assumption that that would give him more time to get on with the planning aspects of his job. (Ironically, being in the House of Lords was one of the reasons that Prime Minister Neville Chamberlain would later give in May 1938 when replacing Swinton with Kingsley Wood. Swinton may have been too aggressively in favour of rearmament for Chamberlain's policy of appeasement.) Churchill thought well of Cunliffe-Lister and his attempt to strengthen the Air Force, but felt that he had made a serious mistake in agreeing to go to the House of Lords. He commented that 'very considerable efforts were made by the British Government in the next four years [from 1935], and there is no doubt that we excelled in air quality; but quantity was henceforth beyond us. The outbreak of war found us with barely half the German numbers.'[19]

With Swinton's absence from the Commons, it was once again in March 1936 Philip's obligation to introduce the Estimates. As such, he was very much the public face of the Ministry. But in the papers of the Air Ministry I have not been able to find evidence of Sassoon's contributions to the making of policy or to the financial positions that it was his obligation to present to the House. The sum now, in 1936, was £43.5 million, the largest since the First World War. The aim, he stated, was 'to make an attack upon these islands too dangerous to contemplate' by having an adequate air force, an adequate number of pilots and an adequate manufacturing industry. He spoke at length and in great detail. Effective as he may have been, one MP felt that the situation was so important that the Secretary of State himself should have presented the Estimates, even though that was not constitutionally permissible. Philip, although briefed by civil servants, and involved with the relevant committees, was undertaking the formidable task of presenting the Estimates yet again with the handicap of being an Under-Secretary outside the Cabinet. In his second speech at the conclusion of the debate he said:

The disarmament to which we subjected ourselves for many years was to give an example to other nations, but they never followed it. We embark to-night on another method of maintaining the world peace, and that is to show the world that Great Britain has the power and the will to make aggression unprofitable .... We are carrying out to-night another task, which is to fulfil an obligation clearly laid on us at the last Election ... of so organising and strengthening our defences that the wealth of the British Empire shall not be a temptation to any aggressor.[20]

The following year the Ministry's budget nearly doubled. Philip presented the Estimates of £82.5 million in 1937, mentioning the problems of increased production and the need to support an ever growing number of air squadrons: compared with 53 squadrons in 1935, there were expected to be 124 squadrons within a few months. He claimed that the sum would result in an air force that was adequate and he based his statement on, he said, confidential government information. He could not reveal his sources, the sort of argument difficult to take issue with but also because of its vagueness not very convincing. The expansion would be 'a matter of trebling a Force and rearming it with modern equipment'. In his speech he wished to assure his listeners that all was going well, with figures to back up that assertion. He mentioned that the Air Force had continued to help maintain order in areas for which Britain was responsible, most notably during the previous year in Palestine. He also reported on satisfactory progress in civil aviation and in the provisions for sending mail. He concluded: 'I make bold to say that so large an expansion in so short a time has never been approached, even remotely, in like circumstances by any other Service Department. It is an expansion without precedent in peace time in the history of our country.'[21]

At this time, Philip had been ill. His old radical antagonist, Montague, recorded his pleasure that Sassoon had returned to the House 'fit and well'. Whatever the state of his health, Philip's days at the Air Ministry were numbered. He was thought not strong enough to handle his increasingly sensitive post. In a move that Stanley Baldwin had envisioned for a year, Philip became First Commissioner of Works in May 1937. The Minister was in charge of the buildings owned by the state and much of their contents. It was a position that in some instances gave its holder Cabinet rank, but in Philip's case rather insultingly it did not. Nevertheless, it was in many ways a superb office for him to have. He was in charge of a large department and at last was not subservient to another politician. Yet one couldn't really consider it a promotion, considering the denial of the place in the Cabinet that his immediate predecessor had had and the fact that questions of air power were much more in the news and much more contentious than those Philip would handle in the future. Baldwin had been considering moving him to the Office of Works for some time.

When writing later, Churchill, who had praised some of Sassoon's work, was rather dismissive of him, although he is anonymous in his reference: 'The Spokesman who was chosen from the Government Front Bench was utterly unable to stem the rising tide of alarm and dissatisfaction.'[22] And of course it was Churchill himself who was causing a great deal of this 'rising tide'. Yet the two men remained quite close personally; and Churchill had spent New Year's Day in 1937 with Philip at Trent Park.

For the next year, until Chamberlain appointed Kingsley Wood, the Air Minister, Swinton, was still in the House of Lords. Lord Winterton, an Irish peer and hence not in the House of Lords, now took the position of Air spokesman in the House of Commons. As Chancellor of the Duchy of Lancaster, he was senior to Philip and even became a member of the Cabinet in March 1938. Possibly it was he whom Churchill referred to, but there was a general feeling that Philip was no longer up to the job. In a sense, though, two men replaced him as there was also a new Under-Secretary of State for Air as well, A.J. Muirhead.

Any speculation that Chamberlain, with his interest in appeasing Hitler, might have thought it would be awkward to have a Jew as Under-Secretary of State for Air is undercut by a more important appointment he made the same year: Leslie Hore-Belisha, another Jew, became Minister for War. Anti-Semitism may have played a part in Hore-Belisha's dismissal in January 1940, but that was after the war had begun. There is little question, though, that the rise of Hitler made the public more aware of both anti-Semitism and of who was Jewish. A feature in a newspaper at about this time called 'Men Who Are Making To-Morrow' referred to Philip more bluntly than was usually the case as 'the third baronet, a Jew, a bachelor, and forty-seven years old' and also mentioned that his work at the Air Ministry emphasized more the commercial and imperial side, which was the special charge of the Under-Secretary, than the military, quoting him as saying that 'flight can give the British empire a cohesion and a permanency which earlier empires lacked . . . . Air power is more important to us, scattered as we are, than to any other nation in the world.'[23] At an anti-Semitic rally of 250 people at Finsbury Square in the East End of London in 1936, for which the speaker was jailed (since he wouldn't pay the fine for causing a disturbance), Hore-Belisha, Sassoon and a generic Rothschild were attacked as candidates for expulsion from England. Two years later, swastikas were daubed on the gates at Trent.[24] There is virtually no evidence of what Philip thought about the Nazis. When he had visited Hermann Goering in Germany because of his position in the Air Ministry, he had allowed him to think that he was a Parsee. It was in February 1933 at the very beginning of the Hitler regime. On another occasion, he offended the British Jewish community by crossing the Atlantic on a German liner.[25] On the other hand, the MP Chips Channon, who supported appeasement of Hitler, reported after his visit to Philip at Port Lympne in August 1936 that 'there was the usual German argument after dinner with Philip and Duff [Cooper] attacking the Nazis with the violence born of personal prejudice'.[26] Apparently Philip supported Chamberlain's appeasement of Hitler at Munich in September 1938, sending him a silver tray 'in grateful admiration for your magnificent work for peace during these fateful weeks'.[27] Sybil rarely voiced political opinions, but, perhaps influenced by Toscanini, she took a very different position on Munich. She wrote to him about it as being 'a nightmare of horror & *shame*' and that he would not be 'lulled into a sense of false security by the turtle-dove cooings of the Gangsters . . . . Now we shall have a few months of respite I suppose but at what price?'[28]

One of the great political events of the period was the Abdication crisis of 1936. Those in the 'know', including Philip, were completely aware of the Prince's affair with and deep love for Wallis Simpson. When George V died in January 1936, the question of what would happen in the personal life of the new King, Edward VIII, took on great urgency. Philip and the Prince of Wales were old friends. He had continued to see the Prince and entertained both him and Wallis Simpson at Park Lane and at Trent Park. Philip was happy to advise Edward on the decoration of his country place, Fort Belvedere, in Windsor Great Park and brought over flowers to be put in the garden. On one trip, to the Prince's intense irritation, he brought a gardener as well, to plant them: Philip indicated where they were to be planted and his gardener put them in. The Prince moved them later, although he admitted to Wallis that Philip had chosen the best spot but he couldn't tolerate leaving them there. Philip knew a lot about the eighteenth century's tradition of courting the man who was bound to be King, a far less powerful force now than then.

With the accession of Edward, Philip's brother-in-law, the Marquess of Cholmondeley, became the Lord Great Chamberlain for the new monarch. (In the spring of 1935, the then Prince of Wales had taken the Cholmondeley villa, Le Roc, on the Riviera for a party of friends. None of the extensive newspaper stories, British or American, of the time about the Prince's stay at Le Roc mentions that Wallis Simpson was in attendance.) One of Cholmondeley's first tasks after the old King's death was to receive the coffin of George V at Westminster Hall, along with David Ormsby-Gore as Commissioner of Works and the Duke of Norfolk as Earl Marshal.

Once Edward was King, it was estimated that about forty Tory MPs supported the idea that he might remain on the throne even if he married Mrs Simpson, but Edward did not encourage this. He knew better than his supporters that, as King and head of the Church of England, it would be impossible for him to marry a twice-divorced American. Through his support of the King, Churchill enhanced his reputation for irresponsibility and hence harmed his pursuit of the cause of rearmament. At the time of the crisis, Philip, as a government figure and loyal to Baldwin, was certainly not part of the King's party. Nevertheless, Sassoon's was one of the names bandied about in clubland as someone who might be part of a Cabinet that would support the King. Osbert Sitwell wrote a poem about the abdication, 'Rat Week', that in effect attacked those who deserted the King; but much more strongly, in an essay he wrote years later, he deeply disapproved of Edward and glorified the Duchess of York. He characterized those who hovered around Edward in clearly anti-Semitic terms as 'the rootless spawn of New York, Cracow, Antwerp and the Mile End Road'.[29] Despite being close to Philip, did he have him in mind?

Once Edward stepped down, Philip seems to have distanced himself from his old friend. The letter he wrote accompanying his wedding present to the Duke and Duchess of Windsor is polite but more cool than genuinely friendly: 'Sir. It has taken me a long time to find a wedding present for you & the Duchess wh. wd. satisfy me. So I can wait no longer & hope that you may be able to find a corner for this old Irish cup which brings to you & the Duchess my respectful & heartfelt good wishes for your health & happiness. I remain, Sir,

Your Royal Highness's faithful & obedt servt. Philip.'[30] Philip did reluctantly visit the Duke in France after the abdication, having been pressed by others to see the fallen monarch.[31]

Works

Being First Commissioner of Works was a dream job for someone with Philip's interests and skills. (The title is rather misleading as it would imply that there are other commissioners. There are not, and the title was changed to Minister of Works in 1940.) The position dated back to the first Norman monarchs, having been established in 1133, and descended from the King's Office of Works, which must have given Philip a certain amount of pleasure. During Philip's term of office, the department grew dramatically, expanding from 3,300 civil servants to 6,400 by 1939.[32] Chips Channon claimed that Philip had lobbied for the job with Edward before the abdication. In the course of recording his grand dinner party at which Emerald Cunard sat next to the King, Chips noted: 'Philip Sassoon, who had not yet been given the job of Commissioner of Works, which he longs for, asked Emerald to say a word for him to the King, which she did.'[33] It was not as if the King had the appointment in his gift, although there was much more contact with the royal family than in any other ministerial positions.

An aesthete, devoted to buildings and their contents, Sassoon was now in charge of much that the government owned in the United Kingdom and abroad: abbeys, castles, palaces, royal parks, monuments ranging from Stonehenge on down, royal palaces, the Tower of London, and embassies. It emphasizes the close-knit nature of British life that if Edward VIII had not abdicated, Philip would have shared responsibility with his brother-in-law for the maintenance of the Houses of Parliament.

In contrast to the years when he was Under-Secretary for Air, Philip's new appointment was certainly quite far removed from the central international concerns of the times. On 7 June he had to cope with one MP, A.C. Bossom, who complained during question time that there was too much hot air in circulation in the House, as evidenced by the fact that on the previous Monday he had noticed that there was a Member asleep on every bench. (Of course, that might have other causes than the lack of air circulation.) The following week, Philip was asked whether the 265 clocks in the House should be electrified so that they no longer need be wound by hand.[34]

Although Philip may have felt bitter for having been pushed out of the Air Ministry and not yet achieving Cabinet standing and his health was not as good as it had been, he threw himself into the deeply satisfying work at hand. It was as if all his previous life had prepared him for this role: his love of beauty and of grandeur, and of the great, with whom he would now deal directly – most notably the royal family, whom he already knew well. The position also put him back in touch with others whom he had met at the beginning of his career. Lloyd George, for example, now had the honorary position of Constable of Carnarvon Castle, one of Philip's charges. Philip wrote to him, addressing him as 'Sir Constable' and remarking that their new connection 'reminded me so much of the old days when I had the privilege to be working for you . . . . Thank you for the kind & generous appreciation of the work of my Dept.' After Philip's death, Lloyd George wrote: 'He had gifts of a very special kind which never had full play until he became First Commissioner of Works. Had he survived a few more years there was every indication that he would be a notable Minister of Public Works.'[35] In its way, though, this was hardly a compliment, stating that it would have taken Sassoon several years to achieve eminence in a position of little political significance.

He was, however, an extremely active minister. Members of the Cabinet appreciated all that he did to make their quarters and ceremonial occasions much more attractive. For instance, Lord Halifax, at the Foreign Office, commented with pleasure that at a banquet for the French President the footmen were dressed in eighteenth-century livery, which Philip had, according to Halifax, either discovered or designed.[36] Sassoon demonstrated an impressive attention to detail. Sir John Simon, the Chancellor of the Exchequer, recorded his thanks for all Philip did to help his wife when they moved into 11 Downing Street, 'restoring the Queen Anne windows which look out on the Horse Guards' Parade and getting two beautiful Adam mantelpieces, which were lying in some Government store, for the two ends of the drawing room'.[37] In an undated letter to the Prime Minister, Philip wrote: 'I have made enquiries into the question of the overflowing pipe at the Foreign Office & I am told that it was due to a fault in the ball-valve of the water waste preventer in Vansittart's [an opponent of appeasement in the Foreign Office] lavatory! This has been put right & I am very grateful to you for calling my attention to this public nuisance!'[38] He was closely involved in the refurbishment of 10 Downing Street itself when the Chamberlains were about to move in. He wrote to Anne Chamberlain about the proposed work: 'As you know, there is nothing I should hate so much as for you to feel that I was not doing everything I can for you, but we must remember the enormous bill which the public have got to pay for the rehabilitation of this house, and it behoves us to be thinking rather how we can save money than how we can spend more.'[39] He also consulted with her about who should paint Chamberlain's portrait. As Cecil Roth summed up his contribution: 'He brought to bear on the property of the public the same trained taste and the same devotion to detail that he had lavished on his own houses, and the results were not dissimilar on a scale immeasurably greater.'[40]

Similarly, in the letter columns of *The Times*, Philip dealt with questions such as cutting branches and widening paths so that Rodin's *Burghers of Calais* could be better seen in its public space. In speeches to the Royal Institute of British Architects and to the Council for the Preservation of Rural England he dwelt on the necessity to build new buildings, such as the caretakers' cottages at Stonehenge, which would not be out of keeping with their surroundings. He fought against litter and unsightly advertising: 'The Englishman's love of England was not merely bestowed on its ancient monuments, the peculiar charm of London, or the orderly attractions of the royal parks, but on the unrivalled beauty of our countryside.'[41]

Philip himself also wrote longish pieces in *The Times*, one on the art of Inigo Jones on the occasion of the reopening of the Royal Chapel at Marlborough House in October 1938. He provided a historical sketch of the Chapel, and there were three photographs of the restored building. The next April he wrote on the new public entrance to the Tower of London (a scheme that had been planned by Lord Stanhope, his predecessor as Commissioner). In the process of its construction, valuable discoveries had been made about the ancient draw-bridge that had been the entrance to the Tower, original thirteenth-century work had been uncovered.[42] Sassoon enjoyed being involved with archaeological digs that were taking place in London and gave a talk about one of them to a society at his old school, Eton, at a time when his nephew, Sybil's elder son, Hugh, was there. The group was so enthusiastic that Philip arranged for it to visit the dig itself and afterwards had the young Etonians to tea at Park Lane. One who was there remembers the occasion vividly, chiefly because one of their number broke a valuable teacup, and Philip handled the situation very graciously, as if it were nothing.

Sassoon played the major role in several projects while he was at the Office of Works. Ironically one of them, involving Lord Haig, harked back to the First World War. When Haig died in early 1928, he was given a state funeral and Parliament voted that year the sum of £5,000 to erect a statue of him in Whitehall. The statue had a troubled history, and had not yet been finished when Philip inherited the problem. The first two efforts of the sculptor, A. F. Hardiman, had been deemed not acceptable. Even the final version was not satisfactory. In the view of the military, the horse was too heroic and terrible liberties had been taken – Haig was not wearing his hat, his Burberry cloak was open and lacked buttons, the stirrups were misrepresented and his boots were too short. The critics wanted Haig dismounted with his back to the wall, echoing the famous dispatch that Sassoon possessed. There was talk that an inscription might be added at the base of the statue. Since such modifications would have required Hardiman's being paid a further fee, the effort was abandoned. As late as 21 June 1937, one Member of Parliament said that the statue should not be erected as no one wanted it. Sassoon replied that it was too late.[43] Although the statue looks to the untutored military eye quite conventional, it created more uproar than had been expressed over a public sculpture since some of Jacob Epstein's works thirty years before.

Philip was friendly with the 2nd Earl Haig, still not 20 and a student at Oxford. But Lady Haig, the widow, had never much cared for Philip, and apparently she did not much care for the statue either. When Philip attempted to communicate with her in July, she couldn't reply as she was making a pilgrimage to the battlefields. Philip later noted in the official file on 29 September 1937: 'I heard from young Haig that his mother is in a nursing home & not likely to be at the unveiling . . . . We need not expect any outbursts.'[44]

Despite the objections, the statue was finally finished that autumn and was unveiled under Philip's supervision. At first this was scheduled for Armistice Day itself, but instead Philip arranged that the Duke of Gloucester, the King's brother, would do so on 10 November with the King laying a wreath at the statue on the 11th. Thousands attended the unveiling, which took place at 3.30 on the 10th. The 2nd Earl Haig has in his scrapbook a fine photograph of the unveiling, showing himself and his two sisters, as well as Philip and the Duke. The Haig statue stands in Whitehall, very close to Lutyens's Cenotaph, the single most important monument for the observance of Armistice Day and where the King would be on the 11th. Even after the unveiling, the questions in Parliament did not cease. On 29 November Philip had to assure one member that representatives of the Royal Academy, the National Gallery, the Royal Institute of British Architects and the Royal Society of British Sculptors had all approved the choice of Hardiman.[45]

It is one of the glories of the parliamentary system that MPs are entitled to ask ministers any questions they wish, no matter how trivial they might appear, and the possibilities were particularly rich in Philip's bailiwick. On 5 July 1937, shortly after taking office, he was asked about the refreshment rooms and the lavatories in the House of Commons, as well as about the lawns at Hampton Court. At a later point he had to field inquiries about the heating of that palace and the rehanging of its pictures. The Labour MP William Wedgwood Benn attacked him on 1 March 1938 over the expenses for George VI's coronation. Wedgwood Benn objected to the Government Hospitality Fund being used to entertain, in connection with the coronation, King Carol of Romania, whom he considered an unacceptable dictator. Sassoon attempted to explain that he did not in fact control the fund, but Wedgwood Benn remarked that 'I am dissatisfied with the Right Hon. Gentleman's answers.'

In the ensuing discussion, Philip was defended by George Lansbury, a former holder of his office, and a former leader of the Labour party. While as a radical Lansbury was certainly no admirer of King Carol, he pointed out that Wedgwood Benn had not objected to the fund when it had been used to entertain Indian princes when he was Secretary of State for India in the Labour government of 1929–31. Furthermore, Lansbury observed that the Commissioner in any case 'has no power over [the fund] at all'. Lansbury went on: 'I am not trying to defend one of my numerous successors but only to explain that the First Commissioner cannot answer the question whether anything will be required for the visit of King Carol . . . . I listened to the rather hefty attack made upon the right hon. Baronet . . . I would like to point out that I had also been a victim.' The radical James Maxton rather gratuitously remarked: 'From what I have heard of the right hon. Gentleman's private hospitality, that he would have a very generous outlook on these matters. I have read in the newspapers about the lavish way in which he entertains people who visit him in his private house, but I should imagine that he, as a private individual, may be a little selective about his guests.' Later on in the debate Wedgwood Benn gave Philip trouble about the building of a munitions factory.

Sassoon also had to report on the increased cost of coal and hence of heating in government buildings. This was discussed at great length and the debate apparently went beyond his control. The Labour MPs enjoyed baiting him, and one said:

When the Minister departs from his brief he has not very much to tell us in the way of detail . . . . The First Commissioner is sharing with the housewife the increases in the price of coal, soap and other utensils . . . . Has soft soap gone up? We have had soft soap from him in his explanatory brief, but we want a little more than the brief . . . . He is only in the same category as at least a million housewives who are having to pay more for their soap, coal, brushes and pails.

It was ironic to have Philip talked about in this way since no doubt he had no idea whatsoever where those objects were to be found in his own houses. But he said that he would try to discover more, as 'it is difficult to refuse a request made in such an alluring tone'. Sir Stafford Cripps was less charming and more demanding: 'we shall expect him to make inquiries in the proper quarters'.[46]

Philip had not been involved with the coronation itself, which had taken place on 12 May 1937 just before he assumed office. But he was in charge of the disposal of the coronation furniture. Traditionally those who attended and sat on the extra chairs provided, most commonly the peers and their wives, had the option to buy the chairs on which they sat. The Office of Works recouped £15,000 from the sale.[47] Philip's method of selling them to fellow guests at dinner parties irritated Bernard Newman, a civil servant in the Ministry, who in general had nothing good to say about his political superiors. He found Sassoon 'a man of unsatiated ambition and a certain temper. I had more than one skirmish with him, culminating in a series at the Coronation of King George VI and Queen Elizabeth . . . . The First Commissioners naturally imagined that they were very important, but the department would have got on just as well without them.'[48]

One of the grandest enterprises that Philip was involved in was the redesigning of Trafalgar Square, the most famous square in London. John Nash had begun to lay out the square in the early nineteenth century, tearing down the Royal Mews that occupied the space. Sir Charles Barry, the architect of the Houses of Parliament, designed its final version. He proposed large equestrian statues of two kings – George IV, who had died in 1830, and William IV, who had died in 1837, to be placed on two massive plinths at the northern corners of the square. George IV made it: a statue by Francis Chantrey; William IV did not; his empty plinth still stands in the square. The square is dominated by a 145-foot-high column, topped by a 17-foot-high statue of Nelson, erected in 1843. Reliefs in bronze of scenes from Nelson's life surround its pedestal, and in 1867 Edwin Landseer's four colossal lions were added. There are two further statues in the square rather arbitrarily celebrating conquests in India: one of Sir Henry Havelock, the deliverer of Lucknow and the other of Sir Charles James Napier, the conqueror of Sind. There were also two fountains and, between them, a statue of General Gordon, the great military hero who had been killed at Khartoum, was erected in 1888. Hamo Thornycroft, a prominent sculptor (and incidentally Siegfried Sassoon's maternal uncle) had executed it. Lutyens had redesigned the square in 1911 as a memorial to Edward VII but nothing came of this scheme. He had proposed a grand staircase in front of the National Gallery, broken in the middle by a statue of Edward VII and culminating in a large fountain.[49]

In May 1936, when William Ormsby-Gore stepped down as First Commissioner, to take on the Colonies portfolio, Stanley Baldwin had considered appointing Philip to the office, only to settle on Earl Stanhope. Rex Whistler was quite furious that Philip had been passed over. He wrote Sassoon a note of condolence:

> What lovely things you would have done & I could cry with annoyment & disappointment at another commissioner of works being appointed as dull & tasteless (probably) as the last one . . . . I had so particularly hoped you would put in hand immediately . . . the laying out of a *piazza* worthy of exquisite St. Pauls . . . & just think what you could have done about the coronation decorations.

Whistler put his ideas about these projects into drawings in the letter. When Philip was actually appointed the next year, Whistler wrote the same sort of letter about Trafalgar Square with a drawing of new fountains:

> I hope London will now be transformed in a year or two into one of the loveliest & most elegant cities in the world. If only you had a completely free rein. But will you *please* dear Philip make the erecting of *two new fountains* in Trafalgar Square one of the *first* things in your programme. Couldn't a great open competition be started for designs for them? The present ones are *so* unworthy of London & I'm sure can have no defenders . . . . Very likely some now unknown Bernini would be discovered through the competition.[50]

Philip was very taken with the idea of doing something about Trafalgar Square and the coincidence of death provided an opportunity. The square was closely associated with the Navy and the two most important naval officers of the First World War had recently died. In December 1935 the House of Commons had voted money to create a memorial to Lord Jellicoe and in May 1936 for Lord Beatty. Before Philip became Minister, there had been some thought of statues on a grass plot near the Admiralty, and then the possibility had arisen of doing something in Trafalgar Square. Complicating matters for Philip, the widows were still alive and Lady Jellicoe was particularly difficult. Among other things, she was determined that there should be no association between her husband and Lord Beatty, who had succeeded him as Commander-in-Chief after Jellicoe had been fired by Lloyd George. She had already emphasized this point in a letter to Lord Stanhope, the previous Commissioner, where she also stressed that the monuments should not be dedicated on the same day.[51] Lady Jellicoe had a point: as she later insisted to Sassoon, there was nothing in Haig's memorial connecting him with French, the man he had replaced. As the Haig matter made clear, memorials moved very slowly. Philip saw the situation as his opportunity to take dramatic action in Trafalgar Square.

The obvious and traditional step would be two statues. On 29 July 1937, Philip had a conference with his colleague from the National Gallery, the Earl of Crawford, in his capacity as chairman of the Royal Fine Arts Commission. Crawford recorded in his diary:

> The difficulty has been Lady Jellicoe who had refused to sanction her husband's statue if Beatty is in the neighbourhood. As a pair of statues is clearly intended she has made every possible difficulty. At last in an unguarded moment she agreed to Trafalgar Square on the

disappointment at another just commission

of works being appointed as dull & tasteless, probably

as the last one.

One of the things I had so

hoped you would put in   particularly

                                                       hand names

was the laying out of a piazza worthy of exquisite St Paul's.

Having acres of those hideous trimmed hedges cut each day

all round, with lines of pleached trees or of trees &

fountains etc.   with perhaps a rest encircling colonnade

cribbed from Bernini.   Now all this has to be

shelved indefinitely   — I just think about you

could have done about the Coronation decorations.

Real nausea comes over me when I even think

of old sealed-lips.   Osbert says he is seriously thinking

of starting a riot. I shall certainly be in the van of the

& could easily raise a body in Fitzrovia

with love sincere & affectionate indeed in   Rex.

67. Rex Whistler, letters to
Philip Sassoon.

elegant cities in the world.

If only you had a completely

free rein.   Won't you

please dear Philip make

the erecting of two new fountains

in Trafalgar Square one of the

first things in your programme?

Couldn't a great open competition

be started for designs for them?

The present ones are so unworthy

of London & I'm sure can have no

defenders — except perhaps a few

Aberdonians who happen to admire

very likely some now unknown

Bernini would be discovered

through the competition.   I should

certainly submit thousands of

designs though this wd a sad bother.

& can hardly wait to begin.

Couldn't they be connected both ...

me in ... if the King is the first to give

(these could ... me in to conquer

in London)   then everyone would

... it.

assumption that Nelson's Column and Landseer's Lions will separate the naval heroes, but now at the last moment a fresh idea is started – namely placing our gallant Jack Tars in the fountains, one each side of General Gordon. Sassoon liked the idea, which emanated in a casual phrase I inserted in the Royal Fine Art Commission report on the subject.[52]

On 6 August Philip attempted to mollify Lady Jellicoe, but his letter was actually rather austere: 'I am very sensible, believe me, that this monument means more to you than to any other person living to-day. But a monument expressive of a Nation's wish to commemorate a Nation's hero is not always capable of conforming to individual predilections.'

Philip was hopeful that he might be able to move forward with the plan to make the square a naval piazza. He had to pursue the idea of new fountains over the objections of some civil servants, who felt, with some justification, that fountains and personal memorials could not be 'married'. On 14 August Duff Cooper, the First Lord of the Admiralty, wrote to Philip that the Navy people would be miffed if there weren't proper statues, but they would feel better about it if the non-naval statues were removed: 'If on the other hand the military statues were removed and their places taken by commemorative fountains, with a view to finally confining Trafalgar Square to Nelson and fountains, each in memory of a great sailor, then I think the views of the Navy would be met and Trafalgar Square would both be beautiful and would fulfil the function of a naval memorial.'[53] In an 18 August internal memorandum, Philip wrote that he thought that all was resolved, and that Napier and Havelock would be removed as the first step towards the Navy takeover:

> We have after long months got the War Office to agree that Trafalgar Square shd. be a *Naval* Piazza & that the military heroes (such as they are) shd. be removed. We have also got the relatives to agree. Do not let us reopen the subject. We shd. *without any delay* proceed to remove Napier & Havelock to their newly appointed stations. We can then proceed to alter the existing fountains into appropriate memorials to Lord Jellicoe & Lord Beatty. From the First Lord's letter this will satisfy the admiralty, as indeed it will please Parliament & the Public.

The new Lord Beatty at first didn't like the idea of the fountains but he was rapidly won over.

Even though it was a good plan to dedicate the square to one service and have fewer statues in it, Havelock and Napier are there to this day. The intended destination for the two generals was somewhere in Chelsea (there is no indication of the exact spot in that borough). By the time Philip wrote to the War Minister, Leslie Hore-Belisha, on 20 August, he was moving against the idea of adding more 'commonplace or definitely unpleasing statues in London and I was overjoyed when it was suggested to me by Reid Dick [a leading sculptor] that there was no need to have statues at all, when in Trafalgar Square itself a splendid opportunity was present of providing memorial fountains which, besides commemorating in adequate fashion the two naval heroes, would themselves be things to delight the eye and ear'. He reported that both the Prime Minister and Duff Cooper were enthusiastic about the idea. The new fountains were to be designed by Sir Edwin Lutyens and set in the old basins.

In September 1937 Luytens brought his sketches to Port Lympne and discussed the design with Sassoon.

The next step was to get the money from the Treasury. Sassoon's Permanent Under-Secretary, Sir Patrick Duff, wrote in November with an estimate of £20,000. On 7 December Philip had to write again to the irate Lady Jellicoe, who had heard that a drinking fountain was going to be her husband's memorial. Philip began by pointing out the splendour of having the memorial at Trafalgar Square and went on that 'the provision of new fountains in Trafalgar Square affords a far more acceptable method than the conventional statues for giving effect to the resolutions of Parliament . . . . The two new fountains are intended each to have a definite individual character, so that their memorial purpose can never for a moment be lost sight of.' [54] In a written answer to a question in Parliament on 24 November 1937, Philip stated:

> The memorials which Parliament resolved should be set up to Earl Jellicoe and Earl Beatty should appropriately and more acceptably take the form of ornamental fountains. No site so suitable for naval heroes can be found as Trafalgar Square: and I am accordingly exploring the possibility of a scheme which while adequately fulfilling the intention of providing memorials to these two great sailors, shall at the same time afford an embellishment of Trafalgar Square itself.

On 6 December he noted in answer to a question that there was no proposal to put anything on the empty plinth.[55] Later that month, Duff Cooper wrote to tell Philip that the Board of the Admiralty would still have preferred statues but accepted that he had already agreed to Philip's scheme and requested that there might be plaques with the admirals' heads placed on each fountain.

There had been earlier talk of removing George IV to Windsor Great Park, but nothing came of that scheme either – he, too, is still in the square. Sir Patrick Duff strongly expressed his opinion on 12 January 1938: 'The best site at Virginia Water for the statue of George IV – as for many other statues – would be the bottom of the Lake!' But he pointed out that moving statues was a very expensive business and that the wise course would be to let the statues stay put for the time being and to concentrate on the memorial fountains. He ventured the opinion that any suggestion that General Gordon be moved would 'bring a hornets' nest about our ears.' (Ironically Gordon's was the one statue that was moved: in 1953, to Victoria Embankment Gardens.)

Little progress was made during the year, with plans languishing until a meeting on 30 November between Philip and a concerned MP, Captain Evans, who was representing the point of view of Lady Jellicoe. He also felt that quite a few of those who were concerned with naval interests were unhappy and that the aim of the scheme was more a beautification of the Square than the creation of memorials to two naval heroes. Philip admitted, in a memorandum about the meeting, that 'the intention was not only to provide fitting memorials to the Admirals but also to effect some improvement in the appearance of the Square'. He argued that, after an exhibition of the plan and publications of the drawings of it, there had been a complete lack of criticism. Philip also pointed out that there were other memorials, in which the personal element was not prominent.[56] Of course, the fact of the matter is that fountains are not usually understood as memorials by observers while statues would obviously have that function.

Philip became quite carried away with the scheme and he even wanted, which would have been charming, flower stalls to be introduced into the Square. The local authority was appalled by that idea, the Town Clerk of Westminster minuting that 'the proposal is not one which will bear serious examination and my Committee desires to make it quite clear that if it is pursued they would have to oppose it strenuously.' That committee was convinced that stalls would bring a great increase in rubbish and untidiness.[55] (When the Socialist George Lansbury was First Commissioner, in 1931, he too had suggested flower stalls in the Square and had also been defeated by officials.) A civil servant in the Office commented on 9 February 1939:

> The Solicitor advises that it is doubtful whether we can legally do this. *The Westminster City Council strongly oppose it.* In my view, it will be very difficult to get such sellers to come; when they come, it will be hard to control them, and hard to get rid of them. Whether it is ultimately done, it is surely wise to get our new fountains going, before providing new subjects for controversy. We have no money for providing or maintaining flower-beds (another suggestion made in this file), and we must remember that Trafalgar Square is the traditional place for political meetings.

As civil servants put up these and other objections, Philip seemed to go along with them yet also remained determined to try to get his own way. He both minuted 'I agree' and added 'I am very anxious that we shd. do this & [shd.] like to talk to you. I think the difficulties cd. be overcome.'

Lutyens's fountains – replacing the old fountains – were finished on 10 September 1939, but with the advent of war, the total plan was not completed until 1948. It was as Philip wished it in its grand design, but without the flower stalls and with none of the other statues removed, except General Gordon. There are two glorious fountains with dolphins, mermaids and mermen. In the wall behind them there are quite obscure memorial busts of the two naval heroes, Jellicoe by Sir Charles Wheeler and Beatty by William MacMillan. In no way is the public made aware that the fountains themselves are the major parts of the memorial work. The admirals and the families were right to be dubious about having the naval figures celebrated in this way. But Sassoon was right too: he vastly improved one of the greatest sites in the world.

Pieces written about Philip after his death cite as one of his great accomplishments the restoration of the Great Painted Hall at the Royal Naval College at Greenwich. It was built as a hospital for naval veterans and had become a college for officer training in 1869. Christopher Wren designed the buildings, with Nicholas Hawksmoor's assistance, in 1704. From 1707 to 1714 James Thornhill embellished the walls and ceilings of the Hall with glorious allegorical paintings. One of the most famous grand rooms in Europe, it had rarely been used for its original purpose: as a place to dine. Thus it was a considerable achievement that Sassoon should have brought this plan, which had started in 1930, to completion. As far as I have been able to determine, little survives in the files about the project. Lady Diana Cooper, who was concerned with the project because her husband, Duff, was First Lord of the Admiralty, did send a suggestion about lighting for the tables in the Hall based on a fixture she saw at John Lewis department store, and Philip acknowledged her letter. There is also a rather charming exchange with Lord Louis Mountbatten about the nature of the candelabra on the tables, their height, and who would pay for them, the Navy or the Office of Works. Lord Louis wrote to Philip on 21 October 1938, thanking him for seeing the Captain of the College and himself the previous day. He was confident that the Navy would be able to raise the difference in cost between the plated candelabra that the Office was willing to supply and the silver ones that were desired.

> I do think you have made the most magnificent job of the painted hall and I would like to assure you that everybody feels that you have been most sympathetic and couldn't possibly have done more than you have done. I personally think that it is up to the officers to put their hands in their pockets to pay the difference between the silver candelabra and the plated ones .... I was most impressed by the sumptuousness of your office, but if the First Commissioner cannot have a sumptuous office, who the Hell can?

Philip replied on 1 November and it turned out that what his Office was willing to do was even less than 'Dickie' had imagined. According to Philip, the Navy would have to bear the expense for everything connected with actual dining. 'While, therefore I still think that candelabra on the tables are the only possible way of lighting the Mess properly, it will, I am afraid, be for the Admiralty, and not for me, to consider whether the cost of these in plate can be borne on public funds (i.e. Navy Votes) and a private contribution accepted to enable silver to be used. Anyhow, the scheme has my blessing, and I hope that it will go through.'[58] In the end, sixty-two grand candelabra, of solid silver, were installed in the Hall but there is no indication of who ended up paying for them.

Another of Philip's major projects was improving the quality of the benches available in the Royal Parks. There were deck chairs for which one paid a fee as well as free benches. Philip wrote a letter on 23 July 1937 to *The Times* suggesting that in order to mark the coronation individuals might like to donate £5 to purchase an oak bench. He planned to have the design based on those he had at Trent and the chairs were to be made by ex-servicemen. He remarked in his letter on the 'conventional ugliness of the old free seats there [in the Royal Parks]. With their cast iron sides and dull green colour, they are in marked and unpleasing contrast to the occasional new seats of teak or oak which are also free .... I have had prepared a new design of seats which, besides being much more attractive and suitable than the old seats, will be also very much more comfortable.' He also stipulated that donors might indicate where they wished the bench to go and an attempt would be made to place it there. On the page on which the clipping is preserved in the file at the Ministry, there is a photograph of two of the benches showing a lady with a pram sitting at one of them.[59] Also preserved in the file is a list of donors who requested locations for the seats they had paid for. Some of Philip's relations gave benches: Mrs M.E. Gubbay, Mrs Meyer Sassoon, the Hon. Mrs N.C. Rothschild. Most requested that the seats be placed in Hyde Park, but also included were Kensington Gardens, Green Park, St James's Park, Regent's Park, Richmond Park and Greenwich Park. There was some toing and froing about whether the donor's name should be on the bench, but the final decision was that, except for the King and Queen, they should not.

The Public Record Office contains the transcript of an interview that Philip gave on television about the benches. British television began in November 1936 for two hours a day, the first regular high-definition television in the world. The unnumbered pages begin the interview abruptly. The announcer asks: 'What gave you the idea?' Philip responds: '. . . I had always taken great interest in the Parks, and as I am something of a gardener myself this is very natural.' He felt that the old seats were very ugly and very durable and as they served their purpose he couldn't justify spending public money on new ones. Finding the right design was not easy. 'We had a specimen made and we all went down to sit on it in a very critical spirit and anxious to find something wrong.' On the air he displayed photographs of both the old and new seats. There were 2,000 old seats; at this point he had replaced 100 of them, he had money to replace about 300 more, and eventually he hoped to replace them all. Philip mentioned that among those who had given money for the seats were the King and Queen, Queen Mary, and the Duke of Kent; there were also generous gifts from Mr Ezra who had given the pelicans in St James's Park, Lord Duveen, the Duke of Westminster, Neville Chamberlain and Anthony Eden. There was some objection to the project. The Ministry kept a clipping from the *Yorkshire Observer* of 24 July 1937 objecting that the plan was undignified and represented ministerial 'niggardliness.' 'Next it will be asking us to do a turn at mowing the grass.'

The duties of Philip's office in assisting the high and mighty with domestic matters gave him some pleasure. He played a role in the decoration of Admiralty House for his old boss, Samuel Hoare, when he was First Lord. He then assisted his friends Duff Cooper and Lady Diana when they settled into the Admiralty briefly. And he helped Hoare redo his grim office in his next post, as Home Secretary. In some cases, these positions came with actual living quarters and in others just working rooms. As a result, there were delicate matters to address – for instance, how much should be spent when a new minister took office. Philip also had to deal with various residences that were occupied by those who had such rights as perquisites, such as Walmer Castle, home to the Marquess and Marchioness of Willingdon, thanks to his position as Lord Warden of the Cinque Ports. There was an extensive correspondence about whether the Office of Works would pay for the creation of a new doorway there, to make the couple's lives easier. Philip felt it was only fair, considering how much of his own money Willingdon had spent on the Castle.[60]

Much of Philip's time was devoted to problems involving the royal family. That he knew them moderately well through his exhibitions and their visits to his residences – to Park Lane to see the exhibitions and to Trent to see the flowers – made the task easier. He and

Queen Mary shared a great interest in antique objects. The Queen was famously not shy about asking for gifts and was happy to accept the stream of small presents Philip sent her way. On 12 July 1937, almost immediately after his appointment, Queen Mary, now a widow, thanked Philip for some carnations and expressed the hope that the estimates for Hampton Court would go through, 'but you must not be too extravagant or else you will get into hot water!' (In 1938 Philip himself gave two antique chairs to Hampton Court.) In her next letter, on 25 March 1938, she is careful to point out that she is no longer in a position of authority but she thinks that there should be some hesitation about transforming some space in Kensington Palace into a display area as it might be needed for a flat. 'Of course this has nothing to do with me *now* .... I hope you will not think I wish to interfere.' The next month, she wrote expressing a wish to visit the storerooms of the Ministry. 'I have always longed to see the contents of the stores of the Office of Works which exist somewhere (perhaps you have never even seen it) wd it be possible for you to take me there, I promise not to ask for anything we may find there?' She also had useful suggestions such as, on 2 July, that some very large standing lighting fixtures might function better at the Foreign Office than at Kensington Palace.

On issues about royal residences, such as a scheme to improve a terrace at Buckingham Palace, Philip dealt with George VI, the new King. Philip wrote a memorandum to his staff that something needed to be done about the terrace on the Garden Front side because at present during the summer 'guests at Garden Parties etc. sink up to the thigh bones in that loose gravel – & apart from that the appearance is deplorable'. The King thought the estimate of £2,445 was too high and opted for spending just between £600 and £700 pounds to pave a small area and leave the rest as it was. A summerhouse in the gardens of the Palace was proposed, but that would have to wait as money needed to be spent first on refurbishing the swimming pool and the squash court. One civil servant recorded in the file: 'I note the First Commissioner's decision as to the colour for the diving board.'[61] There were also issues at Windsor to be dealt with: the private apartments of the royal family and a great deal of discussion about repointing the exterior walls, to be done in the 'Ancient Monument' manner. Philip inspected the result and was very pleased.[62]

The post of First Commissioner of Works was one that was full of detail. On the whole it was just the sort of thing that Sassoon enjoyed and that he did very well. It was a position that tended to be filled by those politicians who had more interest in aesthetics, such as Lord Harcourt, Earl Beauchamp, Earl Crawford, Lord Melchett, and Ormsby-Gore. Philip was able to put his own stamp on the position with both flair and imagination.

Even in this post, however, he remained concerned with preparing for war. He was asked on 20 December 1937, in the House of Commons whether steps were being taken in case of an air raid upon Parliament and upon the Royal Palaces. He assured the Members, in a written answer, that the sandbags being prepared were made in the United Kingdom and were being filled with British sand.[63] The next year, there was a discussion in the Ministry of having allotments in the parks and digging trenches in them, as well as in gardens in public squares and even in private gardens in case of air raids. There were also plans for shelters at Buckingham Palace. Objects from the British Museum, the Victoria & Albert and the Wallace Collection might go to the Aldwych tube station, and the armouries from the Tower of London to the Knightsbridge one. The staff of the Office of Works was to be relocated to Harrogate and Bath. An attempt was made to 'zone' Britain on the basis of how likely various areas were to be attacked. In the files there is little indication of how closely Philip was involved with these decisions but neither before nor after Munich did his office try to pretend that there wasn't a serious possibility of war.[64]

Philip's health was weakening during this period; he never seemed to have fully recovered from having his tonsils removed in 1931. His ill health had an effect on his moods and shortened his temper. His health declined further in the spring of 1939. On 19 April *The Times* reported that he was suffering from influenza and that his doctor had ordered him to cancel his engagements for a fortnight, and then over the next two days in the paper's column of 'Invalids' he was reported to be better. Unfortunately the infection moved to his throat. In the middle of May Sir Patrick Duff wrote to the son of Lord Beatty that 'Sir Philip is still very far from well'.[65] Rather touchingly, Samuel Hoare, who knew how much Philip would hate not to know what was going on, wrote him a letter in the middle of May with political gossip.[66] The Kenneth Clarks, who had become very fond of him, visited him before leaving on a trip to the United States and said that he would be better on their return. ' "No," he replied "I shall never get better." '[67]

Philip had a certain fatalism about his health. But he didn't make it easier on himself by arising from his sick bed, perhaps out of excessive loyalty, an overly strong sense of duty towards his monarch or, some said, snobbism, in order to consult about the work at Windsor on a cold wet day in April.[68] His doctor, Alec Gow, had forbidden him to go out and warned him that if he did his throat infection would go to his lung. Nonetheless, Philip may have felt that he needed to rise from his sick bed, since the King and Queen were leaving shortly on 5 May for a visit to Canada and the United States. In the event, he did develop a fatal infection, and in the age before antibiotics, grew steadily worse. In North America, the King was kept informed about Philip's state of health.

Philip died at his house in Park Lane on 3 June 1939. Sybil and Hannah were with him. Sybil wrote the most affecting letter to Dr Gow (who was also her own and Hannah's doctor), immediately afterwards, thanking him for all he had done on her brother's behalf.

Alec dear . . . The devoted, wonderful, & deeply human way in which you have helped darling Philip through these dreadful weeks & at the same time looked after Hanna & me . . . . Now that the agony of waiting has been changed to the anguish of losing him one can take stock of what has taken place. I feel that he had touched the highest point of human interests & joy – & loved by his friends, adored by his family, keeping his own fine nature untouched by success & prosperity, before anything came to sadden or spoil life for him, he went – leaving a bright track in which we must try to follow him. He died with his hand in yours holding to you in the firm faith that all was going to be alright . . . . We are unhappy beyond bearing, we have lost the most darling brother & cousin . . . . I do not want this 3rd of June to end without writing to you something of what is in my heart. We are going now to take our leave of Philip for the last time as we know him.[69]

The next day, the Clarks' transatlantic liner reached England. 'On our return from America,' Lord Clark wrote years later, 'when the tender came out to meet us in Southampton Water, we heard that he had died the day before. The picnic really was over.'[70] The King was telegraphed that same day that the funeral would be strictly private. Two days later, he was informed that there would be no official London memorial service.[71] The King and Queen sent a telegram to Sybil bemoaning the death of their 'old friend'. Queen Elizabeth later wrote to Sybil about how Philip 'put so much into this world – his exquisite taste, his genius for friendship' and said that Queen Mary would miss her visits to Trent and Park Lane, ending her letter 'God help you dear Sybil.'[72] Sybil replied to a letter from Queen Mary on 6 June: 'It helped me to bear what I felt was nearly too much for my heart to endure . . . . The pain is increasing – the aching longing to see him again, if only *once* more – but God who gave him to us for such happy years of perfect companionship has taken him back & we must wait to see him again . . . . We have such breaking hearts, Hannah & I.' She wrote again the next day, after visiting Queen Mary. 'I must thank Your Majesty for being so wonderfully kind and understanding to me today.'[73] The court appreciated Philip's attentions – in some senses at the end of his life he was almost more of a courtier than a politician.

The few surviving letters from Sybil in reply to those – she received 1,800 sympathy notes – who wrote to her about Philip attest to the siblings' extraordinary closeness. On 23 July she wrote to Bernard Berenson, a connection going back to their youth, indeed childhood, when Philip and Sybil visited BB with their mother. 'Philip & I had such a rare closeness to each other – just *that* divine unspoken intimacy – with its roots in childhood . . . there is no comfort save in the knowledge that what we shared together was perfect & without a flaw. He loved & embellished the world.'[74]

As Sassoon wished, there was a very small private funeral at Golders Green Crematorium on 5 June. According to *The Times*, there were only two relatives present, presumably Sybil and Hannah. His ashes were scattered by plane over Trent Park while fighter planes roared over the house, dipping and circling. (At the express wish of Sybil and Hannah the annual Royal Air Force garden party was held at Trent on 24 July, as it had been the previous year.) On 5 June a memorial service was held in his constituency, at the Folkestone Parish Church. (He had received the freedom of the borough in 1933.) Canon Hyla Holden officiated at this traditional service, with two other Anglican ministers and a Nonconformist minister, Dr J. C. Carlile. The next day, Carlile's obituary of Philip appeared in the *Baptist Times*. There rather interestingly he described Sassoon as 'a Liberal Jew in opinion and a good Christian in character and conduct'. He knew him personally in the locality, described him as a lonely man and said that 'recent events deepened his sadness, his sensitive spirit was hurt, bruised and wounded'.[75] It is unclear whether Carlile had in mind Philip's regret at not holding a higher office or his distress at the turn of international events, or something more personal. At the service, local worthies representing the various political parties were present, as well as the members of the Folkestone Corporation in full regalia. The only London touch was the attendance of William Gibson, the Keeper at the National Gallery, representing the National and Tate Galleries.

The obituary in the *Folkestone Express* of 10 June recorded Philip's local benefactions: the Sassoon Housing Estate and a free dental clinic as well as his presidency of the Royal Victoria Hospital and of the Chamber of Trade. The Town Council passed a vote of condolence and Councillor Wood, who had known Sassoon since he was a small boy, remarked that Philip had 'placed his magnificent ability, his wealth to some extent, and certainly the whole of his time, to public service and the nation's welfare when he could have been on the racecourse or yachting in the Mediterranean'.

The Times recorded on 7 June that, according to Philip's wishes, there would be no memorial service in London. There was also a mention in *The Times* that Neville Chamberlain on behalf of the Cabinet expressed its condolences to Sybil, which was unusual for someone who was not of Cabinet rank. In his letter he wrote that although 'Sir Philip was not a member of the Cabinet his relations with the Cabinet Ministers was so exceptionally intimate that it was felt to be appropriate that on this occasion they should express their feelings in the only way open to them.' In the Cabinet minutes of 7 June 1939 it was noted that the Cabinet approved of the letter being sent as, Philip 'had held a very exceptional position and, moreover, had been a close personal friend of many members of the Cabinet'. In a way, it summed up his political life: he couldn't possibly have been closer to power yet he never possessed it at the highest level.

The Prime Minister pressed Sybil to stand for Philip's seat, since she knew the constituency so well. Her immediate response was that it was out of the question for her to give up private life. Chamberlain tried to have her husband persuade her, because it was important that the seat be retained by the Tories, but Rock said that Chamberlain must convince Sybil himself. Of her difficult interview with Chamberlain Sybil remembered that she said, 'Oh I couldn't possibly go into the House of Commons. First of all, I perhaps wouldn't always agree with the government! So he said "I forgot one had to be legally represented when one spoke to you" and stalked out of the room .... I said my private life means everything to me.' Nevertheless, she did spend part of the next six weeks after her brother's death in Lympne campaigning for the Tory candidate.[76] A brief news item about her decision stated: 'She has many interests, but politics, apart from her brother's career, was never one of the chief. Tennis, motor racing and travel have been in turn her favourite pursuits.'[77]

Most British newspapers mentioned Sassoon's Jewishness, with the *Glasgow Evening Citizen* calling him the foremost Jew in society and the *Daily Telegraph* pointing out that he belonged to one of the most distinguished Jewish families in England. The *Daily Mail* depicted him as combining an English outdoor charm with a subtle oriental beauty derived from his Eastern ancestry. There was an awareness that he wasn't quite English, even though so many aspects of his life shared the style of the highest reaches of English society.

An obituary in the *Univers israélite* of Paris mentioned that Sassoon did not take a direct part in the management of Jewish causes, but that he was a member of the Sephardic synagogue in London. *The Times*'s long obituary of 5 June made no mention of his Jewishness. His death, it said, 'brings to a premature end a political career of distinction that seemed to hold even greater promise, and removes from social life one of the best-known and most remarkable figures of our time . . . . He was a charming host, a notable patron of the arts, and a practical enthusiast in aviation.'

Sir Samuel Hoare wrote an almost equally long personal tribute the same day in *The Times*. In a way it was a curious piece, for it first set up the stereotype of what many may have thought Philip was like: 'the ostentatious millionaire obsessed with social and political ambition, surrounded with Oriental magnificence, living in the luxury of a thousand and one nights.' He then contrasted that to what he considered the truth: 'To his friends he was something very different. But being so sensitive and volatile it is difficult for even those who knew him best to describe his charm or define his character.' Hoare went on to describe what he was not: 'He was not ostentatious at all . . . . There was nothing coarse about him. Vulgarity of all kinds was entirely repugnant to him.' He discussed his perfection as a host and his great success at the Office of Works, 'the rightful culmination of his career. The flowers and seats in the parks, the decorations in the Mall, the Trumpeters in Westminster Hall, the liveries and plate at the Foreign Office banquets, the restoration of Downing Street, the elimination of varnish from the Palace of Westminster, these are among the many evidences that he left of his labour of love in a Government office.' Hoare also emphasized Philip's sensitivity and his nervousness, dating back to his maiden speech before the First World War. The following day Osbert Sitwell (who would also write about him in the *Dictionary of National Biography*) contributed a shorter notice, arguing that he was more an artist than a politician, as shown by his houses, his activities as a collector and as an exhibitor. On 9 June in *The Times* Philip's old friend Evan Charteris focused on the private person, saying that he had never really revealed himself as a politician. 'He spoke rarely from his innermost mind, still more rarely did he disclose the sense of tears that lay below his matchless gift for laughter.'

All this press attention was in keeping with the passing of a major figure, a man who was extremely well known in his own day. Philip Sassoon was at the centre of the English world. The style of the Baghdadi Jews had been to remain in the background, to be a power behind the scenes, not to draw too much attention to themselves, but Philip presented a more paradoxical case than his forebears. His political role was largely as a background figure, as someone who knew 'everyone' and entertained 'everyone'. Yet he was hardly obscure and his actions were tracked in the press. He was a colourful, indeed exotic, figure of the time.

Two assessments of him, by men who knew him well, give, I believe, a good sense of the man. One is rather barbed, by his rival Chips Channon. It's important to note first that, as an American, Channon was something of an outsider himself; he was determined to be at the centre of things but in my opinion was less assured than Philip in his relationship with the English establishment, less his own person. Philip was anxious to be part of the inner world, and he would, no doubt, entertain lavishly and at times wax hyperbolical in that cause. But he did not betray himself while doing that – he remained his own vivid person, unwilling to tone himself down, even if doing so might well have made his acceptance into society easier.

In his diary for 3 June Channon wrote:

Philip Sassoon died today – which is a loss to the London pageant. No-one infused it with so much colour and personality. Philip was sleek, clever, and amiable, kindly yet fickle, gay yet moody, he entertained with almost Oriental lavishness in his three rather fatiguing palaces (of which Trent is the loveliest) . . . . He was always pleasant and witty with me, talking in that clipped sibilant accent which has been so often imitated . . . . Philip was never in the Chamberlain racket and his power waned with Baldwin's retirement, but he never lost his thirst of life. Though Jewish, he hated Jews. What he really loved were jewelled elephants and contrasting colours – the bizarre and the beautiful.[78]

Channon put it too strongly, I believe, about Sassoon's attitude towards Jews. I think he was, unlike his sister, uneasy about being Jewish and perhaps somewhat self-conscious. There is the persistent story that he preferred to be taken as a Parsee and it was quite amazing how many seemed to believe this, despite the well-known fact that the Sassoons were Jewish. But he never converted to Anglicanism (unlike Sybil, who did so after the Second World War). The brother and sister rarely visited their Rothschild relations on their frequent trips to France (here, too, things changed after the war: Sybil would see more of them, particularly her first cousin Elie and his wife Liliane). Sybil's children did not know that they were half-Jewish until the boys went away to prep school. They outraged Philip by coming home with schoolboy anti-Semitic jokes. He insisted that they be told about their heritage, and at the same time, partially through Hannah's insistence, his niece Aline was told as well. Rock remarked to his sons that telling such stories was the sign of the second-rater.[79]

Philip was, contrary to Jewish custom, cremated rather than buried. He had kept up his membership in Bevis Marks, the Sephardic synagogue, although he played no part there. Like many other secular Jews, he recognized that he was Jewish and came, I believe, to terms with that. He was deeply devoted to his sister and his cousin, and saw fairly frequently some other members of the family. He maintained his officially close association, although he was far from active, with the family firm.

More kindly than Channon, Sir John Colville, a consummate insider who served as private secretary to Chamberlain and then Churchill, remarked about Philip that he was

a man who employed his wealth with impeccable taste, who entertained lavishly but not with vulgarity, who pined for royal favour but yet had time for all men, and who deliberately invited totally unlike people to meet each other . . . . He soared like a shooting star through the political and social skies, brilliant and considerate as a host, a tolerant perfectionist, satisfied only with the best for others as well as for himself. His wit was original and even his casual remarks were amusing because of his effective use of stress and accentuation. Skilful entertaining and exquisite taste are transitory. Good conversation and original wit are scarcely less so. Redecorating Government offices and arranging splendid exhibitions are no claim to immortality.[80]

The attempt here has been to try to recapture such a figure: important, intriguing, emblematic, but making less of an obvious mark than some of the others among whom he moved during his life.

Rather surprisingly, although it is not that unknown among the rich, Philip and his solicitors had not thought out his will properly. The two people closest to him, Sybil and his cousin Hannah, were his principal heirs. Philip appeared to be almost unduly concerned about Hannah's future, leaving her an annuity of £11,000 a year. After the death of her husband in 1924, as we have seen, Hannah had devoted much of her time to Philip, serving as his hostess and being extremely active in the exhibitions at Park Lane. She was also very close to Sybil and her family. But Sybil had a husband, three children, Houghton, 12 Kensington Park Gardens, an active sporting, social and cultural life. The problem with Philip's bequest was that his estate, large as it was, was not sufficient to produce £11,000 of annual income for Hannah. This put the will into jeopardy ('abatement' is the legal term). It was as if Philip had died without a will, although his executors did their best to follow his wishes.

The estate as announced in *The Times* of 16 August was of a value of almost £2 million, but estate taxes took more than half of that. The particular bequests mentioned in the article were the Sargent portrait of himself and his drawing of the Duke of Windsor to the Tate,[81] Haig's order of the day to the British Library, and £5,000 to the Treasury Solicitor to establish a prize to be given twice a year at the RAF Cadet College at Cranwell for the best all-round graduate, excluding the cadet who received the sword of honour. (With the onset of the war, this prize was not actually awarded until 1948 but it has continued ever since. Before his death he had already given a great globe to the College, had arranged that pictures were to be lent to it from the Tate, and he had presented a large bronze eagle.[82] He had also established the Sassoon Photographic Trophy, to be awarded annually to the air force unit that produced the best image of a particular area.) He left £5,000 to the Royal Northern Hospital and £1,000 to the Folkestone Hospital. He left £10,000 outright to Hannah, as well as Port Lympne and its contents, including cars and planes. Trent Park and its contents were to go to her for life, and then to Sybil or her heirs after Hannah's death. His two executors received £5,000 each. There were also annuities of £300 to his secretary, Miss Boyce, and annuities of £100 apiece to his matron at Eton, Miss Skey, and to Frank Garton, his butler. His domestic and business employees, if they had been in his employ for a year or more, were to receive one year's wages, a charge upon the estate of approximately £17,000. He was a life tenant of Park Lane, so that residence reverted to being part of the estate of Sir Edward Sassoon. There was approximately £300,000 in his name at the family business, which was ultimately divided between Hannah and Sybil.

The estate became so complicated, largely because it could not totally pay out the sums stipulated, particularly the annuity to Hannah, that there had to be a lawsuit in 1941, with Hannah and Sybil officially suing each other to settle the outstanding questions. Between the war and the various problems with the will, the settlement was not tied up until 1944. The executors were finally able to achieve most of Philip's wishes. The objects and pictures in Park Lane went to Sybil and those in Trent Park went to her after Hannah's death in 1968. Many of these are still at Houghton, but some of the French objects and pictures were sold in the sale of 1994.[83]

Philip had left a legacy of beautiful objects and an intriguing career. Although he had not achieved the political prominence he may have desired, he was at the centre of English public, social and aesthetic life. Nonetheless, his achievements were not necessarily sufficiently satisfying to him, and he seemed to be depressed towards the end of his life. He adored his sister and was very close to his cousin Hannah. He does not appear to have had other intimates – or, if he did, he kept them so private that virtually all traces of them have disappeared. (In this regard, though, it is worth noting that he was so devastated by the death of an airman friend that he attempted to reach him in a seance.)

Philip certainly had a rich and varied social life. He created three extraordinary houses. The exhibitions that he arranged had immense and long-lasting influence and were very important in building up aesthetic interest in the French and English eighteenth century. He did valuable work, in a secondary position, at the Air Ministry and tried to satisfy both those who believed in greater rearmament and those who believed in less. In the last two years of his life he had found the perfect post for someone of his talents as First Commissioner of Works and did an excellent job in improving the aesthetics of the state.

Philip's cousin Siegfried was probably then and certainly now the best known member of the family. But in the press and in the world of high politics Philip was its most prominent member. (His cousin Sir Victor, of the other baronet branch, cut a considerable figure and was far better known in the business and racing worlds than Philip. His stable won the Derby four times.) There were others in the public eye during the period, but Philip was in many ways the most famous English Jew of his time. (This was not a distinction that would have pleased him.) Being a Jew may well have limited the degree to which he was accepted in the world in which he moved, and there was an element of 'poor little rich boy' about him.

Very few of us do all that we might hope. Philip Sassoon achieved a lot. He had served Douglas Haig well during the First World War. He made a mark as Under-Secretary of State for Air and he was an extremely effective First Commissioner of Works. He was one of the great collectors of his age, and he played a highly influential role in the revival of interest in eighteenth-century arts. It was a rich and emblematic life. Philip chose to lead a public life; Sybil, except during wartime, chose to lead a private one. He died young, she lived for another fifty years.

8   *Sybil*

Sybil was forty-five years old when the Second World War broke out; that was the official upper limit for service in the Women's Royal Naval Service so she was able to re-enlist in the WRNS on 12 November 1939, and thus became one of the very few women to serve in the WRNS in both wars. Vera Laughton Mathews, who also had served in the previous war (first in the Army Auxiliary Corps and then in the WRNS upon its formation in November 1917), was the Director during the Second World War, with a rank equivalent to Rear-Admiral. Marina, Duchess of Kent, was the Commandant. Sybil told her grandson David that she had been offered the directorship but declined as she felt it inappropriate that a person with a title should hold the position.[1] There had been 7,000 WRNS in the First World War; by the conclusion of the Second, 74,620 women were in 100 different categories of naval service.

The WRNS had been disbanded after the First World War, but in the mid-1930s the government considered the general question of reviving the various women's units. In September 1937 Katharine Furse wrote to the Admiralty urging such a step; finally, a year later, proposals for the re-formation of the WRNS were approved. In March 1939 Mathews was appointed Director. By December, after the outbreak of war, there were 3,000 in the Service and a year later 561 officers and 9,439 ratings.[2] Their main obligation was to serve in naval shore establishments. At the beginning the women were thought of as 'immobiles'– that is, they would live at home in such places as Dartmouth. But soon bases were established to which women were posted. Throughout the war the Wrens greatly expanded their sphere of operations. Although they rarely went to sea, they did serve in many places abroad. They had three weeks of general training and then a period dedicated to more specialized work such as signalling, conveying orders, housekeeping, supplies, mail, maintenance, and training as drivers on land and of small communicating boats in ports. There was a discussion of the Wrens in the House of Commons on 10 March 1943, during which 'that small band of leaders who fashioned this Service', such as Sybil, were particularly commended. Vera Mathews sent quotations from the debate to those who had been members of the Wrens in 1939. Sybil preserved the memorandum from the Director in her scrapbook alongside a photograph of herself and other Wren officers with Queen Mary in Bristol the previous year.

68. Lee Miller, *The Marchioness of Cholmondeley*, 1945.

Sybil had a rather special position, which was made clear in the layout of *Wrens in Camera*, a 1945 book by the photographer Lee Miller. After a stylish full-page portrait of the Duchess of Kent, there is a single page featuring Vera Laughton Mathews. Then come two pages containing thirteen senior officers: two designated deputy directors; ten with the rank of Superintendent, the equivalent of Captain; and Sybil herself, with the rank of Staff or Chief Officer of the Service. This was the equivalent rank of Commander, and it had been conferred on her on 2 January 1940. (Women had blue braid indicating their rank while the men had gold.)

Sybil was in effect the troubleshooter and a substitute for the Director, particularly during Mathews's frequent illnesses. She also chauffeured the Director about in her own car, mainly from London to Greenwich for the commissioning ceremonies for new officers. Vera Mathews remembered being driven 'alarmingly by Sybil herself in the "beetle" or the "lady-bird", as her grey and later maroon Fiats were successively called.'[3] She appreciated her aide's 'champagne personality' and found her ideal to serve as the liaison with royalty and to arrange ceremonies. Sybil was particularly concerned with vetting possible officer candidates and sat on all the boards that decided whether or not a certain individual had made the grade. She was promoted from Chief Officer to Superintendent on 9 February 1945, and was awarded the CBE (Commander of the British Empire) on 14 June 1946, two weeks before her discharge from the service. She received a letter of commendation from Captain Archie Cooper, the Judge Advocate of the Fleet, commenting on 'her common sense, intelligence, administrative ability and strength of character . . . . Nobody knows better than I what you had to contend with in the early days, the apathy, ignorance, suspicion, the failure to appreciate the tremendous possibilities of such an organisation.' She had received an official citation from Vera Mathews on 11 May 1946: 'Her wise judgment, understanding of human nature and devotion to duty, combined with great sympathy and charm, have been invaluable in the headquarters administration and have gained her the affection and admiration of the whole service.'[4]

With her contacts in the great world, she was invaluable. Even so she could be teased, as in a poem written by David Horner, Osbert Sitwell's friend, who was the ADC to the Duchess of Kent.

> Even among these Ma'amships wild
> Ma'am Cholmondeley is the problem child.
> While urgent minutes fill her tray
> For days and days she goes away
> Corrupting Portsmouth C-in-C
> With endless cups of China tea.[5]

Sybil preserved quite a few of the comic poems about her colleagues in the service. In another by an anonymous author she appears again as one of the three 'Medium Ma'amships' who misbehave when the Super Ma'am, the Director, is not present.

> Ma'am Cholmondeley too, who was so prim,
> Austere, remote and frightfully grim,
> Who worked her staff from dawn till eve,
> And never took a moment's leave.
> Since SUPER MA'AM has gone away
> Now idles through the livelong day.
> Those duty tours of Scapa Flow
> Are made because she has a beau
> Stationed at that outlandish place –
> (She swoons each time she sees his face.)
> And once a week she has to go
> To Greenwich where another beau
> Presides at parties very gay,
> (At least, that's what the gossips say.)

'MS' wrote a poem entitled: 'Lines Written on the Occasion of Chief Officer the Marchioness of Cholmondeley Telephoning for the Name and Address of the Superintendent's Hairdresser in London'. There is a poem that Sybil wrote with 'MS', 'The Laws of the W.R.N.S.' in 1940, marking it 'Secret' and 'The only copy'. It reveals her sense of humour. It had thirteen stanzas; here are the concluding seven:

That letter you wrote the Commander,
Beginning 'My darling half-wit . . .'
Destroy it, and type again neatly
'The honour is mine to submit . . .'

And when you meet on the Parade-Ground
(Though maybe he kissed you last night)
Stand up and salute and say: 'Yes, sir!'
And keep Sex Appeal out of sight.

Remember when purchasing stockings,
Dark knickers, and things of that ilk,
That many a girl's been in trouble
Through wearing a pair that was silk.

That officer down at the Barracks,
That charmer at 'Vernon' or Lee –
Beware how you flutter your lashes
Or carelessly show him a knee.

Though blue may his eye be, and ardent
His pleading, until your head whirls,
While boys may be boys in the Navy
We don't allow girls to be girls.

Remember the lessons they taught you
At Greenwich and break the embrace
Before it's too late and the 'Super'
Says: 'Out, on your ear, in disgrace'.

Oh, these are the Laws of the Women
Who serve with the Navy in war;
Beware how you break them, and ponder
Before you go berserk on shore!

WRNS officer training took place in Greenwich, at the Royal Naval College, where Philip had been so involved in renovating Thornhill's Great Hall in the Christopher Wren buildings. The service's headquarters were in the centre of London, appropriately near Trafalgar Square. Sybil travelled quite extensively in the course of her service, including trips to Hong Kong and Ceylon on WRNS personnel questions. Right after the war, she went with Vera Mathews to Germany. With her innate sense of assurance she was able to cut through red tape. She frequently made decisions without too much consultation with the Admiralty, using the useful phrase 'in anticipation of their Lordships' approval'. She also spent time at Portsmouth, involved with signalling in connection with D-Day. Because of her knowledge of French she was particularly useful for liaison work with Charles de Gaulle.[6] This was one reason, along with her Anglo-French background, why in 1984, the year of her ninetieth birthday, French President François Mitterrand made a special trip to Houghton to award her the Légion d'honneur. (Nevertheless, she disapproved quite deeply of the French Revolution, writing to Ted Walker, the poet, in 1989, about 'the enormous fuss the French government has made to celebrate one of the most horrible events ever perpetrated. I have the feeling that you approve of it!')[7]

While in the WRNS, she served as a liaison with Queen Mary, writing on 2 July 1941 to thank her 'on behalf of all the W.R.N.S. (and especially on my *own*) for the gracious & most enjoyable visit on Saturday . . . . I was delighted to have that little talk & the drive as well! . . . Philip used to note & admire everything your Majesty wore! I miss him more & more as the days go on, he would have been such a help & a cheering influence in these anxious times.'[8] Appropriately, she was the conduit for other ties between royalty and the service. When Princess Marina, the Duchess of Kent, wrote a letter of commendation in December 1940 to the Wren dispatch riders for their 'cheerful and willing service under often very trying conditions' it was sent via Sybil.[9] After the war, she kept up with Wren activities, taking part in the festivities in connection with its Golden Jubilee in 1967 at the Painted Hall at Greenwich and at the Royal Festival Hall. She chaired the WRNS Benevolent Trust for several years. She generally went to the annual Wrens reunion and she had those who had served with her to visit at Houghton.

Sybil had led an extremely full life before the war, one full of various obligations, her family, cultural and sporting events: the busy life of a prominent English figure. But never before, other than during the First World War, had she been obliged to keep a schedule set by others. Now she was working hard in the centre of London from nine in the morning to 7.30 and frequently nine o'clock in the evening, as well as bringing papers home. She found her position both increasingly interesting and more and more exhausting. It was also unusual for her in that she was being paid. She took only one week off during the first thirteen months of her service. Her two sons were in the armed services, Hugh in the Army and John in the Fleet Air Arm. Her husband, Rock, was in Civil Defence. During the war Rock ran an Air Raid Precautions post, in the basement of their London house. On 14 January 1941, he published a letter in the *Daily Express* pointing out that there would be far less damage from air raids in the centre of London if more buildings had fire watchers on their roofs.

Sybil's wartime letters to her friend Arturo Toscanini provide glimpses into her life in the WRNS as well as general conditions in England. She had visited him in New York shortly before the war's outbreak and their friendship continued on cordial terms. In a letter to Toscanini on 3 December 1939, she remarked: 'I am glad that dear Philip did not have to endure this – two wars in one brief life is too much to bear & the complete absence of all culture & spirituality gives one a mental "black-out" which is demoralizing.' She does mention, however, that a mutual friend of hers and Toscanini's had presented opera and ballet at Sadler's Wells and that the general mood is surprisingly good. 'You would admire the spirit of *service* which exists everywhere here. People seem to have become suddenly more human & all round there is a fine sense of steely determination to end this horror & injustice.'[10] The following November, she makes clear what she has given up for the war: 'Sometimes one realizes that all one's private life has gone, that there is no time for reading or music or quiet thought, no privacy of feeling or person.' She also mentioned that she had shared with Churchill a quotation from Garibaldi that Toscanini had sent her. Presumably it was his remark in 1854: 'If ever England should be so circumstanced as to require the help of an ally, cursed be the Italian who would not step forward in her defence.' In 1943 she wrote to him with great pride of Hugh's having spent four days behind the German lines; for this exploit, he won the Military Cross. Sybil sent Toscanini a copy of the citation. The same year she wrote about hearing his concerts on the BBC, listening to them on the radio that David Sarnoff had given her when she had been in New York. (As the head of the Radio Corporation of America, Sarnoff had been the central figure in the formation of the National Broadcasting Company orchestra conducted by Toscanini. Sarnoff saw Sybil in London during the war and Sybil gave a lunch for him to meet Churchill.)

Sybil had been working so hard in the Wrens that she came down with septic bronchial pneumonia in July 1942, and was out of commission until the autumn. She was much happier when she was working as she then had less time to worry about her sons. She hadn't seen Hugh for a very long time. John, whose planes had crashed several times into the sea, had once spent some hours in shark-infested waters. One of her nephews, on Rock's side of the family, had been killed.

During the war, Sybil was on cordial terms with her cousin Siegfried Sassoon. She certainly was aware of his prickliness and his mixed feelings about the Sassoon side of his family. She regarded him as a distant cousin but admired his poetry more than her brother had.[11] In the summer of 1943, she invited Siegfried to dine at her house in Kensington Palace Gardens, in order to meet Lord Wavell, who thought highly of him as a poet and had included some of his poems in his anthology *Other Men's Flowers*. (Wavell had become a very good friend of Sybil's and had written poems to her.) Siegfried enjoyed the evening far more than he had expected, given his prejudice against mixing with the grand. He was surrounded by admirers at the dinner – not only Wavell, but also Desmond MacCarthy, who told him how much he liked his memoirs, and Ivor Brown of the *Observer*, who invited him to review Wavell's anthology. He was also very taken with the strong silent Rock. Siegfried's experience provides a glimpse of the sort of dinner parties Sybil gave. Siegfried viewed the invitation as the equivalent of a royal summons; Sybil felt, with reason, that she could entertain pretty much anyone she might wish to meet. In that, she was similar to her brother.

Sybil wrote to Siegfried shortly after the dinner, on 6 July:

For my part, I am *delighted* to see you at last in my home & I feel sure that we shall have many good meetings in the future . . . . I will certainly come down one evening to meet Hester [his wife] and George [his son] . . . but I don't know if you'll like me as a Lady High Admiral – sounds like a butterfly – or whether you like me at all (after thought) . . . . I am off tomorrow by plane to the Orkneys .... I enclose Hugh's Citation with a slightly shamefaced feeling that a purely British mother would scorn such action as being 'not done' but what matter – I am very proud of him & rightly so – Love from your Coz Sybil.

Two months later, in another letter to Siegfried, she confides that she is 'submerged with work at the moment, trying to conjure astronomical numbers of Wrens out of nothing, for all these new theatres of war, but I hope to see you in the Autumn. I trust your visit in the summer has now broken the ice.'[12] Apparently, however, the cousins did not get together as she had hoped. Sassoon records meeting her once more twenty years later at a cocktail party he wasn't enjoying in London where she was 'effusively affectionate' and consulted him about a granddaughter who wanted to become a Catholic, as Sassoon himself had done. 'A lively girl, apparently, who was sent away from Wardour Castle School for knocking down the Matron.'[13]

After the war, Sybil returned to private life, but she was far from idle, even though she was liberated from a strict schedule. Such a style of living was not restricted to women in the upper classes. The men too, who might be very busy, did not keep regular schedules. When Sybil and Rock visited Florida in 1929, she noticed the difference. Unlike the rich in England, the men in the United States were not at home during the day.

Her brother continued to be a considerable presence in her life. Sybil integrated the great possessions he left to her – the Sargents of their mother and of Sybil, the great pieces of French furniture and many decorative objects and fine eighteenth-century paintings – into the house at Houghton. Many other *objets d'art* and paintings went to her house in London. Meanwhile, historians were in touch with her about her brother's political role. In 1955 she had been rather dubious but allowed Randolph Churchill to browse in Philip's comparatively few papers for the first volumes of his father's life. In the 1970s she assisted historians such as Martin Gilbert and Cameron Hazelhurst in incorporating Philip's political activities into their studies. She was quite rightly upset about the snide portrait of Philip that emerged in Stanley Jackson's general book about the Sassoons published in 1968. (In return for her co-operation she had asked to read the proofs, but he had not sent them to her.) In answer to an inquiry she wrote: 'Stanley Jackson's book has given me the utmost annoyance .... The whole book is written in a most patronizing tone and journalistic style without any sensitivity .... I strongly advise you not to read it.'[14] After that bad experience, she was critical of the idea of studies about her brother, although there had been a possibility that her friend the biographer Kenneth Rose would do one.

She was far less reluctant about historical projects that involved Sir Robert Walpole, who had built Houghton. She co-operated fully with J.H. Plumb, allowing him access to papers for his great work on Walpole, and was instrumental in having Walpole's papers deposited in and eventually sold to the Cambridge University Library.[15] She had a lengthy correspondence, preserved in the Walpole library in Farmington, Connecticut, with Wilmarth Lewis, the leading Horace Walpole collector and scholar, in which she revealed both her extensive knowledge and interest in the earlier history of Houghton and the Walpole family.

In 1964 she established the Philip Sassoon Flying Award in her brother's memory. It had the purpose of enabling engineer airmen who otherwise would not have the opportunity to do so to learn how to fly. Up to four such awards (generally two or three) are given annually; in 1999, as the 100th grant was made, for the first time a woman was among the recipients. (The prize that Philip himself had established, for the second-best cadet in the graduating class at the Air Academy at Cranwell, still continues to be presented.) Sybil monitored her prize carefully, being informed about the recipients and the income from the money she had given.

Sybil felt that the Air Force was much more efficient in producing and spending the income from her donation than was the case with another prize that she gave in her own name, the Cholmondeley Prize for Poetry. On 27 September 1982, she wrote to the poet Ted Walker,

> I spent a very interesting day with the R.A.F., meeting some twenty of my 'Awardees', a very nice and intelligent group of advanced engineer apprentices. I took the opportunity of enquiring into the finances of the Award and was very satisfied to hear that this year the sum amounted to £6,000. As you know, the Poetry Award capital is identical, and I am surprised to find that the difference is so great. However, leave it to me to tackle the Royal Society of Authors!

She was a patron in other ways as well, becoming involved with the arts festival that was established in 1951 in King's Lynn, the nearest large town to Houghton. This happened through one of her greatest friends and neighbours, Ruth, Lady Fermoy. Performers at the festival, such as Yehudi Menuhin and Raymond Leppard, stayed at Houghton and became good friends. Winners of her poetry prize, 'my poets', gave readings at the festival. But she would pick and choose what she became involved in. In 1956 Queen Elizabeth, the Queen Mother, pressed her to become chairman of the Royal School of Needlework. As the Queen Mother's representative wrote: 'Nobody of Her Majesty's acquaintance has knowledge and gifts which wd. so perfectly qualify you for this position and you may readily guess of what consequence it is to her to feel that the post is occupied by somebody who is a close personal friend. I do not think I need stress therefore the deep pleasure which Her Majesty would derive from your acceptance and I really do not know to whom else she could turn were your acceptance to prove impossible.' Sybil tersely noted on the bottom of the letter 'I refused.'[16] She was both self-effacing and firm in her opinions.

A highly cultivated woman, Sybil had been an intense reader, particularly of poetry, all her life. She began thinking about a poetry prize in 1964; it was established in the following year 'for the benefit and encouragement of poets' and was first presented in 1966. John Masefield, the Poet Laureate and the President of the Society of Authors, wrote to her enthusiastically that 'such a gift opens the doors to glorious experiment and breathless discovery, by which the world may be changed and man remade'.[17] She much enjoyed hearing about the committee's work and took a great interest in the awards. But it was up to the committee to select the poets, who were neither nominated nor allowed to submit their work. The committee was to designate those it thought appropriate in terms of quality, and there was also, from time to time, some consideration of need. As with the Philip Sassoon Flying Award, the annual number of prizes given varies. In recent years it has been most often four recipients, generally with £2,500 given to each winner. The first year, 1966, £500 was given to Ted Walker and £300 to Stevie Smith, and the next year Seamus Heaney was one of the three winners, in 1969 Derek Walcott, in 1973 Philip Larkin, whom Sybil thought particularly highly of. William Plomer, the chairman of the committee, wrote to Sybil about Heaney,

> a very good young poet in Northern Ireland . . . . He is believed to be still in his twenties and unlikely to be at all well off . . . . There was a strong feeling that publicity is very useful to young poets, and that announcing the Awards to the Press would be much more effective if a small party could be given at Drayton Gardens [the office of the Society of Authors that administered the prize] . . . . It was thought if you could present the Awards that would greatly please everybody, but I said I thought it unlikely that you would be able or willing to do that.[18]

Sybil's close friendship with Plomer, a novelist and well-known writer of satirical poems, had been a factor in the establishment of the prize in the first place. They had met during the war, when Plomer was in Naval Intelligence and had grown close afterwards, through their mutual friend, Ian Fleming. (Sybil had an unusually wide circle of friends in the literary world, such as the critic Raymond Mortimer and the poet Osbert Sitwell, who was involved as well in planning the poetry award.) Before the war Plomer had replaced Edward Garnett as the reader for the publishing firm of Jonathan Cape. After the war he would have the occasional Cape book sent to Sybil, since he regarded her as a serious reader who could, through her talk in the cultural and social circles in which she moved, help Cape books along.[19] She was characteristically modest about the enterprise of the poetry prize: 'I've never done anything of any importance, involved in anything . . . . I greatly enjoyed my conversation with people like William Plomer, and other writers I've been in touch with. I've given an award to poetry that brought me in touch with many good young poets, but I don't think I would have been capable of ever writing anything.'[20]

Plomer visited her almost annually for a week at Houghton during the summer; he much enjoyed himself, taking particular pleasure in meeting Princess Margaret and the Queen Mother. He wrote to Sybil on 31 July 1952: 'Whatever way the world may be going, there can never be any substitute for the grace of inherited authority, and for the sense of public responsibility. It is such an aesthetic pleasure to see all that, effortlessly functioning.' In 1959 he dedicated a poem about Queen Mary to Sybil. And he must have been pleased to hear from her that Princess Margaret and the Queen Mother had read out his poems to friends and that Sybil had read them to Churchill. She conveys in her letters to him some sense of the quality of her life and her interests, as when she wrote on 20 November 1952, about hearing Edith Sitwell and Dylan Thomas do a public reading of poetry. The hall was 'sparsely filled with – mostly – raincoated, corduroy types & I only knew Osbert and the K. Clarks'. In the same letter she reports that she is visiting Katharine Furse daily in the hospital (she would die that year) and that Charlie Chaplin has been to visit her at Kensington Palace Gardens. 'Chaplin has been here several times. His imitation, lasting ¼ of an hour, of Mrs. Truman launching a seaplane with a bottle which *would* not break was *epic*.' She reported to him how upset she was about Katharine Furse's death. 'Katharine has been my friend for nearly 49 years & I felt so *safe* with her.'[21] She treasured the embroidered work Katharine had given her, as well as the watercolours of flowers by her son Paul Furse, one of Sybil's great admirers.

In 1966 Plomer dedicated his seventh collection of poetry, *Taste and Remember*, to her, and sent her manuscript copies of some of his poems. Plomer was also a good friend of Benjamin Britten's and wrote several of his libretti. She wrote to Plomer that one evening when visiting Aldeburgh, Suffolk, where Britten lived, 'I sat next to Ben at supper & he said such prescient delightful things about you & your wisdom & help & understanding & how he values your friendship that I nearly kissed him!'[22] Their correspondence continued until the very end of his life; Plomer last wrote to her on 19 September 1973 just a few hours before he died. He had visited Houghton the previous month, his fellow guests being the Kenneth Clarks and John Sparrow, the Warden of All Souls, Oxford. 'I have often thought of the view of you, which I cherish, when you looked up from the floor of the Stone Hall & waved to Sparrow and me above, on the way to our beds.'[23] She wrote to Ted Walker about Plomer's memorial service: 'William was the last of my real friends & I shall miss him while I live. What an agony this business of growing old is and losing those one loves. There is no one who can replace him.'[24]

Walker did replace Plomer as the chairman of the prize committee and as the liaison figure with Sybil. In 1976 the amount of the prize was increased, after Sybil complained to the treasurer of the Society of Authors. In her view, the Society kept back too much of the income from the prizes themselves; the only expenses should be for some clerical work and a lunch for the judges. She recommended against caution and holding back money. In the last year of her life she wrote a sharp letter to the Society to instruct its accountant to forget about increasing the capital amount in the prize fund.

In 1978 Walker had written to her that the prize 'is both prestigious and beneficial; it has evolved as a means of honouring the distinguished and encouraging the promising'.[25] She didn't interfere with the judging but she didn't hesitate to let Ted Walker or the administrator at the Society know her opinions. Although she was very pleased with the 1980 winners (George Barker, Terence Tiller and Roy Fuller), the following year was a different story. In a letter, she remarked that Robert Garoich wrote in 'no known tongue (what is Lallans?) [Roy] Fisher is probably a Marxist & Boyle who might well have waited another year! I feel sure that I shd. not like any of their work! But I am a conventional old fuddy duddy .... I can't come to the party on June 3rd as I have a large visitation of Canadian architects here (80).' Nor was she impressed by the 1988 list, writing to Diana Shine at the Society: 'You ask if I approve of this year's list but, for your ear alone, I am not mad about them! I intend to read them more carefully now that I have come home.'[26]

Poetry was on her mind towards the very end of her life. In 1911 Lady Diana Manners had given Eddie Marsh a cheap notebook and from then on he had various mostly very well known poets – ninety-eight in total – write poems in it. On the first page there is a poem by Thomas Hardy, on the last one by C. Day Lewis. After Eddie Marsh's death in 1953, Eton College Library acquired the notebook. Some years after his mother's death, John Julius Norwich had the notion that the notebook should be reproduced. Where was the money to be found? He told the story to Sybil and she 'spontaneously suggested that as a token of her life-long friendship with Eddie and my mother she might be allowed to defray all the expenses'.[27] She contributed £20,000. It was probably also a factor that her husband, brother, sons and grandson had all gone to Eton. Unfortunately the book did not appear until very shortly after she died, but it was a suitable memorial to her love of poetry and that combination of aesthetic and social interests that had made up so much of her and her brother's lives. She also established family trusts to give charitable contributions, with particular attention to churches in Norfolk and Suffolk. It also gave money to help repair the Sassoon Library in Bombay. Part of their funding came after her death as directed in her will from the sale of a Rothschild tiara and necklace that had become a bone of contention at the time of her marriage. An uncle had reclaimed them, an indication of the Rothschild displeasure at her marriage. Its return indicated a family reconciliation.

Her husband, Rock, too led a more public life after the war, in part by choice, in part by inheritance. Sybil had married into very grand aristocratic circles and into the heart of the royal court. That Rock's interests took an increasingly artistic form owed much to Sybil. In 1950 he too established a prize of aesthetic interest, the Cholmondeley Prize for Calligraphy, to be competed for between Eton and Harrow; later Winchester was added. Rock had taken up calligraphy in 1946 with the same enthusiasm with which he had become involved in the Margaret Morris movement. (He continued his keen interest in exercise and worked out daily in the gyms in his houses.) He became a student of Irene Wellington, one of the leading calligraphers of the period. She had been an assistant and pupil of the founder of modern calligraphy, Edward Johnston, a craftsman in the tradition of William Morris. Sybil had become a good friend of Sir Sydney Cockerell, the Director of the Fitzwilliam Museum in Cambridge, formerly William Morris's secretary. He had introduced Rock to Wellington, having earlier piqued Rock's interest in calligraphy by taking him in 1945 to the Johnston memorial exhibition at the Victoria & Albert. Wellington and the Cholmondeleys became such good friends that Sybil offered her a mews flat at Kensington Palace Gardens. Wellington did several magnificent calligraphic compositions for the Cholmondeleys, one in 1948 of Meister Eckhart's slogan, 'Just Like One Who Wants to Learn to Write'; a calligraphic fantasia: 'Upon Being Given a Norfolk Turkey for Christmas' in 1950, and a splendid 'Hopeful Beginning' sent as a Christmas greeting to the Cholmondeleys in 1951 as a 'souvenir of the happy years working together.'[28] Under her guidance Rock totally transformed his hand from a dull if legible script into a beautiful italic, known as the Cholmondeley Italic. He served as President of the Society for Italic Handwriting. He also became in his own right an important collector of Sèvres, beloved of the Rothschilds.

Politically Rock was, not surprisingly, quite conservative. Sitting in Walpole's chair at Houghton, he wrote in 1945 to Churchill praising him for his greatness and bemoaning his defeat in the general election:

> For 6 years our class have been attacked and no one has lifted a voice .... Who are the Col. Blimps? The subalterns who rode with you at Omdurman, that you saw on the Malakand Pass, on the kopjees of S. Africa – their sons were the first in the last war and their grand-sons in this. The old school tie – old families and their houses. Have they done so badly. No one would dare put in print what percentage of deaths and honours the House of Lords have suffered and gained.

Churchill replied in a rather conciliatory way: 'I feel so much sympathy with what you say. But there is no gulf in England (as in France) between the Old world and the New.'[29] The Labour government of 1945–50 was not congenial to the Cholmondeleys. In January 1950 Sybil wrote from Houghton to her friends the American actors Lynn Fontanne and Alfred Lunt, to whom she was grateful for sending food during the austere post-war years, 'We still hope that you will soon be paying us a visit here before the Govt bereaves Rock of his lovely home .... We are busy with our Election & it will probably be what Wellington called Waterloo – "a d—d close-run thing." '[30] Contrary to her hopes, Labour did retain power by a slim majority, but then a year later the Tories won, with Churchill returning as Prime Minister.

Being hereditary Lord Great Chamberlain forced Rock to play a much more public role than he might have preferred. But once in the position, he fulfilled his obligations magnifi-cently. As one of the great officers of state, he was unpaid, and did not regard himself as a courtier. This enabled him, as he didn't like social occasions, to decline many invitations although not those from the Queen that were royal commands. The position had been an inherited one since 1133 when Henry I granted it to Aubrey de Vere. It came into the Cholmondeley family through the marriage of Georgiana, a sister of the eighteenth-century Lord Great Chamberlain, the Duke of Ancaster, to the first Marquess of Cholmondeley. In 1915 Sybil had written to Philip about the post and the losses that the Cholmondeleys had sustained because of the situation. Her mother-in-law told her

> how King Edward [VII] loathed Ld. C & stopped all the Lord Chamberlain's perquisites. The Lord Chamb. always used to have the *whole* of the gold plate used at the Coronation Banquet, all the carpets, & the furniture of the dressing room where the King slept on the night before the Coronation. So Ld C. wrote & asked if he was to have the furniture & King Ed. flew into a rage & stopped all the perks .... It appears that the Ancasters have far more gold plate that we have. I supposed they had richer Kings! ... If the King had sup-ported Ld C. he need never have had that case which cost him £10,000 about the L. Chamberlainship. Asquith won it for him.[31]

Edward VIII made up for it to an extent as he gave Lord Cholmondeley the two neo-Gothic thrones designed by Pugin for Prince Albert and the Prince of Wales (they are now returned from Houghton to Westminster when necessary for Prince Philip and Prince Charles to sit on at the State Openings of Parliament).

Rock's first term as Lord Great Chamberlain, for Edward VIII, was a brief one; despite his personal disapproval of the monarch, he discharged his task conscientiously. The Earl of Ancaster served as Lord Great Chamberlain for George VI from 1937 to 1950 and then resigned for reasons of health in favour of his son, Lord Willoughby de Eresby, for the remaining years of the reign. Rock then returned to the post in 1952 on the accession of Elizabeth II, very proud that he could easily fit into the same uniform he had worn for Edward VIII. The Lord Great Chamberlain is a 'working peer'. As a great officer of the crown, he was the administrator of the royal Palace of Westminster, a position shared with the Ministry of Works as the representative of Parliament. The Ministry's power in theory is suspended when the House is not in session. The Ministry and the Lord Great Chamberlain tended to disagree from time to time, because each tried to assume as much authority as possible while simultaneously imposing as much of the expense as possible on the other. Rock was responsible for the general security of the Palace of Westminster, repairs and renovations, the reception of distinguished visitors, conferences held in the Palace, for the coronation along with the Earl Marshal, visits to Parliament, works of art, and many other aspects of the running of the Houses of Parliament as a royal palace. Rock's Elizabethan obligations began with the lying in state of George VI. He received a letter of thanks from George's widow, Elizabeth:

I found those few minutes that I spent in Westminster Hall more moving than I can say, and also in a strange way, rather comforting. You were so kind, & I felt that you knew how anguished were my thoughts and feelings. And yet, watching those quiet & loving people walking so gently past the King, one realizes how truly they mourned, and that in their English way they had realized the valour and goodness and faith which had carried the King through those fifteen difficult and sometimes agonized years. I was filled with admiration by the beauty of your script, & the exquisite phrasing of the letter you wrote to me.[22]

That was in February 1952 but the appointment was not confirmed until May. It was an extensive and demanding job full of endless small decisions. The Lord Great Chamberlain plays his most conspicuous role at the State Opening of Parliament. He and the Earl Marshal, the Duke of Norfolk, precede the monarch as she processes to the House of Lords in order to deliver her address. He walks backwards, as does the Earl Marshal, holding his white wand of office. He and the Earl Marshal were also responsible for the coronation of Elizabeth II. In particular he arranged lunch for 1,200 distinguished guests, as well as extra lavatories for them.

Rock played an active role in the post and took very seriously his obligations in relation to the state of the Palace and its decorations. He was a very successful Lord Great Chamberlain, dealing with the myriad issues that came under his authority, christenings and marriages in the crypt, introductions of peers to the House of Lords, endless questions about redecoration and the physical state of the rooms in the Palace. He had to fight off moves by obstreperous members of the House of Commons such as Tam Dalyell to take over some of the Lords' rooms for the Commons, and by the Dowager Marchioness of Reading on behalf of peeresses.

69. Sybil and Rock at 12 Kensington Palace Gardens.

Although Rock was very different in so many ways from his brother-in-law, like Philip and Sybil, he concerned himself with aesthetic questions. He took a much closer interest than had previous Lord Great Chamberlains in the art and decoration of the House of Lords. In 1954 he issued an appeal to his fellow peers for portraits of eminent members of the House, tapestries, carpets and pieces of furniture to be given or bequeathed or to be lent for a period of no less than twenty-five years. He felt that the decoration of that part of the Houses of Parliament had been neglected since the death of the Prince Consort in 1861. He set an example himself by donating a portrait.

As a member of the House of Lords, Rock himself rarely spoke; in fact, although he had taken his seat in 1923, he did not make his maiden speech until thirty-two years later (it concerned the extermination of rabbits and lasted four minutes). But in reply to speeches of tribute in the House he did say, on 4 May 1965, shortly before his retirement: 'When I took over this job I found there was scope to do things. The last person who did things in the House in the way of decoration was the Prince Consort. He was unable to finish the job, and I found many bare walls, empty spaces, and so on. I made an appeal to your Lordships and others, and in a short time tapestries and pictures came along and the Palace now looks more "lived in."' His colleagues in the Lords had demonstrated their appreciation of his work through subscribing to a portrait of him in 1963, on the occasion of his eightieth birthday; it was hung in a peers' dining room named in his honour. In 1965 the powers of the Lord

Great Chamberlain were reduced; they now mostly turn on his role in the State Opening of Parliament. Upon Rock's retirement in 1966 for reasons of health, his elder son, Hugh, succeeded him. When Hugh died in 1990, he was succeeded by the present Marquess, who will hold the position for the rest of Elizabeth's reign.

The years between Rock's retirement and his death in 1968, at the age of 85, were times of worsening health, but also of deepening love; Sybil and Rock spent most of their time together at Houghton. In a touching letter to William Plomer in 1963, the year of the couple's golden anniversary, Rock wrote, 'Well William you are one who knows how great my luck has been in having had Sybil as a constant companion always by my side for 50 years helping over everything & educating me.'[23] Sybil received 1,400 letters of condolence upon his death. Answering one, from a daughter of Lady Desborough, she wrote: 'I think Emily Bronte's line "learning to live without joy" best describes irreplaceable loss but it is a small price to pay for 55 years of perfect happiness. He met death as a friend – quite conscious till the very end & holding my hand firmly.'[34] Whatever restlessness she may have felt in the marriage in the period between the wars appeared to have evaporated. She wrote to William Plomer on 24 September 'I held his hand very tightly for many hours & at 6:15 he just said "Syb" and was gone.' The following April Noel Coward had lunch with her in London. He had seen them from time to time, and would come to their London house to play his music, particularly for Rock who did not like going to the theatre. He recorded in his diary that she 'suddenly broke down over Rock .... She soon recovered herself and I felt somehow glad that I had been there and touched that she should have trusted me enough to give way in front of me.'[35]

Rock and Sybil's was a successful partnership. Their houses, the children, their intense interest in sport, and in Bugattis, kept them together and increasingly fond of one another for fifty-five years. She had intense admirers, such as Marshall Balbo as well as prominent men in the arts, whom Rock found uninteresting. No doubt, as in any relationship, there were difficult periods and they were comfortable in spending time apart. Despite her wide interests, in her marriage to him she had made a commitment to join his high aristocratic world and have little to do with the world of the Sassoons and the Rothschilds. Other than Hannah Gubbay, who was very much part of her and Philip's lives, Sybil saw comparatively little of her relations. Even her relationship with Philip lost some of its intensity after the First World War, when her family required more of her time. (Rock appeared to disapprove of Sybil and her children spending too much time with Philip, with his propensity to spoil them.)

Nonetheless the milieu in which Sybil was raised did much to shape her aesthetic interests. She brought its sense of worldliness and style – particularly that of the Rothschilds – into the life she led as Lady Cholmondeley. And of course she brought with her Sassoon and Rothschild money, which allowed the Cholmondeleys to preserve their very English inheritance. Aesthetic interests are far from unknown among the English aristocracy but, on the whole, they lack the intensity and knowledge that Philip and Sybil displayed.

The Cholmondeleys are one of the great families of England. They own two considerable estates, Cholmondeley Castle in Cheshire with its 7,500 acres and Houghton Hall with 8,000 acres. Rock, besides his marquessate, held two earldoms, two viscountcies and three baronies. He was one of the most handsome young men in England and Sybil had not only beauty but a great fortune. The latter would be of much use to a land-rich but cash-poor family. They spent April and September generally in the house, Le Roc, that he built on the Riviera, and Rock would go to the south of France frequently during the winter on his own. In France (as in England) they much enjoyed themselves driving and at times racing Bugattis. They had taken part several times in the Monte Carlo rallies and Rock enjoyed test driving them on the straight drive at Houghton. They took trips together, most notably to the United States in 1929 with the children. As they became older they spent more and more time together at Houghton. They are buried side by side in their own section of the cemetery at the parish church in the grounds at Houghton.

Sybil lived on for fifty years after her brother's death and more than twenty years after her husband's. She felt, wrongly, that she did not have a wide circle of friends. On the contrary, she did mix with intriguing people in London, in the country, and on trips. She had friends among the more interesting royals and aristocrats, among the artistic and political both at home and abroad, such as Jan Masaryk, the Czech statesman. She continued her patronage of musicians. She remained close to old friends, seeing a fair amount of the Winston Churchills and entertaining Churchill in his declining years by playing bezique with him, one of a trio of ladies who did so – Lady Violet Bonham Carter, Asquith's daughter; Clementine's cousin, Silvia Henley; and Sybil – so that Lady Churchill might have a night off. She became involved in charitable activities, particularly the homes run for the disabled and those down on their luck by Leonard Cheshire and Sue Ryder. When Cheshire established the first of these, she promptly sent a vanload of furniture. Cheshire's nickname for her was 'Chum Mum'.[36]

After the war Sybil became a very good friend of the famous travel writer Freya Stark, and took several trips with her, to Greece and Iran, learning Persian for that journey. In the preface to Stark's *Dust in the Lion's Paw: Autobiography 1939–1946* (1961), she thanks Sybil for reading the work in manuscript. Once in the course of a visit by Stark to Houghton, Sybil had heavy entertaining duties: Queen Mary needed to be amused for three hours and later the same day thirty Wrens came to tea. Stark wrote in a letter about the Queen: 'Everyone offered her little bits of the conversation that might please her . . . . Sybil was so kind and had me tell her about the submarines in Aden, and the siege of Baghdad.'[37]

In 1969 Sybil gave Stark a considerable sum of money. The writer told her publisher, John Murray, that Sybil 'said vaguely that she didn't intend to wait till she died but I had no idea this was really to come about. It is lovely, warm and touching to think of . . . . It will cover Nepal, and a little shopping, Delhi on the way, and should make 1970 a nice easy year and that will be rather a blessing.'[38] Sybil much enjoyed Stark's company, telling Ted Walker after a 1974 visit that she is 'a most enchanting woman with a depth & originality of mind and experience which are a joy to listen to – a high artificial style of speech directed by a strong intelligence & commonsense.'[39]

Sybil did a fair amount of other travelling – of course frequently to Paris and a trip to Rome, but also to Munich and Vienna, where she hadn't been since 1934. (On that visit she had had dinner with the Prime Minister, Engelbert Dollfuss, the night before he was assassinated. She was worried about his lack of security, as she warned him.) She and Rock took a trip to Russia in the summer of 1959 to see the paintings at the Hermitage that the Walpoles had sold. She learned some Russian before going there. The pictures 'were quite superb & we enjoyed the trip very much & became fast friends with the Hermitage people'.[40] In 1960 she went with Freya Stark to Greece for the first time. In 1973 she took a three-week trip to Kenya and Uganda with the Australian painter Sidney Nolan and his wife.

One of Sybil's greatest achievements was her care of Houghton. She was undoubtedly the most involved owner since the builder, Sir Robert Walpole. She thought of it as *his* house – and thus as a monument that she needed to preserve. She wished to restore the rooms as they were in Sir Robert's time, although she also needed to find places for what she inherited from Philip and at a later point for what was moved there from the house in London. On 9 August 1982, she wrote about Walpole to Ted Walker: 'He must have been a real countryman as well as all the rest of art & politics & taste. I feel somehow he would have liked me!' (Interestingly, her centrality to English life is suggested in a remark she made about Walpole in the interview she gave for the fine short film her grandson made of her in 1986: 'All the prime ministers that I have known have said he was the greatest one we had.'[41] One wonders if Lloyd George or Churchill actually shared that sentiment.)

Houghton had not been neglected before the war but like all stately homes, it required constant upkeep. Essential repairs could take years; for instance, major work started on the roof before the war was not completed until after. As we have seen, when Rock's father died in a hunting accident in 1923, rather contrary to custom Sybil and Rock remained at Houghton rather than moving to Cholmondeley Castle. That remained his mother's home. And then, when Hugh married in 1947, he and his wife took up residence at Cholmondeley Castle.

Sybil was the chatelaine of the estate for more than seventy years. She did not consider herself a collector; rather she had a collection that she needed to conserve. Philip was a great acquirer, but she played the more aristocratic role of preserver (and, when necessary, the culler). In 1975 she bought Sir Godfrey Kneller's portrait of Joseph Carreras, the only painting sold to Catherine the Great in 1779 that has returned to Houghton. She made her mark on every room through meticulous restoration. For instance, she had the upholstery of one of the original beds redone under the guidance of the eminent decorator John Fowler, using material that she had inherited from her brother. She would have material reproduced based on what she found in the house.[42]

The principal rooms are extremely grand. Most still have the original furnishings, frequently by William Kent, of Walpole's era. The house achieves the ideal of being an integrated work of art. Unlike Philip at Trent, she had, despite the loss of the paintings in the eighteenth century, a great collection to build upon.

70. Sybil at Houghton, 1980s.

Philip's acquisitions enriched what she had. The Sargents added the history of her family. Although quite a few of the great French pieces were sold in 1994 to provide funds to help restore and maintain the house, many objects, particularly English ones, remain. Like Philip's paintings, they are in keeping with the spirit of the house. Although Houghton was not opened to the public until the mid-1970s, Sybil welcomed visitors and took them around the house herself. In 1959 there was an exhibition at Agnew in London, with the proceeds to charity, of the pictures from Houghton, making its collection better known. The house has been written about in magazines such as *Country Life*. Quite often it provided a chapter in the increasing number of books about country houses. It is one of the greatest eighteenth-century houses in England.

Another major project under Sybil's guidance was the restoration of the neo-Palladian Water House, a pump house. The Earl of Pembroke had designed it some time before 1733. Estate craftsmen worked on it very successfully in the early 1980s under the 'good auspices of the Dowager Lady Cholmondeley'.[43] But her greatest mark upon the house was the rebuilding of the great outside staircase on the West Front. The 3rd Earl of Orford had had the staircases on both fronts taken down because of decay (there is also a story that he had lost them by having gambled them away). It was a long-term project and the Cholmondeleys began to think about doing it as early as 1964, when Sybil approached the architect Marshall Sisson about the job. She wrote to Wilmarth Lewis on 1 June 1972: 'I am in a great state because I am planning to replace the steps on the garden front! I have to sell all my Renaissance jewels to pay for this vast project as my "swan song" for Houghton. I am sure it is right & Rock was determined to do it but oh! what a lot of trouble.'[44] The staircase was finished that year. John Sparrow composed the Latin lines carved below the steps' balustrade commemorating the rebuilding of the steps in Rock's memory: *Scalae Quas Perfecit Robertus Walpole Dimouit Nepos Iterum ad MDCCCCLXXII Exstructae Pristinam Aedibus Houghtonianis Formam Reddiderunt Georgium Marchionen Quintum de Cholmondeley Commemorant* (The steps, which Robert Walpole completed and his nephew removed have, rebuilt in 1972, restored to pristine form again the Houghton edifice; they commemorate George, the Fifth Marquess of Cholmondeley.)[45] It was a great accomplishment. Plomer wrote to her on 4 September about them: 'They are not only a memorial to him but a last commemoration of your vision & taste & resolve, as well as of your love.'[46] She was becoming ever fonder of the house. As she wrote to Ted Walker on 18 January 1974, 'It is lovely here & I have a big job to look after the estate and the people who have nearly all been here 30 & 40 years & that keeps me very active.' That May she wrote: 'Houghton is too lovely for words, by far the best season & I *hate* to go to vile London on Monday.'

The house was opened to the public on 2 May 1976, and remains a popular destination to this day. As she wrote to Ted Walker, it had 40,000 visitors that first year. Sybil felt that she had to a considerable extent sacrificed her privacy but it was in keeping with the times. She was not extravagant and she sold selectively some of the family's possessions; she was certainly willing to spend what was necessary to have the house at its finest. To open the house was not a decision she had taken lightly and perhaps she came to it reluctantly: 'I am having a great struggle to keep this great house going,' she told Walker. 'After *60* years it would break my heart to shut down yet survival seems nearly impossible. Luckily I have a lot of things to sell & that is helping me.'[47]

In a talk she gave in 1977 at the opening of the house for its second season, she remarked: 'It shows how times have changed, because when people inquire "what the bag was", they are referring not to game but to the number of visitors one has had!' She was quite straightforward about her reasons for opening the house. People had become more appreciative of a house of beauty and the paintings and objects it contained, there were tax advantages, and the income was needed to maintain the house. 'One must not take the attitude that the whole thing is a frightful bore. One must make the whole venture as attractive as possible so that visitors feel that their visit was well worth while, and that they were welcome . . . . There is no doubt that people still much prefer to find the House is still lived in by the family concerned.'[48]

One suspects that opening the house gave her some pleasure, and she was frequently at the entrance desk, holding out a guidebook to visitors and saying 'I understand you should have one of these.' In 1978, she reported to Ted Walker that on one day 200 came from the King's Lynn Festival and 450 from the National Art Collection Fund, followed by the Queen Mother herself at six o'clock, 'but I expect that it keeps me going'. She must have caused some concern to her family, friends and staff, since even in her eighties she was busy going up ladders to help hang tapestries, but she promised Walker that she was being careful.

Sybil also appears to have developed a slight sense of rivalry with the National Trust. After visiting some of their properties in October 1982, she wrote to Ted Walker: 'I must say they did lack the human touch. Even the staff were not very welcoming.' But they were visiting the West of England and she preferred her own area. Years before, in 1965, she and Rock had made a tour of National Trust houses in her neighbourhood and had been more favourably impressed. She wrote to William Plomer on 21 August: 'We went today for an E. Anglian tour of the houses of the Nat. Trust. Rock is so delightfully unspoilt & we both enjoyed Blickling, Ickworth, Euston & Melford . . . while thinking that Houghton was the best.'[49]

Philip and Sybil were not really outsiders at the beginning of their lives but they were members of a Jewish family that had only comparatively recently come to England. Virtually upon the family's arrival from India, the Sassoons had taken a central position in London and royal life. Their grandfather, Sir Albert, and his brothers became prominent figures in the circle around Edward VII. But it was a world that the older aristocracy regarded as vulgar and one that was marked, or so some thought, by too many Jewish members. Although two generations later Philip occupied a central place in English society and politics, many, including those who knew him well, still regarded him as an outsider. Even Sybil may not have been totally accepted by the Norfolk gentry but more perhaps because she was a grand, more urban aristocrat than they, although being Jewish may well have continued to be a factor.

It is therefore striking that the Sassoons got on so well with royalty. Perhaps royalty, as Hanoverians of German descent, grand as they are, may have a special rapport with those such as the Sassoons in that both families were originally from outside England. The royal family were also neighbours as they spent part of the year, generally August and frequently Christmas, at the nearby estate of Sandringham. Nonetheless, Sybil remarked, 'You can't call royalty a real friend', since there was always a certain constraint in the relationship.[50]

An appropriate concluding point for this story, I believe, is Sybil Cholmondeley's ninetieth birthday party held at Houghton in 1984. Eleven members of the royal family, from the Queen on down, attended the occasion. Sybil may have had slightly mixed feelings about that. She wrote to her former Wren secretary, Mrs Callaghan, on 14 January, 'I am kept very busy looking after this lovely House, and am about to have my ninetieth Birthday . . . & now the entire "Royals" have asked themselves to our family party!' Philip and Sybil had felt closest to Queen Mary who shared with them an interest in beautiful objects. Sybil was fond of the Queen Mother; she found the Queen rather formidable, less so in the country.[51] Prince Charles came for a long chat with Sybil two or three times a year. But she felt that one couldn't call someone a friend whom one saw just a few times. In response to her invitation, he wrote to say he would be delighted to attend but, seeing as Diana was unable to because she had to go to a christening, he wouldn't come if being on his own put the numbers out. Diana herself wrote wishing Sybil a happy birthday and to say how sorry she was that she couldn't be there.[52]

Sybil's son Hugh and daughter-in-law Lavinia gave the party on 30 January 1984. Ninety came, with nine tables for ten in the great Stone Hall; each table had a birthday cake with ten candles. Although Givenchy had given her a special dress to wear, she chose instead a dress that Worth had made for her mother in 1901.[53] Besides her children and grandchildren, the

71. Janet Stone, Sybil at Houghton with her portrait by Sargent, 1980s.

guests included her two closest academic friends, Sir Steven Runciman and Sir John Plumb. There were close Norfolk friends such as Lady Zuckerman, Ruth, Lady Fermoy, and Lady Silvia Combe. Her French relations were represented by her first cousins Baron Elie and Baroness Liliane de Rothschild, who had become close friends after the Second World War.

Sybil had prepared a thank-you speech. On 8 January she had written to Ted Walker and mentioned that in the past William Plomer had been kind enough to make some suggestions about what she might say in such situations. 'As the Queen & Co. have asked themselves I fear they will drink my health & I would like to say three or four little words to thank & perhaps amuse them.' On 14 January she wrote to him saying he had given her 'a very good piece of canvas on which to write a few extra words'. The Duke of Grafton delivered the major toast and there were other speeches.

After dinner, fireworks took place outside the West Front. The Queen Mother wrote afterwards that 'the fireworks were so splendid, & their beauty quite eighteenth century and suitable for Houghton'. The Queen herself said in her thank-you letter to Hugh that 'Sybil looking wonderful in her mother's dress in those beautiful rooms all added up to a memorable occasion. Thank you for inviting Philip and me and such a large number of our family.' It was a glorious occasion. Sybil and her brother, Philip, their parents and grandparents had moved in such circles all their lives. And yet, as the mistress of Houghton, she was now even more at the centre of that life.

Even before her birthday her health was weakening and she had had a series of accidents and broken bones. As captured in the film about her made by her grandson, she went about the estate in a motorized cart, generally accompanied by a long-haired dachshund. She now spent all her time at Houghton surrounded by what she had done so much to create and visited often by family. She died there on 26 December 1989, a month shy of her 96th birthday. Her daughter, Aline, wrote to Ted Walker the next day: 'My mother died on Boxing Day. Luckily she spent a happy time on Christmas Day with great grandchildren etc. She had a nasty cough (pleurisy) and died peacefully the next day while reading a book!'

It was a quieter life – but a very full one – than that of her brother. Both had added immensely to the quality of life of their century – in his case through society, political action and activity in the art world, and in hers by an enriching of the English fabric, and through her family and her friendships. The family had made a long trip from Baghdad. In ways consistent with what they were before, they had moved into other worlds. Philip became better known than his sister, but his was a more troubled life. He knew 'everyone' and was a major figure in England between the wars. Through lavish entertaining and political activities, he moved the business of the world forward. In his efforts to succeed, he seemed to have abandoned his private life. He certainly succeeded in his wish to be at the centre of public life. He was prominent but he never entered the Cabinet. He was an exotic figure who never quite acquired fully the trust of his fellow English. Sybil and Philip were an extraordinary brother and sister, charming, extremely rich, living a life deeply dedicated to serving England, he in politics and in the arts, she as a Wren and fulfilling with great success the duties of her position, going far beyond what might have been expected of her, in particular through her care of Houghton. Sybil in her quieter way came to be more securely in the heart of her country.

Notes

1 India: Establishing a Dynasty

1. M. Rodrigues-Pereira, Honorary Archivist, Spanish & Portuguese Jews' Congregation to author, 14 June 1999.
2. Stanley Jackson, *The Sassoons* (London, 1968), pp. 2–3.
3. Cecil Roth, *The Sassoon Dynasty* (London, 1941), p. 22.
4. See Rachel and Sara Manasseh, 'The Baghdadian Jews of India' offprint in the Cholmondeley Papers, Houghton Hall, King's Lynn, Norfolk, no source given. See also David Solomon Sassoon, *A History of the Jews in Baghdad* (Letchworth, 1949), Gillian Tindall, *City of Gold: The Biography of Bombay* (London, 1982) and Joan G. Roland, *Jews in British India: Identity in a Colonial Era* (Hanover, 1968). Years later in the early 1930s when various forms of voting were being instituted in India, the Baghdadi Jewish community attempted to have themselves considered European rather than Indian, without success. 'Edward Judah, a leading Calcutta Jew residing in London, tried to enlist prominent Britons to assist the cause . . . . Sir Philip Sassoon felt that his own position as a member of the government . . . precluded his involvement . . . . They wanted to be treated like Jews elsewhere in the British Empire, not like Indians. The British acted consistently, refusing to distinguish between Baghdadi and other Indian Jews for purposes of electoral rolls.' Roland, pp. 120–27.
5. *Illustrated London News*, 5 December 1863.
6. Plaque in Synagogue.
7. See Roth, p. 135.
8. Translation by Aron Rodrigue.
9. Plaque in hospital.
10. *Illustrated London News*, 5 December 1863.
11. Quoted Roland, p. 17.

2 England: Becoming English

1. Stanley Jackson, *The Sassoons* (London, 1968), p. 71.
2. Marquess of Cholmondeley, transcripts of interviews with Sybil, Marchioness of Cholmondeley in preparation for his television film about her (n.d.), p. 35. Hereafter cited as SCI.
3. Jackson, p. 93.
4. Mark Bonham Carter and Mark Pottle, eds, *Lantern Slides: The Diaries and Letters of Violet Bonham Carter 1904–1914* (London, 1996) 2–15 November 1904, pp. 10–20.
5. Terence Pepper, *High Society: Photographs 1897–1914* (London, 1998), p. 29.
6. Jackson, p. 117.
7. Quoted in Geoffrey Alderman, *Modern British Jewry* (Oxford, 1992), p. 133.
8. Ian Nairn and Nikolaus Pevsner, *The Buildings of England: Sussex* (London, 1965), p. 449.
9. Quoted in J. Mordaunt Crook, *The Rise of the Nouveaux Riches* (London, 1999), p. 184.
10. Or rather not introducing him to Duveen. Lady Sassoon had taken him to Duveen's gallery in London but on his stipulation that he not be introduced. 'One of the pictures Berenson looked at was first rate, and he decided to try to buy it for Mrs Gardner. "I'll pay you £30,000 for it," he said, without preliminaries to Duveen. Duveen turned to Lady Sassoon. "This fellow knows too much," he said, smiling. Berenson and Lady Sassoon

left the gallery without Berenson's having been introduced and without Duveen's having accepted or rejected the offer. Mrs Gardner never got the picture . . . . Duveen had guessed who the visitor was, and their encounter was to have an enormous effect on Berenson's future.' S.N. Behrman, *Duveen* (Boston, 1972), p. 126.

11. Berenson to Mary Berenson, 10 August 1904 quoted in Ernest Samuels, *Bernard Berenson: The Making of a Legend* (Cambridge, Mass., 1987), p. 16.

12. Quoted in Robert Skidelsky, *John Maynard Keynes* (New York, 1986), I, 172. Berenson kept up with Aline's children and years later there is a charming letter from Sybil to him about meeting him in Paris where she has checked out the rooms in which he is planning to stay at the Plaza-Athénée and ventures the hope that the manager will accept a lesser rate for the suite. She also advises him to have the menu rather than dine à la carte as the latter 'is much more expensive & no better food!' Archives, Villa I Tatti, Florence, Sybil Cholmondeley to Bernard Berenson, 20 September 1936.

13. Mary Berenson, Diary, 14 September 1907, Berenson to Mary, 2 August 1907 quoted in Samuels, p. 49.

14. Barbara Strachey and Jayne Samuels, eds, *Mary Berenson: A Self-Portrait from Her Diaries and Letters* (New York, 1983), p. 144.

15. Archives, I Tatti, Florence, Aline Sassoon to Bernard Berenson, 8 August 1908. I am very grateful to Pamela Bell for transcribing these letters for me. Unless otherwise indicated, the quotations from Aline's letters come from this source.

16. Strachey and Samuels, p. 135.

17. Samuels, pp. 38–39.

18. Ibid., p. 90.

19. See Norman L. Kleeblatt, ed., *John Singer Sargent: Portraits of the Wertheimer Family* (New York, 1999).

20. Quoted in Elaine Kilmurray and Richard Ormond, *Sargent* (London, 1998), p. 169.

21. Evan Charteris, *John Sargent* (New York, 1927), p. 175.

22. Wilfrid Scawen Blunt, *My Diaries 1900–1914* (New York, 1922), p. 171.

23. Neal Blewett, *The Peers, the Parties and the People* (Toronto, 1972), pp. 273, 461.

Information about constituency from miscellaneous clippings at Houghton Hall, King's Lynn.

24. H.G. Wells Papers, University of Illinois Library at Urbana.

25. *Vanity Fair*, 1 February 1900.

26. Archives, Houghton Hall, King's Lynn, Norfolk, Box 19. Sir Edward Sassoon to Philip Sassoon, n.d. Hereafter cited as HH.

27. Raymond Asquith to Lady Diana Manners, 29 January 1905, John Jolliffe *Raymond Asquith: Life and Letters* (London, 1980), p. 123.

28. Osbert Sitwell, *The Scarlet Tree* (Boston, 1948), p. 314.

29. Philip Ziegler, *Osbert Sitwell* (London, 1998), p. 26.

30. Errol Trzebinski, *Silence Will Speak: A Study of the Life of Denys Finch Hatton and his Relationship with Karen Blixen* (Chicago, 1977), p. 38.

31. HH, Box 19, Philip Sassoon to Sir Edward Sassoon, Wednesday 11 February n.y.; Sir Edward Sassoon to Philip Sassoon, 11 May n.y.

32. Box 10, Sassoon to Lord Esher, 4 June 1918, Sassoon's ellipses.

33. See M.H. Brock, 'The Oxford of Raymond Asquith', in M.H. Brock and M.C. Curthoys, eds, *The History of the University of Oxford* (Oxford, 2000), VII, 807.

34. See David M. Lewis, *The Jews of Oxford* (Oxford, 1992).

35. No date. Courtesy Pamela Bell.

36. Gertrude Atherton, *Adventures of a Novelist* (New York, 1932), pp. 431–34.

37. HH, Box 19, 1 December, n.y.

38. Ibid., 14 June, n.y. Cecil Roth has pointed out that the Sassoons might be regarded as an army family as fourteen grandsons and great-grandsons of David Sassoon held commissions. Cecil Roth, *The Sassoon Dynasty* (London, 1941), p. 211.

39. HH, Box 16.

40. Marquess of Cholmondeley, Transcripts of interviews with Sybil, Marchioness of Cholmondeley, 5/4. Hereafter cited as SCI.

41. SCI, 80.

42. HH, Box 19, Frances Horner to Philip Sassoon 25 August, n.y.

43. Frances Horner, *Time Remembered* (London, 1933), p. 188.

44. HH, Box 19.

45. Ibid., Box 20, Sybil Sassoon to Philip Sassoon, no complete dates.

46. SCI, I/16–18.

47. HH, Box 19, two letters from Paris, n.d.

48. SCI, I/18.

49. HH, Box 25. The talk is undated but it must have been before 1917 as Rufus Isaacs, the Liberal politician, was in the chair. If it were after 1917, he would have been referred to by his title, the Earl and later Marquess of Reading.

50. SCI, 5/4.

51. SCI, 16.

52. SCI, 5/4.

53. SCI, I/15.

54. Public Record Office, Kew, London, Copy of will, FO 917/1547. It is presumably to be found in the Foreign Office documents as part of his estate was in Shanghai.

55. Bonar Law Papers, House of Lords Records Office, Steel-Maitland to Bonar Law, 26 May 1912.

56. See Nigel Yates, ed., *Kent in the 20th Century* (Woodbridge, 2001), p. 156.

57. HH, Box 19, 9 June 1912. The irony being that Astor's wife, Nancy, was elected in 1919 and became the first woman to take a seat in Parliament. See the *Folkestone Herald*, 1 June 1912, p.7.

58. Ibid., 15 June 1912.

59. Max Beerbohm, *A Survey* (New York, 1921), no. 20.

60. *Parliamentary Debates*, 5th series, Vol. 43, 7 November 1912, cols 1532–35.

61. Roth, p. 234.

62. Lord Beaverbrook, *The Decline and Fall of Lloyd George* (London, 1963), p. 49. The other side of the coin, so to speak, was that when Duff Cooper made his maiden speech on 16 December 1924, he felt that the acme of recognition was that Philip Sassoon, who had ignored him up to then, asked him what he was doing for Christmas. Alfred Duff Cooper, *Old Men Forget* (London, 1953), p. 139. Lady Diana Cooper wrote to Katherine Asquith about the speech: 'I never heard of a maiden speech being such a success (Times leading article & all) & all the big wigs congratulating & Philip asking him for Xmas.' British Library Add. Ms. 70704, 16 December 1924, f. 172.

63. *Parliamentary Debates*, 5th series, Vol. 43, 1 July 1914, cols 497–501.

64. Ibid., 7 July 1914, col. 982.

65. Diana Cooper, *The Rainbow Comes and Goes* (London, 1958), p. 80.

66. Jackson, p.159.

67. Roth, p. 231.

68. SCI, I/17.

69. SCI 79/54. Lady Aline Cholmondeley wrote to me: 'This [her conversion] did *not* take place till a few years *after* W.W. II, by which time we [the children] were of course grown up & had left home. So it was from conviction *not* expediency.' 7 July 2000.

70. Bruce Arnold, *William Orpen: Mirror to an Age* (London, 1981), p. 283.

71. See Andrew Wilton, *The Swagger Portrait* (London, 1992), p. 210.

72. P. de Figueiredo and J. Treuherz, *Cheshire Country Houses* (London, 1988), p. 52.

73. Andrew Moore, ed., *Houghton Hall: The Prime Minister, the Empress and the Heritage* (London, 1996), p. 6.

74. Christopher Hassall, *A Biography of Edward Marsh* (New York, 1959), p. 231. Bernard Shaw was also there and wrote to Mrs Patrick Campbell about the event: '*Tintagiles* requires, first an eerie silence, second that everyone should see the stage and not see the audience. The chairs scraped on the floor the whole time; and nobody could see the stage except by fitful glimpses through armpits and under ears and over shoulders and through feathers. Of the first act not a word was audible; and when the curtain closed, the audience roared the fact at one another and bellowed ribald speculations as to what the show was about until they opened again and Lillah renewed her struggle with adverse circumstances . . . . Smart ladies hailed me as their oldest pal: I received them with enthusiasm, and wondered who on earth they were.' Alan Dent, ed., *Bernard Shaw & Mrs Patrick Campbell: Their Correspondence* (New York, 1952), 1 July 1913, p. 142.

75. HH, Box 20, n.d.

76. Herbert Baker, *Architecture & Personalities* (London, 1944), p. 139.

77. Arthur Gold and Robert Fizdale, *Misia* (New York, 1980), pp. 218, 125.

78. See Alberto Del Castillo, *José Maria Sert: su Vida y su Obra* (Barcelona, 1947).

79. Mallet Papers, Balliol College, Oxford, Sassoon to Mallet, 13 August n.y. IV, 11 (10). I am grateful to Mallet's great-nephews and the

Librarian at Balliol for granting me permission to see this collection.

80. Michael and Eleanor Brock, eds, *H.H. Asquith Letters to Venetia Stanley* (Oxford, 1982), p. 514.

81. HH, Box 33, Diary of trip to India 2 volumes. All quotations from these volumes.

82. Ibid., Box 20, Sybil to Philip 10 February [1914].

3 Philip and Sybil Serve Their Country

1. Northcliffe Papers, British Library, London Add. Ms. 62160, copy Northcliffe to Sassoon dated in pencil before 24 September 1916, f. 23. All subsequent quotations of letters from Sassoon to Northcliffe are from this source, unless otherwise noted.

2. Archives, Houghton Hall, King's Lynn, Norfolk, Box 15, Geoffrey Robinson to Sassoon, 14 October 1916. Hereafter cited as HH.

3. Ibid., Herbert Henry Asquith to Sassoon, 2 January 1916.

4. Ibid., Lord Stamfordham to Sassoon, 25 September 1916.

5. Details of his war record here and subsequently are from the Public Record Office, Kew, London, WO 374/60414.

6. Esher Papers, Churchill Archives, Churchill College, Cambridge 5/58, 27 March 1921.

7. 14 December 1915, Maurice Baring, *Dear Animated Bust: Letters to Lady Juliet Duff: France 1915–1918* (London, 1981), p. 2.

8. Desborough Papers, Archives, Hertford Record Office, Hertfordshire County Council, County Hall, Hertford, D/Erv C2345/1–14. All letters to Lady Desborough from this source.

9. HH, Box 20, n.d.

10. L.E. Jones, *An Edwardian Youth* (London, 1956), pp. 54–55.

11. Mrs Belloc Lowndes, *A Passing World* (London, 1948), p. 232.

12. Susan Lowndes, ed., *Diaries and Letters of Marie Belloc Lowndes 1911–1947* (London, 1971), p. 49.

13. Humanities Research Center, University of Texas, Austin.

14. Robert Blake, ed., *The Private Papers of Douglas Haig: 1914–1919* (London, 1952), p. 30.

15. Martin Gilbert, ed., *Winston S. Churchill*

Companion Volume Vol. III Part 2 (Boston, 1973), pp. 1383, 1392.

16. Mary Soames, ed., *Speaking for Themselves* (London, 1998), p. 143.

17. John Jolliffe, *Raymond Asquith: Life and Letters* (London, 1980), 26 January 1916, p. 240.

18. Esher Papers. All subsequent quotations of letters from Sassoon to Esher are from this archive unless otherwise indicated.

19. Courtesy Clive Gee, Haig Papers, National Library of Scotland, Edinburgh, ACC 3155. Hereafter HP.

20. John Charteris, *Field-Marshal Earl Haig* (New York, 1919), p. 210.

21. Blake, p. 315.

22. HP, ACC 3155, No. 213d, Sassoon to Lady Haig, 7 September 1916.

23. James Lees-Milne, *The Enigmatic Edwardian: The Life of Reginald, 2nd Viscount Esher* (London, 1986), pp. 280–81. Sassoon to Esher, 6 May 1918.

24. HH, Box 9, Esher to Sassoon, 5 February 1916. All subsequent letters from Esher to Sassoon from this source unless otherwise noted.

25. John Keegan, *The First World War* (London, 1998), pp. 307–8.

26. Ibid., p. 321.

27. John Keegan, interview, *New York Times*, 3 July 1999.

28. Jolliffe, *Raymond Asquith*, 15 March 1916, pp. 248–49.

29. HH, Box 15, Dewar to Sassoon, n.d.

30. Blake, ed., p. 149.

31. Cynthia Asquith, *Diaries*, 18, 20 October 1916, pp. 227–28.

32. HH, Box 31, clipping from *Folkestone Gazette*, 20 January 1917.

33. Quoted, no source given, Stanley Jackson, *The Sassoons* (London, 1968), p. 172.

34. *The Times*, 28 December 1916. Story about constituency ibid., 23 October 1916.

35. HH, Box 13. Undated but likely to be late April 1916.

36. Ibid., Box 9, Esher to Sassoon, 5 and 14 August 1916.

37. Imperial War Museum, London, H.A. Gwynne Papers Vol. IV, Sassoon to Gwynne, 6 January 1916, f. 424.

38. Northcliffe Papers (hereafter cited as NP), all letters Sassoon to Northcliffe, ff. 1–97.

39. HH, Box 15, Geoffrey Robinson to Sassoon, 15

August 1916. All subsequent letters from
Robinson from this source.

40. Ibid., Box 15. All subsequent letters from
Northcliffe to Sassoon, with their dates given
in the text, are from this source.

41. This and all subsequent letters from Derby to
Sassoon, ibid., Box 13. Letters from Sassoon to
Derby, Liverpool Record Office.

42. Quoted in Randolph S. Churchill, *Lord
Derby: King of Lancashire* (New York, 1960),
p. 282.

43. Mallet Papers, Balliol College, Oxford,
Sassoon to Mallet 13 August [1915?].

44. HH, Box 13. All letters from Haig to Sassoon
are from this source.

45. HP, n.d.

46. Ibid.

47. HH, Box 21. All letters from Sassoon to Mrs
Dudeney, unless otherwise indicated, come
from this source.

48. Diana Crook, ed., *Mrs Henry Dudeney, A
Lewes Diary 1916–1944* (n.p., 1998), p.12. See
also Diana Crook, ed., *A Peculiar Devotion:
The Friendship of Sir Philip Sassoon and Mrs
Henry Dudeney* (n.p., 1999).

49. Crook, ed., *Diary*, 10 February 1917, p. 16.

50. Quoted in A.J.P. Taylor, *English History
1914–1945* (Oxford, 1965), p. 53, no source
given.

51. HH, Box 9, Esher to Sassoon, 30 May 1917.

52. Ibid., 14 and 15 November 1917.

53. Quoted Peter Fraser, *Lord Esher* (London,
1973), p. 374.

54. NP, Copy Northcliffe to Sassoon, 17 January
1918, ff. 103–4.

55. HH, Box 15, Geoffrey Dawson to Sassoon, 8
February 1918.

56. British Library Add. Ms. 45,416.

57. A.J.P. Taylor, *English History 1914–1945*
(Oxford, 1965), p. 102.

58. HH, Box 23, 8 May 1918.

59. Ibid., 12 and 27 May 1918.

60. Ibid., 11 May 1918.

61. See Meirion and Susie Harries, *The War
Artists* (London, 1983), pp. 68–69. Also Bruce
Arnold, *Orpen: Mirror to an Age* (London,
1981), pp. 307–80.

62. HH, Box 45.

63. Marquess of Cholmondeley, Transcripts of
interviews with Sybil, Marchioness of
Cholmondeley, 73–74. Hereafter cited as SCI.

64. Sybil in conversation with Bruce Arnold, cited

in Bruce Arnold, ed., William Orpen, *An
Onlooker in France* (Dublin, 1996; first
published 1921), p. x.

65. Quoted in Carl Little, *The Watercolors of John
Singer Sargent* (Berkeley, 1998), p. 14.

66. Evan Charteris, *John Sargent* (New York,
1927), p. 212.

67. HH, Box 23, Diary, 17 July 1918.

68. Ibid., 20 August 1918.

69. E.M. Forster, 'Me, Them, and You' in *Abinger
Harvest* (London, 1942) pp. 27–30; first
published 1936. The piece is misdated 1925 in
the collection. It appeared in the *New Leader*
on 22 January 1926.

70. HH, Box 23, 8 June 1918.

71. Ibid., Box 23.

72. Blake, ed., Sunday, 4 August 1918, p. 321.

73. Jackson, p. 172.

74. HH, Box 23, 24 August 1918.

75. Ibid.

76. Ibid., Box 20, 15 May n.y. Internal evidence
would suggest 1915. All the few surviving
letters from Sybil to Philip are in this box
unless otherwise noted.

77. Ibid., Box 23, Diary, 4 May 1918.

78. Katharine Furse, *Hearts and Pomegranates*
(London, 1940), p. 366. Also see HMS
Dauntless (Furse Papers) Collection, National
Maritime Museum, Greenwich, Boxes 3 and 4.

79. Furse, p. 368.

80. Quoted in M.H. Fletcher, *The Wrens*
(London, 1989), p. 24.

81. HH, Box 13a.

82. Blake, ed., *The Private Papers*, pp. 357–58.

83. Courtesy Clive Gee, HP, ACC 3155, no. 227c.

84. *The Times*, 30 December 1918.

85. *Folkestone Herald*, 23 November 1918.

86. HP, ACC 3155, no. 2n.

87. HH, Box 22, Sassoon to Mrs Dudeney, 23
February 1919.

4 Becoming a Politician in the 1920s

1. Archives, Houghton Hall, King's Lynn,
Norfolk, Box 10, Esher to Sassoon, 19 January
1919. Hereafter cited as HH.

2. HH, Box 13, Trenchard to Sassoon, 19 April 1918.

3. For these and other details of the early
history of the Air Force, see Malcolm Smith,
British Air Strategy between the Wars (Oxford,
1984).

4. HH, Box 13, Haig to Sassoon, 16 November 1919. In the few other letters from Haig to Sassoon he was less gracious. On 14 June 1921, he thanks him for wanting to give him a personal present for his house but he reprimands him for not having subscribed for the house as Sassoon's name is not on the list he has been sent and he urges him to send a sovereign to the Bermersyde Fund at the Bank of England. On 31 May 1923, he admonishes him for not having answered Lord Hardinge's request that he speak to the British Legion in Kent. 'Unless people in your position support the Legion, the ex-servicemen in your district will become bolshie, and it is just people in your class [who] will suffer most of all!!'

5. *Parliamentary Debates*, 5th series, Vol. 116, 5 June 1919, col. 2279; Vol. 121, 21 November 1919, col. 1336; Vol. 122, 1 December 1919, cols 134–36.

6. A.J.P. Taylor, ed., *Lloyd George: A Diary by Frances Stevenson* (New York, 1971), pp. 189, 192, 194.

7. Riddell Papers, British Library Add. Ms. 62,984, ff. 228–30 part published in J.M. McEwen, *The Riddell Diaries 1908–1923* (London, 1986), p. 297.

8. Esher Papers, Churchill Archives, Churchill College, Cambridge. All subsequent quotations of letters from Sassoon to Esher are from this archive unless otherwise indicated.

9. Cecil Roth, *The Sassoon Dynasty* (London, 1941), p. 243. The sort of upper-class malice such an appointment could bring about is suggested in a line that Lady Wemyss wrote to Arthur Balfour. 'Have you been told of Diana Cooper['s] proposed telegram to Philip Sassoon "Christ is risen and wants you for his secretary."' 22 May 1920 Balfour Papers, Scottish National Archives, Edinburgh, GD 433/2/229/1/7 courtesy R.J.Q. Adams.

10. Roth, p. 246.

11. Lloyd George Papers, House of Lords Record Office, Beaverbrook to Lloyd George, 30 March 1922, G4/6/11, note of telephone message left, 4 April 1922, G4/6/12.

12. T.W.H. Crosland, 'Lloyd George and the Jews', in *The Fine Old Hebrew Gentleman* (London, ?1922), pp. 78–84.

13. Taylor, ed., *Lloyd George*, 14 November 1921, p. 237.

14. Ibid., 24 May 1921, p. 217.

15. Roth, p. 256.

16. *Parliamentary Debates*, 5th Series, Vol. 129, 10 May 1920, col. 84.

17. Royal Archives, Windsor Castle, RA GV EE 8/63–73. All quoted letters are from this source, unless otherwise noted.

18. Rupert Godrey, ed., *Letters from a Prince* (London, 1998) 20 March 1920, p. 258.

19. Ibid., 8 April 1920, pp. 269, 271, also for speculation by the editor about Mrs Simpson. Subsequent references to this volume are from pp. 336, 340–41, 353, 356, 358, 303, 233, 384–85, 391, 398.

20. Philip Ziegler, the Prince's biographer, believes Mrs Simpson (then Wallis Spencer) was at the dance. See his *King Edward VIII* (London, 1990), p. 125. But in fact she was in North Carolina at the time. See Benjamin Sacks, 'The Duchess of Windsor and the Coronado Legend', *Journal of San Diego History*, Part I, Fall, 1987, pp. 165–78; Part II, Winter, 1988, pp. 1–15.

21. Mallet Papers, Balliol College, Oxford. 1923 Notebook, 20 December.

22. HH, Box 23, 4 March 1924.

23. Chaim Weizmann, *Trial and Error* (New York, 1949), p. 261.

24. For Hankey's views see Stephen Roskill, *Hankey Man of Secrets* II (London, 1972), pp. 168–80.

25. For Mosley see Oswald Mosley, *My Life* (New Rochelle, NY, 1968), pp. 143–44.

26. HH, Box 23 for all quotations from this diary.

27. Desborough Papers, Archives Hertford Record Office, D/Erv C2345/10.

28. Fritz Stern, *Einstein's German World* (Princeton, 1999), p. 188.

29. Roskill, p. 289.

30. Material about Churchill and quotation are from Martin Gilbert, *Winston S. Churchill: IV: The Stricken World 1916–1922* (Boston, 1975), pp. 507–21.

31. Ibid., p. 783.

32. Ibid., p. 786.

33. See Deborah Cohen, 'Who Was Who? Race and Jews in Turn-of-the-Century Britain' *Journal of British Studies* 41: 4, October 2002, pp. 460–83.

34. Lloyd George Papers, F/45/1/4, Sassoon to Lloyd George, 11 January 1921.

35. Martin Gilbert, ed., *Winston S. Churchill Companion Volume IV, Part 2 July 1919–March 1921* (Boston, 1978), Churchill to Lloyd George, 30 January 1921, p. 1330.

36. Mallet Papers, Balliol College, Oxford, Diary note, 3 April [?1922].

37. Lloyd George Papers, F 7/4/15.

38. Churchill Papers, Churchill College, Cambridge, CHAR 2/118/72–83, 19 December 1921.

39. Martin Gilbert, ed., *Winston Churchill Companion Volume IV, Part 3* (London, 1977), [6 March 1922], p. 1795.

40. 15 March 1922, A.J.P. Taylor, ed., *My Darling Pussy: The Letters of Lloyd George and Frances Stevenson 1913–41* (London, 1975), p. 36.

41. Thomas Jones, *A Diary with Letters* (London, 1954), p. 62.

42. Baldwin Papers 42, quoted in H. Montgomery Hyde, *Baldwin* (London, 1973), p. 119.

43. Lord Beaverbrook, *The Decline and Fall of Lloyd George* (London, 1963), p. 221.

44. Sir Edward Marsh Papers, Berg Collection, New York Public Library [C. K. Scott-Moncrieff] *A Servile Statesman*, Privately Printed (London, 1923).

45. HH, Box 45, Typed transcription of letter in French. Translation by Philippe Tapon.

46. HH, Box 18, Diary letters on trip, quotations from 25, 26 and 28 March, 2 and 6 April.

47. Lloyd George Papers, G/17/10/1 1 February 1922.

48. HH, Box 21 [April 1928].

49. All quotations from [Philip Sassoon], *Letters to Sybil* (London, n.y. [?1924]).

50. HH, Box 18, Diary, 2 March and 3 May 1924.

51. *The Times,* 15 March 1924, p. 6.

52. *Parliamentary Debates,* 5th series, Vol. 171, 1 April 1924, cols 2118–20.

53. Ibid., Vol. 174, 18 June 1924, cols 2236–38.

54. Ibid., Vol. 161, 11 March 1924, cols 2232–34; Vol. 174, 28 May 1924, col. 490.

55. *Folkestone Express and Hythe Advertiser,* 1 November 1924.

56. Viscount Templewood, *Empire of the Air* (London, 1957), pp. 187–88.

57. Michael Howard, review of Viscount Templewood, *Empire of the Air,* in *New Statesman & Nation,* 26 January 1957.

58. HH, Box 23, Copy in Philip's hand, 16 November 1924.

59. Churchill Papers, CHAR 2/136/51–52 in Martin Gilbert, *Winston S. Churchill: The Exchequer Years 1922–1929. Companion Vol. V Part 1* (Boston, 1981), p. 251.

60. HH, Box 18 'Monday', n.d. [?Spring 1924].

61. Ibid., Box 23.

62. *The Times,* 22 February 1926. The other events cited are recorded in *The Times* as well.

63. Lord Templewood Papers, Cambridge University Library, V 2 (13) (early March 1925?).

64. Ibid., V 2 (24) n.d. (late 1925?).

65. HH, Box 15, Ronald Waterhouse on behalf of Stanley Baldwin, 17 December 1924. The letters from Stanley Baldwin and W. Mitchell-Thomson are also in this location.

66. Templewood Papers, V 6, 1926.

67. Siegfried Sassoon, Unpublished 1926 Diary referred to in John Stuart Roberts, *Siegfried Sassoon* (London, 1999), p. 203.

68. Templewood Papers, XVIII 2 (47) n.d. (October 1927?).

69. *The Times,* 26 April 1927.

70. Ibid., 8 December 1927.

71. *Parliamentary Debates,* 5th series, Vol. 211, 7 December 1927, cols 1377–78.

72. Ellen Wilkinson, *Peeps at Politicians* (London, 1930), pp. 75–76.

73. 29 June 1928.

74. *Parliamentary Debates,* 5th series, Vol. 211, 1 June 1929.

75. *Folkestone Herald,* 18 and 25 May 1929.

76. Baldwin Papers, Cambridge University Library n.d. ?June 1929, 36, ff. 204–5.

77. Templewood Papers, V 2 (84) (13 June n.y.).

78. Mrs Belloc Lowndes, *A Passing World* (London, 1948), p. 234.

79. H. Montgomery Hyde, *British Air Policy between the Wars 1918–1939* (London, 1976), pp. 211–12.

80. Ralph Barker, *The Schneider Trophy Races* (Shrewsbury, 1981), p. 220.

81. *The Times,* 5 February 1931.

82. See Leslie Hunt, 'The Millionaires' Mob', *Aeroplane Monthly,* April 1976, pp. 202–6; Tom Moulson, *The Flying Sword: The Story of the 601 Squadron* (London, 1964), pp. 27–29; *The Aeroplane,* 19 August 1936, pp. 236–37.

83. Manuscripts, Royal Air Force Museum, Hendon, Logbook AC 91/8/16.

84. Royal Archives, Windsor Castle, RA GV EE 8/73.

85. Dermot Boyle, *My Life* (London, ?1989), pp. 51–55.

86. Diana Crook, ed., *A Peculiar Devotion: The Friendship of Sir Philip Sassoon and Mrs Henry Dudeney* (Lewes, 1999), p. 28.

87. Mrs Belloc Lowndes, *A Passing World* (London, 1948), pp. 235–37.

88. HH, Box 18, Travel diary, written for Sybil, 2–29 October 1928. Subsequent quotations are from this source. The letters provided the raw material for his book. See also a typescript, Arthur Longmore, 'The Diary of Six Weeks Air Tour 1928.'

89. Translation courtesy Erich Gruen.

90. Philip Sassoon, *The Third Route* (London, 1929) pp. 33–34; subsequent quotations from pp. 33–34, 60, 60–61, 106, 118–20, 151, 206, 239–40, 242, 289.

91. See Claudio G. Segrè, *Italo Balbo: A Fascist Life* (Berkeley, 1987).

92. Baldwin Papers, Cambridge University Library, October ?1928, 163, ff. 243–44.

93. HH, Box 19, C. Stobart to Miss Edwardes, 5 April 1963.

94. Ibid., Box 45, 29 April 1929; 15 May 1929.

95. David Garnett, ed., *The Letters of T.E. Lawrence* (London, 1938), 30 March 1933, p. 765.

96. J.L. Garvin Papers, Humanities Research Center, University of Texas, Austin, 12 August n.y.

97. *The Times,* 30 April 1929.

98. See Christine Sutherland, *Enchantress: Marthe Bibesco and Her World* (New York, 1996), pp. 188, 191.

99. HH, Box 21.

100. Mrs Belloc Lowndes, p. 235.

101. HH, Box 19 for this and other Wilder letters except for Wilder to Sassoon 17 January 1930, which is in Box 45.

102. Philip Sassoon, *The Third Route,* with an introduction by Thornton Wilder (New York, 1929), pp. xi–xv.

103. *Parliamentary Debates,* 5th series, Vol. 239, 18 March 1930, cols 1990–94.

5 Setting the Stage in London and in the Country

1. See Mary Soames, *Clementine Churchill: A Biography of a Marriage* (Boston, 1979), p. 288.

2. Philip Tilden, *True Remembrances* (London, 1954,) p. 40.

3. Ibid., p. 44.

4. James Knox, 'Sir Philip Sassoon, Bt. Aesthete, Conoisseur, Patron', in *Works of Art from Houghton* (London, 1994), p. xxiv.

5. Tilden, p. 39.

6. J. Mordaunt Crook, *The Rise of the Nouveaux Riches* (London, 1999), p. 184.

7. Tilden, p. 40.

8. These pieces passed to Sybil upon Philip's death in 1939. Some are illustrated in all their lavishness in the catalogue for the 1994 Houghton sale.

9. David Cecil, *Max* (London, 1964), p. 333.

10. See Elaine Kilmurray and Richard Ormond, eds, *John Singer Sargent* (London, 1988), p. 174.

11. Archives, Houghton Hall, King's Lynn, Norfolk, clippings *Morning Post,* 29 April 1922; *Daily Sketch,* 24 April 1922.

12. HH, Bound book of letters from William Orpen to Sybil Cholmondeley, 31 January 1925.

13. Quoted without a source in William Howe Downes, *John S. Sargent* (London, 1926), p. 225.

14. Martin Birnbaum, *John Singer Sargent: A Conversation Piece* (New York, 1941), pp. 32–33.

15. See F.J.B. Watson, *The Wrightsman Collection: Furniture, Gold Boxes* (New York, 1970), pp. 22–31. John Cornforth in conversation 14 August 2000; also his *The Inspiration of the Past* (London, 1985).

16. María del Mar Arnús, *José María Sert* (Madrid, ?1987), p. 100.

17. Knox, 'Sir Philip Sassoon, . . .', in *Works of Art . . .*, p. xx.

18. Arnús, *Sert,* p. 100. Translated by Philippe Tapon.

19. John Cornforth, *The Search for a Style* (London, 1988), p. 192.

20. HH, Box 23, 26 August 1918.

21. 17 July 1918, to Mrs Dudeney in Diana Crook, ed., *A Peculiar Devotion* (Lewes, 1999), pp. 17–18.

22. Tilden, p. 43.

23. Information about visitors to Port Lympne unless otherwise indicated comes from the Port Lympne Visitors' Books in the possession of Lady John Cholmondeley. I am deeply grateful to her for showing them to me.

24. Kenneth Clark, *Another Part of the Wood* (London, 1974), pp. 220–22.

25. Quotations without sources are from Knox, p. xxiv.

26. Robert Rhodes James, ed., *Chips: The Diaries of Sir Henry Channon* (London, 1967), 29 January 1935, ellipses in published version, p. 24.

27. Ibid., 5 June 1936, ellipses in published version, p. 63; 1 and 2 August 1936, p. 73.

28. Ibid., quoted in Introduction with no date given, p. 7.

29. Susan Lowndes, ed., *Diaries and Letters of Marie Belloc Lowndes 1911–1947* (London, 1971), letter to her daughter, 10 August 1935, pp. 128–29.

30. Cecil, *Max*, p. 422.

31. Anon., 'Port Lympne', *Country Life*, LIII, 19 May 1923, p. 681.

32. Philip Sassoon, in *Architectural Review*, LIII, 1923, col. 134.

33. Stanley Jackson, *The Sassoons* (London, 1968), p. 189.

34. G. C. Taylor, 'The Gardens at Port Lympne', *Country Life* LXXIX, 14 March 1936, p. 276. See also his highly enthusiastic second article, in vol. LXXII, 10 September 1932, pp. 285–87.

35. Jane Brown, *The English Garden in Our Time* (London, 1986), pp. 98, 171.

36. HH, Box 40, 4 September 1967.

37. Quoted in J.G.P. Delaney, *Glyn Philpot* (London, 1999), p. 48.

38. Quoted in Laurence Whistler, *The Laughter and the Urn: The Life of Rex Whistler* (London, 1985), p. 159.

39. Siegfried Sassoon, *Diaries 1923–25* (London, 1985), 24 May 1925, p. 255.

40. Rupert Hart-Davis, ed., *Siegfried Sassoon: Letters to Max Beerbohm & A Few Answers* (London, 1986), Diary, 13 April 1937, p. 47.

41. Jackson, p. 242.

42. Whistler, p. 159.

43. Ibid., 10 November 1931, pp. 160–61.

44. Charles Chaplin, *My Autobiography* (London, 1964), p. 302.

45. HH, Box 21, 25 August 1917.

46. Mary Soames, *Winston Churchill: His Life as a Painter* (Boston, 1990), pp. 48–50.

47. Diana Crock, ed., Mrs Henry Dudeney, *A Lewis Diary 1916–1944* (n.p., 1996), pp. 33–34, 38–39, 45, 60–61, 70, 81, 178.

48. HH, Box 21, Sassoon to Mrs Dudeney, 1 November [1925].

49. Interview, June 1999, House of Lords.

50. Michael Holroyd, *Lytton Strachey* (New York, 1968), II, 469, 534.

51. Lytton Strachey Papers, British Library, London, Add. Ms. 60, 696, Sassoon to Strachey.

52. Nigel Nicolson and Joanne Trautmann, eds, *The Letters of Virginia Woolf* (New York, 1978), IV, 47.

53. Anne Olivier Bell, ed., *The Diary of Virginia Woolf* (New York, 1980) III, 15 June 1929, p. 233.

54. 13 June n.y. Woolf Insert Papers Collection, 1875–1974, Washington State University Libraries, Pullman, Washington, Cage 674, folder 45.

55. Philip Hoare, *Noël Coward* (London, 1995), p. 225.

56. Nigel Nicolson in conversation, 5 September 1999.

57. HH, Box 45, Lawrence to Sassoon, 31 August 1933.

58. Courtesy Duchess of Devonshire, Thomas Mitford to Lady Redesdale, 17 August 1930.

59. Thomas Jones, *A Diary with Letters 1931–1950* (London, 1954), Baldwin to Jones, 20 April 1933, p. 104.

60. HH, Box 15.

61. Thomas Jones, *Whitehall Diary* (London, 1969), 21 June 1929, II, 194.

62. Courtesy Philip Williamson, Arthur Bryant memorandum [March 1937] Liddell Hart Centre for Military Archives, King's College, London, C62.

63. Anne de Courcy, *The Viceroy's Daughters* (London, 2000), p. 41.

64. Unless otherwise indicated, information on the house comes from Patrick Campbell, *Trent Park: A History* (London, 1997), Stephen Doree, *Trent Park: A Short History to 1939* (n.p., ?1974) and *Trent Park: History Trail and Mansion Tour* (n.p., n.y.)

65. I am grateful to Robert Batchelor for this idea.

66. Christopher Hussey, 'Japanned Furniture at Trent Park', *Country Life*, LXVIII, 18 October 1930, pp. 497–500.

67. Christopher Hussey, 'Trent Park', *Country Life*, LXIX, 10 and 17 January 1931, pp. 40–47, 66–72.

68. W. Somerset Maugham, *The Complete Short Stories* (New York, 1932), I, 748. Ironically,

when the story was made into a film the fact that the family was Jewish was left out. See also Stephen Doree, 'The Sassoons of Trent Park', *Heritage*, I (1942).

69. Crook, *The Rise*, p. 281. He uses the story as the last line, and as a summation, of the Victorian and Edwardian parvenu. Although Philip was a member of the first generation born in England, his was fourth-generation wealth and he was a post-Edwardian.

70. See Francis Pitt, 'Water Fowl at Trent Park', *Country Life*, LXXXI, 8 and 15 May 1937, pp. 506–8, 542–44.

71. Churchill Papers, Churchill College, Cambridge. Copy Churchill to Sassoon, 9 June 1927, Sassoon to Churchill, 10 June 1927; copy telegram Churchill to Sassoon, 28 December 1934.

72. Robert Boothby, *Boothby: Recollections of a Rebel* (London, 1978), p. 72.

73. Osbert Sitwell, *The Scarlet Tree* (Boston, 1946), p. 160.

74. Explicitly stated in Clive Aslet, *The Last Country Houses* (New Haven, 1982), p. 80.

75. There are always, at the very top, exceptions to conformity: Disraeli, even Gladstone, Lloyd George and Churchill: all of them had detractors who treated them as quite unstable, eccentric, and not to be trusted. Indeed, if Gladstone's drive to save prostitutes and Lloyd George's affairs (and his child by Frances Stevenson) had been better known, they might have hurt them politically. Disraeli lived his personal life according to pre-Victorian values. Although he had converted to Christianity when he was 13 – he couldn't have had a political career if he hadn't – his Jewishness antagonized many, even as he climbed to the top of the 'greasy pole'. Churchill was, as far as one knows, faithful to his wife, perhaps tamed by his parents' licentiousness.

76. No source given, Knox, p. xxiv.

77. *A Lewes Diary*, 6 and 22 July 1936, pp. 160–61.

78. They are in the archives at Houghton.

79. HH, Box 16.

80. A.J.P. Taylor, ed., Frances Stevenson, *Lloyd George: A Diary* (New York, 1971), pp. 200–1.

81. Meryle Secrest, *Somewhere for Me: A Biography of Richard Rodgers* (London, 2001), pp. 12–13.

82. Lord Haig, interview, London, 17 December 1998.

83. Mary Soames, ed., *Speaking for Themselves* (London, 1998), 8 September 1936, p. 416.

84. Mrs Belloc Lowndes, *Diary*, 29 December 1927, p. 109.

85. Ibid., Diary, a retrospective on the abdication, 20 January 1937, p. 143.

86. Marquess of Cholmondeley, Transcripts of interviews with Sybil, Marchioness of Cholmondeley, V/I. Hereafter cited as SCI.

87. Mrs Belloc Lowndes, *Diary*, Easter Monday, 1938, p. 161.

88. HH, Box 45. T.E. Lawrence papers, Bodleian Library, Oxford MS Eng C 6738 Sassoon to Lawrence, n.d. ff.174–75.

89. HH, Box 45. Photocopied from an unknown book about T. E. Lawrence, pp. 27–28.

90. Michael Ignatieff, *Isaiah Berlin* (London, 1998), pp. 34–35.

91. Harold Nicolson, *Diaries and Letters 1930–39* (London, 1966), 1 June 1931, p. 76.

92. Robert Boothby, *I Fight to Live* (London, 1947), pp. 48–49.

93. Boothby, *Boothby*, p. 71.

94. Boothby, *I Fight*, pp. 49–50. In the later version of this description of Trent in *Boothby: Recollections of a Rebel* (London, 1978), he inserted before the last sentence 'No pomp, no ceremony, no formality, and no white ties – just dinner jackets', p. 71.

95. Campbell, p. 53.

96. David Cholmondeley to author, 2 April 2000.

97. For the quotation and the history of the house, see F.H.W. Sheppard, ed., *Survey of London* (London, 1973), XXXVII, 167–70.

98. See Crook, *The Rise*, p. 171.

99. HH, Box 23, Diary, 4 June 1918.

100. Artur Rubinstein, *My Many Years* (New York, 1980), pp. 163, 223, 276, 320.

101. I am grateful to Percy and Joan Baldwin for their memories and much information on life at Houghton. He was its estate agent from 1937. Interview 11 September 1999.

102. Royal Archives, Windsor Castle, RA GV CC 47 1248, 1882.

103. SCI V/I.

104. See Mary Clarke and David Vaughan, *The Encyclopaedia of Dance & Ballet* (London, 1977), p. 241.

105. The Marquess of Cholmondeley, 'Introduction', in Margaret Morris, *Basic Physical Training* (London, 1937).

6 The Role of Art: Making an Aesthetic

1. Courtesy Deborah Cohen n.d. Archive of Art and Design, Victoria & Albert, London, 1/6–1981.
2. Esher Papers, Churchill Archives, Churchill College, Cambridge.
3. *Parliamentary Debates*, 5th series, Vol. 54, 29 May 1922, cols 1786–89; Vol. 157, 3 August 1922, cols 1857–60.
4. Archives, National Gallery, London, NG 26/106, carbon Charles Holmes to Sassoon, 11 October 1922.
5. *The Nation & the Athenæum*, XXXIX 9 July 1921, p. 541; 30 July 1921, p. 648.
6. Quotation and information from Malcolm Warner, 'The Decline and Rise of the Pre-Raphaelites', *Quarterly*, Spring 2000, pp. 47–50.
7. See Frances Spalding, *The Tate: A History* (London, 1998). Also David Buckman, *James Bolivar Manson* (London, 1973) and Tate Gallery Archives, London, Minute Books.
8. Alan Clark, ed., *A Good Innings: The Private Papers of Viscount Lee of Fareham* (London, 1974), pp. 286, 291.
9. John Vincent, ed., Earl of Crawford, *The Crawford Papers* (Manchester, 1984) 17 February, 26 June 1927; 26 July 1930; 30 March 1935, pp. 519, 534, 560.
10. Clark, *A Good Innings*, p. 321.
11. Kenneth Clark, *Another Part of the Wood* (New York, 1974), p. 224.
12. Ibid., p. 226. Interestingly the Gallery has recently been trying an experiment of illuminating some of the rooms by natural light.
13. Ibid., p. 228.
14. Archives, The British School at Rome, Rome.
15. *The Times*, 29 February 1931, 1 June 1935, 9 November 1936, 19 April 1937; John Rothenstein, *Summer's Lease* (New York, 1965), p. 226.
16. Royal Northern Hospital Archives, London Metropolitan Archives, London, H3/RN/AO/32/87.
17. Archives, Houghton Hall, King's Lynn, Norfolk, Box 23, 2 March 1924. Hereafter cited as HH.
18. *The Times*, 11 February 1927.
19. *Country Life*, LXIII 3 March 1928, pp. xxxiii–xxxvi; 24 March 1928, p. 421; 10 March 1928, pp. 328–33 with nine illustrations.
20. All information about the fund-raising events and the sums achieved come from the Annual Reports of the Hospital to be found in the London Metropolitan Archives.
21. *The Times*, 2 July 1928.
22. Information and quotations from the unillustrated and unpaginated catalogue, March 1930.
23. HH Box 16, Letters from the Royal Family. Subsequent letters from Queen Mary are from this collection.
24. Royal Archives, Windsor Castle, RA GV CC 47 1030–31.
25. Christopher Hussey, *Country Life*, LXVII 15 February 1930, pp. 264–66; M. Chamot, ibid., LXVIII, 8 March 1930, pp. 344–46.
26. C. Reginald Grundy, 'Conversation Pieces in Park Lane', *Connoisseur*, LXXXV, March 1930 pp. 193–94.
27. George C. Williamson, 'Conversation Pieces', *Apollo*, XI March 1930, pp. 163–70.
28. National Gallery Archives, NG 26/106.
29. Ibid.
30. Ralph Edwards 'The Four Georges Exhibition: Furniture', *Country Life*, LXIX, 28 February 1931, pp. 257–61.
31. Frank Rutter, *International Studio*, XCVIII, April 1931, pp. 53–55.
32. C. Reginald Grundy, *Connoisseur*, LXXXVII, March 1931, April 1931, pp. 191, 259–60.
33. V. de Serbe, *Country Life*, LXXI 8 March 1932, pp. 258–60.
34. C. Reginald Grundy, *Connoisseur*, LXXXIX, March 1932, pp. 195–99.
35. Vincent, ed., *Crawford Papers*, 6 March 1932, pp. 544–45.
36. *Country Life*, LXIII, 25 February 1933, pp. 204–6.
37. This picture entered the National Gallery in 1994 in lieu of inheritance tax. This was in accordance with Sybil's wish that it should do so in memory of her brother. Judy Egerton, *The British School* (London, 1998), p. 64.
38. Lord Rothschild, lecture, Filoli, Woodside, California, 11 February 2000.
39. Kenneth Clark Papers, Tate Gallery Archives, London, 8812.5.1.2.
40. *Art News*, 26 February 1938.
41. See Eric C.O. Jewesbury, *The Royal Northern Hospital* (London, 1956), p. 119.
42. Jeffrey Meyers, *The Enemy: A Biography of Wyndham Lewis* (London, 1980), pp. 208–10.

43. All quotations from Sybil Cholmondeley letters to Wyndham Lewis, Cornell University Library.

44. Harvey Sachs to author, 21 July 2000. Sybil's letters, courtesy Harvey Sachs, from Fondazione Sergio Dragoni, Milan and Stiftung Omina-Freundeshilfe, Vaduz. For Toscanini's reaction see Harvey Sachs, ed., *The Letters of Arturo Toscanini* (London, 2002): 'I always thought she admired me as an artist, but it seems that she admires the man, too. I've tried to give her paternal advice, but it's all been futile'. Toscanini to Ada Mainardi, 27 July 1937, p. 272.

7 The Bomber Always Gets Through: Politics in the 1930s

1. *Hythe Reporter*, 31 October 1931.
2. *Folkestone Herald*, 17 October 1931.
3. *Parliamentary Debates*, 5th series, Vol. 309, 4 March 1936, cols 1369–72.
4. Bodleian Library, Oxford, T.E. Lawrence papers, Sassoon to Lawrence, n.d. MS Eng d. 3341 f. 1347.
5. Archives, Houghton Hall, King's Lynn, Norfolk, Box 45. All quotations from T.E. Lawrence. Hereafter cited as HH.
6. Ibid., Box 23.
7. *Parliamentary Debates*, 5th series, Vol. 298, 27 February 1935, col. 1118.
8. Ibid., Vol. 275, 14 March 1933, cols 1795–1938.
9. Churchill Papers, Churchill College, Cambridge, copy Churchill to Londonderry, 15 March 1933, CHAR 2/192/74.
10. *Parliamentary Debates*, 5th series, Vol. 286, 8 March 1934, cols 2027–152.
11. Martin Gilbert, *Winston S. Churchill: The Wilderness Years 1929–1935. Companion Vol. V, Part 2* (Boston, 1981), pp. 862, 874.
12. *Parliamentary Debates*, 5th series, Vol. 299, 19 March 1935, cols 1015–93.
13. Ibid., Vol. 300, 9 April 1935, col. 967.
14. Ibid., Vol. 302, 22 May 1935, cols 475–82.
15. Quoted in Robert J. Caputi, *Neville Chamberlain and Appeasement* (London, 2000), pp. 30–31.
16. I am grateful to Dr C.S. Sinnott for elucidation on these points.
17. *Folkestone Herald*, 2 November 1935.
18. *Folkestone Express*, 9 November 1935.
19. Winston S. Churchill, *The Gathering Storm* (Boston, 1948), p. 129.
20. *Parliamentary Debates*, 5th series, Vol. 310, 17 March 1936, cols 259–76.
21. Ibid., Vol. 317, 15 March 1937, cols 1666–822.
22. Churchill, *The Gathering Storm*, pp. 231–32.
23. Wallace Collection, London, Sassoon file, unidentified clipping.
24. Gisela C. Lebzelter, *Political Anti-Semitism in England 1918–1939* (London, 1978), pp. 36–37.
25. Cecil Roth, *The Sassoon Dynasty* (London, 1941), p. 270.
26. Robert Rhodes James, ed., *Chips: The Diaries of Sir Henry Channon* (London, 1967), p. 73.
27. Chamberlain Papers, University of Birmingham, Sassoon to Chamberlain, n.d. NC 7/11/31/239.
28. Quoted in Harvey Sachs, ed., *The Letters of Arturo Toscanini* (London, 2002), pp. 348–49.
29. Osbert Sitwell, *Rat Week* (London, 1984), p. 57.
30. Royal Archives, Windsor Castle, RA GV EE 10/3372, n.d.
31. Philip Ziegler, *Edward VIII* (London, 1990), p. 370.
32. Public Record Office, Kew, Works 22/30 History, Powers, Duties of the Commissioners of Works. Hereafter PRO.
33. Rhodes James, ed., *Chips*, p. 64.
34. *Parliamentary Debates*, 5th series, Vol. 324, col. 1410; Vol. 325, col. 201.
35. Lloyd George Papers, House of Lords Record Office [20 July 1937], G/17/10/2 and n.d. G/17/10/4.
36. Earl of Halifax, *Fulness of Days* (London, 1957), p. 203.
37. *Retrospect: The Memoirs of the Rt. Hon Viscount Simon* (London, 1952), p. 227.
38. Chamberlain Papers, NC 7/11/32/226.
39. Ibid. Sassoon to Mrs Chamberlain, 20 December 1937, NC 11/1/801.
40. Roth. p. 255.
41. *The Times*, 20 August 1937, 12 February 1938, 14 May 1938, 16 July 1938.
42. Ibid., 28 November 1938, 27 April 1939.
43. *Parliamentary Debates*, 5th series, Vol. 325, col. 836.
44. PRO, Works 20/186.
45. *Parliamentary Debates*, 5th series, Vol. 329, col. 1706.
46. Ibid., Vol. 332, 1 March 1938, cols 974–1035.

47. PRO, Works 21/109.
48. Bernard Newman, *Speaking from Memory* (London, 1960), pp. 54–55.
49. Margaret Richardson to author, 9 November 2000.
50. HH, Box 45 both letters. n.d.
51. PRO, Works 20/229, 10 March 1937, and Works 20/207.
52. John Vincent, ed., Earl of Crawford, *The Crawford Papers* (Manchester, 1984), p. 581.
53. PRO, Works 20/229.
54. PRO. All relevant documents unless otherwise indicated are in Works 20/229. Sassoon's letters cited are carbons.
55. *Parliamentary Debates*, 5th series, Vol. 329, 24 November 1937, col. 1246; Vol. 330, 6 December 1937, col. 47.
56. PRO, Works 20/207.
57. Ibid., Works 20/209, 3 August 1938.
58. Ibid., Works 14/951.
59. Ibid., Works 16/1031.
60. Ibid., Works 14/540.
61. Ibid., Works 19/1003, 1004.
62. Ibid., Works 19/1081.
63. *Parliamentary Debates*, 5th series, Vol. 330, 6 December 1937 col. 1615.
64. PRO, see Works 16/1527, 19/799, 28/11, 28/18, 28/20, 28/21, 28/48.
65. Ibid., Works 20/207, 12 May 1939.
66. Templewood Papers, Cambridge University Library, X, 4 carbon, 13 May 1939.
67. Kenneth Clark, *Another Part of the Wood* (New York, 1974) p. 277.
68. Meryle Secrest, *Kenneth Clark* (New York, 1984), p. 140.
69. HH, Box 34. Ian Gow, the MP who was later assassinated by the IRA, gave the letter to his father to Kenneth Rose who kindly placed it with the family papers at Houghton.
70. Clark, *Another Part of the Wood*, p. 277.
71. Royal Archives, Windsor Castle, PS GVI 03884.
72. HH, Box 34, 7 June 1939; 3 June 1939.
73. RA GV CC 47 1783, 1784.
74. Bernard Berenson Archives, I Tatti, Fiesole, 23 July 1939.
75. HH, all quotations from obituaries come from the Diary, i.e. clippings, 1938–43 as well as the letter from Neville Chamberlain, 7 June 1939.
76. Marquess of Cholmondeley, Transcripts of interviews with Sybil, Marchioness of

Cholmondeley, 7–8. A Tory, Commander Rupert Brabner, was elected to his seat in July. He was a banker who joined the Fleet Air Arm once war was declared. In November 1944 he became himself Under-Secretary of State for Air, but the next year he died when his plane disappeared near the Azores. The eccentric and pro-Fascist St John Philby, the Middle East expert, and father of Kim Philby, also ran for the seat for the anti-Semitic British People's Party, and lost his deposit.
77. *Daily Mirror*, 20 June 1939.
78. Rhodes James, *Chips*, p. 202.
79. Lady Aline Cholmondeley in conversation, 12 August 2000.
80. John Colville, *Footprints in Time* (London, 1976), pp. 69–70.
81. Sybil presented the drawing to Queen Mary at Christmas 1939 and it is now in the Royal Collection. It must have been a rather bittersweet present.
82. *Journal of the Royal Air Force College*, Autumn 1939, p. 151.
83. HH, Boxes 47 and 48 for financial details.

8 Sybil

1. David Cholmondeley to author, 22 February 2001.
2. See M.H. Fletcher, *The Wrens* (London, 1989).
3. Vera Laughton Mathews, *Blue Tapestry* (London, 1948), p. 163.
4. Archive, Houghton Hall, King's Lynn, Norfolk, Box 34, 22 June 1946, 11 May 1946. Hereafter cited as HH.
5. Interview with her naval assistant, Mrs Callaghan, Bourne End, 3 June 1999.
6. Marquess of Cholmondeley, Transcripts of interviews with Sybil, Marchioness of Cholmondeley, 80. Hereafter cited as SCI.
7. Ted Walker Papers, Chichester Institute of Higher Education, Chichester, Sussex, 1989.
8. Royal Archives, Windsor Castle, GV CC 47 1934.
9. Fletcher, p. 31.
10. This and subsequent letters in the Toscanini Legacy, New York Public Library for the Performing Arts. See also Harvey Sachs, ed., *The Letters of Arturo Toscanini* (London, 2002), pp. 375–76 for the Garibaldi quotation.

11. SCI 17.
12. British Library, Add. Ms. 9375, ff.136, 137.
13. John Stuart Roberts, *Siegfried Sassoon* (London, 1999), pp. 282, 326.
14. HH, Box 34, copies, Sybil to Stanley Jackson, 19 February 1965; to Amy Curtis, n.d.
15. While doing research at Houghton, Plumb made a discovery. On the shelves was *Scriptores Rerum Germanicarum Septentrionalium, Vicinorumque Populum Diversi*, edited by Erpoldus Lindenbrogium and published in 1609. Robert Walpole's father had borrowed it from the library at Sidney Sussex College, Cambridge in 1667. It was returned in January 1956, thus establishing a record, almost three hundred years, for the longest recorded borrowed book.
16. HH, Box 34, Arthur ?? to Sybil, 25 July 1956.
17. Ibid., Clippings, 1962–1968, John Masefield to Lady Cholmondeley, 6 June 1965.
18. Ibid., Box 40, William Plomer to Sybil Cholmondeley, 16 June 1967.
19. See Peter F. Alexander, *William Plomer* (London, 1989).
20. SCI 1/24.
21. HH, Box 40 for this and the previous letter.
22. Quotations from the William Plomer Papers, Durham University Library, Files 36 and 247.
23. HH, Box 40.
24. Walker Papers, Chichester, 20 December 1973.
25. HH, Box 40, 4 June 1978.
26. Cholmondeley Prize File, Society of Authors Archives, London.
27. John Julius Norwich, Introduction, Michael Meredith, ed., *Eddie Marsh's Little Book* (Eton, 1990), p. 14.
28. See Heather Child et al., *More than Fine Writing: Irene Wellington: Calligrapher (1904–84)* (London, 1986).
29. Churchill Papers, Churchill College, Cambridge, Cholmondeley to Churchill, 4 September 1945; copy Churchill to Cholmondeley, 16 September 1945.
30. Lunt/Fontanne Papers, State Historical Society of Wisconsin, Madison, Wisconsin, 4185–3–405M 97–98 Reel 3, 19 January 1950.
31. HH, Box 20, 21 November 1915.
32. Ibid., Box 34, Elizabeth to Lord Cholmondeley, 28 February 1952.
33. Plomer Papers, 2 August 1963 35/2.
34. Desborough Papers, Archives, Hertford Record Office, Hertfordshire County Council, County Hall, Hertford, 5 October 1968, D/EC494/2.
35. Graham Payn and Sheridan Morley, eds, *The Noël Coward Diaries* (Boston, 1982), p. 675.
36. Richard Morris, *Cheshire* (London, 2000), pp. 250, 326.
37. Lucy Moorehead, ed., *Freya Stark Letters: The Broken Road 1947–1952*, Vol. VI (London, 1982) to Stewart Perowne, 5 August 1951, p. 247.
38. Caroline Moorehead, ed., *Freya Stark Letters: Traveller's Epilogue 1960–1980*, Vol. VIII (London, 1982) to John Grey Murray, 18 July 1969, p. 167.
39. Walker Papers, Chichester. To Ted Walker, 8 June 1974.
40. Walpole Library, Farmington, Connecticut. To Wilmarth Lewis, 19 January 1960.
41. SCI 65.
42. See John Cornforth, *The Inspiration of the Past* (London, 1985), pp. 198–99. I am also deeply grateful to him for talking and writing to me about Philip and Sybil.
43. Rosemary Bowden-Smith, *The Water House* (Woodbridge, 1987), p. 19. She calls the Water House the 'Jewel in the Crown of the Houghton Estate' (p. 34).
44. Walpole Library, Farmington, Connecticut.
45. Translation courtesy George Brown.
46. HH, Box 40.
47. Walker Papers, Chichester for all letters to Ted Walker.
48. HH, House file.
49. Plomer Papers.
50. SCI 6/14.
51. SCI III/5.
52. HH Box 35, folder on the ninetieth birthday. I am also grateful for the reminiscences of Lady Zuckerman and Lady Silvia Combe.
53. She was a regular client of French couturiers. In 1974 she had given some of her clothing to the V & A, including dresses by Paquin, Vionnet and Mainbocher as well as hats by Caroline Reboux.

Index

Abdication crisis (1936), 175, 226
Aga Khan, 49
'Age of Walnut, The' exhibition (1932), 199–200
Air Ministry: established, 91; PS serves as Under-Secretary, 116–20, 199, 213–25, 246
Albert Gate, London, 30
Aldington, Richard, 210
Alexandra, Queen of Edward VII, 99
Alfonso XIII, King of Spain, 135
Alien Act (1905), 2, 16
Allen, Maud, 79
Allenby, Field Marshal Edmund Henry Hynman, 1st Viscount, 113
Amiens, battle of (1918), 80
Amrani dialect, 6
Ancaster, Gilbert Heathcote-Drummond-Willoughby, 2nd Earl of, 259
Ancaster, Robert Willoughby, 4th Duke of, 40, 258
Annunzio, Gabriele d', 206
anti-Semitism: in British society, 1, 11, 106; at Oxford, 25; and political right, 207; and rise of Fascism, 225; *see also* Jews
Architectural Review, 153
Armistice (1918), 86
Arras, battle of (1917), 69–70
Ashley Park, Surrey, 6, 9
Aspinall, John, 162
Asquith, Lady Cynthia (*née* Charteris), 61
Asquith, Herbert Henry, 1st Earl of Oxford and Asquith: visits Port Lympne, 47; letter to PS on Raymond in war, 52; visits Haig in war, 58; campaign to depose in war, 63–64; Lloyd George replaces as PM, 66–67; decline in political influence, 69, 74, 91; at Park Lane party, 106
Asquith, Margot, Countess of Oxford and Asquith (*née* Tennant), 16, 29, 83, 144
Asquith, Raymond, 24, 52, 56, 60–61
Asquith, Lady Violet *see* Bonham Carter, Lady Violet
Astor, Nancy, Viscountess, 114, 126, 162
Astor, Waldorf, 2nd Viscount, 66
Astor, William Waldorf, 1st Viscount, 32

Atherton, Gertrude, 25–26
Attlee, Clement (*later* 1st Earl), 219
Auric, Georges, 180
Auxiliary Air Force and Air Force Reserve Act (1924), 117

Baghdad: Jews from, 4–6, 10; PS visits on flight to and from India, 131, 134
Bailey, Sir Abe, 77
Baker, Sir Herbert, 44, 47–50, 132, 149
Balbo, Air Marshal Italo, 126, 128, 130, 206, 208, 261
Baldwin, Lucy, 108, 163, 201
Baldwin, Stanley (*later* 1st Earl): on post-war coalition government, 91; denounces Lloyd George, 108; premiership, 109, 116, 222; PS entertains, 109; on election defeat (1929), 123; on PS's indifferent parliamentary manner, 124; and PS's flight to India, 130; PS lends Trent Park to, 162; on National Gallery Board, 189; in National Government, 213; on 'bomber always getting through', 216–18; speaks on air policy, 217, 219; hopes for disarmament plan, 219; on size of German Air Force, 221–22; on inefficacy of disarmament, 222; appoints PS to Office of Works, 224, 231
Balfour, Alfred James (*later* 1st Earl): Declaration on Palestine, 16, 101; as member of the Souls, 16; Aline invites with Lady Elcho, 22; and Post-Impressionist Exhibition, 28; at Park Lane entertainment, 44; visits Haig at HQ, 57; as Foreign Secretary, 67; at Trent Park, 178
Balfour, Captain Harold, 214, 217
Ballet Russe, 41, 46
Banks, Robert Richardson, 179
Baring, Maurice, 52, 75, 162
Barker, George, 256
Barnato, Barnett Isaacs (Barney), 16, 140
Barry, Sir Charles, 179, 231
Basra, 5, 132–33
Beaton, Sir Cecil, 152, 156
Beatty, Admiral of the Fleet David, 1st Earl, 232, 234, 236
Beauchamp, William Lygon, 7th Earl, 239

Beaverbrook, William Maxwell Aitken, 1st Baron, 32, 93–94
Beer, Frederick, 186
Beer, Rachel (*née* Sassoon), 186
Beerbohm, (Sir) Max, 32, 141, 153, 162
Belcaire *see* Port Lympne
Bell, Vanessa, 160
Bellevue (house), Kent, 139
Belloc, Hilaire, 55, 207
Bene Israel, 5
Benn, William Wedgwood (*later* 1st Viscount Stansgate), 230
Benson, Edward Frederic, 199
Berenson, Bernard: relations with Aline, 17–19, 25; Kenneth Clark visits, 190; letter from Sybil on PS's death, 241
Berenson, Mary, 18
Bergson, Henri, 28
Berlin, Sir Isaiah, 176
Bermersyde (house), Scotland, 85
Berners, Gerald Tyrwhitt-Wilson, 14th Baron, 152, 154, 156, 171, 176
Bevan family, 163
Bevan, Francis, 163
Bevis Marks synagogue, London, 3
Bibesco, Princess Marthe, 135, 162
Billing, Noel Pemberton, 79
Birdwood, Sir George, 7
Birkenhead, Frederick Edwin Smith, 1st Earl of, 56, 60, 62–63, 126
Blackett, P.M.S., 217
Blake, Robert, Baron, 56
'Bland, Sir Freddy', 167
Blixen, Karen (Isak Dinesen), 24
Blunt, Wilfrid Scawen, 19
Boehm, Sir Joseph Edgar, 7
Bombay: Sassoons in, 3, 5, 7; Jews in, 5, 7; synagogue in, 7; Sybil visits on honeymoon, 48
Bomberg, David, 185
Bonham Carter, Lady Violet (*née* Asquith; *later* Baroness Asquith), 15, 262
Bootham, Flight-Lieutenant J.N., 126
Boothby, Robert (*later* Baron), 151, 168, 177
Boraston, Lieutenant-Colonel J.H., 88
Borotra, Jean, 174, 181
Bossom, A.C., 227
Boudin, Stéphane, 146
Bowra, Sir Maurice, 151
Boyce, Grace, 195, 245
Boyle, Flight-Lieutenant (Sir) Dermot, 127
Brabazon, John Theodore Cuthbert Moore- (*later* 1st Baron), 221
Brett, Dorothy, 79
Briand, Aristide, 57, 94
Brighton: Sassoons in, 12, 16, 22
British Gazette (news-sheet), 121
British Jewry Book of Honour, 81
British School at Rome, 191

Britten, Benjamin, Baron, 256
Brooke, Rupert, 44, 51, 53, 77
Brown, Ivor, 252
Brown, Jane, 154
Brown, John Lewis, 158
Bryant, (Sir) Arthur, 163
Bugatti, Ettore, 183
Bullock, Malcolm, 171, 178
Bushire, Persia, 3, 5, 133
Byculla, Bombay, 7

Callaghan, Mrs (Sybil's WRNS secretary), 266
Cambrai, battle of (1917), 71–72
Cameron, D.Y., 187
Campbell, Colen, 40
Campbell, Patrick, 178
Canada: PS visits, 122
Carlile, Dr J.C., 241–42
Carlton Club: 1922 meeting, 108
Carnarvon, George Herbert, 5th Earl of, 113–14
Carol, King of Romania, 230
Carpentier, Georges, 99
Carrington, Dora, 160
Carson, Edward Henry, Baron, 62–63
Carter, Howard, 113
Cassel, Sir Ernest, 12
Castlereagh, Charles Vane-Temple-Stewart, Viscount *see* Londonerry, Charles Stewart Henry Vane-Tempest-Stewart
Cathcart-Jones, Owen: *Aviation Memoirs*, 220
Cecil, Lord Hugh, 153, 162
Chamberlain, Anne, 176, 228
Chamberlain, Sir Austen, 102, 107, 126
Chamberlain, Neville: visits Port Lympne, 162; visits Trent Park, 176; as Chancellor of Exchequer, 216; replaces Swinton with Kingsley Wood, 223; appeasement policy, 225; donates money for park bench, 238; sends condolences on PS's death, 242
Chancellor, E. Beresford, 197
Channon, Sir Henry ('Chips'), 146, 152, 171, 225, 227, 243–44
Channon, Lady Honor (*née* Guinness), 152
Chaplin, (Sir) Charles, 157, 198, 256
Charles, Prince of Wales, 181, 259, 266
Charteris, Evan, 19, 28, 76, 187, 243
Charteris, General John, 57, 67, 70–71
Chartwell, Kent, 138, 168
Cheshire, Leonard, VC, 262
Chesterfield, Philip Dormer Stanhope, 4th Earl of, 165
Chesterton, G.K., 207
China: and opium trade, 6, 33
Cholmondeley family, 39, 261
Cholmondeley, Lady Aline (Sybil's daughter): portrait, 35; birth, 83, 181; told of Jewish ancestry, 244; on mother's death, 268
Cholmondeley, David, 7th Marquess of: appearance, 7; inherits title, 40, 261; and Sybil's service in WRNS, 247

Cholmondeley, George, 4th Marquess of, 258

Cholmondeley, George Horatio Charles, 5th Marquess of ('Rock'): as Lord Great Chamberlain, 2, 40, 181, 184, 226, 258–60; marriage to Sybil, 2–3, 33–35; background, 33–34; occupies Houghton, 40; visits Port Lympne, 45; honeymoon in India, 48–50; war service, 83; on PS's difficult behaviour, 172; builds and occupies house in France (Le Roc), 181, 226, 262; sports, 181, 183; visits USA, 181, 253, 262; inherits title, 182; motoring, 182–83, 262; land and property owning, 183, 262; local activities in Norfolk, 183–84; collecting, 206, 257; and Sybil's entertaining, 206; on anti-Semitism, 244; in Civil Defence during war, 251; calligraphy, 257; post-war public life and interests, 257; political views, 258; aesthetic interests, 260; portrait of, 260; speaks in Lords, 260; devotion to Sybil, 261; retirement and death, 261; titles, 262; visits Russia, 263; memorial steps at Houghton Hall, 265

Cholmondeley, George James, 4th Earl and 1st Marquess of, 40, 163

Cholmondeley, Georgiana, Marchioness of (née Bertie), 40, 182

Cholmondeley, Lord Hugh (later 6th Marquess), 229, 251–53, 261, 266, 268

Cholmondeley, Lady John (née Maria Cristina Solari), 171

Cholmondeley, Lord John (Sybil's son), 171, 181, 251–52

Cholmondeley, Lavinia, Marchioness of (Hugh's wife), 266

Cholmondeley, Mary, Countess of (née Walpole), 40

Cholmondeley, Lady Rose, 180

Cholmondeley, Sybil Rachel Bettie Cécile, Marchioness of (née Sassoon): background and career, 2; restores and occupies Houghton Hall, 2, 39–40, 179, 182, 210, 263–66, 268; marriage and honeymoon, 3, 33–35, 47–50; birth, 15; education, 15; and parents' death, 27; Jewishness, 28–29, 170, 266; marriage prospects, 28–29; private life and friendships, 28, 30, 181–82, 206–8, 212, 246, 252, 255–56, 262–63; wariness of Rothschilds, 28–29, 261; inheritance from father, 30; moves to Albert Gate, 30; converts to Church of England, 35, 244; Orpen's relations with, 35, 39, 75–76; portraits and sculpture of, 35, 39, 41, 140, 144, 194, 207–8, 211, 248, 253; relations with Hannah Gubbay, 35, 170–71, 261; and Rothschild emeralds, 35; at Park Lane entertainments, 44, 79; visits Port Lympne, 45–46, 162; shooting, 48; on Billy Grenfell's death, 54; suffers miscarriage, 76; visits France in wartime, 76; relations with PS, 81–82, 246, 261; wartime life and activities (1914–18), 82–85; artistic and cultural interests, 83, 205, 254; children, 83, 181–82; helps found WRNS, 83–84, 92; supports PS in 1918 election campaign, 89; friendship with Geddes, 92; as hostess for PS, 102, 106; letters from PS in Rome and Egypt, 112–14; visits Chequers, 124; Balbo's infatuation with, 126; sees PS off on flight to India, 128; letters from PS on flight to India, 131–33; T.E. Lawrence writes to about *The Seven Pillars of Wisdom*, 133; US edition of *The Third Route* dedicated to, 136; sells art objects from Park Lane, 140; letter from Osbert Sitwell on Siegfried Sassoon, 155; meets Siegfried Sassoon, 156; with Chaplin at Port Lympne, 159; social exclusion, 159; visits Trent Park, 169; dislike for Prince of Wales, 175; London house (12 Kensington Park Gardens), 179–80; musical interests, 180–81, 205; motoring, 182–83, 262; infatuation with Toscanini, 205, 211–12, 251–52; relations with Wyndham Lewis, 207–8, 210–12; and PS's death, 240–41; declines to stand as PS's successor at Hythe, 242; inheritance from PS, 245–46, 253; longevity, 246, 262; serves in WRNS in Second World War, 247–51; awarded CBE, 248; awarded French Légion d'honneur, 251; good relations with Siegfried Sassoon, 252–53; pneumonia, 252; visits USA, 253, 262; establishes prizes and awards, 254; will, 257; devotion to Rock, 261; relations with Rothschild and Sassoon families, 261; death and burial, 262, 268; travels, 263; ninetieth birthday party (1984), 266–68

Cholmondeley, Winifred, Marchioness of (Rock's mother), 263

Cholmondeley Castle, Cheshire, 39, 182, 261, 263

Cholmondeley Prize for Calligraphy, 257

Cholmondeley Prize for Poetry, 254–56

Christ Church, Oxford: PS attends, 25–26

Churchill, Clementine, Lady, 158, 161, 174, 262

Churchill, Lady Randolph (later Porch; Jenny; Winston's mother), 56, 74

Churchill, Randolph (Winston's son), 219, 253

Churchill, Sarah, 158

Churchill, (Sir) Winston: in First World War, 53, 56, 62–65, 70; Esher on, 70; on mother's remarriage, 74; admires Siegfried Sassoon's poems, 81; Haig dines with at PS's, 89; as Secretary of State for War (1919), 91; as Colonial Secretary, 105; and peace negotiations (1920–22), 105–6; PS entertains, 105, 158, 178, 219, 225; recommends PS for political promotion, 107; supports Lloyd George, 108; becomes Tory, 118–19; as Chancellor of Exchequer, 118–19; correspondence with PS on appointment to Air Ministry, 118; relations with PS, 118–19; advocates rearmament, 119, 216; produces *British Gazette* in General Strike, 121; reduces Air Estimates, 121; T.E. Lawrence forbidden from seeing, 126; acquires Chartwell, 138; visits Port Lympne, 151, 161–62; paints PS's homes and gardens, 154, 158; Lytton Strachey meets, 160; opposes Indian independence, 168, 221; PS sends black swans to, 168; on development of Air Force, 218–19, 221–22; estimate of PS as minister, 224; supports Edward in Abdication crisis, 226; correspondence with Rock, 258; resumes premiership (1951), 258; Sybil's friendship with, 262

Clandon Park, Surrey, 21

Clark, Jane, Lady, 151
Clark, Kenneth, Baron: friendship with PS, 149; on
    PS's entertaining, 151; as Director of National
    Gallery, 189–91; memorandum on PS's 'Thomas
    Gainsborough' exhibition, 202–3; visits ailing PS,
    240; learns of PS's death, 241; attends poetry
    reading, 255; visits Houghton, 256
Clemenceau, Georges, 57, 73
Coalition Liberals, 91
Coalition Unionists, 91, 108, 191
Cochin, 5
Cockerell, Sir Sydney, 257
Cohen, Hannah Mildred, Lady, 203
Colefax, Sir Arthur, 31
Colefax, Sibyl, Lady, 31, 162
Collie, Alexander, 179
Colman, Grace, 123, 213
Colville, Sir John ('Jock'), 1, 137, 244
Combe, Lady Sylvia, 267
Coming, John, 163
Conservative Party: fights and wins 1922 election,
    108–9; forms government (October 1924), 116;
    resigns government (1929), 123
Constable, W.G., 197
Cooper, Alfred Duff (later 1st Viscount Norwich), 201,
    225, 234–35, 237–38
Cooper, Captain Archibald Frederick, 248
Cooper, Lady Diana (née Manners), 34, 52, 201, 237–38,
    256
Copley, John Singleton, 195
Cornford, Frances, 77
Country Life, 153–54, 166, 192–93, 196, 264
Coward, (Sir) Noel, 153, 160–61, 208, 261
Crawford, David Alexander Edward Lindsay, 27th Earl
    of, 188–90, 200, 232, 239
Cripps, Sir Stafford, 222, 231
Crosland, T.W.H.: The Fine Old Hebrew Gentleman,
    93–94
Cunard, Emerald (Maud Alice), Lady, 102, 162, 227
Curzon, George Nathaniel, Marquess of, 16, 53, 77, 83,
    104, 109, 112, 116
Curzon, Grace, Marchioness (née Duggan), 163

Dale, Alec, 168
Dalmeny, Harry Primrose, Lord (later 6th Earl of
    Rosebery), 28
Dalyell, Tam, 259
Daniel, Sir Augustus, 189
Daud Pasha, 5
David Sassoon Building, Bombay, 9
David Sassoon General Hospital, Poona, 9
David Sassoon Industrial and Reformatory
    Institution, Bombay, 9
David Sassoon Infirm Asylum, Poona, 9
David Sassoon Library and Reading Room, Bombay,
    7–8, 257
Davidson, Tavish, 89
Davies, J.T., 66

Davies, Sir Martin, 202
Dawson, Geoffrey (earlier Robinson), 52, 62–63, 66, 72
De Valera, Eamon, 105
Deedes, William Francis (later Baron), 159–60
de Laszlo, Philip, 52
Dent, J.M. (publishers), 88
Derby, Edward George Villiers Stanley, 17th Earl of,
    58, 64, 66–67, 69–70, 94, 108
Desborough, Ethel (Ettie), Lady: in the Souls, 16;
    friendship with PS, 24; takes interest in PS and
    Sybil, 29–30; visits Port Lympne with Asquith,
    47–48; sons killed in war, 53–54; wartime letters
    from PS, 53, 83; letter from PS at Spa meeting, 104;
    with party at Port Lympne, 153; entertains PS and
    Siegfried Sassoon, 155
de Serbe, V., 199
Devonshire House, Piccadilly, 164
Dewar, George, 60, 62
Diaghilev, Serge, 41, 46
Diana, Princess of Wales, 266
Dick, Sir William Reid, 234
Dickens, Charles, 186
Digby, Matthew Wyatt, 179
Disraeli, Benjamin, 131
Dobbs, Sir Henry, 134
Dollfuss, Engelbert, 263
Doree, Stephen, 167
Doubleday (US publishers), 136
Draper, Ruth, 92
Driberg, Tom (later Baron Bradwell), 156
Dudeney, Mrs Henry (Alice): PS's friendship with, 68–69,
    78, 89, 95, 113, 127, 148, 159; visits Port Lympne, 157–58;
    and PS's behaviour, 172; Head of the Family, 157
Dudley Ward, Freda, 95–99
Duff, Lady Juliet, 52, 112, 114, 139, 201
Duff, Sir Patrick, 235, 240
Duggan, Grace see Curzon, Marchioness
du Maurier, George, 2
Duveen, Sir Joseph, Baron, 17, 39, 162, 187, 189–91, 238

'Early English Needlework and Furniture' exhibition
    (1928), 192
East India Company, 5
East Kent Yeomanry, 27, 52
Eaton Square: Sybil occupies flat in, 179
Eden, Sir Anthony (later 1st Earl of Avon): visits Port
    Lympne, 153, 162; Toscanini dines with, 211; and
    Hitler's claim to air parity, 221; donates money for
    park bench, 238
Edinburgh, Prince Alfred Ernest Albert, Duke of, 9
Edinburgh, Prince Philip, Duke of see Philip, Prince
Edward VII, King (earlier Prince of Wales): Sassoon
    family's relations with, 1, 6; Bombay statue, 7;
    recovers from illness, 9; social circle, 12, 15–16;
    names yacht for Aline, 15; acquires Sandringham,
    40; proposed Trafalgar Square statue, 231; dislikes
    4th Marquess Cholmondeley, 258
Edward, Prince of Wales (later King Edward VIII and

Duke of Windsor): in First World War, 57; friendship with PS, 93, 95–99, 226–29; PS entertains, 93, 174–76; travels, 95–98; Lady Cunard entertains, 102; liking for Samuel Hoare, 122; on PS's flying lessons, 127; Sargent portrait of, 144; in Abdication crisis, 175, 226; accession, 184; on National Gallery Board, 189; attends PS's charitable ball, 192; and PS's appointment as First Commissioner of Works, 227; gives thrones to Cholmondeley, 258; and Cholmondeley as Lord Great Chamberlain, 259

Egypt, 112–14

Elcho, Mary, Lady (*later* Countess of Wemyss), 22

Eliot, T.S.: 'The Love Song of J. Alfred Prufrock', 110

Elizabeth II, Queen (*earlier* Princess): visits Trent Park, 174; visits Houghton, 182; coronation, 259; at Sybil's ninetieth birthday party, 268

Elizabeth, Queen of George VI (*earlier* Duchess of York): Boyle takes flying, 127; PS entertains at Trent Park, 127, 169, 174, 178; friendship with Hannah Gubbay, 175; lends to 'Old London Town' exhibition, 204; donates park seat, 238; on PS's death, 241; fails to persuade Sybil to become chairman of Royal School of Needlework, 254; compliments Rock as Lord Great Chamberlain, 259; at Sybil's ninetieth birthday party, 268

Ellis, Richard, 223

'English Conversation Pieces' exhibition (1930), 194–96

Esher, Reginald Baliol Brett, 2nd Viscount: PS writes to comparing French with Haig, 52; PS's wartime correspondence with, 57–59, 62–63, 65–66, 68–77, 80, 84, 174; career, 58; in Paris during war, 62; on Churchill, 70; supports Haig, 72; on Robertson's resignation, 73–74; on politics and soldiers, 74; on Strachey's *Eminent Victorians*, 79; enquires about Siegfried Sassoon, 81; on Haig's honours, 85–86; congratulates PS, 87; and PS's campaign in 1918 election, 88–89; on Churchill's appointment as Secretary of State for War, 91; PS describes Port Lympne to, 93; PS writes to on life in Downing Street, 94; letter from PS on Prince of Wales, 99; PS analyses political situation to (1922), 108; advises PS not to marry, 109; and PS's pessimism over gaining office, 116; letter from PS on Churchill, 119; letter from PS on Sargent's portrait of Sybil, 144; letters from PS on life at Port Lympne, 152; visits Trent Park, 175; letter from PS on appointment as trustee of National Gallery, 185; as trustee of Tate Gallery, 187

Esher Trophy, 118

Essex, Adele, Countess of, 141

Eton College: PS attends, 23–25; acquires Diana Cooper/Edward Marsh notebook, 257

Evans, Captain (MP), 237

Faisal, King of Iraq, 131

Faringdon House, Berkshire, 156

Fascism: rise of, 216

Fermoy, Ruth, Lady, 254, 267

Finch Hatton, Denys, 24

Firle Place, Sussex, 159

First World War (1914–18): PS's role in, 51–52, 89–90; conscription introduced, 62; tanks used in, 65; casualty figures, 66, 69, 80; Armistice, 86

Fisher, Roy, 256

Fleming, Ian, 255

Fleming, J. Ronald, 185

Fletcher, Alan, 61

Foch, Marshal Ferdinand: in First World War, 57, 63–64, 73, 80; at peace conferences, 102, 105

Folkestone Express, 242

Folkestone Herald, 89, 123

Folkestone Hospital, 217, 245

Fontanne, Lynn, 258

Forster, E.M., 77

Forsyth, Robert, 88–89

Fort Belvedere, 99

'Four Georges, The' exhibition (1931), 197

Fowler, John, 263

France: and peace negotiations, 100–2, 104–5; *see also* First World War

French, Field Marshal Sir John, 52, 59

Frere, Sir Bartle, 8–9

Fry, Roger, 28

Fuller, Colonel F.A., 8

Fuller, Roy, 256

Furse, Charles, 206

Furse, Katharine (*née* Symonds), 84, 211, 247, 255–56

Furse, Paul, 256

Gabard, E., 125

Gage, Henry Rainald Gage, 6th Viscount, and Alexandra, Viscountess, 159

Gainsborough, Thomas, 197–98, 202–3

Gallop, Constantine, 116

Gardner, Isabella Stewart, 19

Garibaldi, Giuseppe, 252

Garnett, Edward, 255

Garoich, Robert, 256

Garton, Frank, 30, 245

Garvin, James Louis, 134

Gate of India, Bombay, 10

Gaulle, General Charles de, 251

Geddes, Sir Eric Campbell, 72, 83–84, 92, 108, 214–15

General Elections: (1910), 31; (1918), 86, 88; (1922), 108; (1923), 114; (1924), 116; (1929), 123; (1931), 213; (1935), 223

General Strike (1926), 120–21

Genoa Conference (1921), 105–6

George IV, King: statue, 231, 235

George V, King (*earlier* Prince): visits Thulchan Lodge for shooting, 12; supports Haig, 70; relations with son Edward, 95, 97–98; and Schneider Trophy races, 125; death, 181, 226; visits PS's exhibitions, 198, 200; lends Gainsboroughs to PS exhibition, 202

George VI, King (*earlier* Duke of York): visits Trent Park, 127, 169, 174, 176, 178; death, 181; lends to 'Old London Town' exhibition, 204; coronation, 230–31; donates money for park bench, 238; and improvements to Buckingham Palace, 239; and PS's decline and death, 240–41; lying in state, 259

Germany: and peace negotiations (1919–20), 100–2, 104–5; as inter-war threat, 119, 217, 219, 221; PS visits, 177; size of Air Force, 221–22

Gibbs, James, 40

Gibson, William Pettigrew, 242

Gilbert, Sir Alfred, 118

Gilbert, (Sir) Martin, 253

Gladstone, William Ewart, 8

Gloucester, Alice, Duchess of, 203

Gloucester, Prince Henry, Duke of, 204, 229

Gloucester, William Henry, Duke of, 163

Goering, Hermann, 177, 225

Gordon, General Charles George: statue, 235–6

Gosford, Louisa Augusta Beatrice, Dowager Countess of, 168

Gow, Dr Alec, 240

Grafton, Hugh Denis Charles Fitzroy, 11th Duke of, 267

Granville Barker, Harley, 44

Graveney, William C., 188

Graves, Alderman (of Sheffield), 191

Graves, Robert, 51

Great War *see* First World War (1914–18)

Greenwich *see* Royal Naval College

Grenfell, Billy, 23–24, 53–54, 61

Grenfell, Julian, 23–24, 26, 51, 53, 61

Grey, Sir Edward (Viscount Grey of Fallodon), 138

Grosvenor, Lord Edward, 118, 129

Grundy, C. Reginald, 196, 198–99

Gubbay, David, 21, 30, 99, 132, 158, 162

Gubbay, Hannah (*née* Ezra): relations with PS, 21, 35, 81, 99, 170, 246; inheritance from Sir Edward, 30; relations with Sybil, 35, 170, 261; wartime work, 83; Prince of Wales's devotion to, 99; as hostess for PS, 102, 106, 206; meets flying officers, 127; PS writes on Karachi to, 132; meets Kenneth Clark at Port Lympne, 151; at Port Lympne, 157–59, 161–62; Mrs Dudeney on, 158–59; inherits from PS, 162, 170, 178, 245–46; at Trent Park, 170; friendship with Prince of Wales, 175; helps PS with art exhibitions, 191–92, 194–95, 198–99, 201; charitable work, 193; defends admission price to PS's exhibitions, 203; at PS's death, 240; and Aline's being told of Jewish ancestry, 244

Gubbay, Mrs M.E., 238

Guest, Frederick Edward, 222

Guinness, Lady Evelyn, 139

Gwynne, Howell Arthur, 62–63

Hahn, Reynaldo, 181

Haig, Dorothy Maud, Countess, 58, 75, 229

Haig, Field Marshal Douglas, 1st Earl: PS serves as private secretary, 1, 51–52, 56–61, 67, 70–73, 78, 104, 109, 246; Esher praises, 59; and battle of Somme, 60–61; letter from PS on secret session in Parliament, 62; reputation, 62; Churchill's and F.E. Smith's grievance against, 63; relations with Lloyd George, 64, 85, 93; politicians' attitude to, 66; welcomes Lloyd George's appointment as PM, 67; on Lord Derby, 69; and French army mutinies, 70; survives Passchendaele disaster, 70; generalship questioned, 71–72; complains of lack of manpower, 73; issues order of the day (11 April 1918), 73; indifference to political interference, 74; PS changes view of, 74–75; Orpen portrait of, 75; taste in house decoration, 75; proposes ecumenical religious service, 80; post-war honours and rewards, 85–88; signs Armistice, 86; dispatches published, 88; PS maintains relations with after war, 89; death and funeral, 174, 229; statue, 229–30, 232

Haig, George Alexander Eugene Douglas, 2nd Earl, 174, 229–30

Haldane, Richard Burdon, Viscount, 58

Halifax, Edward Frederick Lindley Wood, 1st Earl of (*earlier* Baron Irwin), 132, 228

Hampton Court, 95

Hankey, Maurice (*later* 1st Baron), 101–2, 104–5, 214

Harcourt, Lewis, 1st Viscount, 239

Hardiman, Alfred Frank, 229–30

Hardinge, Sir Arthur, 112

Hardinge (of Penshurst), Charles, 1st Baron, and Winifred Selina, Lady, 49–50

Harlech, William Ormsby-Gore, 4th Baron, 189–90, 231, 239

Harmsworth, Desmond, 207, 211

Hart, Sir Israel, 21

Havelock, Sir Henry, 231, 234

Hawksmoor, Nicholas, 236

Hazelhurst, Cameron, 253

Heaney, Seamus, 255

Heath, Sir Herbert, 84

Heinemann, William (publishing house), 134

Hendon air show, 124

Henley, Sylvia, 262

Hever, Kent, 154

Hill, A.V., 217

Hitler, Adolf: Wyndham Lewis on, 207, 211; rise to power, 215, 225; on size of German Air Force, 221

Hoare, Lady Maud (*née* Lygon), 116, 161

Hoare, Sir Samuel (*later* Viscount Templewood): as Secretary of State for Air, 92, 116–17, 119–20, 213; and General Strike, 121; PS writes to after 1929 election defeat, 124; supports Schneider Trophy, 125; visits Port Lympne, 161; as Secretary of State for India, 221; and decoration of official residences, 238; writes to ailing PS, 240; obituary tribute to PS, 243; *India by Air*, 121

Hofmannsthal, Raimund von, 176

Holbein, Hans: *A Lady with a Squirrel and a Starling*, 182

Holden, Charles, 163
Holden, Canon Hyla, 241
Holland, Hester, 123, 213
Holmes, Sir Charles John, 186, 188–89
Holmes, Martin, 204
Hong Kong, 6
Hope, Constance, 203
Hore-Belisha, Leslie (*later* Baron), 225, 234
Horne, Sir Robert (*later* Viscount), 174, 186
Horner, David, 249
Horner, Edward, 23, 61
Horner, Frances, 16, 27, 29, 162
Houghton (house), Norfolk: Sybil restores and
    occupies, 2, 39, 179, 182, 210, 263–66, 268; style, 140;
    Oudry painting stolen from, 153; sale (1994), 178,
    246; art objects in, 253, 263–64; Sybil entertains at,
    254; in Cholmondeley ownership, 261–62; opened
    to visitors, 264–65; Water House, 264
Houston, Dame Fanny Lucy (Lady), 126
Howard, Sir Michael, 117
Hussey, Christopher, 166, 196
Hutchinson (publishers), 220
Hythe conferences (1920), 102, 105
Hythe, Kent: parliamentary constituency, 21, 30–32; PS
    represents as MP, 31–32, 123–24; PS visits in war, 61

Illustrated London News, 7
Imperial Airways, 128, 131, 214–15, 217–19
India: PS visits, 2–3; Jews migrate to, 5; opium trade,
    5–6, 33; Sassoons leave, 10; Sybil honeymoons in,
    47–50; Prince of Wales visits, 95–99; flights to, 128,
    130–34; Churchill opposes independence for, 168,
    221
Inskip, Sir Thomas, 222
International Conference for Air Navigation (1927),
    122
International Disarmament Conference (1933), 217
Iraq: RAF's role in, 119, 214, 218–19; PS visits, 131, 134;
    see also Baghdad
Irish Free State: established, 107
Irish Treaty (1921), 105
Irwin, Baron *see* Halifax, 1st Earl of
Italy: terror in, 114; Air Force, 117; wins Schneider
    Trophy, 125; Fascism in, 128

Jackson, Stanley, 3–4, 81, 253
James, Henry: Sargent portrait of, 35
James, Mrs William, 15
Jansen (decorating company), 146
Jebb, Sir Richard, 163
Jellicoe, Admiral of the Fleet John Rushworth, 1st
    Earl, 57, 72, 232, 234, 236
Jellicoe, Florence, Countess (*née* Cayzer), 232, 234–35
Jews: status and rights in Britain, 1–3, 11; in India, 5, 7;
    social acceptance in England, 11, 170; in Parliament,
    22; at Oxford, 25; in Cabinet, 64, 106; in First World
    War, 81; T.W.H. Crosland attacks, 93–94; *see also*
    anti–Semitism

Joffre, Marshal Joseph, 57, 59–60, 63, 76
John, Augustus, 153, 207
Johnson, Jack, 153
Johnston, Edward, 257
Johnston, Sir George Lawson, 192
Jones, Inigo, 229
Jones, L.E., 55
Jones, Thomas, 162–63
Jouvet, Louis, 206

Karachi, 128, 132
Keegan, Sir John, 60
Kensington Palace Gardens (No.12), London: Sybil
    occupies, 179
Kent, Emma Crew, Duchess of, 165
Kent, Prince George, Duke of, 165, 176, 192, 203, 204,
    238
Kent, Princess Marina, Duchess of, 165, 176, 203,
    247–48, 251
Kent, William, 40, 164, 263
Keppel, Alice, 15
Kerr, Philip Henry (*later* 11th Marquess of Lothian),
    101
Keynes, John Maynard, Baron, 17
Kirkwood, David, Baron, 122–23
Kirkwood, Joe, 178
Kneller, Sir Godfrey, 263
Knox, James, 147
Knox, Ronald, 23

Labour Party: strength in 1919, 91; government (1924),
    114; loses October 1924 election, 116; and (National)
    government (1931–37), 116, 213; election victory
    (1929), 123–24; government (1945), 258
Lambert, Baron Leon, 30
Lambton, John Frederick, Viscount, 26
Lancaster, Sir Osbert, 46
Landseer, Sir Edwin, 231
Lansbury, George, 230, 236
Larkin, Philip, 255
Lascelles, (Sir) Alan ('Tommy'), 55
Lausanne, Treaty of (1924), 115
Lavery, Sir John: *The Red Hat* (painting), 140
Law, Andrew Bonar, 31, 60, 92, 94, 108–9
Lawrence, D.H., 79
Lawrence, T.E., 126, 132–33, 160–61, 175, 214–15; *The
    Seven Pillars of Wisdom*, 133, 136
Lee, Arthur Hamilton, Viscount Lee of Fareham, 175,
    189–90
Lees-Milne, James, 58–59
Leigh, Vivien, 151
Lenglen, Suzanne, 181
Leppard, Raymond, 254
Leslie, Lady (Churchill's aunt), 138
Lewis, Wilmarth, 253, 264
Lewis, Wyndham, 207–8, 210–12
Liberal Party: in 1919 government, 91; in 1929 election,
    123

Lindbergh, Charles, 120, 124, 192
Lindemann, Frederick Alexander (*later* Viscount Cherwell), 217
Lindsay, Norah, 152–54, 169
Lipatti, Dinu, 181
Lister, Charles, 23, 61
Lloyd George, David (*later* 1st Earl): PS serves as parliamentary private secretary, 1, 87, 93–94, 100, 102, 104, 109, 116; introduces Insurance Bill, 31; PS attacks in Commons, 33; visits Haig's HQ, 60, 64; Esher criticizes, 62; as Asquith's successor, 63, 67; relations with Haig, 64, 85, 93; complaints about conduct of war, 65; Northcliffe warns against interfering with army, 66; administration, 69; and conduct of First World War, 70–71; denounces PS as intriguer, 71; view of Haig, 72; withstands Maurice's accusations, 74; calls general election at war's end ('Khaki' or 'Coupon election'), 86, 88; and Haig's honours and rewards, 86–87; heads coalition government (1919), 91–92; PS entertains, 92–94, 100, 109; and Prince of Wales's travels, 97–98; in peace negotiations, 100–2, 104–5; and Irish question, 105, 107; PS confesses political ambitions to, 106; criticizes Montagu, 108; political twilight and death, 109; letters from PS abroad, 112; PS criticizes in 1929 election, 123–24; Churt home, 138; appoints PS trustee of National Gallery, 185; as Constable of Carnarvon Castle, 227–28
Lloyd George, (Lady) Megan, 86, 106
Lodge, Sir Oliver, 128
London: bombed in First World War, 92; *see also* Park Lane
Londonderry, Charles Stewart Henry Vane-Tempest-Stewart, 7th Marquess of, 213, 216–18, 221–22
Long, Walter, 1st Viscount, 67
Longcroft, Cecil A., 30
Lonsdale, Emily Susan, Dowager Countess of, 145
Low, (Sir) David, 122
Lowndes, Mrs Belloc: on PS in war, 55; friendship with PS, 68, 162; on PS's constituency work, 124; and PS's grief at death of airman friend, 127–28; visits and praises Port Lympne, 153, 162; visits Trent Park, 174–75; on Prince of Wales and Mrs Simpson, 175; at PS exhibition, 201
Lunt, Alfred, 258
Lushington, Sir Henry, 163
Lutyens, Sir Edwin, 44, 49, 132, 231, 234–36
Luxmoore, H.E., 24, 162
Lyautey, Louis Hubert Gonzalve, 111
Lympne, Kent: airfield, 118; *see also* Port Lympne
Lys, battle of the (1918), 73

MacCarthy, (Sir) Desmond, 252
McCarthy, Lillah, 44
MacDonald, James Ramsay, 116, 126, 188–89, 201, 213, 222
Maclean, Neil, 218, 222
Macmillan, Lady Dorothy, 177

Macmillan, Harold (*later* 1st Earl of Stockton), 222
MacMillan, William, 236
Mallet, Sir Louis: PS writes to on Port Lympne decoration, 46; and Venetia Stanley's marriage, 65; at Park Lane, 68; sees Sybil's baby daughter, 83; on trip to Egypt with PS, 112–14; meets PS in Marseilles, 128; Thornton Wilder meets, 136; background and career, 138, 176; takes Tilden to Port Lympne in war, 138, 148; artistic taste and interests, 139; and PS's dissatisfaction with Sert, 147; stays at Port Lympne, 158, 162; on PS's difficult behaviour, 172; visits Trent Park, 175; and Wyndham Lewis, 211
Manners, Lady Diana *see* Cooper, Lady Diana
Manship, Paul, 144
Manson, James Bolivar, 188
Margaret Rose, Princess, 182, 255
Marlborough House Set, 12, 16
Marsh, Sir Edward, 44, 81, 110, 256–57
Mary, Queen of George V: visits Port Lympne, 148; visits Trent Park, 174, 176; friendship with Sybil, 181–82; visits Houghton, 182, 210, 262; visits PS's exhibitions, 195–96, 200, 203; offers to guide PS round Windsor Castle, 196; lends to PS's exhibitions, 198–99, 202; donates money for park bench, 238; and PS as First Commissioner of Works, 239; Sybil visits after PS's death, 241; photographed with WRNS officers, 247; Sybil liaises with during WRNS service, 251; Plomer and, 255
Mary, Princess Royal, 203
Masaryk, Jan, 262
Masefield, John, 254
Mathews, Dame Vera Laughton, 247–50
Maugham, Syrie, 153
Maugham, William Somerset: 'The Alien Corn', 167
Maurice, General Sir Frederick Barton, 74
Maurois, André, 211
Maxton, James, 230
Mellon, Walter, 203
Menuhin, Yehudi, Baron, 254
Meyers, Jeffrey, 207, 210
Meynell, Francis, 19
Millais, John Everett: *Christ in the House of His Parents* (*The Carpenter's Shop*), 186
Miller, Lee: *Wrens in Camera*, 248
Millerand, Alexandre, 101, 104–5
Milner, Alfred, Viscount, 72, 74
Minto, Gilbert Elliot, 4th Earl of, 34, 48
Mitchell-Thomson, W., 121
Mitchison, Naomi, 207
Mitford, Thomas, 161
Mitterrand, François, 251
Mond, Sir Alfred (*later* 1st Baron Melchett), 94–95, 106, 239
Montagu, Edwin Samuel, 47, 64–65, 106, 108, 224
Montagu, Venetia (*née* Stanley), 47, 64, 161
Montague, Frederick, 126
Moorhouse, Captain Samuel, 31–32
Morocco, 111–12

Morrell, Lady Ottoline, 79, 155
Morris, Margaret, 183–84, 257
Mortimer, Raymond, 255
Mosley, Diana, Lady (*earlier* Guinness), 139, 161–62
Mosley, Sir Oswald, 101–2, 162
Mountbatten, Lord Louis (*later* 1st Earl), 149, 237
Muirhead, A.J., 225
Munich, 25–26
Munich crisis (1938), 225
Murdoch, Sir Keith, 97
Murray, John, 262
Mussolini, Benito, 112–14

Namier, (Sir) Lewis Bernstein, 25, 140
Napier, Sir Charles James, 231, 234
Nash, John, 231
Natanson, Misia Godebska (Sert's wife), 45–46, 111
National Gallery, London: PS serves as trustee, 185–91;
    PS urges Treasury support for, 186; and PS's art
    exhibitions, 196–97, 202
National Government (1931), 116, 213, 223
National Trust, 265–66
New Delhi, 49, 132
Newman, Bernard, 231
Nicolson, Sir Harold, 161, 176–77
Nicolson, Nigel, 161
Nissim, Meyer, 48
Nivelle, General Robert, 70
Nolan, Sidney, 263
Northcliffe, Alfred Harmsworth, Viscount, 52, 61–63,
    65–67, 69, 71–72
Norwich, John Julius Cooper, 2nd Viscount, 176, 257

Obolensky, Sergius, 25
Observer (newspaper), 66
'Old English Plate' exhibition (1929), 193
'Old London Town' exhibition (1938), 204
O'Neill, Maire, 44
opium trade: in India, 5–6, 33
Opium War, First (1839–42), 6
Orford, 1st Earl of *see* Walpole, Sir Robert
Orford, George Walpole, 3rd Earl of, 364
Ormsby-Gore, William *see* Harlech, 4th Baron
Orpen, Grace, Lady (*née* Knewstub), 35
Orpen, Sir William: portraits of Sybil and PS, 35, 39,
    41, 43, 194; relations with Sybil, 35, 39, 75–76, 206; as
    war artist, 75; PS entertains, 75; painting of Park
    Lane interior, 140; praises Sargent's portrait of
    Sybil, 144; visits Port Lympne, 157, 162
Oudry, Jean-Baptiste: *The White Duck* (painting), 153, 188
Owen, Wilfred, 51
Oxford *see* Christ Church

Paget, Lady Elizabeth (*later* von Hofmannsthal), 176
Palestine: proposed as Jewish national home, 16; and
    Balfour Declaration, 101; PS's little interest in, 101,
    110; Royal Air Force in, 224
Panter, Gilbert, 192

Paris Peace Conference (1919–20), 100
Park Lane, London: Sir Edward Sassoon's residence
    in, 16–17, 140; PS occupies, 30, 43, 75, 92–93, 140;
    entertaining at, 44, 100, 106, 109, 206; PS improves,
    138, 140–41, 146–48; art exhibitions in, 140, 191–204;
    art and paintings in, 144, 153, 185; demolished, 146,
    148; charitable balls at, 192; reverts to estate of Sir
    Edward on PS's death, 245
parks *see* royal parks
Parsees, 2, 10
Passchendaele *see* Ypres, 3rd battle of
Paul, Prince of Serbia, 25
Peel, William Robert Wellesley, 1st Earl, 107
Pembroke, Reginald Herbert, 15th Earl of, 188
Pembroke, Thomas Herbert, 8th Earl of, 264
Persia, Shah of *see* Shah of Persia
Pétain, Marshal Philippe, 70, 73
Peto, Samuel Morton, 179
Philip, Prince, Duke of Edinburgh, 259, 268
Philip Sassoon Flying Award, 254–5
Philpot, Glyn: portrait of PS, 41, 81; PS as patron of,
    41, 185; portrait of Siegfried Sassoon, 81; friendship
    with Sybil, 83; paints frieze at Port Lympne, 148,
    162; draws in Port Lympne Visitors Book, 157;
    homosexuality, 171; on Tate Board of Trustees, 187
Pius XI, Pope, 113
Plas Newydd, 154, 176
Plomer, William, 255–56, 261, 265–66; *Taste and
    Remember*, 256
Plumb, Sir John H., 170, 253, 267
Poincaré, Raymond, 57, 63
Polignac, Charles de, 28
Poona, 7, 9, 48
Pope, Squadron Leader, 175–76
'Porcelain through the Ages' exhibition (1934), 202
Porch, Montagu, 74
Port Lympne (house), Kent: and PS's origins, 2; name,
    44, 68; PS builds and decorates, 44–48, 75, 147; Sybil
    visits in wartime, 83; PS occupies, 93; Prince of
    Wales visits, 97–98; PS entertains at, 100, 117, 127,
    148–62, 174, 206; Lloyd George meets Millerand at,
    101–2; PS improves and redecorates, 138, 148–49, 151,
    153–56, 162, 166; garden, 152–54; PS's life at, 152–53;
    Visitors' Book, 157; Hannah Gubbay inherits, 162,
    245; later owners, 162; gardens opened for charity,
    192
Porteus, Hugh Gordon: *Wyndham Lewis: A Discursive
    Exposition*, 210
Poulenc, François, 180
Pound, Ezra, 207
Primrose, Neil, 28
Proust, Marcel, 12, 110–11

Rathenau, Walther, 105
Rawlinson, General Sir Henry, 52–53, 55, 67
Reading, Rufus Isaacs, 1st Marquess of, 64, 93–94, 106
Reading, Stella, Dowager Marchioness of, 259
rearmament, 119, 216, 223

Rembelinski, Count, 19
Reynolds, Sir Joshua, 203
Rhodes, Cecil, 44
Rhondda, Margaret Haig Thomas, Viscountess, 211
Ribbentrop, Joachim von, 222
Riddell, Sir George, 93
Rinder, Frank, 187
Rivera, Diego, 46
Robertson, General Sir William, 66, 72–73
Robinson, Geoffrey *see* Dawson, Geoffrey
Rocksavage, George Horatio Charles Cholmondeley,
    Earl of *see* Cholmondeley, 5th Marquess of
Rodgers, Richard and Dorothy, 174
Roman Catholics: political emancipation, 3
Rome, 112–13
Rose, Kenneth, 253
Ross, Robert, 41, 155
Roth, Cecil, 5, 32, 34, 93, 228
Rothenstein, John, 191
Rothenstein, Sir William, 187
Rothermere, Harold Sidney Harmsworth, 1st
    Viscount, 91
Rothschild family, 3, 6, 12–13, 17, 19, 28–29, 35
Rothschild, Cécile de (*née* Anspach; Gustave's wife),
    12, 27
Rothschild, Baron Elie de, 134, 244, 267
Rothschild, Baron Gustave de, 12, 27
Rothschild, James de, 12, 140, 202
Rothschild, Leopold de, 12, 56
Rothschild, Baroness Liliane de, 244, 267
Rothschild, Lionel Nathan, 11
Rothschild, Lionel Walter, 2nd Baron, 16, 203
Rothschild, Marie de (*née* Perugia; Leopold's wife), 12
Rothschild, Meyer Amschel de, 21
Rothschild, Mrs N.C., 238
Rothschild, Victor (*later* 3rd Baron), 202
Royal Air Force: established, 91–92; PS's interest in
    and advocacy of, 115–16, 119–20; development and
    status, 116–17; role in Iraq, 119, 214, 218–19; inter-war
    condition and development, 214, 216–18, 220–24; in
    Palestine, 224
Royal Flying Corps, 91
Royal Naval College, Greenwich: Great Painted Hall,
    236–37; wartime WRNS training at, 250
Royal Northern Hospital, Holloway Road, London,
    192–93, 199, 203–4, 245
royal parks: benches, 237–38
Royal School of Needlework, 254
Rubinstein, Artur, 144, 181, 205, 208
Ruhr, 101, 105
Runciman, Sir Steven, 267
Russia (USSR): proposed reconciliation with, 105–6;
    Sybil and Rock visit, 263
Rutter, Frank, 198
Ryder, Sue, 262

Sackville-West, Vita (Lady Nicolson), 161
St Donat's (house), 154

Salmond, Sir John, 127
Samuel, Herbert Louis, 1st Viscount, 64, 101, 106
Sandringham, Norfolk, 266
Sargent, John Singer: PS as patron of, 1, 185; Aline
    and, 19; portrait of Sybil, 35, 39, 253; PS meets on
    leave from war, 53; proposes bust of Julian Grenfell,
    54; visits western front, 76–77; war paintings, 77–78;
    friendship with Sybil, 83; portrait of Prince of
    Wales, 99; at Park Lane, 141; portraits hung in Park
    Lane, 144; portrait of Jack Johnson at Port Lympne,
    153; visits Port Lympne, 157; PS lends paintings to
    Churchill, 158; musical parties, 180; painting of
    Sitwell children, 195; *Gassed* (painting), 77
Sarnoff, David, 252
Sason, Abraham, 4
Sasson ben Saleh, 5
Sassoon family: origins, 3–5; and Rothschilds, 17
Sassoon, Abdullah *see* Sassoon, Sir Albert, 1st Bt
Sassoon, Sir Albert, 1st Bt (PS's grandfather): settles
    in England, 3, 6, 10; honours, 5; business interests,
    6–7; gives statue of Edward Prince of Wales to
    Bombay, 7; social life, 12, 266; death, 16, 19, 140
Sassoon, Alfred, 13, 25, 186
Sassoon, Aline, Lady (*née* de Rothschild; PS/Sybil's
    mother): marriage, 12, 15; jewellery and art
    interests, 15, 17, 19, 144; social life, 15–16; residence
    in Park Lane, 16–17, 140; friendship with Berenson,
    17–19, 25; Keynes disparages, 18; death, 19, 27, 82;
    Sargent portrait of, 19; correspondence with H.G.
    Wells, 22; and PS at Oxford, 25
Sassoon, Arthur, 6, 12–13, 16, 24, 30
Sassoon, David: in Bombay and Poona, 3, 5–10; birth
    and background, 7–8; statue, 7–8; descendants, 81
Sassoon, Sir Edward Albert, 2nd Bt (PS/Sybil's father):
    Jewish observance, 3; marriage, 12, 15; social life, 15;
    residence in Park Lane, 16, 140; in Rome, 18;
    background and career, 19, 21; political activities,
    21–22, 31; and PS's schooling, 23, 25; letter to PS at
    Oxford, 26; death, 27, 31, 41; and wife's death, 27;
    will and estate, 30, 245; acquires Trent Park lease,
    163
Sassoon, Elias David, 6
Sassoon, Flora, 34
Sassoon, Frederick, 21, 30
Sassoon, George (Siegfried's son), 252
Sassoon, Hester (Siegfried's wife), 252
Sassoon, Sir Jacob, 7
Sassoon, Louise (*née* Perugia; Arthur's wife), 12, 16,
    30–31, 47, 99, 170
Sassoon, Mozelle (*née* Gubbay; Mrs Meyer Sassoon),
    170, 175, 202, 238
Sassoon, Sir Philip Albert Gustave David, 3rd Bt:
    background and career, 1–2; as Haig's private
    secretary, 1, 51–52, 56–61, 67, 70–73, 78, 89–90, 109,
    246; as parliamentary private secretary to Lloyd
    George, 1, 87, 93–94, 100, 102, 109; Jewishness, 2–3,
    106, 159, 170, 177, 190, 225, 242, 244, 246; visits India,
    2, 132; birth, 15; inherits parental pearls, 15, 144; and

Jewish immigration, 16; in Park Lane house, 17, 30, 43, 92–93; and mother's attachment to Berenson, 18; collecting interests, 19, 144–46, 153, 170, 185, 193, 204, 212, 263–64; education, 23–27; in Germany, 25–26; lively manner, 25–26; commissioned in East Kent Yeomanry, 27, 52; and death of parents, 27; inheritance from father, 30, 43; enters Parliament, 31–33; as MP, 31–32, 51, 62, 70, 123–24; public speaking, 32, 123, 160; portraits of, 39, 52, 77, 140, 144, 194; interest in art and architecture, 41, 139–41, 185–92, 212; property holdings, 43; builds and decorates Port Lympne, 44–46, 148–54; entertaining, 44, 79, 92–94, 100, 106, 117, 138, 170, 172–78; Sybil buys present for in India, 50; as Rawlinson's ADC, 52–53, 55, 67; appearance, 59, 106; sexual orientation, 59, 79, 81, 106, 156, 171; honours and awards, 61, 109; dealings with press, 62–63; excuses for not marrying, 68; criticizes Haig, 74; relations with cousin Siegfried, 80–81; close relations with Sybil, 81–82, 246, 261; lacks close personal relations, 81–82, 172, 246; and Haig's post-war honours and rewards, 85–88; election victory (1918), 88–89; demobilized, 89–90; maintains relations with Haig after war, 89; parliamentary activities, 92, 95, 115–16, 119–20, 122, 127, 137, 214, 218, 223–24, 230, 235, 239; as parliamentary private secretary to Geddes, 92; gives presents to Prince of Wales, 98–99; attends peace negotiations (1920), 100–2, 104–5; lacks religious belief, 100; superstitions, 100; coolness on Palestine issue, 101, 110; diaries, 102, 104; political ambitions, 106–7; memorandum on political situation (1921), 107–8; at Carlton Club 1922 meeting, 108–9; re-elected (1922), 109, (1923), 114; (1924), 116; (1929), 123; (1931), 213, (1935), 223; Scott-Moncrieff abuses, 110–11; travels to Spain, Morocco and Egypt (1922–23), 111–14; as Under-Secretary of State of Air, 116–20, 199, 213–25, 246; as commander of 'The Flying Swords', 118, 127; tennis-playing, 120; in General Strike, 121; Ellen Wilkinson's view of, 122–23; visits USA and Canada, 122; political style, 124, 137; and T.E. Lawrence, 126; learns to fly, 127; flies to India, 128–34, 136; art exhibitions, 137, 140, 192–204; extravagant style, 151–52, 160, 170–72, 177, 188–89; social life, 151, 160, 174; style of speech, 152; writes on Port Lympne for *Architectural Review*, 153; meets cousin Siegfried, 155; excess energy, 159; as outsider, 159, 177; private flying, 162, 174, 178; melancholic disposition, 172, 176; temper, 172, 240; visits Nazi Germany, 177; disputes with Duveen, 190–91; charitable activities and fund-raising, 192–95, 199, 203–4; tonsillitis operation, 199, 240; overseas tours (1933–34), 215–16, 219; favours disarmament, 217–18; as First Commissioner of Works, 224, 227–40, 246; ill health, 224, 240; supports Chamberlain's appeasement, 225; in Abdication crisis, 226; and redesign of Trafalgar Square, 231–36; death, funeral and obituary notices, 236, 240–43; television interview, 238; achievements and assessment, 243–46, 268; will and estate, 245–46; place in English life, 266; *The Third Route*, 128, 133–36, 160

Sassoon, Reuben, 6, 11–12, 24

Sassoon, Sassoon David, 3, 6, 11, 13, 81

Sassoon, Siegfried: reputation, 1, 246; birth and parentage, 13; Philpot portrait of, 41; and Edward Marsh, 44, 81; war poetry, 51–52; protests about war, 80; relations with PS, 80–81; Churchill admires poetry, 81; war experiences, 90; in General Strike, 121; T.E. Lawrence on, 133; friendship with Rex Whistler, 155; PS meets, 155; meets Sybil, 156; and controversy over Millais painting, 186–87; good relations with Sybil, 252–53; 'Monody on the Demolition of Devonshire House', 164; *The Old Huntsman*, 80–81

Sassoon, Sybil *see* Cholmondeley, Sybil, Marchioness of

Sassoon, Theresa (*née* Thornycroft; Alfred's wife), 13

Sassoon, Sir Victor, 1, 246

Sassoon, David & Co.: PS's role in, 2; founded, 6; Edward works with, 19; safeguarded in Edward's will, 30

Sassoon, E.D. & Co., 6–7

Sassoon Mechanics Institute, Bombay, 8

Schiff, Sydney, 210

Schneider, Jacques, 125

Schneider Trophy, 124–26

Scott, Sir Samuel, 87

Scott-Moncrieff, C.K., 110–11

Sephardic Jews, 4–5

Sert, José Maria, 45–47, 111, 146–48, 185

Shah of Persia (Nasr-ed-Din), 6

Shaw, George Bernard, 178

Shepherd, E., 140

Shine, Diana, 256

Shorncliffe Lodge, Sandgate, Kent, 21

Shoshans (of Toledo), 4

Simon, Sir John, 47–48, 221, 228

Simpson, Ernest, 175

Simpson, Wallis *see* Windsor, Duchess of

Sims, Charles, 83, 144

Sisson, Marshall, 264

Sitwell, (Dame) Edith, 255

Sitwell, (Sir) Osbert: as PS's fag at Eton, 24; friendship with Siegfried Sassoon, 80, 155–56; at Port Lympne, 153, 162; friendship with Rex Whistler, 155; PS's friendship with, 156, 171, 178; describes Trent Park, 169–70; on Sassoon ownership of Millais painting, 187; on Abdication crisis, 226; obituary notice of PS, 243; friendship with Sybil, 255

Sitwell, (Sir) Sacheverell, 194

Skey, Miss (House Dame at Eton), 24, 245

Smith, F.E. *see* Birkenhead, 1st Earl of

Smith, Logan Pearsall, 82

Smith, Stevie, 255

Smuts, General Jan Christian, 92

Smyth, (Dame) Ethel, 162

Snowden, Philip, Viscount, 126
Soames, Mary, Lady (*née* Churchill), 158
Society of Authors, 254, 256
Somme, battle of the (1916), 60–61, 65–66
Souls, the (group), 15–16
Spa, Belgium, 102, 104
Spain, 111–12
Sparrow, John, 256, 265
Stamfordham, Arthur John Bigge, Baron, 52, 80
Stanhope, James Richard, 7th Earl, 229, 232
Stanley, Venetia *see* Montagu, Venetia
Stanley, Lady Victoria, 28
Stark, Freya, 262–63
Steel-Maitland, Arthur, 31
Steer, Philip Wilson, 185
Stevenson, Frances (*later* Countess Lloyd George),
    92–94, 100, 104, 108, 174
Stewart, Patrick Shaw, 23, 61
Stinnes, Hugo, 105
Strachey, Lytton, 18, 160; *Elizabeth and Essex*, 136;
    Eminent Victorians, 78–79, 160
Stratford de Redcliffe, Stratford Canning, 1st
    Viscount, 138
Stravinsky, Igor, 180
Surat, India, 5
Sutherland, George Sutherland-Leveson-Gower, 5th
    Duke of, 117
Swinton, Philip Cunliffe-Lister, 1st Earl of, 222–23, 225

Taplow Court, near Windsor, 29
Tate Gallery, 186–88
Tatham, Herbert, 23–24
Taylor, A.J.P., 73
Taylor, G.C., 154
Ten Year Rule: revoked (1932), 215
Tennant, Stephen, 155
Thomas, Dylan, 255
'Thomas Gainsborough' exhibition (1936), 202–3
Thomson, Christopher Birdwood, Baron, 122, 126, 135,
    215
Thornhill, James, 236
Thornycroft family, 13
Thornycroft, Sir Hamo, 13, 231
'Three French Reigns' exhibition (1933), 200
Tilden, Philip, 45, 117, 138–41, 148–49, 154
Tiller, Terence, 256
Tizard, Sir Henry Thomas, 217
Toscanini, Arturo, 205, 211–12, 251–52
Trafalgar Square: redesigned, 231–36
Transport, Ministry of, 92
Trenchard, Air Marshal Hugh, 1st Viscount: Orpen
    portrait of, 75; dispute with Rothermere, 91; and
    Auxiliary Air Force, 117; and PS's appointment to
    Air Ministry, 119; T.E. Lawrence sends message to,
    133
Trent Park, New Barnet: put in trust under Sir
    Edward's will, 30; Cholmondeleys acquire (Trent
    Place), 40; PS inherits lease, 43; entertaining at,
93–95, 97, 100, 109, 117, 120, 170, 172–78, 206; PS
    renovates, 138, 153–54, 163–70; PS's use of, 162–63;
    history, 163; exotic birds at, 168, 170; garden, 169;
    ownership and fortunes after PS's death, 178, 245;
    requisitioned during Second World War, 178;
    gardens opened for charity, 192
Trent Place *see* Trent Park
Tring, Hertfordshire, 28
Troy, J.F. de: *A Reading from Molière* (painting), 145,
    193–94
Tulchan Lodge, Strathspey, Scotland, 12

United States of America: PS visits, 114, 122; Rock and
    Sybil visit, 181, 262
Univers israélite (Paris), 243
Ur (Sumer), 133
Uzzielli, Major, 76

Vanity Fair (magazine), 12, 22
Vansittart, Sir Robert (*later* Baron), 228
Vaughan Williams, Ralph, 44
Verdun, battle of (1916), 60
Vernon, George, 61
Versailles, Treaty of (1919), 104

Waddesdon Manor, 202
Waite, Colonel, 162
Walcott, Derek, 255
Walewska, Marie, 135
Walker, Ted, 251, 254–56, 262–63, 265–68
Wallace Collection, London, 188
Wallace, Sir Richard, 188
Walmer Castle, Kent, 238
Walpole family, 39
Walpole, Horace (4th Earl of Orford), 39–40, 165, 168
Walpole, Sir Robert (1st Earl of Orford), 2, 39–40, 253,
    263, 265
Waterhouse, Ellis Kirkham, 202–4
Waterhouse, Sir Nicholas, 210–11
Watson, Mrs Chalmers, 84
Waugh, Alec: *The Loom of Youth*, 208
Wavell, Field Marshal Archibald Percival, 1st Earl, 252
Weizmann, Chaim, 101
Wellington, Arthur Wellesley, 1st Duke of, 40, 85
Wellington, Irene, 257
Wells, Herbert George, 22
Wertheimer family, 19
Westminster, Hugh Grosvenor, 2nd Duke of, 238
Weygand, General Maxime, 102
Wharton, Edith, 159
Wheeler, Sir Charles, 236
Whistler, Rex: friendship with Siegfried Sassoon, 80,
    155; illustrates PS's *The Third Route*, 128; at Port
    Lympne, 153; decorates Plas Newydd, 154, 176; paints
    Tent Room at Port Lympne, 154–56; Tate murals,
    154, 190; anti-Semitism, 156; decorations at Trent
    Park, 167–68; PS acts as patron to, 185; designs jacket
    for Sacheverell Sitwell book on conversation pieces,

194; designs posters for PS's exhibitions, 197, 199; anger at passing over PS for Office of Works, 232; designs for London squares, 232

Wigston, John, 163

Wilder, Thornton, 136

Wilkins, Captain H. St Clair, 9

Wilkinson, Ellen, 122

Wilkinson, Norman, 44

William IV, King, 231

Williamson, George C., 196

Willingdon, Freeman Freeman-Thomas, 1st Marquess, and Marie Adelaide, Marchioness 49, 238

Willoughby de Eresby, Gilbert James, Lord (*later* 3rd Earl of Ancaster), 259

Wilson, General Sir Henry, 73–74, 102, 104–5

Wilton Diptych, 188

Windsor, Edward, Duke of *see* Edward, Prince of Wales

Windsor, Wallis, Duchess of (*earlier* Simpson), 96, 102, 175–76, 226

Winterton, Edward Turnour, 6th Earl, 225

Witt, Robert, 187

Women's Royal Naval Service (WRNS): Sybil helps found, 83–84; Sybil serves in Second World War, 247–51

Wontner, Arthur, 44

Wood, Councillor (of Folkestone), 242

Wood, Sir Kingsley, 223, 225

Woolf, Virginia, 160

Woolley, Sir Leonard, 133

Woolner, Thomas, 8

Works, Office of: PS serves as First Commissioner of, 224, 227–40, 246

Wren, Sir Christopher, 236

WRNS ('Wrens') *see* Women's Royal Naval Service

Yockney, A., 197

York, Duchess of *see* Elizabeth, Queen of George VI

York, Duke of *see* George VI, King

Younger, Sir George, 108

Ypres, 3rd battle of (Passchendaele, 1917), 70, 72

Zionism: Sybil's view of, 29; PS's indifference to, 101, 110

Zoffany, John, 168, 194

Zuckerman, Joan, Lady (*née* Isaacs), 267